What Americans Know about Politics and Why It Matters

What Americans Know about Politics and Why It Matters

Michael X. Delli Carpini

and

Scott Keeter

Yale University Press

New Haven and London

Designed by James J. Johnson and set in Melior and Syntax types by the Marathon Group, Inc., Durham, North Carolina.
Printed in the United States of America

Library of Congress Cataloging-in-Publication Data

Delli Carpini, Michael X., 1953-
What Americans know about politics and why it matters / Michael X. Delli Carpini and Scott Keeter.
p. cm.
Includes bibliographical references and index.
ISBN 0–300–06256–7 (cloth: alk. paper)
978-0-300-07275-4 (pbk.: alk paper)

1. Political participation—United States. 2. Politics, Practical—United States. 3. Political culture—United States. I. Keeter, Scott. II. Title.
JK1764.D453 1996
323'.042'0973—dc20 95–24248
CIP

A catalogue record for this book is available from the British Library.

The paper in this book meets the guidelines for permanence and durability of the Committee on Production Guidelines for Book Longevity of the Council on Library Resources.

10 9 8 7

To Jane and Rosemary

Contents

Preface ix

INTRODUCTION Political Knowledge, Political Power, and the Democratic Citizen 1

CHAPTER ONE From Democratic Theory to Democratic Practice: The Case for an Informed Citizenry 22

CHAPTER TWO What Americans Know about Politics 62

CHAPTER THREE Stability and Change in Political Knowledge 105

CHAPTER FOUR Who's Informed? Individual, Group, and Collective Patterns of Political Knowledge 135

CHAPTER FIVE Explaining Political Knowledge 178

CHAPTER SIX The Consequences of Political Knowledge and Ignorance 218

CHAPTER SEVEN Informing the Public's Discretion 268

APPENDIX ONE Overview of Data Sources 291

APPENDIX TWO The Conceptualization and Measurement of Political Knowledge 294

APPENDIX THREE Knowledge over Time 307

APPENDIX FOUR Details of the Structural Analysis Used in Chapter 4 329

APPENDIX FIVE Methodology of the Analysis of Information's Impact on Opinion in Chapter 6 334

Notes 337

Bibliography 367

Index 387

Contents

Preface

During summer 1994, the progress and travails of health care reform received widespread attention from the media. This issue, which appeared suddenly on the national political agenda in the early 1990s, was a centerpiece of Bill Clinton's 1992 campaign platform. Now the battle was being waged in Congress, and it was a battle that included concerted efforts from all sides to mobilize public opinion. Whether a health reform bill would become law and, more important, the specific nature of the reform would depend in large part on who could convince the American public of which plan—if any—was most in their individual and collective interests.

This debate was, potentially, democracy at its best. The issue tangibly affects the quality of life for most Americans. It reached the public agenda because it resonated with citizens in a number of state-level races. A new party controlled the White House in part because of the promise of sweeping change, change that included health care reform. In justifying their positions on the issue, members of the House and Senate regularly referred to public opinion polls, conversations with constituents, or letters they had received. Interest groups flooded the media with advertising for and against various aspects of health care reform. And the media reported the debate from a variety of angles.

The quality of the public debate on such issues as health care, however, and thus ultimately the quality of the reforms that emerge, depend on two things: the nature of the information brought to the public marketplace and the ability of citizens to use that information to discern their interests and to articulate them effectively. On the first point, the evidence from the health care debate is discouraging. An analysis of paid political advertising found that more than half the ads on television were unfair, misleading, or deceptive, as were more than one-fourth of the print ads.[1] And although journalists devoted considerable attention to the issue, their coverage focused inordinately on the game itself and the strategies of the players. Journalists spent less than 10 percent of their reporting on the fairness or accuracy of paid advertisements, concentrating the majority of their time on the political motives and strategies of the groups sponsoring the ads. While coverage of strategy and motive has merit, citizens can learn little from it about the issue itself and quite likely will come away skeptical of the motives of everyone involved and more cynical about politics in general—a very accurate description of the electorate just after the health care debate ended in late summer.

How well citizens are able to discern and articulate their interests depends not only on the immediate information environment in which any issue is debated, but also on their ability to put this new information into a broader personal and political perspective. Consider, for example, the opening two paragraphs of the following article by Adam Clymer from the *New York Times* of August 6, 1994:

> "Liberals Back Senate Health Bill in Hope of Gains Later." Liberal senators and organizations unhappy with elements of Senator George J. Mitchell's health insurance bill are coalescing behind a strategy of defending the bill while it is on the Senate floor and hoping to get something out of a House-Senate conference committee later.
>
> Most of them speak of trying to strengthen the bill with amendments that move toward universal coverage sooner, or enhance its benefit package. A few insist that their ultimate support cannot be taken for granted unless the bill moves in their direction, although even Senator Paul Wellstone, a very liberal Minnesota Democrat, stops short of saying he will vote against it if his amendments fail.

The paragraphs are filled with potentially useful information regarding the health care debate. But to be useful, a citizen must bring additional information to his or her reading of the article. This includes some understanding of broad concepts like "liberal" and "conservative" and some understanding of more substantive issues, such as what is meant by "universal coverage" or what the Mitchell bill (and its competitors) says about this issue. A reader's understanding of the article is also enhanced by some knowledge of who George Mitchell and Paul Wellstone are, where they stand on health care, or what the fact that Wellstone is "a very liberal Democrat" indicates about his stance. The article also assumes some understanding about the law-making process, such as its bicameral nature, the amendment process, and the function of conference committees. Without this information, the article would be nearly incomprehensible.

Although the issue of health care reform no longer dominates the national agenda, the larger issue it illustrates—the role of an informed citizenry in democratic politics—remains. As its title indicates, this book is an exploration of what citizens know about politics and why it matters to the functioning of the American political system. Our analysis is descriptive, analytic, and interpretive. In presenting it, we use a vast amount of evidence from surveys and related sources. Many scholarly and popular conclusions regarding the state of political knowledge are based on relatively small and idiosyncratic collections of facts. By drawing on a large array of data—much of it collected specifically for this study—we present a more comprehensive portrait of what Americans know about national politics. As such we hope the book will serve as a resource for academics, journalists, and interested citizens and as an antidote to the sometimes overly simplistic caricature of the American public that is often presented. Beyond this, we attempt to clarify the dynamics of political learning and how these dynamics affect the individual and collective distribution of political knowledge in the United States. As part of this analysis we show that factual knowledge is an important political resource that assists individuals in their civic actions, helps explain group differences in political access, and serves as a collective good, strengthening the likelihood that the polity functions both responsively and responsibly.

Ultimately, however, we draw on our specific descriptions and analyses to weave a broader and more normatively based interpretation of the relation between political knowledge, democratic citizenship, and political power in the United States. This argument is consciously rooted in the philosophies of progressive modernism and the Enlightenment. We believe that social understanding emerges out of, and is sustained by, informed, rational discourse. Our argument is also rooted in the democratic tradition that runs, though sometimes circuitously, through the works of Jean Jacques Rousseau, John Stuart Mill, John Dewey, Jürgen Habermas, and William Connolly. Despite their often sizable differences, all these theorists argue for the importance of citizen input in the determination and implementation of the public good. They also argue for the importance of informed discourse, which they see as both instrumental and self-fulfilling in its own right. Finally, they all understand the contextual nature of an informed citizenry, arguing that the social, political, and economic institutions of a democracy must educate and inform citizens in the broadest sense and must provide a public sphere that allows and encourages civic discourse. We further argue that for this process to be fully democratic and enlightened, it requires an exchange that approximates Habermas's (1984) "ideal speech situation" and thus requires citizens who are more or less equally informed.[2]

While arguing from a perspective akin to what Benjamin Barber (1984) calls "strong democracy," we also contend that competitors to this perspective—from theories of limited, protectionist democracy through postmodern challenges to rational discourse—are also normatively dependent on an informed citizenry, though in different and less developed ways. We do not pretend that a consensus on the true meaning of democracy nor on the specific requisites of citizenship could or should ever be reached; we share Connolly's (1983) view that concepts like democracy and citizenship are inherently ambiguous and essentially contestable. We do argue, however, that an informed citizenry is a common thread that implicitly ties together all theories of democracy.

As we read the existing research regarding citizenship in America, we find consistent support for the idea that given the appropriate information, citizens are capable of making rational political choices. Evidence of political ignorance is not proof that citizens are fools. In the absence of adequate and equally distributed information, however, evidence that citizens can reason or that aggregate opinion is rational is not proof that the public interests are being served. And evidence that the American polity is stable and long-lived is not proof that it is democratic. It is possible for the American system, designed as a "machine that would go of itself," to function with no input from most of its citizens most of the time. But democracy without citizens is no democracy at all.

During the seven years we worked on this project we incurred a number of debts that we would like to formally acknowledge. Scott Althaus, Stephen Bennett, Jim Caraley, Susan Carroll, Doris Graber, Herbert Hirsch, Neil Henry, Robert Holsworth, Susan Howell, David Kennamer, Jane Mansbridge, Benjamin Page, Wendy Rahn, George Rabinowitz, Robert Shapiro, and Cliff Zukin provided useful (and often quite critical) insights into our theoretical, conceptual, and methodological approach. So, too, did numerous anonymous reviewers of articles we published along the way. Although this book will not satisfy all the concerns raised by our colleagues, it is the stronger for their critiques. We would also like to thank the Board of Overseers for the National Election Studies (NES) for allowing us to include several of our knowledge items on their 1991 pilot survey and for their useful comments on early versions of our proposal. We are indebted to the staffs of both the NES at the University of Michigan and the Roper Center at the University of Connecticut for their prompt and efficient help in much of our data collection. The staff of the Survey Research

Laboratory at Virginia Commonwealth University went above and beyond the call of duty in helping to design and administer the local, state, and national surveys we conducted for this project. So did Nell Dillon-Ermers of Barnard College in helping with a number of administrative tasks associated with the project. Research assistant Leonard Bernado aided in data collection and was invaluable in seeking out correct answers to the many often-obscure political facts of which both authors readily admit ignorance. Joy Greene provided assistance with the bibliography. We thank both Barnard College and Virginia Commonwealth University for their generous support (both grants and time release) without which this project could never have been completed. We thank Eliza Childs for her careful and insightful copyediting of our manuscript and Margaret Otzel for her cheerful management of the manuscript's production. And we thank John S. Covell, senior editor of Yale University Press, for his support and encouragement. Of course, in the end this book is the work of its two authors, and we take full responsibility for any and all errors it contains.

INTRODUCTION

Political Knowledge, Political Power, and the Democratic Citizen

If a nation expects to be ignorant and free, in a state of civilization, it expects what never was and never will be.—THOMAS JEFFERSON, letter to Charles Yancey

Knowledge is power.—FRANCIS BACON, *Sacred Meditations*

This book is an exploration of what Americans know—and don't know—about politics. Driving this exploration is a deceptively simple argument: that democracy functions best when its citizens are politically informed. Factual knowledge on such topics as the institutions and processes of government, current economic and social conditions, the major issues of the day, and the stands of political leaders on those issues assists citizens in discerning their individual and group interests, in connecting their interests to broader notions of the public good, and in effectively expressing these views through political participation. In addition, the more equitably information is distributed among citizens, the more likely it is that the actions of government will reflect the public interest and, thus, that the public will be supportive of those actions. In short, a broadly and equitably informed citizenry helps assure a democracy that is both responsive and responsible.

The assumption that political knowledge, political power, and socioeconomic power are inextricably linked in the real world is fundamental to our argument. Knowledge is both an important political resource in its own right and a facilitator of other forms of political and thus, indirectly, socioeconomic power. At the same time, knowledge is easier to obtain for those who are already politically, socially, and economically powerful. Consequently, those least advantaged socially and economically are least able to redress their grievances politically.

Although rooted in commonly held notions of democratic theory and practice, these assumptions are surprisingly controversial, with many scholars arguing against either the possibility or the necessity of a broadly and equitably informed citizenry. Indeed, this simple argument opens a

Pandora's box of unresolved questions regarding the nature of citizenship, the promise and performance of democracy, and, ultimately, the meaning of democracy itself.

Democracy was held in disrepute for most of the 2,500-year-old debate over what form of government is most just. A primary reason for this was the belief that the average citizen was intellectually and morally incapable of self-government. Even those who championed the public's right to self-rule expressed grave reservations about citizens' ability to exercise this right effectively. "What are the matters," wrote Aristotle, "over which freemen, or the general body of citizens—men of the sort who neither have wealth nor can make any claim on the ground of goodness—should properly exercise sovereignty? It may be argued . . . that it is dangerous for men of this sort to share in the highest offices, as injustice may lead them into wrongdoing, and thoughtlessness into error" (1946: 124).

During the last two hundred years opinions about democracy have come full circle, and today one would be hard pressed to find a citizen, intellectual, or world leader who would not endorse the notions of popular sovereignty and popular rule. But democracy's rehabilitation has shifted rather than ended the debate about the competency of the masses. Modern democracy is designed to balance what James Morone (1990) has called a "dread" and "yearning"—a dread dating back to Socrates that democracy inevitably decays into some form of despotism and a yearning, traceable to Pericles' Athens, for direct rule by the people. This combination of fear and faith in the public's collective wisdom has resulted in political institutions and processes designed to allow citizens to have a voice in their own governance, while at the same time limiting the impact of that voice. These systems of checks and balances serve to safeguard against the potentially negative impact of mass opinion, but in the absence of informed civic input, at best such checks assure only stability—not democracy.

How one balances democratic dread with yearning depends in large part on how sure one is that citizens are individually and collectively capable of self-rule. Not surprisingly, those who defend a limited, elite-based democracy (for example, Schumpeter, 1942; Berelson, 1952; Schattschneider, 1960; Neuman, 1986; Mueller, 1992) point to evidence of low levels of public knowledge about politics to support their arguments. However, many defenders of more mass-based models of democracy argue that citizens need not be as politically informed as is implied by democratic theorists in order to participate effectively. These arguments take several forms. For some, the absence of a broadly informed citizenry is

countered by the presumed existence of numerous "attentive publics," each of which brings information about specific aspects of the political and social world to the marketplace of ideas (Miller, Suchner, and Voelker, 1980; Miller, 1983). Others suggest that citizens are able to use their limited information in ways that lead to relatively efficient individual (Key, 1966; Popkin, 1991; Sniderman, Brody, and Tetlock, 1991) and collective (Converse, 1990; Page and Shapiro, 1992) political decisions. Citizens are able to make reasonably good low-information decisions, and indeed are rational in doing so, because the demands of citizenship in contemporary democracies like the United States are presumed to be few, as are the tangible payoffs for engaging in politics.

The Case for an Informed Citizenry

We take issue with these perspectives and make the case for the importance of a broadly and equitably informed citizenry. Although we agree that the actual level and distribution of political knowledge in the United States falls short of this normative goal, this state of civic affairs is neither inevitable nor benign. Rather, it *results from* systematic distortions in the development and practice of democracy in America. And it *results in* substantial inequities in who participates, in how effective their participation is, and, ultimately, in who benefits from the actions of government.

Our argument is built on four propositions, which serve as both normative assumptions that drive the argument and (especially for the latter three) as empirical assumptions that we test throughout this book. The first is that the American political system is based on an amalgam of often inconsistent normative theories. This results in a polity that provides many opportunities for civic participation, that requires an often underestimated amount of citizen input if it is to operate democratically, but that makes few formal demands on citizens. The second is that factual knowledge about politics is a critical component of citizenship, one that is essential if citizens are to discern their real interests and take effective advantage of the civic opportunities afforded them. Our third proposition is that how much citizens know about politics, what they know, and how knowledge is distributed among different groups and classes of citizens is the product of both individual characteristics and systemic forces. And the fourth is that the varied opportunities to participate; the centrality of information to effective participation; and systematic biases in the ability, opportunity, and motivation to learn about politics combine to produce a stratified political system that affords different access to political power—

and thus one that is more or less democratic—depending on where in the knowledge hierarchy one falls.

Civic Demands and Opportunities in American Democracy

Citizenship in the United States is often described as "thin," meaning that expectations of civic responsibility are low and that the political system can operate effectively without a great deal of public input. This characterization is based on the assumptions that the United States is a liberal democracy; that liberal democracy expects little from its citizens beyond the occasional (and noncompulsory) act of voting for representatives; that both "the public" and "the public good" are unitary; and that citizens have relatively equal access to the public sphere. All four assumptions are overly simplistic. Although the U.S. system undeniably draws on liberal democratic theory for its core institutional structures and processes, the tangible influence of both direct, communal notions of democracy and of centralized, socialistic ones is often profound (Morone, 1990; Hanson, 1985). Further, liberal democracy, especially as instituted in the United States, assumes more civic input from its citizens than is often understood or articulated. Indeed, even the act of voting, if it is to be meaningful, requires a surprisingly active and engaged citizenry.

In the world of American politics, citizens are asked to undertake a wide array of civic activities: select qualified representatives (both within parties and in general elections) for local, state, and national offices; serve as the pool from which representatives are selected; reward and punish officeholders for their past performances; vote directly on policy issues through initiative and referenda; fill the thousands of voluntary, appointed, and bureaucratic civic roles required for the machinery of campaigns, elections, and government to work effectively; help shape local, state, and national political agendas through numerous outlets from public opinion polls to public demonstrations to direct contact with public officials; support and cooperate with the implementation of public policies; navigate government bureaucracies for information, goods, and services; attend local government and civic meetings; and more. Further, the explosion of new technologies and the growing popularity of such new political forums as instant polls, interactive media, electronic town meetings, and talk show politics have all expanded the opportunities for civic participation.

Knowledge as a Critical Component of Effective Citizenship

The complexity of contemporary American democracy and the numerous ways individuals can become politically involved suggest a potentially "thicker" definition of citizenship. For citizens to engage in politics in a way that is personally and collectively constructive, however, they must have the resources to do so. A central resource for democratic participation is political information.

We understand that effective citizenship requires more than just factual knowledge—information is a resource that can be used wisely or foolishly. Among other things, citizens must also be able to reason, be committed to such fundamental democratic principles as freedom of speech and assembly, share a sense of community, and be willing and able to participate. Nor do we assume that informed citizens would always arrive at a common understanding of the public good. To the contrary, many of the fundamental issues of politics are, as Connolly says, "essentially contestable" (1983, 10–41) and so can never be resolved to everyone's satisfaction. Finally, politics requires passion along with reason, and so it cannot be reduced to the technical calculus of informed experts.

Nonetheless, knowledge is a keystone to other civic requisites. In the absence of adequate information neither passion nor reason is likely to lead to decisions that reflect the real interests of the public. And democratic principles must be understood to be accepted and acted on in any meaningful way. A primary justification for the cultivation of the "intellect and judgment of mankind" is, according to John Stuart Mill, "learning the grounds of one's own opinions" (1859: 35). More generally, it is a fundamental tenet of democracy that the validity of ideas about what is proper and just in a society should be established through the exchange of informed opinions. It is *because* the public good emerges out of the often unstable combination of individual, group, and collective interests that information is critical. As Walter Lippmann noted, "public opinion is primarily a moralized and codified version of the facts" (1922, 81–82). Civic knowledge provides the raw material that allows citizens to use their virtues, skills, and passions in a way that is connected meaningfully to the empirical world.

More specifically, the real interests of an individual—and by extension of a group and of the polity as a whole—are reflected in the choices one would make if he or she were fully informed about the consequences. Thus, following the work of Connolly, what citizens "aspire to, but do not expect to attain completely, is a choice between alternative experiences that is *fully informed* about the factors entering into those experiences and helping to make each what it is. . . . One who chooses in the light of such self-awareness does not necessarily give [each piece of information] full reign: He simply chooses after confronting these facts about himself and his setting. Since it is inevitable that no choice will ever be *fully* informed in this way, we must say that the most informed choice available to one in a particular context constitutes a judgement in serious pursuit of one's real interests" (1983: 68–69).

The "alternative experiences" from which an individual chooses need not be motivated solely by narrow notions of self-interest: especially in the public realm individuals may prefer options that achieve some notion of the greater good, even if it comes at some personal expense. Nothing in our (or Connolly's) emphasis on individual choice and real interests is incompatible with more collective notions of the public interest. Nor does it suggest that informed choices would lead to particular preferences that could be determined independent of the affected individual. It does suggest, however, that "any current choice whose import undermines one's capacity to make future choices or seriously restricts opportunities to act upon a range of possible future choices weighs heavily against the real interests of the person or class of persons involved" (69). In short, the informed opinions, participation, and consent of citizens is by definition the best measure of what is in the public's interest. And the opportunities provided citizens to make such informed choices is the best measure of how democratic a system is.

Connolly's notion of informed choice goes a long way in helping to establish why information is a critical component of democratic politics. But politics often involves the clash of disparate individual and group interests (or definitions of the public good). Habermas (1984) suggests that the measure of a working democracy is the extent to which individuals and groups enter the public debate with relatively equal amounts of information. If the collective interests of a polity are ultimately based on the aggregation of individual and group choices that are as fully informed as possible, then this condition of relative equality is essential. Having relatively equal amounts of information assures neither a consensual nor a particular outcome (though nothing would prevent such an outcome in certain circumstances), but it does assure that whatever decisions are reached provide the most democratic approximation of the public will.

Political knowledge is also a critical and distinct facilitator of other aspects of good citizenship. A well-informed citizen is more likely to be attentive to politics, engaged in various forms of participation, committed to democratic principles, opinionated, and to feel efficacious. No other single characteristic of an individual affords so reliable a predictor of good citizenship, broadly conceived, as their level of knowledge. Thus, political knowledge not only aids in the construction of real interests, but it also helps assure that those interests become part of the governing process.

The Individual and Systemic Roots of Political Knowledge

The importance of political knowledge to effective citizenship suggests that those concerned about issues of democratic politics are well served by a close examination of what citizens know. But studies that attempt to gauge the level and distribution of valued civic requisites raise issues that are normatively charged. This is especially true when such studies conclude that citizens fall short of some standard of civic competence. Further, the tendency to treat low levels of knowledge as a psychological or a cognitive trait implies that the problem is intractable. For example, Herbert Hyman and Paul Sheatsley, after reviewing public knowledge of foreign affairs, claimed that "there is something about the uninformed which makes them harder to reach, no matter what the level or nature of the information" (1947: 413). Russell Neuman begins the concluding chapter of his book on political sophistication with Albert Einstein's comment that "politics is more difficult than physics" (1986: 169), implying that most people lack the wherewithal to understand it. Eric Smith, though equivocal, concludes there is little that could be done to increase current levels of political knowledge in the United States (1989: 219–23). Robert Luskin makes the most explicit case for equating knowledge with inherent traits and abilities: just as "ordinary people who enjoy music do not compose great symphonies," many ordinary citizens who might be interested in politics lack the ability to engage in it effectively. This is especially true, he argues, because politics is "simply harder material than, say, sports or cooking." He concludes that intelligence is a major determinant of political knowledge or sophistication (1990: 335–36).

Much of the evidence we provide could be seen as supporting these claims—we, too, found that what citizens know about politics has remained remarkably resistant to societal changes that, on the surface, should have led to a more broadly and equitably informed public. Ultimately, however, the conclusions one draws from any exploration of political competence depend as much on the normative assumptions and conceptual framework one brings to the data as on the data themselves. The emphasis on inherent ability found in most studies of political knowledge is reminiscent of the classical republican belief that citizens differ in their capacity for civic virtue. It is also consistent with more modern attempts to categorize citizens by their natural proclivity to engage in politics—consider Robert Dahl's classic distinction between "political man" and "civic man" (1961: 223-26). In all these cases, the dominant heuristic has emphasized individual motivation and ability to learn over the opportunity provided by the political environment to do so. This focus on the individual derives in part from the assumption that the information environment within which citizens act is both adequate and reasonably equitable. Thus, the determining factor regarding who knows what about politics is reduced to the psychological rather than the social or political.

Our conceptualization of this construct differs from the mainstream in subtle but important ways. We treat political knowledge as a resource rather than a trait. Political information is to democratic politics what money is to economics: it is the currency of citizenship.[1] And as with other currencies, the ability to acquire it is only partially and imperfectly the result of the personal abilities of individuals. The opportunity to learn about the political world is also influenced by social, economic, and political forces that are beyond the short-term control of individual citizens and that have different effects on citizens situated in different places on the socioeconomic ladder. Further, ability and motivation—often treated as purely individual characteristics—are initially shaped by and continually responsive to these larger forces. Arguing that political knowledge results from the interaction of ability, motivation, and opportunity—and that, in turn, all three are determined by a combination of individual and systemic factors—produces a more realistic view of why citizens are or are not adequately informed than is often proffered.[2]

Our conceptualization does not eliminate the normative implications of low levels of political knowledge. Nor does it excuse citizens for their political ignorance. It does, however, shift the emphasis from the competence of an individual or group to larger issues of access and opportunity. And although one might reasonably disagree with our specific weighting of these factors in this book, in the end it is clear that political knowledge is produced by the *interaction* of human observation of the political world with how the political world organizes and presents itself to the public. What people know about politics tells us much about citizens *and* about the political environment in which they operate. Just as the distribution of income and wealth is a telling statistic concerning the economic equity of a nation, so too the distribution of knowledge is informative as to a nation's potential for political equality. Political knowledge is a public resource as much as a private one.

Political Knowledge and Stratified Democracy

The varied but noncompulsory opportunities for civic participation, the importance of political knowledge for participating effectively, and the systemic roots of political knowledge and ignorance combine to produce a system that is more or less democratic depending on where in the information hierarchy one falls. For those who are relatively well informed, the system operates much as in textbook descriptions of representative democracy. The less informed one is, however, the less likely one is to participate, and the less likely it is that one's participation will be effective.

The stratified nature of democracy in America should be reason for concern in its own right because much of democracy's normative force derives from the noninstrumental benefits of self-determination and public engagement (Pateman, 1970). There are, however, more tangible costs to stratified democracy. Because the likelihood of being politically informed is at least partially determined by access to other economic and social resources, the public sphere often becomes a mechanism by which differences in economic, social, and political power are perpetuated and even exacerbated, rather than serving as an arena in which socioeconomic differences are discounted and in which citizens engage each other on relatively equal footing (the underlying premise of "one person—one vote" and other notions of majority rule).

The fact that some citizens do participate extensively in politics is often used to suggest that an active minority can substitute for or represent those who are less politically engaged. To be plausible, however, such arguments must assume that the public is a single, homogeneous mass (with singular, homogeneous interests), that the activist minority is representative of the varied interests of the less engaged majority, or that this minority is willing to ignore its own interests for the interests of those who are less willing or able to participate. Although these assumptions have some validity, ultimately they ignore the contestable, socially determined nature of the public good, the conflictual, zero-sum nature of much of politics, and the often sizable and systematic group differences in political power. Those who participate are advantaged—as individuals and as members of certain groups and classes—in the process of deciding who gets what from government and, ultimately, in the determination of the public good.

Conceptualizing and Measuring Political Knowledge

The concept of political knowledge is at the center of our critique of the promise and performance of American democracy. We are not alone in making this claim—many political theorists and practitioners throughout the ages have argued for the importance of an informed citizenry. As Neuman has noted, however, "Democratic theory has never been terribly explicit about the precise requirements of knowledge and cognitive skill that must be exhibited by each citizen for the system to work as intended" (1986: 8). Political theorists generally discuss the various requisites of citizenship as if they were indistinguishable, a tendency that has carried over to empirical research. As a result, political knowledge is often treated as one of a variety of interchangeable constructs measuring what is essentially civic competency. According to John Zaller: "Variables purporting to measure 'political awareness,' 'political expertise,' 'political sophistication,' 'cognitive sophistication,' 'political information,' 'political involvement,' 'media exposure,' and 'political interest' appear regularly in the public opinion literature and are used (along with education) more or less interchangeably to explain the same general family of dependent variables. Questions thus arise: Are these alternative measures different in any important ways? If so, what are the differences? If not, what is the basic concept of which they are all indicators, and how is this concept best measured?" (1990: 126).

There are some obvious reasons for this conceptual blurring. Both statistically and substantively, knowledge of politics is closely related to other aspects of citizenship, the former both depending on and affecting the latter. Yet ultimately they are not equivalent. Indeed, the failure to treat political knowledge as a distinct concept, and thus to treat the qualities of good citizenship, even of human actualization, as interchangeable is responsible for much of the distortion that has occurred as scholars move from theory to practice to prescription in the study of American democracy and citizenship.

Defining Political Knowledge

We define *political knowledge* as the range of factual information about politics that is stored in long-term memory. This definition, while still broad, distinguishes political knowledge from other forms of knowledge and from other requisites of citizenship.

The emphasis on *information* distinguishes political knowledge from such other key concepts of mass politics as attitudes, values, beliefs, and opinions. It also distinguishes knowledge from logic, reasoning, discourse, participation, and other important components of democratic citizenship. Political knowledge is a type of cognition, but not all cognitions constitute factual information about politics. The emphasis on *factual* information distinguishes political knowledge from cognitions that are incorrect or that are not subject to reasonable tests of correctness.

Establishing something as a fact is an admittedly problematic enterprise. One cannot state as a fact why certain people are poor and others are not. One cannot state as a fact how many people are poor in America. One cannot even state as a fact what it means to be poor. One can say, however, with reasonable assurance how the federal government defines poverty, what percentage of the American public currently lives below the federally defined poverty line, and whether that percentage has increased or decreased over the past four years. The reduction of weighty issues like poverty to clinical facts about official statistics leads many to argue that the enterprise is trivializing. If the debate were to end there, we would agree. But our point is that facts prevent rather than lead to the trivialization of public discourse. Such facts as the percentage of the American public living below the poverty line, how the line is determined, and how the percentage has changed over time provide a foundation for deliberation about larger issues. They prevent debates from becoming disconnected from the material conditions they attempt to address. They allow individuals and groups with widely varied experiences and philosophies to have some common basis of comparison—some common language with which to clarify differences, identify points of agreement, and establish criteria for evaluation. They tether public discourse to objective conditions while allowing for debates over what objectivity means (for example, is the poverty line a valid definition of poverty).

The emphasis on information that is *stored in long-term memory* distinguishes political knowledge from information that is never cognized or that is used in short-term memory but then discarded. This is important to our argument, in that it allows us to focus on information that citizens bring to their interpretation of the political world, rather than solely on the information that is provided as new issues emerge and events unfold. It is this kind of information that gives citizens—as individuals, members of particular groups, and as a collectivity—the ability to think and act with greater autonomy and authority.[3]

The notion of *range* is included in the definition to distinguish the broad concept of political knowledge from the more specific facts that comprise it. This allows us to speak about different levels of political knowledge by adding additional qualifiers. For example, one can conceptually distinguish among knowledge about a particular president, knowledge about the presidency, knowledge about national political institutions and processes, and knowledge about politics more generally. Thus we can speak to the issue of whether citizens are specialists who are informed about particular aspects of politics but uninformed about others, or generalists who are more broadly informed. We can also explore the extent to which specific information is more or less relevant to certain groups or in certain circumstances.

Finally, our definition of *politics,* taken from David Easton (1965), is the authoritative allocation of goods, services, and values. The use of Easton's definition allows us to distinguish knowledge about politics from other kinds of knowledge (for example, music, literature, or science) but does so in a way that does not close off discussion about what constitutes politically relevant information. For example, poststructuralists and neo-Marxists see the culture industry as reproducing (and occasionally challenging) patterns of domination and subordination in society through television, popular music, and the like. Certain kinds of information regarding popular culture are relevant to the authoritative allocation of values and so might be included in a particular consideration of political knowledge. (The case could be made, that information about rappers Ice T and Sister Souljah and about the television character Murphy Brown was politically relevant in the 1992 presidential campaign). The same logic applies for information about such subjects as economics, geography, and history. In this way, our definition sets rules for justifying the inclusion or exclusion of certain kinds of information without being overly rigid regarding the specific content.

This definition—and our use of it—is subject to several criticisms (see, for example, Graber, 1994). It is, in some ways, both too restrictive and too broad. The determination of correct answers is often subjective and open to bias: indeed, the notion that there are any objectively determined facts is a rebuttable presumption. In some cases data limitations prevent us from measuring political knowledge as subtly as we conceptualize it. Nonetheless, we believe this definition has much to offer. By treating knowledge as the aggregation of facts that citizens bring to their individual and collective decision making it serves as an indicator of their agency in the construction and implementation of the public good.

Knowledge as Situational, Relative, and Collective

Our definition provides a mechanism by which to decide whether a particular piece of information constitutes a political fact. It does not, however, provide much guidance in establishing which facts are important for citizens to know. This is, in part, a conscious decision. Any attempt to assemble a specific list of critical facts is sure to fail. Research about what citizens know can be put to questionable purposes, serving as litmus tests for determining whose opinions matter most, and even for who is deserving of the mantle of citizenship. The presumed inability of the masses to know either their own interests or the public interest has been one of the most powerful arguments against democracy. Such arguments have been used to restrict the participation of women, the poor, and blacks in the United States (consider, for example, the role of civic knowledge exams in restricting the voting rights of the poor and of blacks in the postbellum South). The very endeavor of identifying what citizens should know seems patronizing and antithetical to the notion that democracy is rule by the people. According to E. E. Schattschneider, the effort to establish informational standards for effective citizenship "is dangerous because it creates confusion in high places. . . . It is possible that we shall abolish democracy before we have found out what it is!" (1960: 136).

One solution to this problem is to avoid preconceptions altogether and let the data speak for themselves. There are good reasons for this approach—a slavish attachment to pure theory can lead one to deduce the absurd. Inductive reasoning, in which theory is constructed from specific evidence, can lead to conclusions that are more firmly grounded in the possible. Russell Neuman, Marion Just, and Ann Crigler make the case for such a *constructionist* approach:

> Constructionism is non-evaluative in character. The paradigm [of] the uninformed voter . . . set[s] up an idealized model of rational citizenship in a rich information environment. When measured against the Madisonian ideal, the voter . . . comes up short. Even when researchers in these traditions testify for the defense, asserting that voters are not fools, they do so within the original paradigm. Constructionist theory turns the original question on its head. One does not start with an idealized model of rational issue-voting and design studies to see if the voter measures up. It focuses on what motivates people to pay attention to some public issues rather than assuming that civic duty simply requires attention to all matters political. One asks, simply, how do people become informed about the political world around them, and how do they use the information they have acquired? (1992: 18)

We share much of the sentiment expressed by Neuman and his colleagues and follow their advice to a great extent throughout this book. As Schattschneider argues there is a danger in setting standards that are unreachable: "We become cynical about democracy because the public does not act the way the simplistic definition of democracy says that it should act. . . . The trouble is that we have defined democracy in such a way that we are in danger of putting ourselves out of business" (1960: 134–36).

Nonetheless, if an overdependence on idealized models can lead to cynicism, an overdependence on existing norms and practices runs an equal risk of treating the current world as the only and best possible one. For example, Schattschneider moves from an attack on "pedants" who attempt to measure what citizens know about politics to the conclusion that "real" democracy is by definition "a form of collaboration of ignorant people and experts" (1960: 136–37). For this reason, we believe it is necessary to say something more specific about what one should know to be an effective citizen. After all, though the responsibilities of citizens are varied, they are broadly identifiable. And although it is true that citizens cannot be experts on all aspects of politics, a general familiarity with (1) the rules of the game (the institutions and processes of elections and governance); (2) the substance of politics (the major domestic and international issues of the day, current social and economic conditions, key policy initiatives, and so forth); and (3) people and parties (the promises, performances, and attributes of candidates, public officials, and the political parties) is critical to the maintenance of a healthy democracy.

There is a tension between constructionist and prescriptive approaches to informed citizenship. We address this tension by arguing that the value of political information is situational, relative, and collective. The value of knowledge is *situational* in that it depends on the particular use to which it is put. For example, knowing how a presidential veto works is of little use in determining how to vote on a local school bond. Our emphasis on a broadly informed citizenry is based on the assumption that government addresses a wide array of issues of direct or indirect relevance to citizens and involving various actors and institutions: the instrumental utility of this knowledge is dependent on the context, however.

The value of knowledge is also *relative* in that, all other things being equal, more information is better than less information. For example, the more our citizen knows about the school bond issue, the clearer she will be on what her interests are (however she defines them), and the more likely she will be to cast a vote consistent with those interests. Knowledge is also relative across time: politics is an ongoing process, and new or

more accurate information allows citizens to continually refine their political opinions and behaviors so that they better match their real interests. And political knowledge is relative across groups: in the competition over scarce resources, those with more information are likely to be advantaged over those with less, regardless of the absolute amount of information involved—to second graders, third graders are geniuses. It is for these reasons that Habermas argues that democracy requires relative equality in the conditions under which political discourse occurs (1984). By treating political knowledge as a relative good, we can evaluate the informational state of individuals, groups, and the citizenry as a whole without need of some absolute standard of knowledge.

Finally, the value of knowledge is *collective,* in that the greater the aggregate amount of information possessed by a group, and, ultimately, by the citizenry as a whole, the more likely that the actions of government will accurately reflect the will of the people. This is true regardless of whether the underlying issue is, in Jane Mansbridge's terms, adversarial or unitary (1983). When group interests differ, the allocation of scarce resources will be determined in part by the relative knowledge (and thus the political effectiveness) of the groups involved. Even when the underlying public interest is unitary (or consensual), greater information increases the likelihood that this common interest will be discerned and acted on effectively.[4] Treating political knowledge as a collective good allows us to examine individual and group levels of knowledge without losing sight of the ultimately social and communal nature of politics and the ultimately social and communal value of political knowledge. Acknowledging the situational, relative, and collective utility of political knowledge, while also identifying the broad categories of knowledge likely to be most relevant to the responsibilities of citizenship combines the advantages of both idealized and pragmatic approaches to the study of political knowledge and avoids many of their limitations.

Much of the evidence presented in this book is based on survey data of citizens' knowledge about particular facts or sets of facts (see chapter 2 and appendix 1 for detailed descriptions). In spite of our hesitancy to provide a list of critical facts that citizens know, we are necessarily limited in the extent we can tap the full range of possible information citizens have with such data.

Although this is a potentially devastating limitation to the empirical exploration of political knowledge, this endeavor is valid for two reasons. First, our analyses are limited to a finite set of facts, but this set includes a very large number of survey questions on a very wide range of political topics. Second and more important, in much of our analysis we use our

measures of specific political facts as purposive samples of what citizens know. Although we discuss the content of individual items and evaluate their potential relevance for effective citizenship, we also argue—and demonstrate—that fairly simple measures can be constructed that are good indicators of what people know more generally about politics. Thus we are able to talk about citizens' level of political knowledge and yet avoid some of the pitfalls associated with ranking the substantive importance of particular pieces of information.

An Overview of This Book

In the chapters to follow we develop the arguments introduced here, describe current levels of political knowledge in the United States, and provide evidence regarding the causes and consequences of political knowledge and ignorance. We begin chapter 1 with a review of classical political thought and demonstrate that support for democracy has always been tempered by concerns about the capacity of most citizens to know what is in their own and the public's interest. As a result, democracy has been instituted cautiously and selectively in Western societies, with significant limits placed on the civic roles played by the general citizenry and on which citizens could fill even these limited roles. Over time, the moral logic of self-rule coupled with theories that made a stronger case for the civic potential of the general public have expanded both the role of citizens and the range of citizens eligible to fill these roles.

The U.S. system is built on these competing, often contradictory views regarding the possibility of democratic governance. Aspects of the system that encourage civic engagement assume that a knowledgeable citizenry is necessary for the system to operate effectively. But skepticism regarding the competence of the public, beliefs in the appropriateness of social and economic hierarchy, and biased notions regarding the nature of the public good continue to place significant limits on the commitment to democracy in America. The result is a political culture that allows for a great deal of civic involvement, but one that sends mixed messages regarding the importance of this involvement and has provided mixed opportunities for different groups to engage the system effectively.

The combination of a system of government built on the assumption of an informed citizenry and mounting evidence that citizens are often woefully underinformed about the details of politics has seemed paradoxical to many observers of contemporary democracy. Researchers have attempted to resolve this paradox in a variety of ways, including arguing against the necessity—and even the rationality—of a broadly informed

public. But these theories depend on overly simplified notions of the public, the public interest, and the nature of civic participation. They also often assume a more knowledgeable citizenry than they explicitly acknowledge and so fail to truly resolve the paradox. A close examination of the varied responsibilities of citizens and of the resources citizens need to effectively perform these responsibilities suggests that there is no way around the necessity of a broadly informed public in a democracy. We conclude that there is no paradox; rather, for citizens who are informed the American political system does operate as intended, while for those who are not, the system is far from democratic. Although the political system can operate without a great deal of informed input from its citizens, it operates more democratically as the range and depth of information held by citizens increases and as the distribution of knowledge becomes more equitable.

In chapter 2 we present a detailed portrait of what Americans actually know. Compared with what people ought to know as determined by a textbook model of citizenship, the public is ignorant about much of the detail of government and politics—just as conventional wisdom holds. In contrast, and compared with what we would expect people to know in light of arguments that acquiring and retaining political knowledge is fundamentally unnecessary, even irrational, the level of knowledge about certain aspects of politics is surprisingly high. An examination of the pattern of misinformation suggests that rather than being apathetic, many citizens actively attempt to understand the political world and often give answers that, although wrong, are plausible or that reflect biases in the information environment.

In chapter 3 we continue with our overview of what Americans know about politics, focusing on how levels of public knowledge in the United States today compare to those of the past. Drawing on several hundred knowledge questions that have been asked more than once over the past half century, we conclude that the public's level of political knowledge is little different today than it was fifty years ago. Given the ample reasons to expect changing levels of knowledge over the past fifty years, this finding provides the strongest evidence for the intractability of political knowledge and ignorance. The specific impact of societal changes, however, is hotly contested by those who study the state of postindustrial America. For some, they add up to a better, more competent citizenry (Inglehart, 1977), whereas for others they have led to the "closing of the American mind" (Bloom, 1987). We conclude that positive and negative systemic changes occurring over the past fifty years have offset one another. This conclusion is bolstered by several specific examples of significant, short-

term shifts in knowledge of particular facts. We interpret these patterns as evidence that learning (and forgetting) is very much dependent on the context in which it occurs, and that given the appropriate mix of motivation and opportunity, aggregate levels of political knowledge can be increased.

The conceptual arguments presented in chapter 1 and the aggregate overview of the "state of the masses" presented in chapters 2 and 3 form the backdrop for more specific analyses in subsequent chapters. In chapter 4 we begin with an examination of the patterns and distribution of political knowledge. The aggregate variation in knowledge of specific facts described in chapter 2 can result from several different patterns in what people know about politics more generally, each of which have different implications for the way in which democracy operates. We explore whether citizens specialize in what they know, or whether they tend to be generalists who are more or less equally informed (or uninformed) about most areas of politics. With a few important exceptions, data from a wide range of surveys indicate that citizens who are the most informed about one aspect of national politics tend to be the most informed about other aspects. To the general question of whether the U.S. public is composed of information specialists, the answer is no.

Evidence that people tend to be generalists is consistent with our theoretical argument regarding the demands of citizenship in the United States. It also raises the possibility that the citizenry is divided into those who are information rich and those who are information poor. In discussing what Americans know and don't know, it is important to remember that the public is not a single, undifferentiated mass of people. We conclude chapter 4 by examining the distribution of political knowledge and find, much as with other aspects of the subject, a complex picture that defies simple labels of "good" or "bad." On the one hand, there are sizable differences in what the most and least informed citizens know. On the other hand, the overall distribution of knowledge very much approximates a normal curve, with the majority of citizens, while not very informed, also not very uninformed. Thus, a common view of what Americans know, which sees a small knowledgeable elite and a vast ignorant public, appears to be incorrect. Instead, sizable proportions of citizens can be found at most points along the continuum from high to low knowledge. In addition, we find significant, often dramatic group differences in levels of political knowledge, with groups that are most disadvantaged in the social and economic spheres (women, blacks, low-income citizens, and younger citizens) also the least informed, and thus least equipped to use the political system to redress their grievances. Further, these knowledge gaps show little evi-

dence of declining over time. Indeed, levels of knowledge among white, middle-class, educated males—citizens who arguably have been afforded the greatest opportunity to develop the skills and incentives to learn about politics—are remarkably high. If, as economic models of politics suggest, it is rational for citizens to remain mostly ignorant of politics, can we accept that the wealthiest, best-educated, and most powerful citizens are also the most irrational?

Why are some citizens reasonably well informed about politics, others modestly informed, and still others oblivious to all but the most elementary of facts? In chapter 5 we attempt to answer these questions, focusing on differences in citizens' ability, motivation, and opportunity to learn about politics. A great variety of individual and systemic factors interact to determine how much an individual knows about politics, including—among others—interest and engagement in politics, formal education, occupational experiences, and the media environment. Continued structural disadvantages, the legacy of past exclusion from politics, and the perceived irrelevance of much of what constitutes mainstream national politics also depress current levels of knowledge for members of certain groups (for example, blacks and women). Individual, systemic, and contextual factors have a reciprocal relation: they feed one another, and this mutual influence, by promoting a spiraling of knowledge, is one reason there are great disparities in knowledge levels between individuals. These findings are central to the argument that the distribution of political knowledge in the United States should be viewed as an issue of political power and access rather than simply as a matter of personal choice and ability.

Driving our research is the assumption that political knowledge matters. In chapter 6 we turn to this bottom line, using several public opinion surveys to demonstrate that better-informed citizens are significantly more likely to participate in politics, are better able to discern their "self-interest, properly understood" (de Tocqueville, 1850: 525), are better able to connect their enlightened self-interest to specific opinions about the political world, are more likely to hold opinions that are internally consistent and stable over time, and are more likely to connect their opinions to their political participation in meaningful, rational ways. More informed citizens are also more likely to demonstrate other requisites of good citizenship, such as political tolerance. In short, informed citizens are better citizens in a number of ways consistent with normative and pragmatic notions of what constitutes good citizenship.

The relation between knowledge and effective participation holds for members of socially and economically disadvantaged groups. But because members of these groups are less informed in the aggregate than their more advantaged counterparts, they are often less able to use the political system effectively. This should concern those who believe that in a democracy citizens from all walks of life should be engaged in politics; it is of special concern because the interests of disadvantaged groups often differ from those of more advantaged ones. In the process by which the public good is established and by which the specific allocation of goods, services, and values is determined, knowledge is power. And that power is distributed in ways that call into question how truly democratic the U.S. system is.

In 1922, Joseph Tussman asked, rhetorically, "Why . . . dream of impossible tribunals manned by thoughtful, devoted, disinterested angels deliberating about the common good? There is a better plan, which takes men as they are and asks of them only what is possible and pleasant" (1970: 18). In answering his own question, Tussman wrote: "There is more to life than politics, even for the political animal. But there is more, also, than the private pursuit of happiness; and nothing is more central to the spirit of democracy than this conviction. The democrat turns his back resolutely on the temptation to divide men into pursuers of happiness and bearers of responsibility. He summons every man to his place in the public forum" (28). We conclude (chapter 7) with a summary and discussion, focusing on ways in which political knowledge levels and, by extension, the public's level of political engagement, might be increased. There is no silver bullet to slay apathy and ignorance among citizens, prevarication and neglect by public officials, or ineffective and misguided reportorial methods by journalists. Nor is there a simple way to induce the schools to give greater weight to education for citizenship. But just as our research suggests that citizens come to understand the political world through a wide variety of means and influences, so too may some improvement in the level of citizen knowledge result from many small efforts, each of which is achievable in the real—rather than ideal—world. The very existence of relatively high levels of political knowledge among some citizens, in view of compelling arguments that it is rational to remain ignorant, is cause for optimism.

Improving citizenship in the United States will require citizens to change, but the heart of the problem is not with the individual. We subscribe to V. O. Key's oft-quoted notion that "the voice of the people is but an echo. The output of an echo chamber bears an inevitable and invariable relation to the input" (1966: 2). To this we would add that it also bears an "inevitable and invariable relation" to the shape of the chamber itself. Accordingly, the impetus for change needs to come largely from

those who speak into and control the chamber. Citizens do need to be more engaged in politics, but the reasons for paying attention need to be clearer to them, the benefits of stronger citizenship must be more evident, and the opportunities to learn about politics more frequent, timely, and equitable.

CHAPTER ONE

From Democratic Theory to Democratic Practice: The Case for an Informed Citizenry

A popular government, without popular information or the means of acquiring it, is but a prologue to a farce or a tragedy, or perhaps both. —JAMES MADISON, letter to W. T. Barry

The most familiar fact to arise from sample surveys is that popular levels of information about public affairs are, from the point of view of the informed observer, astonishingly low.—PHILIP CONVERSE, *Handbook of Political Science*

It seems remarkable that democracies have survived through the centuries. . . . That is the paradox. Individual voters today seem unable to satisfy the requirements for a democratic system of government outlined by political theorists.—BERNARD BERELSON, PAUL LAZARSFELD, and WILLIAM MCPHEE, *Voting*

Debates over the importance of an informed citizenry are rooted in the collision of theory and practice. In theory, a democracy requires knowledgeable citizens to avoid becoming Madison's "tragedy" or "farce." In practice, it appears that a majority of people lack even the most basic political information. Indeed, the belief that citizens were incapable of self-government led to great skepticism regarding the wisdom of democratic governance—as C. B. Macpherson notes, "from Plato and Aristotle down to the eighteenth and nineteenth centuries, democracy, when it was thought of at all, was defined as rule by the poor, the ignorant, and the incompetent" (1977: 9–10).[1] But for the last 200 years the United States has survived as a stable democracy, despite continued evidence of an uninformed public. This is the paradox of modern democracy.

Much of contemporary democratic theory and research has been an attempt to resolve this paradox. There is a consensus that most citizens are politically uninformed, but there is no consensus on the causes or implications of this state of civic affairs. Many observers, starting from the premise that an informed citizenry is the sine qua non of democracy, conclude that American politics is in crisis: that the tensions inherent in its

theory and practice have made it either ungovernable, undemocratic, or both. Robert Entman, in his aptly titled book, *Democracy without Citizens,* argues that "people who participate regularly and knowledgeably form a distinct minority," and, thus, the U.S. system "represents the general public less well than Americans deserve" (1989: 28). Paul Blumberg puts it more starkly: "America's embarrassing little secret . . . is that vast numbers of Americans are ignorant, not merely of the specialized details of government which ordinary citizens cannot be expected to master, but of the most elementary political facts—information so basic as to challenge the central tenet of democratic government itself" (1990: 1).

Not everyone agrees that low levels of civic knowledge constitute a threat to democratic politics. Starting from a realist's view, many believe that the need for a generally informed citizenry is overstated. For these scholars the solution to the paradox of democracy is not to change citizens—or the system in which they operate—but to change the definition of democracy: "It is an outrage to attribute the failures of American democracy to the ignorance and stupidity of the masses. The most disastrous shortcomings of the system have been those of the intellectuals whose concepts of democracy have been amazingly rigid and uninventive" (Schattschneider, 1960: 135–36). In this evolving view, real democracy functions through some combination of control by elites, the availability of attentive publics, resourceful use of heuristics and information shortcuts by citizens, and the beneficent effects of collective rationality wherein the whole of citizen awareness is greater than the sum of its parts.

Much of this research is motivated by a desire to salvage liberal democracy from its critics, to show that "ordinary citizens are not to be feared" and that "skepticism and disdain [for the civic capacity of the public] are not well founded" (Page and Shapiro, 1992: xi, 1). But in attempting to rehabilitate the image of ordinary citizens, scholars sell these citizens short. Further, these theories ultimately fail to show that a political system can operate effectively and democratically without an informed citizenry. The paradox, it seems, remains.

Much of the difficulty in addressing this paradox is that the propositions being juxtaposed—that democracy requires an informed citizenry and that American citizens are uninformed—are too general. What constitutes a "democracy" or an "informed citizen"? Why is it presumed that citizens should be informed? What does it mean to say that the public is uninformed? Political thinkers have been remarkably vague on these issues, and as a result the evidence used to gauge citizens' performance, and the standards against which that performance is measured, are often inadequate or inappropriate.

Democratic Theory and the Informed Citizen

"There is no democratic theory," writes Robert Dahl, "there are only democratic theories" (1956: 1). At the same time, as Schattschneider correctly notes, "Whether we know it or not *all* speculation about American politics rests on some image of democracy" (1960: 129, emphasis added). The range of available democratic theories makes it easy to argue selectively when characterizing the opportunities and obligations of citizenship and when appraising citizens' performance. This is true regardless of whether one is challenging or defending the American citizen. By not explicitly acknowledging the range of normative theories on which American politics is based, one runs the danger of selling democracy short by expecting too much or too little from its citizens.

Advocates of democracy have made their case on three grounds: the inherent and equal right of all citizens to self-determination regarding their collective actions; the greater likelihood of maximizing the public good (however it is defined) if the public is centrally involved in its determination and implementation; and the self-actualizing benefits that derive from participating in public life. At the same time, political theorists have often doubted the ability of citizens to govern themselves wisely. Most citizens were believed to lack the civic virtues and knowledge to discern either their own interests or the public good more broadly, or to effectively translate these interests into political action. The tension between the belief that citizens should govern themselves and the belief that they are incapable of doing so has been resolved in one of three ways: rejecting democracy as a viable form of government; acknowledging the inherent right of citizens to govern themselves but limiting the scope of that participation as a concession to the assumed civic shortcomings of most citizens; or advocating for strong versions of democracy that are designed not only to allow citizens to participate, but to provide them with the resources necessary to do so effectively.[2] Each of these approaches has influenced the theory and practice of democracy in America.

More specifically, we argue that American politics is shaped by five competing traditions: a deep-seated skepticism of democracy; a republican belief in civic virtue; a liberal faith in the individual and the private sphere; a protectionist belief in participation as a check on the excesses of centralized power; and a communalist belief (found in both the Greek city state and in the writings of some eighteenth- and nineteenth-century theorists) in the self-actualizing educative role of participation in the public sphere. Collectively, these five traditions help to determine the range of what citizens are expected to know in the United States, the conditions

under which they are expected to know it, and the way in which their failure to meet these informational requisites is interpreted.

Citizenship, Civic Competence, and Democracy in the Greek City States

Western notions of democracy can be traced to the political transformation that occurred in Greece in the fifth century B.C., when "several city-states, which from time out of mind had been governed by various undemocratic rulers, whether aristocrats, oligarchs, monarchs, or tyrants, were transformed into systems in which a substantial number of free, adult males were entitled as citizens to participate directly in governing" (Dahl, 1989: 13).

Although no comprehensive theoretical treatise exists that codifies the normative logic underpinning this transformation, enough is known to reconstruct the nature of the polis in democratic Greek city states like Athens. Several of these characteristics are of special relevance to our exploration of the nature of democratic citizenship (Dahl, 1989: 18–19). First, it was assumed that the citizens of a democracy were similar socially, culturally, and economically, thus limiting the scope and depth of disputes regarding the nature of the public good and helping to assure that the public good was compatible with more private interests and pursuits. Second, all citizens were expected to participate directly in public life. This included not only participating in collective deliberations, but also filling the numerous roles designed to implement policy and administer the law. According to Dahl, "every citizen [of Athens] was almost certain to occupy some office for a year, and a large number would become members of the highly important Council of Five Hundred, which determined the agenda for the Assembly" (19). And third, in order to participate effectively in public life, it was critical that citizens be able "to acquire the knowledge of their city and their fellow citizens, from observation, experience, and discussion, that would enable them to understand the common good" (19). Developing such an informed citizenry was not left to chance; it was a central goal of both formal education and the design of the public sphere more generally.

But a homogeneous, informed public capable of governing itself was achieved by allowing only a minority of those living in the Greek city states to wear the mantle of full citizenship: women, long-term resident aliens, and slaves were all excluded from most forms of participation. Although the reasons for this exclusion are uncertain, it seems reasonable to assume that it resulted from the belief that such residents lacked the common interests and civic capacity deemed necessary for effective citizenship in a democracy. Greek city states were designed as strong democracies for the few, rather than the many.

Even this circumscribed notion of direct democracy was viewed by many as placing too much faith in the civic virtue and wisdom of the public. Doubts about the ability of average citizens to make informed decisions have been raised since Plato's tale of the cave. Indeed, Socrates and Plato were among democracy's harshest critics; they doubted both the civic ability and civic authority of the general public. Public opinion was equated with misguided beliefs that had little to do with the truth. Democracies were believed doomed to seek a uniform level of incompetence and were considered inherently unstable, tending first toward oligarchy and despotism and then back toward democracy in an endless cycle of tyranny of the minority or the majority.

For Socrates and Plato, the public good emerged from a just society, defined as one that was in harmony with nature. Since hierarchy was natural, the key was to design a system in which citizens found their proper niche. This natural order could be determined through a combination of observation and reason, and so society should be designed and ruled by those most knowledgeable about the social and physical world. Members of Plato's republic were divided into three classes—the general citizenry; a more select group of "Auxiliaries," who executed and enforced the law; and "Guardians," who had ultimate authority to rule. Membership in the Auxiliary or Guardian class was based strictly on ability, as determined through a series of examinations. Those who achieved the status of Guardian were "philosopher kings" whose every action furthered the public good.

Aristotle also doubted the individual civic capacity of most citizens. Unlike his teacher, however, he concluded that ultimate political authority rested with the general citizenry. For him, politics was among the "number of arts in which the creative artist is not the only, or even the best judge. These are the arts whose products can be understood and judged even by those who do not possess any skill in the art. A house, for instance, is something which can be understood by others besides the builder: indeed the user of the house—or in other words the householder—will judge it even better than he does. In the same way a pilot will judge a rudder better than a shipwright does; and the diner—not the cook—will be the best judge of a feast" (1946: 126). Aristotle also believed that it was possible for citizens to participate—directly and indirectly— in governing the polity and that under the proper circumstances rule by the many was both more just and more stable than other forms of government. Key to this argument was his faith in collective judgments: "There is this to be said for the

Many. Each of them by himself may not be of a good quality; but when they come together it is possible that they may surpass—collectively and as a body, although not individually—the quality of the few best" (123).

Drawing on this notion of collective judgment, Aristotle argued that in the ideal state the general citizenry would both select its leaders and deliberate on the wisdom of their political decisions (125–26). Embedded in his writings, however, are many concerns that place important limits on democracy's scope. For Aristotle, a "good ruler" must also be a "good man," in that both require moral wisdom (101–7). In a society in which all citizens possess this quality, all citizens could act as rulers. But like Plato, Aristotle believed in natural differences in individuals' civic and ethical capacities (see, for example, *Nicomachean Ethics,* VI xiii). Whereas all citizens have both rights and obligations, these will vary depending on a citizen's ability to contribute to the general good—the ultimate purpose of government (116–21).

This notion of "distributive justice" led Aristotle to circumscribe citizenship in two important ways. First, in his ideal system, which he calls a *polity,* leaders (both magistrates and judges) could be selected in a variety of ways: by all citizens from all citizens; by some citizens from all citizens; by all citizens from some citizens; and by some citizens from some citizens (198–99; 202). The particular mix of who selects leaders and from what pool they are selected is determined by the social, economic, and civic quality of the citizenry in question.[3]

Second, Aristotle's definition of citizenship leaves out a large portion of those who reside within the polis. The greatest opportunity to participate in political deliberation and governance is reserved for middle-aged members of the leisure class. Slaves, foreigners, women, laborers, farmers, craftsmen, merchants, and the like are either excluded from the citizenry or have very limited political functions (300–303). Aristotle ultimately defines a polity as a mixture of oligarchy and democracy (175) and views this form of government as closely related to aristocracy, or rule by "the best" (172–74).

The Roman republic (and later, the Renaissance city states, such as Florence) built on Aristotle's political vision. This republican tradition assumed that full human potential emerged out of social and political associations, that civic virtue was a fragile concept that needed to be cultivated, and that the best political system was one in which citizens were relatively equal in their political, social, and economic status. As with the Greeks, however, this relative equality was achieved by excluding a majority of residents from the full rights and obligations of citizenship. These republics were also designed to balance the interests and abilities of

the one (usually a monarch), the few (an aristocracy or oligarchy), and the many (the general citizenry) through a carefully designed constitutional structure that echoed Aristotle's notion of distributive justice.

Liberalism and the Emergence of the Private Sphere

Capitalism added a new dimension to the already complicated debate over the role of the citizen. According to John Locke, all human beings have the right to life, liberty, and the pursuit of property. Yet natural differences in people were reflected in their ability to add value to the material world through their labor, and so some individuals would accumulate more than others. It was the fear of losing the fruits of one's labor that necessitated government. Atomistic individuals entered into a social contract so as to assure that their lives, liberty, and property were protected from those who had less.[4] Political leaders existed to create and administer the law, but ultimate authority resided with the public.

As in the republics of Plato and Aristotle, hierarchy was natural. But in the Greek republics, hierarchy was centrally political and civic. Natural differences were emphasized only in terms of their relevance to the creation of an organic community that furthered the common good. Differences in social and economic status were encouraged only insofar as they furthered this collective good and assured that citizens were capable of filling the various roles of the political hierarchy. For English social contract theorists, economic hierarchy was the centerpiece. Differences in public roles existed to assure the protection of private rights and wealth. It was, in many ways, the mirror image of Plato's republic. For Plato, authority resided with an elite guardian class, but that authority was used for achieving the public good. In the liberal state ultimate authority resided with the people themselves, but power was used for the purpose of protecting private rights and property.

For liberal social contract theorists, the centralization of political power was a necessary evil. The type of public sphere that emerges from this concession to human nature is a matter of some debate, however. Such writers as Carole Pateman and C. B. Macpherson present the most negative view of public life in liberal societies. Civic virtue is nowhere to be found: left to their own devices those in power would use it for personal gain. Thus, political institutions should be designed so as to limit the possibility of leaders exercising power indiscriminately. Citizens' civic power was largely negative—the power to dissolve the social contract if their inalienable rights were not protected by the state.

The extent to which liberalism is driven solely by "possessive indi-

vidualism" can be overstated. Richard Ashcraft (1987) and James Tully (1979) argue that Locke allows for a more egalitarian, communal notion of both property and civil society than is often assumed. They emphasize Locke's notion of "positive community," in which all property is ultimately common. They also point to Locke's belief that it is the obligation of all citizens to act in ways consistent with the public interest, and that notions of the public good (consistent with natural rights but determined, at least indirectly, by a majority of citizens) can outweigh private interests. Finally, they note his arguments against the unlimited accumulation of private wealth, his criticism of the potentially destabilizing effects of a capitalist economy, and his insistence on the importance of charity. The work of Robert Holsworth (1980) on contemporary political movements also suggests that liberalism is compatible with broader notions of the public interest and collective action.

Regardless of how extensive a public sphere one sees emerging in liberal societies, however, notions of inherent ability surface in ways that suggest not all citizens will be able to perform their civic functions effectively. Consistent with his view of human nature, Locke believed that knowledge was the result of a combination of natural abilities and labor. By extension, citizens were likely to vary in how politically informed they were. As Ashcraft notes: "'All reasoning,' Locke insists, is simply 'the labour of our thoughts,' which 'requires pains and application.' God has only furnished us with natural materials, and, just as we must employ our 'faculties and powers industriously' in building houses or bridges, so, Locke argues, the employment of those powers of the mind (reason) is the only means by which we come to have knowledge. 'We are born ignorant of everything,' and therefore whatever we acquire as knowledge is the product of our 'labour, attention, and industry'" (1987: 239). Just as citizens would vary in the property they accumulated, they would vary in the amount of information they "accumulated" and, thus, in their ability to serve as a check on the excesses of government. Indeed, since knowledge is a prerequisite to the successful accumulation of property, and since those with the most property would also have the most to lose from a corrupt government, the same class of citizens would dominate the private and public spheres.

Protectionist Democracy and the Reluctant Extension of Political Authority

The election of public officials was introduced into liberal political theory and practice as a check on government. Locke allows that the first

legislature of any system would be selected by citizens themselves. He further suggests that such legislatures might be periodically dissolved without dissolution of the entire polity. Elections of this sort were designed to be purely protective in function and were not originally intended as expressions of the public will more broadly.

Although liberal theory constrained the role of most citizens to voting for representatives, it also provided a compelling argument for extending this limited role to a much broader segment of the population. The logic and ethic of social contract theory clearly stated that all citizens had a stake in the actions of government and that initially at least, this stake was equal. This argument was codified by Jeremy Bentham and James Mill. For both, the public interest was defined in utilitarian terms: that which produced the greatest happiness for the greatest number of citizens. Much as in the philosophy of Locke, people's natural tendencies were to maximize their pleasure at the expense of others. Hence the need for government: "That one human being will desire to render the person and property of another subservient to his pleasures, not withstanding the pain or loss of pleasure which it may occasion to that other individual, is the foundation of government" (Mill, 1825; sec. VI, 17).

Government's task was to regulate the private accumulation of wealth in a way that brought about the greatest good to the greatest number. But government would be run by pleasure-maximizing individuals, and what would prevent them from using power for their own ends? The system already in place in England embodied a modified version of Locke's theory, complete with institutional checks and periodic elections. The franchise was limited to adult males with substantial property, however. If the ultimate goal was the greatest good to the greatest number, who spoke for the vast majority of disenfranchised citizens? What prevented government from acting against their interests?

The theoretically consistent answer was that no one did and that the franchise should be extended to include all citizens. Bentham and Mill, however, remained concerned that the majority of citizens were too ignorant to exercise their franchise in a responsible way. They initially argued that "all those individuals whose interests are indisputably included in those of other individuals may be struck off without inconvenience" (James Mill, 1825: 45). Because they believed that a capitalist market system was in everyone's best interest, this allowed them to keep the franchise from those deemed too incompetent to use it effectively. For Bentham this crude rationalization allowed him to advocate a franchise that excluded dependents, the uneducated, the poor, and women. Mill also made the case for a limited franchise that excluded all women, the poorest

one-third of the population, and men under the age of forty. But such views proved difficult to justify in any convincing manner, and both theorists eventually advocated near universal adult suffrage. This shift in position was eased by evidence from America, where the vote had, by the early nineteenth century, been extended to those "without property sufficient for their maintenance" (Bentham, 1830: v. 9, 143) without the underclass using this power to take property from the wealthy. To the surprise of most theorists, universal suffrage was also made more palatable by the institutionalization of the party systems in England and the United States. Rather than acting as the instruments by which ideological factions did political battle, parties served as an additional check on the masses by limiting the electoral choices to two or three moderate alternatives. The mitigating role played by parties eventually became a central component of the theory of limited democracy (Schumpeter, 1942; Schattschneider, 1942).

Participatory Democracy: Empowering the Public

Not all eighteenth- and nineteenth-century theorists were willing to concede the limited civic role that emerged from the writings of Locke, Bentham, and James Mill. The most developed defense of a more participatory democracy is found in the writings of Jean Jacques Rousseau.[5] For the English social contract theorists, order was achieved by structuring the ways in which individual interests clash. Rousseau also saw the need for individuals to band together to protect their interests from each other's baser instincts. Like the Greeks, however, Rousseau believed that human nature was partially shaped by the context in which it developed and operated. Rather than simply reflecting presumably immutable behaviors, political and social institutions could be designed to educate citizens to a higher plane of thought and action.

Rousseau acknowledges that individuals are both self-interested and desirous of property. He also acknowledges that outside of civil society these motivations lead to intolerable conflict. Because of this it is only in a community that individuals are truly free. Rousseau's citizens act in the public sphere neither as self-interested individuals nor as self-sacrificing ones, but as part of a collectivity in which cooperation is as natural as the cooperation between the parts of a human body. In short, the polity is organic.

Such collective behavior does not happen automatically, of course—citizens must be "forced to be free" in Rousseau's infamous phrase (1762: 64). This requires an environment that encourages cooperation and makes

the domination of one individual over another unlikely.[6] Under Rousseau's social contract, citizens participate directly in the making of laws. This political participation serves to protect the private interests of citizens. Beyond this, however, direct participation serves an educative function. By forcing citizens to deliberate about public policy, they come to understand the point of view of others, the need for cooperation and compromise, and the full impact of what is being legislated. This increases the likelihood that legislation will reflect "the general will" and that citizens will cooperate with its implementation. Such participation, because it is empowering, is viewed by Rousseau as fulfilling in its own right, and so democracy is less likely than most political systems to degenerate over time.

Participatory democracy is usually dismissed as unworkable because, as in the theory of Rousseau, it is often tied to small homogenous agrarian polities. The notion of participatory democracy has been adapted to liberal societies, however.[7] John Stuart Mill provides the most developed description of and justification for such a system. Mill, like his father, was both a liberal and a utilitarian. He advocated universal suffrage and saw the vote as necessary for protecting the interests of all citizens. Mill, however, differed from other utilitarians in ways that hearken back to Rousseau. He believed human fulfillment derived from more than economic consumption and that all citizens were capable of developing their human potential if given the opportunity. In order to do this, citizens needed to be educated in the broad sense. Political institutions were important to this education and should be judged by "the degree in which they promote the general mental advancement of the community, including under that phrase advancement in intellect, in virtue, and in practical activity and efficiency" (1861: 195). While Mill understood that large societies would require representative government, he argued for a more participatory public sphere: "A democratic constitution not supported by democratic institutions in detail, but confined to the central government, not only is not political freedom, but often creates a spirit precisely the reverse" (1871: 944). The educative function of participation meant that the simple casting of a vote was not enough: "A political act, to be done only once in a few years, and for which nothing in the daily habits of the citizen has prepared him, leaves his intellect and his moral dispositions very much as it found them" (1835: 229).

Mill was not a full egalitarian. Consistent with Locke, he argued that people should be rewarded in proportion to what they produced and fully expected this would lead to some economic disparity.[8] And reminiscent of Plato and, to a lesser extent, Aristotle, Mill believed in a hierarchy based

on inherent abilities. National political leaders would emerge from a formally educated elite because they would be the "wisest and best." Although he advocated universal suffrage, he also advocated that votes be weighted based on educational attainment. Nonetheless, Mill's citizens were public spirited and critical thinkers who followed the lead of their wiser brethren not out of deference, but because they discerned it to be the best course of action. Citizens were expected to engage in open and free debate regarding public issues. Indeed, it was through this ongoing public debate that the truth was constructed and reinforced:

> If all mankind minus one, were of one opinion, and only one person were of the contrary opinion, mankind would be no more justified in silencing that one person, than he, had he the power, would be in silencing mankind. Were an opinion a personal possession of no value except to the owner; if to be obstructed in the enjoyment of it were simply a private injury, it would make some difference whether the injury was inflicted on a few persons or on many. But the peculiar evil of silencing the expression of an opinion is, that it is robbing the human race; posterity as well as the existing generation; those who dissent from opinion, still more than those who hold it. If the opinion is right, they are deprived of the opportunity of exchanging error for truth; if wrong, they lose, what is almost as great a benefit, the clearer perception and livelier impression of truth, produced by its collision with error. (1859: 18).

Public life and public discourse served more than the instrumental purpose of protecting individual interests. The right to free speech, a free press, and open assembly were all designed to assure, according to Mill, that the truth was learned and reaffirmed.

The theories of democracy that emerged over the centuries contain several consistent themes. The answer to the critical question of "Who governs?" has always been resolved by answers to two prior questions: "Who has the ultimate authority to rule?" and "Who has the civic ability to do so?" Although political theorists increasingly concluded that ultimate political authority rested with the citizenry itself, they also assumed that most citizens lacked the virtue and knowledge to do so effectively. Belief in the political authority of the general public, combined with concern over the public's civic competency, inevitably resulted in circumscribed notions of the rights and responsibilities of citizenship. In addition, the greatest limits on citizenship were placed on the less affluent, women, minorities

(or foreigners), and the young and were justified by the conflation of political ignorance with low social and economic status and the conflation of the public good with the interests of socioeconomic elites.

In spite of these similarities, the theories we have examined differ in their explanations for the perceived shortcomings of the general public and in their proposed solutions. For Plato, differences in civic ability were natural, and governance was left to a select few who proved themselves the wisest. For supporters of the Athenian model, there was a clear distinction between those classes that were deemed incapable of self-governance and those that, through education and a well-developed public sphere, were capable of direct and complete self-rule. Like the Athenians, Aristotle believed some classes were incapable of governing themselves. Unlike the Athenians, however, he also allowed that those who did participate could vary in their specific rights and responsibilities, with different citizens eligible for different civic functions. Again, these distinctions were based on the perceived civic capacity of different classes of citizens.

As can be seen in the writings of Bentham and James Mill, concerns over the civic capacity of average citizens survived into the eighteenth and nineteenth centuries. The logic of social contracts and natural rights, however, increased the pressure for a more inclusionary political system. The solution was a sharp distinction between the power to choose who governed and the power to actually govern. The franchise was reluctantly extended (in theory and eventually in practice) to all adults. At the same time, executive, legislative, and judicial functions were reserved, by law or custom, largely to citizens whose class or education indicated their superior civic virtue and knowledge. The incentive and opportunity to participate were further limited by the shrinking of the public sphere and its separation from the pursuit of private interests.

The theories of Rousseau and John Stuart Mill combined the more inclusive notions of citizenship found in ancient and liberal theories of democracy. Drawing on utilitarian, protectionist, and liberal tenets, they concluded that citizens from all classes had the right to participate. Mill also accepted the notion that some participation would be limited to the selection of representatives, and that these representatives would be the most educated, civically capable citizens. Like the democratic Greeks, however, they believed in the importance of a well-developed public sphere and the centrality of civic participation to human fulfillment. They advocated for a more participatory democracy that extended well beyond the periodic selection of leaders. Both Rousseau and Mill shared a fear that many citizens would lack the skills, virtue, and knowledge to partic-

ipate directly, but they saw this as the unacceptable result of a class system that created too great a disparity in social, economic, and, thus, political resources, rather than the inevitable result of immutable differences in ability. Citizens from all walks of life could be educated (formally and informally) in ways that would enhance their civic capacity.

The Hybrid Design of American Democracy

The framers of the U.S. system "were conversant with the great works of Western philosophy and political science, and quoted Aristotle, Plato, Locke, Montesquieu, and scores of other thinkers with great facility and frequency" (Greenberg and Page, 1992: 52).[9] Rather than design a system that reflected the thinking of any one school of thought, they created one that was a creative, though often inconsistent blend of ideas.

The framers concurred with Locke that concentrated power without proper institutional checks served the interests of those in positions of authority. Thus, the role of government was carefully circumscribed. Many of the most celebrated characteristics of the American political system—the constitutional protection of individual civil rights, an extensive private sphere largely outside the purview of government, an elaborate system of checks and balances among the various levels and branches of local, state, and national government—were designed to limit the power of government and protect the private interests of citizens.

This design made relatively few civic demands on the general public because it was intended to limit the excesses of government primarily through institutional checks rather than through the civic virtue of leaders or a vigilant, informed citizenry (hence the notion of the U.S. Constitution as "a machine that would go of itself"). This limited public sphere was consistent with liberalism's emphasis on private life, but it was also based on more deep-seated doubts about the ability of citizens to rule themselves wisely. John Adams summarized this view bluntly: "The proposition that [the people] are the best keeper of their liberties is not true. They are the worst conceivable, they are no keepers at all. They can neither act, judge, think, or will" (1788: 7).

At the same time, however, the framers believed in the ultimate authority of the public and in the importance of civic input as a further protection against the abuses of centralized power. They balanced these inconsistent views by allowing for the limited and indirect participation of the public. The primary responsibility of most citizens was voting for representatives, and even this form of participation was restricted in significant ways. Of the four major officers in national government—House members, senators, justices, and the president—only the first was directly elected by the people. Elections were staggered so as to further protect against the "mischiefs of faction."

Consistent with the theories discussed above, the framers tended to equate socioeconomic status with civic ability. This is evident in the voting restrictions established by the states after the ratification of the Constitution. The franchise was initially limited to white male property owners—citizens deemed the most competent, stable, and supportive of the status quo. As a result, less than 20 percent of the adult population was eligible to vote in the first national elections. Further, it was assumed that positions of political leadership would be dominated by this same class of citizens. Hamilton acknowledges that "there are strong minds in every walk of life that will rise superior to the disadvantages of situation and will command the tribute due to their merit, not only from the classes to which they particularly belong, but from the society in general." He saw these as "exceptions to the rule," however, and he assures his readers that the national legislature will "consist almost entirely of proprietors of land, of merchants, and of members of the learned professions" (Hamilton, Madison, and Jay, 1961: 217). Skepticism regarding the civic capacity of citizens continued even as the franchise expanded. Arguments against suffrage for the poor, for blacks, for women, and for the young centered on concerns over their ability to use the vote wisely. Universal suffrage was viewed with great suspicion and was seen as a threat to the stability of Western democracies. "The electoral mass," according to Joseph Schumpeter, "is *incapable* of action other than a stampede" (1942: 283, emphasis added).

The nature of citizenship in the United States is further complicated by the grafting of republican theories onto classical liberal tenets and skeptical attitudes about the public's civic capacity. In part, the melding of these ideas provided additional support for a limited, elitist vision of democracy. For example, according to Madison, the Congress was designed to "enlarge the public views by passing them through the medium of a chosen body of citizens, whose wisdom may best discern the truest interest of their country and whose patriotism and love of justice will be least likely to sacrifice it to temporary or partial considerations. Under such a regulation it may well happen that the public voice, pronounced by the representatives of the people, will be more consonant to the public good than if pronounced by the people themselves, convened for the purpose" (Hamilton, Madison, and Jay, 1787–88: 82). The emphasis on the public good, the distinction between it and the public voice, the hierarchy of civic

responsibilities, the assumption that representatives would be the wisest of citizens—these are republican notions in the classical sense.[10] Such notions abound in the framers' design and allow them to combine their belief in the public's ultimate authority with their skepticism of democratic politics. For example, the constitutional age requirements for representatives, senators, and presidents are justified by Madison on the grounds that the greater the responsibility of office, the more time an individual needs to acquire the "information and stability of character" required for the job (Hamilton, Madison, and Jay, 1787–88: 376). Similarly, the state-imposed restrictions on suffrage and indirect methods of elections discussed above were at least partially designed to assure that only the best of citizens were involved in the selection of leaders.

At the same time republican—as opposed to purely liberal—justifications for a hierarchy of civic responsibility required a more developed concept of the public sphere and a greater appeal to the civic virtue and ability of citizens. The framers assumed that the quality of representatives, and thus of the discerned public good, depended on the proportion of citizens who were civically competent. It is commonly and correctly understood that Madison favored a large republic because a broad range of interests would help prevent tyranny of the majority (1787–88, 83–84). Yet the framers also believed that a large number of voters would assure that virtuous leaders were selected and that self-interested behavior was observed and punished. Further, since representatives were selected from the general citizenry, some portion of that citizenry needed to be capable of filling these roles. Madison makes clear that the larger the pool of citizens who are capable of governing, the better the chances that government would successfully pursue the public interest.

The American political system is also rooted in more directly participatory democratic theories. As James Morone (1990) has demonstrated, the colonists and early citizens of the United States were taken by "the democratic wish" to rule themselves directly. This desire for an engaged citizenry is exemplified by—but goes well beyond—the New England town meeting. Jefferson advocated dividing the country into wards that were small enough to allow for citizens to act "directly and personally" in the business of government (1944: 670). State legislatures were treated as concessions to geography and demography and, when unavoidable, should be, in John Adams's words, "an exact portrait, in miniature, of the people at large, . . . it should think, feel, reason, and act like them" (1776: 86).[11]

This democratic sensibility was strongest in the late colonial and the revolutionary war periods. Although suffrage was limited by certain prop-

erty restrictions, it is estimated that as much as 70 percent of white adult males were eligible to vote in state and local elections—often two to three times the percentage eligible after 1789. And as Morone notes: "the colonists linked constituents as closely to their representatives as they could. The revolutionaries broadened their franchises, multiplied constituencies (on average the assemblies doubled in size), mandated periodic reapportionment of seats (in five states), guaranteed the right to instruct representatives (in four states), erected visitors' galleries in the assemblies. One proposal, in Pennsylvania, would have all laws posted for a year in the public houses before the legislature acted on them" (40).

The rhetoric of state and local politics was suffused with republican notions of civic virtue and the common good. At this intimate level, such notions became more Rousseauian than Aristotelian: "The ideal was not simply the sum of individual private interests, but a distinct public interest with an objective existence of its own. Like Rousseau's general will, the common good would harmoniously integrate the entire community. The community was a single, organic body" (Morone, 1990: 41–42).

None of this is to suggest that colonial and revolutionary America was Rousseau's Geneva writ large. Seventy percent of white adult males having the franchise still meant that the vast majority of adults did not. Notions of a natural hierarchy dominated by white male property owners were prevalent and gave local republicanism a decidedly liberal hue. Nonetheless, citizens were assumed to be self-reliant, virtuous, knowledgeable, and the ultimate determiners of the public good.

As Morone, Gordon Wood (1980; 1992), and others have demonstrated, the period during and immediately after the ratification of the national constitution was marked by the triumph of liberalism over democracy in the United States. The increasing nationalization of politics and the growth of the bureaucratic state severed many of the most direct ties between the citizen and government. Still, these early experiences were very significant for the theory and practice of democracy. It is important to remember that the American experience encouraged Bentham and James Mill to advocate universal suffrage. More significantly, much of John Stuart Mill's advocacy of local participatory democracy, of free speech, and of a free press emerged out of his reading of de Tocqueville's account of American democracy and society. Notions of communal democracy, republican virtue, and the common good remain potent symbols that have been used to shape American politics. The expansion of suffrage first to all white adult males, then successively to black males, women, and eighteen- to twenty-year-olds; the Jacksonian, Populist, Progressive, civil rights, new left and women's movements; the politics of the

New Deal and the Great Society; Reagan's New Federalism and conservative populism; even the diverse, grassroots appeal of Ross Perot and Bill Clinton in the 1992 presidential campaign—all are legacies of America's longing for participatory democracy.

The power of this vision of democracy—and its relevance to notions of an informed citizenry—is most clearly seen in the tradition of public education. Civic knowledge has been a constant theme in American education, as this seventeenth-century ditty (cited in Postman, 1985: 33) suggests:

> From public schools shall general
> knowledge flow,
> For 'tis the people's sacred
> right to know

Progressive educators like John Dewey (1916), Henry Adams (1920), and Charles Merriam (1931) saw civic education, broadly defined, as the keystone to democracy. They also argued, consistent with Rousseau's communalism, that democracy required a well-developed public sphere that encouraged civic discourse. Despite recent evidence of the decline of civic education and this progressive ideal, the importance of an informed citizenry remains a guiding principle in American schools.[12]

Citizenship in the United States has been called "thin" by such political theorists as Benjamin Barber (1984). Pamela Conover, Donald Searing, and Ivor Crewe provide a cogent summary of thin citizenship:

> Within this contractual context, political participation becomes mainly instrumental and mainly serves private interests rather than a common good. Hence, the liberal conception emphasizes the privileges of citizenship—in the language of liberalism, "rights"—and interprets them most often in terms of "negative freedoms," as protection for the individual against interference from government or society with his or her autonomy. Duties are usually relegated to the background because they constitute obligations that restrict freedom. . . . Liberal citizen identities are "thin" and occupy only a small part of the self, for liberal citizens are autonomous individuals who are neither rooted in nor encumbered by their public lives. (1991: 802)

Citizens of the United States have much in common with this characterization. For most Americans, involvement in politics is indirect—the actual making and implementing of public policy is done by representatives who are selected through periodic and highly structured elections.

Citizens' central responsibility is to vote for these representatives, and even this is fully voluntary. Indeed, *The Oxford English Dictionary* defines a U.S. citizen as "a person, native or naturalized, who has the privilege of voting for public offices, and is entitled to protection in the exercise of private rights" (1971: 442).

But even thin citizenship requires an electorate informed enough to protect its interests in a meaningful way: "the very right to vote imposes on me the duty to instruct myself in public affairs" (Rousseau, 1968: 49). Further, and consistent with the interpretation of liberalism offered by James Tully (1979) and Richard Ashcraft (1987), Americans demonstrate a commitment to—or at least a longing for—greater involvement in the public sphere (Bellah et al., 1985; Conover, Searing, and Crewe, 1991). As Robert Holsworth (1980) argues, "defensive liberalism" of the sort underpinning Ralph Nader's consumer movement requires "a politicized society with consumers vigorously and constantly asserting their own interests" (33). Finally, the impact of both republican and, especially, participatory theories of democracy suggest a "thicker" definition of citizenship in the United States than is often assumed.

Rather than creating a single vision of citizenship, the combination of political theories described above has produced competing visions, each of which can be justified within the confines of the American system. *All* adult citizens are afforded a great range of opportunities to participate, from the simple act of voting to much more complex and direct forms of political action. This participation is intended to serve a number of functions: the protection of private interests, the selection of competent leaders, the expression of the public good, and the making and implementing of public policy. At the same time, there are no obligations and few expectations that citizens will engage in these activities—the right not to participate is as firmly ingrained as the right to do so. How engaged any individual or group is depends largely upon their own motivation and ability, along with the opportunities that present themselves. Together these competing views lead to a complex, sometimes contradictory political environment that allows for a great deal of civic involvement while encouraging many citizens to opt out of these responsibilities; that reveres both the common good and the pursuit of individual interests; that values political competence while often doing little to help citizens develop their civic skills; and that depends on informed participation while insulating itself from the impact of political ignorance. The result is a hierarchy of political classes that loosely parallel socioeconomic classes and that provide very different de facto opportunities for democratic governance depending on where in the hierarchy one falls.

Democratic Theory and Practice in Contemporary America

Questions regarding the promise and performance of democratic governance remain the subject of intellectual and practical debate—an extension of the debate begun 2,500 years ago. As in the past, much of this debate focuses on the ability of citizens to perform the various functions required of them. The variable nature of citizenship in the United States complicates this debate: as with the individual theories on which the U.S. system is based, citizens are expected to perform different functions based on their ability to do so effectively. Whereas institutional checks and balances are designed to protect against the negative consequences of ill-informed public input, the effectiveness of those checks and balances depends in large measure on the quality of the political elites—which in turn depends on the ability of citizens to select and monitor leaders wisely. Initially, the means for assuring that citizens chose wisely included restricting the vote to a select few and selecting most leaders indirectly. Such changes as the expansion of the franchise, the direct election of senators, and the growing role of public opinion and the mass media have increased the public's role in the selection of leaders and expanded the ways citizens can participate more directly. This extension of democratic input has increased the importance of an informed citizenry. This is true even if one focuses exclusively on the thin aspects of American citizenship, but it is especially true if one considers the full range of participation available to citizens.

Until recently, however, evidence regarding the civic-readiness of the general public had been highly speculative and idiosyncratic. Public opinion studies of the 1940s through 1960s provided the first systematic evidence of the civic state of the masses. The characterization of the citizenry provided by scholars of the period was discouraging: the average American citizen was portrayed as apathetic, uninterested in politics, unconcerned about who wins or loses presidential elections, only marginally interested in voting. The public also held few strong political opinions, and the opinions they did hold conflicted with each other and changed in seemingly random ways over time. In addition, opinions were not particularly influential in determining how most citizens voted. Little evidence was found to suggest citizens were politically sophisticated. For example, only 10 percent of the public could define the meaning of "liberal" or "conservative" (Converse, 1964), and an even smaller percentage actually used such ideological categories in evaluating candidates and parties (Campbell et al., 1960).

Most central to our concerns, the public demonstrated low levels of

knowledge concerning public affairs and the basic workings of parties, politics, and government. Although survey questions tapping factual knowledge were asked infrequently, studies done throughout the 1940s and 1950s consistently concluded that the public was not very politically informed. Subsequent research has, in general, confirmed this view. Russell Neuman notes that "even the most vivid concepts of political life . . . are recognized by only a little over half the electorate" (1986: 16). According to Stephen Bennett, "Using the standard academic grading system, the typical grade [for the American public in 1984] was a D+, hardly a sterling performance given the leniency with which some items were 'graded'" (1988: 481). So well established is this characterization of the American public that, according to Converse, "the most familiar fact to arise from sample surveys . . . is that popular levels of information about public affairs are, from the point of view of the informed observer, astonishingly low" (1975: 79).

Salvaging Democracy (by Weakening Its Meaning)

Evidence gleaned from surveys fueled the ongoing debate over democracy, but it is the theories discussed above that gave—and continue to give—these data meaning. Ironically, in an effort to salvage democracy, contemporary studies have often gone further than classical theorists in circumscribing the role of citizens or the need for them to be informed about politics. This tendency is exacerbated by a failure to consider the full range of theories that have been incorporated into the design of American democracy.

Drawing implicitly on a skepticism of democracy and a belief in republican civic virtue, many scholars have used evidence of an uninformed citizenry to argue that the "irony of democracy is that elites, not masses, govern in America" (Dye and Zeigler, 1990: 3). Many of the institutions of American politics are designed to filter mass opinion through elite opinion. Highly structured elections and moderate political parties provide the mechanisms for both responsiveness and stability. The minority of citizens who are informed and active often serve as guardians for the general public, articulating the public will to the governing elite and assuring that those who govern do so in a responsible manner (Schumpeter, 1942; Berelson, 1952; Schattschneider, 1942; 1960; Neuman, 1986). For some theorists, elite democracy represents the only approximation of democracy that is possible. For its strongest proponents, however, limited participation is not only unavoidable, but preferable, in that it assures that conflict is managed, that political demands are limited, and, thus, that economic and social order is maintained.

Elite democracy is put forward as a realistic alternative to the romanticized vision of participatory democrats, but as our discussion above (and below) maintains, it is as normatively driven as any model of citizenship and politics. Indeed, how true to the actual practice of contemporary democracy is it? Empirical evidence suggests that more people participate in politics than are informed about it. For example, although voters are more informed than nonvoters, many still remain ignorant about the issue stands of candidates and parties. The elite model is also challenged by the increasing importance of public opinion polls in the process of governing. It is no longer necessary for citizens to actively engage in politics for their voices to be heard. Increasingly, popular support, as measured by public opinion surveys, determines the success or failure of both officeholders and specific policies. Yet, as numerous studies have found, the number of respondents willing to give an opinion about an officeholder or issue far exceeds the number of people who are informed about either. In addition, theories that justify limited participation—even if the limits are voluntary—reopen the same questions that led nineteenth-century theorists to slowly break down the barriers to universal suffrage: Can (and will) the few speak for the many? How are individual and group interests accounted for when these individuals and groups are underrepresented in the activist public? How is the public good to be determined if much of the public is silent?

Alternative readings of the state of the masses have attempted to address the normative and empirical shortcomings of elite democracy. One such approach is to distinguish aggregate from individual public opinion. Benjamin Page and Robert Shapiro, echoing and refining the view first expressed by Aristotle, describe the process by which a polity can move from "individual ignorance to collective wisdom":

> At any given moment an individual has real policy preferences, based on underlying needs and values and on beliefs held at the moment. Furthermore, over a period of time, each individual has a central tendency of opinion, which might be called a "true" or *long-term preference,* and which can be ascertained by averaging the opinions expressed by the *same individual* at several different times. If the individual's opinions fluctuate randomly around the same central tendency for a sustained period of time, his or her true long-term preferences will be stable and ascertainable, despite observed momentary fluctuations in opinion.
>
> If this picture of individuals' opinions is correct, then at any given moment the public as a whole also has real *collective* policy

> preferences, as defined by any of various aggregation rules. . . . Moreover—and this is the key point—at any given moment, the random deviations of individuals from their long-term opinions may well cancel out over a large sample, so that a poll or survey can accurately measure collective preferences as defined in terms of the true or long-term preferences of many individual citizens. (1992: 16)

Thus collective public opinion (and, by extension, collective political participation) can be rational even if much of the individual opinion or behavior underlying it is not because the random views of uninformed citizens cancel each other out, leaving the true choices of more informed citizens to carry the day.

Although collective rationality is evocative of John Stuart Mill's argument that truth is produced from its "collision with error," in fact it makes no such claims. Rather, it argues that *error is eliminated in its collision with error.* A polity may have little to fear from uninformed mass opinion or participation, but only because the opinions and behaviors of most of the masses are inconsequential. Such a notion is not inevitably elitist, in that it is possible that most Americans do make informed judgments. But the low levels of political knowledge that motivate scholars like Page and Shapiro to come to democracy's rescue also suggests that most Americans do not make informed decisions. Further, as in all theories that depend on the few to speak for the many, the representativeness of the voices that emerge out of the din produced by the collision of ignorance is critical (Miller, 1986). Proponents of collective rationality are forced to argue, implicitly, that "all those individuals whose interests are indisputably included in those of other individuals may be struck off without inconvenience," an argument no more compelling today than it was when James Mill made it in the early nineteenth century.

A different approach to rehabilitating the democratic citizen has been to challenge the notion that citizens need to be politically informed. Arguing, in V. O. Key's classic phrase, that "voters are not fools," this school of thought sees method where others see madness. Consistent with a liberal, protectionist philosophy, the average citizen's responsibility is portrayed as limited, as is the expected payoff for his or her vigilance. Thus, while citizens may be capable of sophisticated political thought and action, it is not rational for them to expend the personal resources necessary to do this. Rather, they engage in what Samuel Popkin calls "low-information rationality" (1991: 7). Through the use of "heuristics," or informational shortcuts, citizens can reach decisions about where they stand on certain issues or whom they will vote for in a given election.

These shortcuts usually consist of following the lead of a group or an individual that citizens believe have their interests at heart or that have interests similar to their own.

Although this is an appealing argument, the information necessary for a citizen to engage in these decision-making shortcuts is precisely the kind that many citizens lack. Where political parties, public interest groups, prominent public figures, and other potential cue givers stand on specific issues or in broader ideological terms is often a mystery to many citizens.

Research by political psychologists offers yet a different way out of the dilemma raised by survey evidence of a poorly informed public. Most relevant here is the "impression-driven" or "on-line" model of information processing offered by Milton Lodge and his colleagues (Lodge, McGraw, and Stroh, 1989; McGraw, Lodge, and Stroh, 1990). This model suggests that individuals make political evaluations at the moment information is presented, storing their affective impressions in memory and then "'forgetting' the actual pieces of evidence that contributed to the evaluation" (1989: 401). Affective judgments—rather than factual information—about particular candidates or officeholders are mentally stored in a running tally that is updated when new information is encountered.

On its face, the on-line model appears to deny the importance of factual information about politics stored in long-term memory—the type of information of central concern to us in this book. A closer look at this research, however, suggests that this is not the case. When experimental conditions encourage forming immediate impressions (for example, when subjects are told, before being given information about the candidates, that they will be asked to evaluate them) political "sophisticates" (significantly, those defined as scoring the highest on a test of factual political knowledge) are most likely to process new information on-line. But when the experimental conditions are altered (for example, when subjects are not told they will be asked to make an evaluation until after information is presented) or when the topic being evaluated is relatively complex (for example, a policy issue rather than a candidate), political sophisticates are the most likely to draw on information that is stored in memory. This latter set of findings is critical, given that the design and implementation of democracy in America often requires more than the ability of atomistic individuals to form immediate impressions of candidates and officeholders. In any event, individuals who are the most knowledgeable to begin with are best able to use new information, regardless of whether this information is processed "on the fly" or is stored and used more deliberatively at some later point.[13] Conversely, those who are least knowledgeable are also least efficient at processing and using new information under either condition.

There are additional problems with all of these attempts to develop a "realistic" definition of democratic citizenship. In its most extreme form, the elite model is quite patronizing of the average citizen, and its link to rule of and by the people is tenuous, at best. Both collective and low-information rationality avoid some of these normative shortcomings by suggesting that relatively uninformed citizens can still make reasonably informed choices. Both also allow for the possibility of greater citizen input than the elite models of Schumpeter and Berelson. And although the on-line model demonstrates that more knowledgeable citizens are better at processing and using new information, it does provide evidence that under some circumstances less knowledgeable citizens can use the immediate information environment to make political evaluations. In all three approaches, however, "the voice of the people is but an echo" of the elites who dominate the information environment at any given time (Key, 1966: 2). The opinions and behaviors of most citizens are treated as either uninterpretable background noise or the mere reflections of a more informed minority. All three models assume the "unavoidable dependency of [the mass public] on elite discourse" (Zaller, 1992: 311). Most researchers who draw on these models conclude that "there is more meaning to voting, and less manipulation of voters, than . . . the traditional civics information focus would have us believe" (Popkin, 1991: 20). Nonetheless, many remain equivocal on whether such systems produce outcomes that reflect the choices the public "would make if it were fully and completely informed" (Page and Shapiro, 1992: 356). The key is the quality of the information provided by the various levels of elites who shape public opinion: "Individuals or institutions that influence public opinion by providing correct, helpful information, can be said to *educate* the public. On the other hand . . . those who influence public opinion by providing incorrect, biased, or selective information, or erroneous interpretations, may be said to *mislead* the public. . . . If government officials or others mislead the public consciously and deliberately, by means of lies, falsehoods, deception, or concealment, we say . . . that they *manipulate* public opinion" (Page and Shapiro, 1992: 356).

Yet one of the main justifications for citizen participation in liberal democracies is to serve as a check on the tendency of those in power to use their position for their own gain. Herein lies the catch-22 of any model of democracy that makes citizens solely dependent on information filtered through political elites—even through competing elites. Some have addressed this by suggesting that citizens are "not so passive" and "not so dumb" as tests of factual knowledge suggest (Gamson, 1992: 4). Qualitative explorations of citizens' discourse about political issues do suggest that, under certain circumstances and for certain issues, they can draw on a combination of personal experiences and popular wisdom to resist the messages of elites and even construct their own, oppositional interpretation of the political and social world. But even the most encouraging of these analyses concludes that although "the raw material" for critical, independent thinking is present in many citizens, only "a small minority" actually achieve this level of political thought (Gamson, 1992: 175).

So powerful is contemporary democracy's catch-22 that some have challenged the notion that factual information exists independent from its source: "There is a conventional [wisdom] that can be captured in a sentence rather than a volume: citizens who are informed about political developments can more effectively protect and promote their own interests and the public interest. [This] takes for granted a world of facts that have a determinable meaning and a world of people who react rationally to the facts they know. In politics neither premise is tenable, a conclusion that history continually reaffirms and that observers of the political scene are tempted to ignore" (Edelman, 1988: 1). According to Murray Edelman and others (Lasch, 1979: 391–97), all knowledge is relative, constructed out of social beliefs rather than residing in some objective reality. Since elites control how the facts of public affairs will be constructed, ignorance—not knowledge—of these facts is the ironic mark of a healthy citizenry:

> Public indifference is deplored by politicians and by right-thinking citizens. It is the target of civics courses, oratory, and television news shows and the reiterated theme of polls that discover how little political information the public has and how low politics rates among public concerns. . . . That indifference, which academic political science notices but treats as an obstacle to enlightenment or democracy, is, from another perspective, a refuge against the kind of engagement that would, if it could, keep everyone's energies taken up with activism: election campaigns, lobbying, repressing some and liberating others, wars, and all other political activities that displace living, loving, and creative work. Regimes and proponents of political causes know that it takes much coercion, propaganda, and the portrayal of issues in terms that entertain, distort, and shock to extract a public response of any kind. . . . Indifference to the enthusiasms and alarms of political activists has very likely always been a paramount political force. . . . Without it, slaughter and repression of diverse groups in the

name of nationalism, morality, or rationality would certainly be even more widespread than it has been. (Edelman, 1988: 7–8)

However, this relativist perspective can also justify the very atrocities it is intended to resist, allowing them to continue unchecked.[14] Edelman acknowledges that indifference to public affairs is only "partially effective . . . because it is a nonaction" (8). Citizens must also engage in constructing their own social reality. Further, Edelman argues that "there are multiple realities because people differ in their situations and their purposes. The reality a destitute black person constructs respecting the nature of poverty has little validity for a conservative political candidate or a conservative political scientist or even for the same black when he is trying to achieve high grades in a business school. Every construction of a world is a demanding activity. *It can be done badly or wrong.* To understand that multiple realities are prevalent is liberating, *but such understanding in no way suggests that every construction is as good as any other"* (6; emphases added).

In arguing that some interpretations of the world are better than others, Edelman begs the question of how one determines this, even for oneself. Further, his argument clearly assumes that the actions of political elites have real-world implications that affect one's ability to "live, love, and create." One does not escape this fact by ignoring it. One cannot argue that people have real, if diverse interests, that *all* facts are socially constructed, *and* that factual knowledge is unimportant. To do so is as likely to produce the "slaughter and repression of diverse groups" as any appeal to rationalism. Indeed, appeals to "nationalism, morality and rationalism" are not precluded by Edelman's brand of relativity. It is an awareness that knowledge is socially constructed that leads Rousseau, J. S. Mill, Dewey, and Habermas to argue for the importance of a public sphere in which equally informed citizens can engage each other in public debate.

For all our disagreement with Edelman, there is much to his argument. In a system where political action is reduced to a parody of authoritative civic engagement, indifference may be a citizen's most effective weapon. We would argue, however, that this indifference—this resistance—needs to be an *informed indifference* to be meaningful. Virginia Woolf (1938) describes this view in her explanation for why women may, given their second-class status, choose to be indifferent to men's decision to go to war. The "duty" of "the educated man's daughter" is "not to incite [her] brothers to fight, or to dissuade them, but to maintain an attitude of complete indifference. But the attitude expressed by the word 'indifference' is so complex and of such importance that it needs even here further definition. Indifference in the first place *must be given a firm footing upon fact. . . . The outsider will make it her duty not merely to base her indifference upon instinct, but upon reason*" (107, emphasis added). Circumstances may not always allow for citizens to participate in meaningful ways, but in politics as in most important aspects of life, the readiness is all.

The Case for an Informed Citizenry

The paradox of modern democracy cannot be resolved by eliminating the need for a broadly and equitably informed citizenry. In the end, the paradox itself is illusory—to the extent that citizens are uninformed, the system *is* less democratic. This is true regardless of which variant of democracy one subscribes to, but it is especially true in the complex form of democracy that has emerged in the United States. In our view, truly salvaging democracy requires that scholars confront "the more pessimistic aspects of their data" (Burdick, 1959: 146). In confronting these data, however, we must also guard against overgeneralizations that caricature what is a fairly complex pattern of knowledge and ignorance. And we must be cognizant that these data are contextual in nature, with much of what emerges reflecting the design of the system rather than proving that this design is the best that can be achieved. In essence, rather than simply examining what citizens currently know and using that as evidence for the possibility of democracy, we must treat democracy—and its requisite for an informed citizenry—as a nonnegotiable end to be sought, using the data to understand where we fall short and why (Barber, 1993: 71–72).

Information and a Minimalist Model of Democracy: The Competent Voter

The strongest arguments against the need for an informed public draw on liberal, protective theories of democracy. Because it is assumed that there is little that a citizen is required to do, it follows there is little a citizen is required to know. From a purely individual perspective, there is no minimum criterion—a politically uninformed citizen is perfectly acceptable, so long as he or she understands the possible consequences of that ignorance. It is on the thin reed of voting's protective function that any sense of an obligation to be informed rests. Further, whether motivated by self-interest or civic duty, the incentives for being informed are limited. Because the impact of a single person's vote is negligible, it is not individually rational to devote much effort to the task. And, given a system designed to limit the impact of both minority and majority factions, the incentive to participate as an informed member of a group, class, or party is also diminished.

It would be a mistake, however, to equate weak incentives and low expectations with the absence of an informational requisite to competent voting. For the vote to serve as a reasonable first approximation of the public will, as a useful mechanism for selecting public leaders, and as a credible check on the behavior of those leaders, voters need to have at least some minimal information regarding all three.

Consider the alternatives. We will avoid, for the moment, the thorny issue of how to define a person's interest. For now we simply define a competent vote as one that fulfills the three requirements outlined above. The vote least likely to achieve these ends is one that is misinformed—that is cast for the wrong candidate because the voter is unintentionally misled or intentionally manipulated. Also unsettling is an ignorant vote, which in essence is a random vote. In the typical two-person race this decision rule does leave a 50 percent chance that the voter's interests will be served (at least as well as allowed by the choices available). Clearly, however, neither of these alternatives is acceptable if voting is to be anything more than symbolic.

A more acceptable alternative is for voters to be *specialists,* each focusing his or her civic efforts on a limited set of concerns. For example, a citizen primarily concerned about abortion rights might cast an informed vote based solely on her own stands, the stands of the candidates, and, if relevant, the prior behavior of the incumbent. Although the information costs for being a specialist vary, they are likely to be relatively low for most issues. In addition, specialists, by definition, are more likely to be motivated to pay these costs. Finally, aggregating the votes of specialists might serve as a reasonable approximation of the public will and an acceptable way of selecting and evaluating public leaders. This method is not without its shortcomings, however. In the example above, our voter behaved as if she were voting in a referendum on abortion, but this is not the case. In casting a vote for a candidate, she is in reality voting for all the things that candidate will do in office. Our voter does not include these other factors in her calculus, but the behavior of that elected official affects her material interests just the same. There is no guarantee that specialists will accurately approximate either the voter's or the public's interest.

At the opposite extreme are *generalists,* whose votes are determined by a wider range of informed personal and candidate issue positions. Elections in which voters are generalists are the most likely to approximate the public will and to assure responsive and responsible leaders. But the information costs required to be a generalist are obviously high and eventually become prohibitive, given the depth and breadth of issues addressed by government.

A Closer Look at the Use of Informational Shortcuts

Much of the literature falling under the rubric of *economic voting, rational voting, low-information voting,* and *heuristic decision making* are explorations of the ways citizens resolve this cost-benefit tradeoff and the implications of these solutions for the individual and the polity. Although specific theories vary, all trace their roots to Anthony Downs's classic work, *An Economic Theory of Democracy*. Downs is clear in saying that "political information is valuable because it helps make the best possible decisions" (1957: 258). In a world of perfect, costless information, all citizens would be generalists. Information costs and low expected utility, however, lead citizens to make decisions that are only partially informed. As a result, citizens strike a compromise of sorts by turning to information shortcuts. These shortcuts—or heuristics—involve distancing oneself from the raw data by depending on someone else's synthesis of information regarding a particular issue or candidate, or by knowing how certain reference groups feel about them. For example, a citizen may not know enough about the voting record of his U.S. representative to make an informed decision about whether to support her in an upcoming election. However, he knows that his local paper has endorsed the representative and that he generally supports the editorial views of the paper. So he saves the cost of finding out about the representative's voting record and simply follows the cue of the local paper. Heuristics can be more indirect than this kind of specific endorsement. For example, a citizen might know that a candidate is a member of the Religious Society of Friends and infer from this the candidate's likely views regarding the use of military force.

The argument that citizens use heuristics in making political decisions is often used to counter laments over the low levels of civic knowledge found in most surveys of the American public. Consider the view of Paul Sniderman, Richard Brody, and Philip Tetlock: "Our argument, most broadly put, is this: Citizens frequently can compensate for their limited information about politics by taking advantage of judgmental heuristics. Heuristics are judgmental shortcuts, efficient ways to organize and simplify political choices, efficient in the double sense of requiring relatively little information to execute, yet yielding dependable answers even to complex problems of choice. . . . Insofar as they can be brought into play, people can be knowledgeable in their reasoning about political choices without necessarily possessing a large body of knowledge about politics" (1991: 19).

The distinction between the "civic knowledge" and "heuristic" schools is less sharp than often supposed.[15] We argue this for three related reasons. First, as Downs notes, almost all politically relevant information is filtered in some way—through news organizations, academics, public officials, friends, coworkers, and so forth. We all use shortcuts in making political decisions; no one ever has all the relevant information. This is Schattschneider's point in claiming that "nobody knows enough to run government" (1960: 136). The use of shortcuts describes a human condition rather than a particular form of decision making. The issue, then, for both schools of thought, is not whether we use partial information to make political decisions, but the reliability and validity of the specific information we do use.[16]

Second, the heuristic model is based on *low* information rationality, not *no* information rationality. As the earlier quote from Downs suggests and as the evidence from numerous studies show, more information is better than less information even in heuristic decision making. Further, when one examines the kinds of heuristics citizens are purported to use in forming opinions or in deciding who to vote for, they are not unlike many of the facts included in civics quizzes: information about the party attachments, ideological leanings, issue stands, and personal characteristics of public figures; ideological and policy differences between the parties; knowledge about the connection between personal circumstances and government action (or inaction); general information about national and international events.

And third, low-information decision making is no guarantee of good decisions for either the citizen or the polity. At some point the amount or the quality of the information used for making decisions can become so limited as to be useless or misleading. Indeed, much of the pioneering work on cognitive heuristics by Daniel Kahneman and Amos Tversky (1972; 1973) focused on the likelihood of making errors in judgment when using overly simple shortcuts (see Mondak, 1994). For Downs, the irony of contemporary democracy is that the logic of individual rationality leads citizens to be woefully underinformed. As a result, citizens sacrifice both their own long-term interests and the collective interests of the polity:

> It arises from the simultaneous truth of two seemingly contradictory propositions: (1) rational citizens want democracy to work well so as to gain its benefits, and it works best when the citizenry is well-informed; and (2) it is individually irrational to be well-informed. . . .

> This paradox exists because the benefits men derive from efficient social organization are indivisible. . . . [An individual's] vote is not decisive: it is lost in a sea of other votes. Hence whether he himself is well-informed has no perceptible impact on the benefits he gets. If all others express their true views, he gets the benefits of a well-informed electorate no matter how well-informed he is; if they are badly informed, he cannot produce these benefits himself. Therefore, as in all cases of indivisible benefits, the individual is motivated to shirk his share of the costs: he refuses to get enough information to discover his true views. Since all men do this, the election does not reflect the true consent of the governed. (1957: 246)

Sniderman et al., following Downs, also argue that the differential cost of becoming informed means that some citizens—especially those who are better educated and who are financially better off—will have greater influence and so reap more benefits than the many others who are less informed.

In the end, the real value of the heuristic model is in demonstrating that a citizen need not know everything about a particular issue to reach a decision of some kind. It also points to the kind of proximate information that citizens can and do use in making certain kinds of decisions. However, demonstrating that certain heuristics are used is not the same as demonstrating that they are the best—or even modestly effective—decision rules. Nor does it eliminate the value of an informed citizenry.

Minimally Competent Voting in the Context of a Two-Party System

Are there heuristics that can approximate our generalist? As we noted above, the information required of citizens depends on the institutions and processes within which democracy operates. This requirement is eased significantly in the United States by the institutionalization of an ideologically moderate two-party system. Because voting in the United States is reduced to periodically choosing between two candidates or parties, a voter's responsibility is reduced to a series of dichotomous choices. In this context, there is little need for a detailed understanding of one's self-interest or of the public good. One need only know enough to determine which of the two parties comes closest to those interests. It is for this reason that a unidimensional conception of ideology remains so valuable in American politics—not because it can accurately or efficiently aggregate political reality or the public's range of political views, but because in a two-party system politics is necessarily reduced to a single dimension, and then further reduced to three points on that continuum: the two parties and the individual choosing between them.[17] The competition between two parties also increases the likelihood that the stands of the parties will converge (Downs, 1957). Although it may be more accurate to argue that individuals have diverse, even unique belief systems, at the systemic level it must be possible to reduce these belief systems to two. In the United States these two broad philosophies are labeled liberalism and conservatism, though the labels matter less than their relation to each other and to the two parties.

A misinformed or ignorant voter is unlikely to go too far astray in such a system. But unless one argues that it makes no difference which party governs—a perspective that would challenge the notion that the United States is a democracy—political parties do not eliminate the need to be informed. A partisan voter needs to know, for example, both that he is a Democrat and that a particular candidate is a Democrat. These two pieces of information are enough to produce a competent vote if our hypothetical voter's interests are closer to the Democratic party. But is the likelihood of this happy circumstance greater than if our voter had simply flipped a coin?

Perhaps. If party platforms and party identification were consistently tied to the interests of particular socioeconomic groups, one might argue that a voter need know nothing about politics to vote in a way that protects his or her interests. Voters would inherit their partisan affiliation as young adults and use it as a simple and efficient cue to future votes. There is some evidence for the reasonableness of this assumption. Partisanship does appear to form early in life (Easton and Hess, 1962; Greenstein, 1965) and, once formed, to be relatively stable (Converse, 1964; Converse and Markus, 1979). In periods of political calm, party identification is transmitted from generation to generation through parents (Jennings and Niemi, 1974), but in periods of uncertainty or change, first-time voters develop attachments more finely tuned to their new economic and social interests (Beck, 1974; Burnham, 1970; Andersen, 1979). Partisanship is at least partially rooted in such socioeconomic conditions as region, class, and ethnicity (Berelson, Lazarsfeld, and McPhee, 1954; Lazarsfeld, Berelson, and Gaudet, 1944; Nie, Verba, and Petrocik, 1979). Further, on at least some key issues, the Democratic and Republican parties do consistently tie their platforms—and their behavior in office—to the perceived interests of distinct socioeconomic groups (Sorauf and Beck, 1987: 413).

Does this mechanistic model satisfy our three requisites of competent voting? Assuming there is a link between one's socioeconomic circumstances and one's interests, it provides some approximation of the public will and also serves as a mechanism for selecting leaders to refine and act on that will. It does not, however, provide a credible check on the behavior of officeholders because there is nothing in this model that allows citizens to evaluate past performance.[18] And even the first two goals of competent voting will go unmet if citizens' socioeconomic circumstances change over time or if party platforms shift because the ability to adjust one's party identification to these new circumstances would necessarily require additional information. Further, the modestly ideological nature of U.S. parties, the often weak programmatic coherence among candidates and officeholders from the same party, the crosscutting nature of many issues and socioeconomic circumstances, and the rapidly changing political agenda in postindustrial America make an unreflective dependency on party affiliation of the sort we describe here too crude and unreliable a method to assure even minimally competent voting.

Clearly, greater surveillance of the political terrain is required. Even for the simple act of voting citizens need to stay in touch with their own interests, with the articulated stands of the candidates and parties, and with their actual performance when in office. Heuristics, such as partisanship, can serve as schema through which new information is more easily evaluated, thus bridging the gap between the inordinate information costs associated with being a generalist and the unsettling narrowness of the specialist who leaves too much of the authoritative allocation of public resources to chance. With any heuristic, however, citizens still need to have more specific information about public officials, political parties, and public policy—much of it also heuristic in quality. Without such information any shortcut to political decision making will lose its efficacy. The use of such cues allows citizens to extrapolate from information that is somewhat dated and only indirectly relevant to the decision at hand. In essence, it spreads out the information costs over a wider period of time, thus lowering them significantly. But it does not eliminate the need for such information.

Expanding the Role of Information: The Competent Democrat

Thus far our focus has been on the information requirements for thin citizenship. The case for an informed public is strengthened as one moves from thin to thicker definitions of citizenship in the United States. Even liberal democracy can be interpreted as requiring more than minimally efficient voters. Further, American politics is also premised on republican and participatory theories that go beyond this simple protectionist model. Arguments in favor of a broadly informed citizenry are often dismissed by claiming that normative theories exaggerate the actual responsibilities of the general public. A closer look at these responsibilities suggests that calls for a more informed citizenry are very much grounded in the real world of contemporary democracy.

To begin with, within the confines of protectionist democracy additional information is still valuable: the more one knows about politics, the more effective—the more instrumentally rational—one's vote is likely to be. The task of assigning responsibility for the successes and failures of government policy is more complex than the party model would suggest. Especially in races for lower-level offices, candidates often take stands that are at odds with the party. In addition, split-party government, the federated system of power, and the intricacies of checks and balances across the branches make it easy to misplace reward and blame. Indeed, many economic and social trends are outside the control of government, and so the very notion of responsibility may be inappropriate in certain cases. And some issues are either ignored by both parties or are part of a bipartisan consensus, and so party cues are of little value in guiding one's vote choice.

Further, in the current electoral system citizens not only select between the two candidates put forward by political parties, but they are encouraged to become directly involved in the selection of the party nominees. This occurs through party caucuses and, especially, through primary elections. The goals of expressing the public will, of selecting qualified leaders, and of protecting against the sinister excesses of government apply as much here as in general elections. In the many electoral communities where one party dominates the other, the primary election is more significant than the general election. And given the usually large array of generally not-well-known candidates, the informational requirements are often greater in primaries than in general elections (Brady, 1987). For example, the 1988 Democratic presidential primaries featured as many as eight legitimate candidates, and the 1985 Democratic gubernatorial primary in New Jersey featured twelve candidates and no clear frontrunner. In primary elections voters cannot fall back on party cues and often need more subtle knowledge about ideological and policy differences among the candidates. It would be naive to suggest that all citizens must engage in these selection processes. But the logic and ethic of democracy suggests that the greater the number of primary voters, the more representative of the rank and file they are, and the more informed they are, the better the chances that a qualified, representative candidate will emerge. Indeed, the proper functioning of the minimalist model described above depends on the extent to which the nominating process produces candidates who reflect the interests of citizens who identify with the party.

At a more general level, campaigns and elections are intended as periods of public deliberation and as broad referenda on the state of American society. This is important in a system that is as culturally and economically diverse as the United States. During these periods of self-assessment individual, party, and public priorities are articulated and deliberated: parties (and other elites) that serve as cue givers for the public also take their cues from the public. The quality and range of this dialectic depends on the quality of these periodic national political conversations. But as Entman (1989) makes clear, the public's knowledge of politics sets the parameters of public discourse. The less informed citizens are, the more likely that campaigns will devolve into sensationalism and demagoguery, as the media and political leaders play to the public's baser instincts or seek to capitalize on their inability to distinguish between fact and fiction.

The process of choosing representatives is more citizen-intensive than often suggested. But a citizen entering the polling booth is increasingly required to do more than simply vote for candidates (Cronin, 1989). For example, in the November 1992 election forty states and the District of Columbia had at least one statewide initiative or referendum, and several had over a dozen. The issues addressed were varied, important, and complex: term limits for elected officials; expansion of or limitations on abortion rights, gender rights, and gay rights; the death penalty; physician-assisted suicide; legalized gambling; school voucher systems; tax and spending caps; technical changes in state constitutions; state search and seizure laws; environmental standards; bond issues; and more. The number and range of such plebiscites are even greater at the local level: in 1990 the residents of Los Angeles were asked to vote on twenty-eight ballot initiatives, and San Francisco's official information pamphlet, published to assist voters in evaluating the city's eleven 1990 ballot initiatives, was 162 pages long!

In addition, campaigns and elections require a number of civic roles beyond voting. Short of residency and age requirements, most public offices in the United States are open to all citizens. In theory there is not a distinct class of elites who rule, and the general public serves as the pool from which public officials are selected. Because the civic requisites of effective public leadership are greater than those for voting, at least some portion of the general citizenry needs to be better informed. One would be hard pressed to establish a specific percentage of citizens for whom this greater knowledge should be required. We hold no illusions of a system in which effective leaders can be selected by lot from the general citizenry.[19] Nonetheless, it seems reasonable to suggest, as Madison does, that the larger the pool of qualified, representative citizens, the better the chances of qualified, representative leadership. This is all the more true when one considers that governing requires not only elected leaders, but also appointed ones. This logic can be extended to the many thousands of other civic roles that must be filled for the machinery of campaigns and elections to operate: party officials, campaign staff, volunteers, and so on.

Thus far we have focused only on citizens' varied roles in the electoral process. But what about the politics between elections? The actual work of government takes place in this period, and this work involves civic input at several levels (Lemert, 1992). Both private and public interests constantly lobby government officials, committees, and agencies. Although many of these groups depend exclusively on professional lobbyists, many do not. In addition, much of the power of these groups comes from their ability to mobilize citizens to put direct and indirect pressure on government—through letters, phone calls, campaign donations, petitions, rallies, and so forth. As Benjamin Ginsberg and Martin Shefter (1990; Ginsberg, 1982) argue, elections have become increasingly symbolic affairs; the real battle for who gets what in contemporary America is fought between elections and "by other means."

The battle between branches of government is increasingly fought through the mobilization of public pressure. Presidents use the media to rally public opinion and to put direct and indirect pressure on Congress. Presidential favorability ratings serve as indicators to Congress as to whether he should be followed. Agendas are revised and policies succeed or fail depending on the ability to rally public support. Issues that were unanticipated during an election campaign emerge and require public support—few who voted for Richard Nixon expected him to freeze wages and prices or to thaw relations with Communist China; few who voted for Lyndon Johnson expected him to commit the United States to a protracted war in Southeast Asia.

The implementation of policies also depends on public cooperation and, thus, on at least a modicum of public understanding of such matters as the relation between oil consumption and geopolitical conflict, between taxes and spending, between education and productivity, and between crime rates and the economy. A policy based on informed civic input is more likely to reflect the public interest. This is true in the simple sense of aggregating the individual interests of citizens and in the broader sense expressed by Rousseau and the younger Mill. A citizen who understands the context surrounding a particular issue may be more likely to think in public, rather than purely private, terms. As a result, a citizen who participates in, or who simply follows, the development of national policy and who understands the logic of that policy is better able and, when appropriate, more willing to support the policy's implementation.

All the complexities of national civic engagement apply as well at the state and local levels of politics. In addition, some kinds of involvement are both more common and more necessary at these levels. Local civic action is more dependent on voluntary participation for which there is little or no direct compensation. Decisions on such matters as the public schools, zoning laws, and property taxes are often made in public meetings where substantial and substantive citizen input is required. Although local politics today may not be the hotbed of direct democracy found in the colonies, it remains reasonably dependent on informed civic input.

Finally, civic knowledge is ultimately more than simply instrumental, but is a good in and of itself. An informed citizen is one who is politically and socially oriented and so more fulfilled (Putnam, 1993). Socrates argued that the "unexamined life was not worth living," and that "there is only one good—knowledge, and only one evil—ignorance." He was, of course, speaking about the individual, but a similar case could be made for people in their public life. One of the ends of public life, of political education, is to know one's civic self.

The American political system was designed to balance a belief in the public's civic authority with doubts about the public's civic competence. The negative consequences of uninformed input were originally controlled through legal restrictions on the participation of the public, with the greatest restrictions aimed at particular classes of citizens thought to lack the necessary qualities of good citizenship. The public voice was tempered further through an elaborate system of checks and balances. At the same time, however, the inherent equality of citizens, the importance of civic virtue, and the tradition of participatory democracy were important undercurrents in American political thought. Driven largely by these undercurrents, de jure restrictions on political participation have slowly disappeared, and today all citizens are given a great deal of latitude in how, and how much, they participate in the public sphere.

The opportunities for political participation have resulted in a system that can be very responsive to the interests of civically engaged citizens. But to take even modest advantage of these opportunities, citizens need a number of political resources. Central among these resources is political information. In a public sphere that is only partially designed to facilitate informed civic input and a public philosophy that sends mixed messages regarding the importance of such input, there are few assurances that the voice to which government responds is spoken by or for the general public. Many citizens lack the de facto ability to participate, especially in more costly but more influential ways. Further, when they do participate—either directly through the vote or indirectly through opinion polls—low absolute and relative levels of information lower the likelihood that this participation will accurately reflect the individual, group, and collective interests of the public.

Suggestions that the negative consequences of low levels of political information can be offset by an informed elite, collective rationality, or heuristic decision making underestimate the importance of political information to these very theories. For elites to represent the general public effectively, they must still be accountable to the public. For collective opinions and decisions to accurately reflect the public interest, either all citizens must be able to discern and articulate their interests, or the portion who can do so must not be a biased sample of the citizenry. And for citizens to use simplifying strategies in reaching their individual decisions, they must have enough information to assure that these cues effectively tie their interests to their political behavior. This would be true even if political interests were always consensual or if those with information were representative of those without it. It is all the more important when interests clash and when the disparities in information are closely tied to different conceptions of the public good.

One cannot resolve the paradox of modern democracy by assuming away the importance of an informed public. What is required is a closer look at what citizens actually know and how information is distributed among different classes of citizens. The fundamental question is not if the American system is democratic, but how democratic it is and for whom. In the end the paradox of democracy is no paradox at all. For citizens who are the most informed, democracy works much as intended, while for those who are the most uninformed, democracy *is* a tragedy or a farce.

The modern world is bewilderingly complex, and mastering the facts relevant to the myriad of issues addressed in national politics is admittedly impossible—Schattschneider is correct in saying that by some absolutist standard nobody knows enough to run government. But Schattschneider and others who mirror the thrust of his argument draw the wrong conclusion from this fact. Being informed is not an either-or proposition, it is a more-or-less proposition. True, the American political system is well insulated from many of the negative effects of nonparticipation and of participation by citizens who are poorly informed. The political system does not collapse when a president is elected with less than half the popular vote and less than a quarter of the eligible vote. Nor does it go into crisis when a majority of citizens express an opinion regarding aid to the Contras without knowing where Nicaragua is relative to the United States or who the Contras are. But none of this suggests that the authoritative allocation of goods, services, and values—decisions about who gets what, where, when, and how—would not be significantly altered if more citizens participated in more informed ways. Finally, it is true that many citizens show remarkable resourcefulness in using partial, often meager information to extrapolate to opinions and decisions that, on the face of it, would appear to require more complex deliberation. But this ability still requires some information, and it in no way assures that the decisions made are satisfactory for the individual or the polity, or that such decisions would not be improved by more information.

We are not arguing that contemporary democracy requires that all citizens be expert on all facets of national politics, but we do suggest that the more citizens are passingly informed about the issues of the day, the behavior of political leaders, and the rules under which they operate, the better off they are, the better off *we* are. Similarly, we acknowledge that even democracies require information elites—experts who are especially informed about particular issues and to whom the rest of the citizenry turns for advice or leadership. But the greater the range of these experts, and the greater the percentage of the general public that is able to fulfill these roles (even as intermediaries in the flow of information), the more democratic that flow of information is likely to be.

During a public lecture on astronomy in which he described the earth's orbit around the sun, Bertrand Russell was challenged by an elderly woman in the audience who exclaimed, "What you told us is rubbish. The world is really a flat plate supported on the back of a giant tortoise." Russell, thinking he had the woman trapped by her own logic, asked, "But what is the tortoise standing on?" "You're very clever, young man, very clever," was the woman's response, "But it's turtles all the way down!"[20] In some ways this exchange captures the shortcoming of arguments intended to demonstrate that democracy can operate without benefit of citizens who meet the civic requisites assumed by political theorists. Competent civic decision making may rest "on the backs" of elites or some simple heuristic shortcuts. But on what do these elites rest? These heuristics? To argue it is "elites all the way down" is to define away the meaning of even limited democracy. And to suggest it is "heuristics all the way down" is to destroy their conceptual utility—that they are information shortcuts. In the end one cannot use these models to argue that democracy can operate effectively without an informed public because, ultimately, democracy rests on the backs of its citizens.

CHAPTER TWO

What Americans Know about Politics

If, then, there is a subject concerning which a democracy is particularly liable to commit itself blindly and extravagantly to general ideas, the best possible corrective is to make the citizens pay daily, practical attention to it. That will force them to go into details, and the details will show them the weak points in the theory.—ALEXIS DE TOCQUEVILLE, *Democracy in America*

The facts ma'am—nothing but the facts.—JOE FRIDAY, *Dragnet*

Efforts to gauge what Americans know about politics have been made for as long as public opinion surveys have been conducted. Since the 1940s, scholarly studies have consistently found that the public is poorly informed. This conclusion has been reinforced by popular press accounts of public ignorance, such as a 1986 ABC *Washington Post* poll taken shortly after the widely covered Geneva summit between Ronald Reagan and Mikhail Gorbachev that discovered a majority of Americans could not name the leader of the Soviet Union. A similar, if less scientific, example was given in a 1991 *New York Times* column: "'That's *U.S.* Senator.' Several members of the New York State Senate reported last week that they had received dozens of calls from constituents with urgent advice on how they should vote on the nomination of Clarence Thomas to the Supreme Court. The trouble was, the nomination was in the hands of the United States Senate."

Such books as Allan Bloom's *The Closing of the American Mind,* Diane Ravitch's and Chester Finn's *What Do Our 17-Year-Olds Know,* and E. D. Hirsch's *Cultural Literacy* have also contributed to this negative image of the American public. Indeed, D. Charles Whitney and Ellen Wartella conclude that a "virtual cottage industry has arisen in the past few years in making out the American public as a bunch of ignoramuses" (1988: 9). This characterization is so well established that, according to John Ferejohn, "Nothing strikes the student of public opinion and democracy more forcefully than the paucity of information most people possess about politics" (1990: 3). In spite of indications that the public was more interested in "fact-slinging" than "mudslinging," evidence from the 1992 presidential campaign did little to rehabilitate the American voter's image. A 1992 report by the Center for the Study of Communication at the University of Massachusetts found that 86 percent of a random sample of likely voters knew that the Bush's family dog was named Millie and 89 percent knew that Murphy Brown was the television character criticized by Dan Quayle, but only 15 percent knew that both candidates favored the death penalty and only 5 percent knew that both had proposed cuts in the capital gains tax.

In spite of the apparent unanimity with which scholars and other observers characterize the American public's knowledge of politics, there have been relatively few systematic studies of this topic.[1] This inconsistency is noted by Neuman: "The situation is a little like the discussion of sex in Victorian times. Everybody is interested in the subject. There are many allusions to it. But they are all inexplicit and oblique. . . . Ironically, the issue of mass political sophistication has moved from a puzzling discovery to a familiar cliché without ever being the subject of sustained empirical research" (1986: 8–9).

Although recent studies have made this criticism somewhat less applicable, the scope of the issue and the gravity of the conclusions continue to outweigh the empirical evidence. In this chapter we will draw on more than fifty years of survey research data and review the evidence more systematically. A careful search of public opinion polls reveals a surprisingly rich and varied set of questions tapping public knowledge. And the public's performance on these items suggests that the answer to the question "what do Americans know about politics" is more complicated than often assumed.

A Closer Look at What Citizens Should Know

The role of the citizen in contemporary American democracy is multifaceted and carries with it the responsibility to be politically informed. Emphasizing the importance of an informed citizenry does not contradict the notion that citizens use shortcuts in making political decisions. Rather it suggests that citizens are better able to make choices and respond to relevant cues if they have a broader range of information to draw on. Within this context several more specific and common sense guidelines can be developed. James David Barber argues that citizens "need to know what the government *is* and *does*" (1973: 44, emphasis added). According to Neuman, knowledge of what the government is includes "the basic structure of government—its basic values, such as citizen participation, majority rule, separation of powers, civil liberties, and its basic elements, such as the two-party system, the two houses of Congress, the role of the judiciary, and the organization of the cabinet" (1986: 196).

Much of what citizens are expected to do requires an understanding of the rules. A citizen may blame the majority party in Congress for what he perceives to be a failure to act, but an understanding of the relative powers of the executive and legislative branches, of the implications of divided government, and of what a veto is and the size of the majority necessary to override it may lead to very different conclusions. A citizen who is concerned about deteriorating public services but who understands the different responsibilities of local and national government may vote differently in both local and national elections than if she were less aware of these relations. A citizen who is reasonably well versed in the logic of the First Amendment might react to government attempts to censor the press differently than someone less familiar with this logic. A citizen concerned about abortion is well served by a familiarity with how the Supreme Court operates and how justices are appointed and confirmed. A citizen trying to determine why the savings and loan industry collapsed is aided by knowledge of who is responsible for government oversight in such cases, and why such oversight failed. And so on. Information of this kind might be used in forming and expressing opinions, in determining who to vote for, in deciding who to contact to register a complaint or offer a suggestion, or for maintaining the kind of informed indifference discussed in chapter 1. Regardless of how it is used, such information is valuable in making sense of the political world.[2]

Relevant knowledge of what the government does, the second half of Barber's definition, is described by Bernard Berelson et al.: "The democratic citizen is expected to be well-informed about political affairs. He is supposed to know what the issues are, what their history is, what the relevant facts are, what alternatives are proposed, what the party stands for, what the consequences are" (1954: 308).

It is not hard to see why information of this kind is useful if citizens are to be engaged meaningfully in politics. A citizen's grasp of contemporary domestic politics is strengthened by knowing, for example, whether the United States has a budget deficit or surplus or what the trends in unemployment and inflation are. An understanding of America's foreign policy is enhanced by the knowledge that the United States is dependent on imported oil or an awareness of what the United Nations is and what it does. As Berelson's definition suggests, citizens should also have some ability to put issues in historical context and to evaluate the success or failure of certain policies and philosophies. Was Russia our ally or our enemy during World War II? Did the Great Society programs increase or decrease poverty among the elderly? Who was helped and hurt by the Reagan economic program? Did the Clean Air Act of 1970 actually improve air quality? The contestable nature of answers to these questions does not lessen the need for citizens to have facts about them. Without such information citizens are unable to follow the debate and are highly vulnerable to manipulation. Knowledge of substantive politics is critical to the formation of reasoned opinions and to effective participation.

To Barber's two categories of "what government is" and "what it does" we add a third—"who government is." Given that one of the central responsibilities of citizens in a representative democracy is to select and periodically reevaluate leaders, citizens also need specific information about these leaders, both as individuals and as members of key political groupings. For example, citizens should be familiar with where parties and leaders stand on the important issues of the day. Does the president support or oppose raising taxes? Did one's senators vote for or against the use of force in the Persian Gulf? Do the Republicans want to increase or decrease defense spending? Do Democrats favor or oppose a voucher system for education? As with knowledge of substantive issues, citizens should be able to put parties and leaders into some historical context. Which party was responsible for the New Deal? The War on Poverty? Was Richard Nixon a Democrat or a Republican? In addition, because non-elected public figures and groups (for example, a religious leader like New York's John Cardinal O'Connor or a public interest group like Greenpeace) also serve as cues for making political evaluations, knowledge about their general philosophies and their particular stands can be valuable.

Taken as a whole, these three broad areas—what we call *the rules of the game, the substance of politics,* and *people and parties*—provide reasonable organizing principles for discussing what citizens should know about politics. The more citizens can draw on knowledge from these areas (breadth) and the more detailed the information within each area (depth), the better able they are to engage in politics.

Assessing Political Knowledge: 1940 to 1994

The analysis in this chapter is based primarily on the percentage of respondents correctly answering factual questions about politics on national surveys.[3] Two issues of validity warrant attention. First, the percentage who answered correctly is, of course, not necessarily the same as the percentage who knew the answer. Because of guessing (discussed in more detail below), these marginal percentages may overstate the extent of knowledge on many items, especially those with only two or three obvious choices. Offsetting this is the possibility that the survey setting (especially in telephone interviews) may cause some respondents to miss items that they actually know.[4] For simplicity's sake we will often refer to the percentage who knew a fact, but it should be kept in mind that the survey process is not perfectly reliable.[5]

A potentially more serious problem of validity is survey nonresponse. In addition to accurate measurement, a valid assessment of what the public knows depends on obtaining a representative sample. Even the very best national surveys, such as the National Election Study, are unable to obtain interviews with one-fourth to one-third of the sample. Many of the surveys we use (both our own and many of those obtained from the Roper Center) employ postsurvey weighting techniques to compensate for nonresponse and sample noncoverage errors (for example, nontelephone households in telephone surveys), but the effectiveness of these techniques is not fully known. One implication of nonresponse bias is that we will overestimate political knowledge levels because, as John Brehm has demonstrated, nonrespondents tend to be less engaged in politics than are respondents. Another implication is that our analyses of the consequences of political knowledge will understate knowledge's impact because the range of variability is attenuated (Brehm, 1993: chap. 5). Where appropriate, we will discuss the implications of nonresponse.

The items discussed below and in chapter 3 were gathered from several sources. The majority were drawn from the Roper Center archives. The Roper Center's collection of public opinion surveys is by far the most comprehensive in existence today. It includes over 200,000 survey questions dating to the 1930s. Of these questions, approximately 5 percent address some aspect of public information. Most of these focus on exposure to information (for example, "Have you read or heard anything about the recent arms negotiations between the United States and the Soviet Union?"), self-reports on sources of information (for example, "How often do you watch the national news?"), and self-assessments on how informed respondents are (for example, "Do you feel you have enough information to understand the changes currently taking place in Eastern Europe?"). Less than 2 percent of the questions archived by the Roper Center—and presumably of the questions generally asked on public opinion surveys—directly measure factual knowledge about public affairs, and over a third of these are devoted to knowledge of public health issues. Despite this relative lack of attention, however, this translates into over 3,500 factual questions asked over the last fifty years.[6] In addition, although the percentage of factual items has decreased over time, the explosion in the number of surveys in recent years has meant that the absolute number of such items has generally increased.

We supplemented the items collected by the Roper Center with those from several other sources. The National Election Studies (NES) and our 1989 Survey of Political Knowledge were the most useful of these (Miller, 1992; Miller, 1988; American National Election Study, 1984). We also included items gleaned from the national news media, convention papers, published works, and miscellaneous polls we happened upon. In the end we were able to collect nearly 3,700 individual survey questions that tapped factual knowledge of some kind.

Although there are few systematic patterns to the specific items included on public opinion surveys, overall they address a wide range of public concerns. About a third of the items address issues of public health; of these, nearly 90 percent pertained to AIDS, while the rest dealt with such topics as cancer and smoking or the causes of heart disease. Four percent of the items measure knowledge of geography, and 3 percent tap knowledge of history; 2 percent measure knowledge about organized religion, and 1 percent concern cultural figures and topics. Three percent of the items covered a wide range of miscellaneous information (for example, knowledge of vocabulary or the metric system).

At some level all information has political relevance, and certainly knowledge of such topics as public health, geography, and history aid in understanding, responding to, and influencing the political world. We are especially interested, however, in facts that are more directly tied to the processes, participants, and policies of government. The remaining 56 percent of our items, amounting to over 2,000 questions, measure knowledge of these more clearly political facts. Eleven percent—or 405 of the items—query knowledge about political and economic institutions and processes. Twenty-one percent, or 773, of the questions deal with knowledge about contemporary public figures, political parties, and other public organizations or groups. Nine percent (332 items) address domestic policy and social conditions. And the remaining 15 percent (553 items) address issues of foreign policy, international affairs, and global conditions. All told, the survey questions available through the Roper Center, supplemented by items from the NES, our original survey, and other miscellaneous sources, provide a reasonably varied pool of data from which to construct a picture of how informed the American public is on a wide array of political and politically relevant topics.

An Overview of What Americans Know about Politics

In table 2.1 we sort questions about institutions and processes, public figures and groups, domestic politics, and foreign affairs according to the percentage of the public able to answer them. The more top-heavy the figures, the better able the public is in the aggregate to answer the items in that domain. Of course the items on which these distributions are based do not (and could not) represent a random sample of the universe of facts about politics. But they do represent over a half century of survey research judgment as to what political facts matter. Although conclusions drawn from these distributions should be made cautiously and tentatively, they provide useful information concerning how much Americans collectively know about politics.

Table 2.1 Aggregate Distribution of Political Knowledge by Subject of Question

Percent of Sample Able to Answer	Institutions and Processes	People and Players	Domestic Politics	Foreign Affairs	General Political Knowledge
90–100	***	**	*	***	**
80–89	*****	*****	*****	*****	*****
70–79	************	********	**********	*********	**********
60–69	***********	**********	************	*********	**************
50–59	*******************	************	*********	****************	**************
40–49	*****************	***********	************	**************	*************
30–39	**************	**************	***********	**************	**************
20–29	*********	*************	************	*************	************
10–19	********	************	*********************	**********	************
0–9	*	*************	********	*******	********
	median = 49	median = 38	median = 39	median = 44	median = 41

Source: compilation of political knowledge questions from various sources, including the Roper Center, National Election Studies, 1989 Survey of Political Knowledge, and other miscellaneous surveys. *Note:* each asterisk represents 1 percent of survey questions.

Based on both the overall distribution of answers and the median percent correct, citizens have done best at answering questions about the institutions and processes of politics. This might simply reflect a tendency to ask easier questions about this area than others, but it is consistent with the fact that institutions and processes tend to be fairly stable and thus require less regular monitoring of the political landscape. In addition, this is the one domain of politics consistently taught in the schools.

The distributions of knowledge about political leaders, domestic politics, and foreign affairs are more similar to each other than they are to knowledge of institutions and processes, although of the three domains, citizens have done somewhat better on questions about foreign policy. For all four areas of civic knowledge, the distributions tend to be skewed toward the middle to lower deciles, and in no case does the median score top the 50 percent mark. Clustering at the lower ends of the distribution is most pronounced for knowledge of domestic politics, and least for knowledge of institutions and processes and of foreign affairs. The overall distribution of knowledge, based on all the items included in the more specific domains, is, quite naturally, a composite of the other distributions, neither as bottom-heavy as knowledge of domestic politics nor as diamond-shaped as knowledge of institutions and processes. Taken as a whole, these figures suggest that the American public, while not as politically informed as one might hope, is also not as uninformed as some characterizations have suggested. This general finding is supported by our more detailed examination of specific facts.

Knowledge of Specific Facts: A Portrait of the American Public

Although table 2.1 provides useful information concerning the aggregate distribution and level of political knowledge, it makes no distinction concerning the specific facts involved. What facts are most commonly known by citizens? What facts are more obscure? We now draw on the constructivist approach advocated by Neuman, Just, and Crigler (1992) to provide a detailed, narrative description of what Americans know—and don't know—about politics.[7]

Knowing the Rules of the Game

Whether as a spectator or a player, to be a part of a game one must understand the rules. This is as true for the game of politics as it is for the game of baseball. What do Americans know about political rules? Table 2.2 presents the percentage correctly answering a representative sample from our collection of survey questions about political (and politically relevant) institutions and processes.[8] Items in this and subsequent tables are ordered from most to least known.

Table 2.2 Knowledge of Institutions and Processes (Percentage Correct)

Survey Item	%	Survey Item	%
U.S. is a member of the U.N. (1985)	96	Define cold war (1950)	58
Warrants allow police searches (1986)	94	How does U.N. veto work (1947)	57
Length of president's term (1952)	93	Third in line for presidency (1985)	57
What is purpose of U.N. (1976)	90	Free speech protected on all media (1984)	56
Define presidential veto (1989)	89	Convicted felon not assured vote (1986)	55
United States is a democracy (1948)	88	Substance of *Brown* decision (1986)	55
Define press release (1985)	85	# of senators from each state (1945)	55
Right to trial by jury guaranteed (1986)	83	Define newsleak (1986)	55
States can have a death penalty (1983)	83	Define newspaper chain (1985)	55
No religious test for office seekers (1986)	81	Who sets monetary policy (1984)	54
Convicted persons can appeal (1983)	81	Define farm price supports (1953)	54
Define inflation (1951)	80	Purpose of the Constitution (1986)	54
Treaties need Senate approval (1986)	79	# of women on Supreme Court (1988)	53
Define federal deregulation (1984)	78	Define filibuster (1963)	53
What Constitution says on religion (1989)	77	Define federal budget deficit (1987)	52
Constitution can be amended (1986)	76	What does FCC do (1979)	52
Gulf war reports were censored (1991)	76	Effect of unbalanced budget on prices (1959)	52
Define Dow Jones index (1984)	76	What effect do tariffs have (1946)	51
How presidential campaign is funded (1979)	76	Congress can't require president to believe in God (1964)	51
Small papers depend on wire services (1985)	76	Accused are presumed innocent (1983)	50
First Amendment protects free press/speech (1985)	75	How presidential delegates are selected (1978)	49
President employs White House press secretary (1985)	75	Define reciprocal trade agreement (1945)	48
Purpose of U.N. (1951)	74	Define certificate of deposit (1987)	48
All states have trial courts (1977)	74	No right to own handgun (1986)	48
Not all cases heard by jury (1983)	74	What is Voice of America (1951)	46
Name a cabinet position (1960)	72	Define liberal (1957)	46
Define party platform (1952)	71	Define conservative (1957)	46
Define depression (1983)	69	What is N.Y. Stock Exchange (1987)	46
Define a monopoly (1949)	69	States can't legislate silent prayer (1986)	46
Popular votes don't determine president (1986)	69	TV more regulated than print (1985)	45
Define wiretapping (1949)	67	Substance of *Miranda* decision (1989)	45
Need warrant to search noncitizens (1986)	66	Congress declares war (1987)	45
Define impeachment (1974)	66	% vote to override presidential veto (1947)	44
Congress can't ban opposition (1964)	65	Name a branch of government (1952)	44
English not official national language (1986)	64	Who sets interest rates (1984)	42
Define foreign trade deficit (1985)	63	Name a U.N. agency (1976)	41
Need Congressional approval for military aid (1986)	62	Define Bill of Rights (1986)	41
Effect of dollar's value on import prices (1978)	62	Purpose of NATO (1988)	40
President can't adjourn Congress (1986)	59	How are presidential candidates selected (1952)	40
Who determines law's constitutionality (1992)	58	Define free trade (1953)	39
		Can't force pledge of allegiance (1986)	39
		# of states choosing U.S. representatives (1954)	37
		Define primary election (1952)	36

Table 2.2 Knowledge of Institutions and Processes (*continued*)

Survey Item	%	Survey Item	%
Define welfare state (1949)	36	Define fiscal policy (1983)	21
Pool system used in Gulf war (1991)	36	Define collateral damage (1991)	21
Define electoral college (1955)	35	Name two First Amendment rights (1989)	20
Describe economic system in U.S. (1951)	33	What is Food & Drug Administration (1979)	20
Governors don't OK court rulings (1977)	33	Define the Foreign Service (1955)	19
Insider trading is illegal (1987)	33	Define supply side economics (1981)	19
Name a U.N. agency (1975)	35	Name all three branches of government (1952)	19
Substance of *Roe v. Wade* (1986)	30	Define monetary policy (1983)	18
Length of House term (1978)	30	Define sampling error (1987)	16
Substance of *Webster* decision (1989)	29	What is the Common Market (1961)	13
Libel law differs for public figures (1985)	27	Not all federal cases reviewed by Supreme Court (1986)	12
Name two branches of government (1952)	27	Define politically correct (1991)	7
Define bipartisan foreign policy (1950)	26	Name two Fifth Amendment rights (1989)	2
Define prime rate (1985)	26		
Length of senator's term (1991)	25		
No guarantee for high school education (1986)	23		

Simple characterizations cannot do justice to the range of political knowledge and ignorance demonstrated by the public. Some facts about political institutions and processes are known by a substantial portion of Americans: more than one in seven of these survey items was correctly answered by at least three-quarters of those asked. Many are rudimentary—but potentially important—facts about the United States Congress and presidency, such as knowing the definition of a presidential veto or that a president cannot make foreign treaties without Senate approval. Commonly known facts also include information about the bureaucracy, such as what the term *deregulation* means. Some facts about the relation between state and national government are widely known (for example, that the president appoints judges to federal, but not state courts), as are a number of facts about civil liberties and the United States Constitution (for example, knowledge of the constitutional right to a trial by jury; that states have the right to institute a death penalty; that the Constitution can be amended). Awareness of what the United Nations is and that the United States is a member of it is also almost universal. Basic knowledge about the press and its relation to government is quite common: for example, that the White House press secretary is an employee of the president; that during the Persian Gulf war news stories were censored; and that press rights are guaranteed by the First Amendment to the Constitution. Knowledge of economic institutions and processes appears to be a little less common. Of the nearly eighty questions about economics, less than 5 percent were correctly answered by at least three-quarters of the public (for example, defining the term *inflation*).

There is no obvious pattern to the particular facts citizens are more or less likely to know. Not surprisingly, however, as the amount of detail requested increases and as less visible institutions or processes are asked about, the percentage of the public able to correctly answer questions declines. Still, an additional 34 percent of the items could be correctly answered by at least half of those surveyed. Most Americans are able to define such terms as *party platform* and *filibuster,* know the number of U.S. senators from their state, or can name at least one United States cabinet position. At least a majority of those asked understand that Congress cannot pass a law preventing people who disagree with it from meeting or talking with each other, that the popular vote does not determine who wins a presidential election, and that a president cannot adjourn Congress whenever he chooses. Over half know that the federal courts have the power of judicial review, that (in 1988) one member of the Supreme Court was a woman, and that before the decision in *Roe v. Wade,* the legality of abortions was determined by the states. This level of knowledge is also reached on several questions pertaining to other constitutional rights: for example, identifying at least one right guaranteed by the Fifth Amendment or knowing that the Bill of Rights protects speech regardless of whether it is written, spoken, or broadcast. Questions pertaining to economic institutions and processes that were correctly answered by half to three-quarters of the public include defining such terms as *recession, foreign trade deficit,* and *monopoly.*

Although this level of knowledge is encouraging, just over half the questions about institutions and processes could not be answered by a majority of those asked. Included among the questions answered correctly by only a quarter to just under a half of the public (37 percent of all questions) are many items that seem critical to understanding politics in the United States. Significantly, less than half the public can define either *liberal* or *conservative* with any degree of accuracy. Less than half the public can define such terms as *NATO, bipartisan foreign policy,* or *primary elections.* Less than a majority can volunteer the percentage required for Congress to override a presidential veto, say how long a House member's term is, or note that all congressional seats are contested at the same time every two years. Similarly small percentages know that (since 1979) presidential elections are publicly financed or how their own state selects delegates to the national conventions. A minority of Americans know that governors do not have to approve the decisions made by their highest state court or that states cannot pass laws requiring silent prayer in school. Only between a quarter and half of those asked could describe the decisions reached in *Roe v. Wade* or *Miranda v. Arizona* or know that television is regulated more than newspapers. Economic terms correctly defined by a quarter to a half of the public include *prime rate* and *welfare state.*

Finally, one in seven of the questions about institutions and processes were correctly answered by less than a quarter of the public. Included among these obscure facts is the ability to name more than one right guaranteed by either the First or Fifth Amendments, knowing that not every lower court decision is automatically reviewed by the Supreme Court, and identifying all three branches of national government. Less than a quarter of those questioned could, in the midst of the Persian Gulf war, define the term *collateral damage.* In the midst of the debate over Reaganomics, less than a quarter of those asked could define *supply side economics.* And fewer than a quarter could define terms like *fiscal policy* or *monetary policy* or describe what is meant by "free trade between nations."

Knowing the Players: Public Information about People, Parties, and Groups

Citizens in a representative democracy need basic information about who their representatives are and where those representatives stand on issues of the day. Public figures and political organizations in general, and political parties and partisans in particular, are among the most common heuristics used by citizens in making political decisions. We collected nearly 800 survey questions testing knowledge about public figures, political parties, and political organizations over the period from 1940 to 1994. Whereas most of these questions involved identification of national political figures, some asked about foreign leaders, as well as about public leaders from business, labor, and the media. In addition, many went beyond simple identification and focused on more in-depth knowledge, such as party identification, issue stands, or public statements. Finally, a small number of questions tested knowledge about independent groups and organizations involved in politics.

How much do Americans know about the individuals, parties, and groups that make or influence public policy? The most accurate answer to this question is "it depends"—on who you are asking about, on when you ask, and on how much detail you ask for. Of the 773 questions, 85 (11 percent) were answered correctly by three-quarters or more of those surveyed over the years (table 2.3). Not surprisingly, the most readily identifiable leaders were the most visible of their day: U.S. presidents and vice presidents, presidential candidates, and, less frequently, important members of

Congress and of the president's administration. The governor of one's own state was the only elected official other than the president and vice president whom 75 percent or more of *constituents* could name. A few members of Congress who were not also running for president were known to over three-quarters of those surveyed (for example, Senators Joe McCarthy and Ted Kennedy). Nonelected government officials, such as General Douglas MacArthur, Secretary of State George Marshall (architect of the European Recovery Program that informally bore his name), Federal Bureau of Investigation (FBI) director J. Edgar Hoover, and Iran-Contra operative Oliver North were also identified by 75 percent or more of the public. Private citizens (not including the popular culture figures discussed below) who made the top quarter of identifiable public leaders included labor leaders John L. Lewis (of the United Mine Workers) and Dave Beck (of the Teamsters), consumer advocate Ralph Nader, and television journalists Walter Cronkite and Barbara Walters. Among the few foreign leaders about whom three-quarters or more of those surveyed demonstrated some knowledge were Chiang Kai-shek (leader of Nationalist China) in the 1940s and 1950s, and Nelson Mandela, Manuel Noriega, and Saddam Hussein in the 1990s.

Table 2.3 Knowledge of People and Players (Percentage Correct)

Survey Item	%	Survey Item	%
U.S. president (1986)	99	George Wallace (1967)	69
Douglas MacArthur (1947)	97	Party supported by most blacks (1985)	69
Walter Cronkite (1975)	93	Know Bush reversed stand on taxes (1990)	68
John L. Lewis (1957)	93	Progressive party presidential candidate (1948)	67
Know Nelson Mandela is free (1990)	91	Orval Faubus (1957)	67
Name your governor (1970)	86	Carter's stand on ERA (1979)	66
Chiang Kai-shek's country (1954)	84	Verdict in J. Hazelwood trial (1990)	66
Dean Rusk (1964)	82	Tip O'Neil (1983)	66
Henry Kissinger (1973)	78	Dukakis stance on abortion (1988)	64
Clinton's stand on gays in the military (1993)	77	Winner of Nicaraguan election (1990)	63
Joe McCarthy (1954)	77	Who are the freedom riders (1961)	61
J. Edgar Hoover (1960)	75	What is the NAACP (1985)	59
Leader of Iraq (1990)	75	John Foster Dulles (1953)	59
Ralph Nader (1976)	75	Is your governor a Democrat or Republican (1985)	59
Charles de Gaulle (1964)	73	Franco's nation (1949)	58
Dean Rusk (1967)	73	Republican party stance, nuclear testing (1988)	58
Head of China (1943)	72	Nehru's country (1954)	58
Margaret Thatcher	72	Barry Goldwater (1963)	58
Bush's stance on SDI (1988)	71	Republican party more conservative (1988)	57
Mikhail Gorbachev (1990)	71	Truman's stand on taxes (1947)	57
Party control of House (1978)	71		
Walter Reuther (1957)	70		
Truman's stance on communists in U.S. government (1947)	69		

Table 2.3 Knowledge of People and Players (*continued*)

Survey Item	%	Survey Item	%
Secretary of state (1958)	57	How one senator voted on Panama Canal (1978)	29
How representative voted on Gulf war (1991)	57	County clerk (1965)	28
Cyrus Vance (1977)	54	State senator (1965)	28
Warren Burger (1984)	51	Who said "thousand points of light" (1988)	27
CIO stance on FDR (1944)	51	Secretary of defense (1959)	27
President of Russia (1994)	47	Name one of "Keating Five" (1991)	27
Andrew Young (1977)	48	Who are the Black Muslims (1963)	27
Gorbachev stance on multiparty system (1990)	47	Reagan's stand on ERA (1979)	27
Harold Stassen (1952)	46	Ivan Boesky (1987)	26
Moral Majority's general stances (1981)	46	A person critical of Gulf war (1991)	25
Incumbent House candidate (1966)	46	Attorney general (1970)	24
J. Birch Society stance: ERA (1979)	45	Gerald Ford's party (1974)	22
Ed Meese (1984)	42	Socialist party presidential candidate (1948)	21
U Thant (1964)	42	Republican party stance: pro-life amendment (1980)	21
Dukakis vetoed pledge bill (1988)	41	Louis Farrakhan (1990)	20
Marshal Tito (1951)	40	Eugene McCarthy (1967)	19
Jim Wright's party (1990)	39	Country Pollard spying for (1990)	19
Reagan stance on balanced budget in '82 (1981)	39	Julius Rosenberg (1950)	18
Kurt Waldheim (1980)	39	Zbigniew Brzezinski (1977)	17
Anthony Eden (1952)	38	Robert McNeil (1980)	16
Truman's stance on war criminals (1947)	37	Robert Bork (1987)	15
Gamal Nasser (1958)	37	Sukarno (1964)	15
Name both your senators (1985)	35	Ross Perot (1971)	14
Harold Washington (1984)	34	Prime minister of Canada (1989)	11
President of France (1986)	34	U.S.'s U.N. representative (1947)	11
President of CIO (1944)	34	Vaclav Havel (1990)	10
Carter's stance on defense spending (1979)	32	Secretary general of U.N. (1953)	10
Superintendant of local schools (1987)	32	Charles Percy's party (1974)	9
Elizabeth Dole (1983)	32	Mark Hatfield (1963)	7
RFK-LBJ differences on Vietnam (1967)	31	Prime minister of Italy (1986)	6
Anthony Eden (1954)	31	Elmo Roper (1960)	5
Ted Kennedy stance on wage and price controls (1980)	30	Head of HUD (1977)	5
Jesse Helms (1984)	29	Lane Kirkland (1980)	5
		President of Mexico (1991)	3
		Hodding Carter (1979)	3
		Prime minister of Norway (1986)	1

Questions asking for more detailed information about public leaders and organizations were generally less likely to be answered correctly. Nonetheless, fully 90 percent of those asked knew that once the fighting started (in January of 1991), both political parties supported the use of force in the Persian Gulf. More than three-quarters of the public knew that Exxon was the company responsible for the massive oil spill in Alaskan waters in 1989. Over the fifty years of survey items we examined only two issue stands of public officials could be identified by more than three-quarters of those surveyed. One was Bill Clinton's "don't ask . . . don't tell" proposal for ending the ban on gays in the military. Tellingly, the other "issue stand" was George Bush's 1989 disclosure that he hates broccoli!

An additional 201 questions, or 26 percent of the total, were answered correctly by between half and just under three-quarters of those surveyed. Included among these are many of the same public figures found in the top quartile discussed above, usually just before or just after their fifteen minutes of fame. Also found here are most vice presidential candidates, as well as many senators and House members who sought but failed to attain their party's presidential nomination. Other members of Congress who achieved this level of public notoriety included Senator John Bricker (author of "the Bricker Amendment," a controversial proposal for amending the Constitution to curb the president's treaty-making powers) during the 1940s and Speaker of the House Tip O'Neill during the 1980s. So, too, did several administration officials throughout the years: for example, Harold Stassen (U.S. delegate to the founding convention of the United Nations) during the Truman administration; Secretary of State Dean Rusk during the Kennedy and Johnson administrations; Secretary of Agriculture Earl Butz (better known for his politically incorrect jokes than his farm policies) during the Nixon-Ford years; and former national security advisor, Navy admiral, and Contragate principal John Poindexter during the Reagan-Bush years.

Other political figures identified by between 50 percent and 74 percent of those asked were Chief Justice Earl Warren, Governor Orval Faubus (the segregationist who defied Eisenhower's executive order in Little Rock, Arkansas), and Mayor Richard Daley (of Chicago). Over half of those surveyed could also usually identify their own mayor, name at least one of their U.S. senators, and say which party controlled the U.S. House and Senate. Private figures like pollster George Gallup, corporate executive Lee Iacocca, and labor leader Harry Bridges (whose conviction for perjury in the McCarthy-era witch hunts was overturned by the Supreme Court) were known to over half of those polled. So, too, were foreign figures, such as Vidkun Quisling (the Norwegian fascist, executed for aiding Germany's invasion of his country and for serving as premier during its occupation), Francisco Franco (the long-lived fascist dictator of Spain), Charles de Gaulle (World War II hero and president of France in 1945–46 and again from 1959 to 1969), and, more recently, British Prime Minister Margaret Thatcher, Soviet President Mikhail Gorbachev, Russian President Boris Yeltsin, and Rumanian dictator Nicolae Ceauçsescu (who reached this level of recognition posthumously).

In most years, at least half of the public knew that the Republican party was the more conservative of the two parties—a key piece of information for being at least a minimally competent voter. A substantial range of general issue stands taken by the national parties, presidential candidates, or sitting presidents was also known by 50 percent or more of those asked. For example, Truman's stands on relations with the Soviet Union and on tax increases were known by over half those polled in the 1940s, as were the views of Jimmy Carter, Ted Kennedy, and Eleanor Smeal regarding the Equal Rights Amendment (ERA) in the mid-1970s. During the 1988 presidential campaign, party or candidate stands on such issues as the Strategic Defense Initiative, relations with the Soviets, and abortion rights were known by half or more of those asked. And over half those surveyed during the 1992 presidential campaign knew the relative stands of the parties or candidates on such issues as federal jobs programs and defense spending. In addition, more than half those polled could provide some biographical information about presidential candidates, such as Ronald Reagan's age, that George Bush once headed the Central Intelligence Agency (CIA), or that Michael Dukakis speaks three languages. More than half those surveyed could also say, when pushed, how their two U.S. senators voted on the 1991 Persian Gulf resolution. And fully 70 percent of those asked knew that President Clinton's health care proposal required businesses to provide insurance for all their workers. Finally, half to three-quarters of those surveyed demonstrated some knowledge of political groups and organizations: for example, identifying (in the 1960s) who the Freedom Riders were or knowing (in the 1970s) the stand taken on the ERA by several political and social organizations.

Although, as with knowledge of institutions and processes, these patterns of information holding provide some cause for optimism, fully 62 percent of the questions about people and parties asked from 1940 to 1994 were answered correctly by fewer than half of those surveyed. Of these, 239 questions (or 31 percent of the total) were correctly answered by a quarter to just under half of those asked. As before, some of these officials were people who achieved (or would achieve) greater notoriety at other times (for example, Senate Majority Leader Lyndon Baines Johnson before his initial bid for the presidency in 1960). Less than half the public could name vice presidential candidates early in most presidential campaigns. Presidential candidates from third parties who achieved this level of recognition were doing better than most (for example, Socialist party nominee Norman Thomas).[9] Members of Congress known by less than half but at least a quarter of those surveyed included the conservative Senator (and brother of polar explorer Richard Byrd) Harry Flood Byrd during the Roosevelt and Truman administrations; Senator William Fulbright (an early, vocal opponent to the war in Vietnam) during the Kennedy-Johnson era; and House Speakers Carl Albert during the Nixon-Ford years and Tom Foley during the Bush and Clinton years. In the midst of the savings and loan scandal of the late 1980s and early 1990s, only about a quarter of those asked could name one or more of the senators known collectively as the "Keating Five." State and local officials known by a quarter to a half of those interviewed included Chicago Mayor Jane Byrne during the 1970s and New York Governor Mario Cuomo during the 1980s and 1990s. More generally, less than half those asked could name their U.S. representative, both of their U.S. senators, or such local officials as county clerk, state legislator, or school board superintendent.

Appointed officials identified by 25 to 49 percent of those asked included infamous communist-hunter Roy Cohn during the Eisenhower years and born again Secretary of the Interior James Watt during the Reagan era. Less than half of those asked could identify Sandra Day O'Connor as a member of the Supreme Court during the Reagan years, recall the name of a single member of the Supreme Court beyond the chief justice during the Bush administration, or identify newly appointed Supreme Court Justice Ruth Bader Ginsburg during the Clinton administration.

Between a quarter and a half of those surveyed had some knowledge of such foreign officials as Josip Tito (president-for-life of Yugoslavia), Anthony Eden (British foreign minister who resigned rather than accept what he saw as Neville Chamberlain's appeasement policy toward Germany and who later became prime minister), Egyptian President Gamal Abdel Nasser, West German Chancellor Konrad Adenauer, French President François Mitterand, United Nations Secretary General U Thant, or the scandalized British cabinet member John Profumo.

Knowledge about many of the specific issue stands taken by candidates, parties, and officeholders also fall in this range. For example, between 25 and 49 percent of those asked knew Truman's stand on the Taft-Hartley Act. A similar percentage could articulate the differences between Robert Kennedy and Lyndon Johnson concerning the Vietnam war, summarize Jimmy Carter's views on defense spending, or say how one of their U.S. Senators voted on the Panama Canal treaty. Only a little more than a third of those asked knew that before the start of the bombing in January 1991, the Democrats were less supportive of the use of force in the Persian Gulf than were the Republicans. And only this percentage of citizens could identify Gorbachev's stand on multiple parties in the Soviet Union, the Moral Majority's basic political philosophy, or several key differences between the Democratic and Republican parties, or between the presidential candidates, in 1988 and 1992.

The remaining 31 percent, or 240 questions, were correctly answered by fewer than one-quarter of the public. Included here are most presidential and vice presidential candidates for third and fourth parties, for example, the Socialist, Progressive, and States Rights parties. Such senators and House members as Henry "Scoop" Jackson, Eugene McCarthy (before his 1968 presidential bid), and Jack Kemp could be identified by fewer than 25 percent of those asked. Similarly small numbers could identify such appointed officials as trustbuster Thurman Arnold in Franklin Roosevelt's tenure; Secretary of State Christian Herter in the Eisenhower era; cabinet member William Simon in the Nixon-Ford years; Commerce Secretary Juanita Kreps during the Carter administration; and Secretary of Defense Caspar Weinberger during Reagan's tenure as president. Before the Persian Gulf war, fewer than 15 percent could identify either General Colin Powell or Secretary of Defense Dick Cheney. Indeed, when asked to name the person (for example, "who is the current attorney general") rather than the position (for example, "who is Ed Meese—what does he do"), fewer than a quarter of those asked were able to identify the holders of any but the most visible and prestigious cabinet posts, especially early in a presidential term. In the midst of public hearings on the Reagan administration's mismanagement of the Department of Housing and Urban Development, fewer than one in ten people could identify Samuel Pierce, who headed that department during the years in question. Among private citizens, union leader Lane Kirkland, businessman Ross Perot (before his 1992 independent presidential bid), Church of Islam leader Louis Farrakhan, journalist Walter Lippmann, and pollster Lou Harris were all identified by fewer than a quarter of those asked. Finally, foreign officials such as Sukarno (Indonesia's first president), Vaclav Havel (Czechoslovakia's first freely elected leader since before World War II), the prime ministers of Japan, Canada, and Sweden, the president of the European Economic Community, and the French and British delegates to the United Nations could all be identified by fewer than one in four Americans.

The Substance of Politics: Knowledge about Domestic Politics

Knowledge of public figures and of the institutions and processes of government serves little purpose if citizens are not also informed about the substance of politics itself. We identified more than 300 survey items that tested the public's knowledge of domestic issues, policies, and conditions (see table 2.4).[10] Of these, 36 (11 percent) were known by three-quarters or more of those asked. These well-known facts included awareness that Medicare legislation was passed in 1965 and that Social Security taxes are not saved for the specific contributors' own retirement. Seventy-five percent or more of the public also knew (during the Truman administration) what the steel dispute was about, and what the stands of both industry and the unions were in that dispute. Similar percentages were usually aware whether the federal government had a budget deficit (though sometimes less than half knew this) and that taxpayers were going to bear the brunt of paying for the savings and loan crises of the late 1980s and early 1990s. And at least 75 percent of those asked demonstrated knowledge of facts relevant to understanding domestic politics, such as that oil was in short supply in the mid-1970s or that pesticides and fertilizers could pollute areas some distance from where they were used.

Table 2.4 Knowledge of Domestic Politics (Percentage Correct)

Survey Item	%	Survey Item	%
What is the steel dispute about (1952)	96	Voting rights legislation passed (1965)	67
Social Security doesn't provide job training (1974)	89	Effect of tax law on mortgage deductions (1987)	63
Minimum wage (1984)	86	Government doesn't require religious broadcasting (1945)	61
Budget deficit increased since 1981 (1985)	83	Public school curricula vary by state (1989)	61
Oil is in short supply (1974)	81	Who is eligible for draft pardon (1975)	61
Aware of recent coal strikes (1944)	81	Causes of acid rain (1981)	60
Industry's position in steel dispute (1952)	80	Excise tax legislation passed (1965)	60
Who will pay for S&L bailout (1990)	79	# of points Dow Jones index fell (10/20/87)	59
Union's position in steel dispute (1952)	78	Birth control pill–health problem link (1978)	57
Pesticides can pollute away from source (1979)	78	Road beautification bill passed (1965)	55
Social Security revenue spent, not saved (1978)	78	What is Watergate about (1973)	54
There is a federal budget deficit (1984)	77	Why nuclear plants built by water (1980)	52
Medicare legislation passed (1965)	76	Why Hubbel telescope in news (1990)	51
What is national health insurance (1978)	76	Government regulates radio (1945)	51
Medicare part of social security system (1974)	75	Major cause of childhood death (1989)	51
What happened at Three Mile Island (1980)	74	Illiteracy rate in U.S. (1990)	51
Medicare doesn't cover all medical costs (1987)	72	Bush vetoed plant closing bill (1990)	50
Size of oil spill off Alaska (1989)	72	What is greenhouse effect (1988)	50
Farmers having economic problems (1979)	71	Size of federal budget (1989)	49
There is a federal budget deficit (1983)	70	Leading cause of death in U.S. (1952)	48
Food preservatives linked to health problem (1978)	69	Current unemployment rate (1984)	48
Fresh water not unlimited (1979)	69	Likely effect of Taft-Hartley (1946)	45
Military personnel tested for AIDS (1987)	68	Major cause of air pollution (1980)	45
Electricity in short supply (1974)	68	Population of U.S. (1988)	43
Describe Nixon economic plan (1971)	68	Current inflation rate (1985)	42
		Food stamps not part of Social Security (1979)	41
		Steel is in short supply (1974)	41
		Government doesn't set # of radio ads (1945)	41

Table 2.4 Knowledge of Domestic Politics (*continued*)

Survey Item	%	Survey Item	%
College education bill passed (1965)	41	Government considering suit against AT&T (1975)	18
Primary education bill passed (1965)	40	% of federal budget to health care (1978)	17
Value of dollar compared to 1939 (1951)	39	% of gross taxes paid by top 25% (1978)	17
Government doesn't set radio profits (1945)	38	Effect of tax law on capital gains (1987)	16
Not all federal employees pay social security (1979)	37	How are stock profits taxed (1989)	16
# of Americans unemployed (1984)	37	% of poor that are black (1985)	15
What are synthetic fuels (1980)	37	% of U.S. power from nuclear (1979)	14
Black and white blood the same (1944)	36	Urban affairs bill passed (1965)	14
Immigration legislation passed (1965)	35	Costs or wages rising faster (1958)	14
Average net industry profit (1969)	35	Required car mpg by 1985 (1979)	13
Westmoreland suing CBS (1985)	33	Corporate income tax rate (1945)	13
What is affirmative action (1985)	31	What is Dixon-Yates proposal (1954)	12
Black relative unemployment rate (1977)	31	Average cost per school child (1979)	12
What is the Hoover Commission (1950)	31	How is Superfund funded (1986)	12
% U.S. citizens who are millionaires (1979)	28	% of population that is Hispanic (1990)	12
Social Security one of top two federal budget expenses (1989)	27	Meese porno report conclusion (1986)	12
Average coal miner's salary (1944)	26	What are right-to-work laws (1955)	11
What is acid rain (1980)	26	% of workers employed by government (1976)	11
What does FICA deduction mean (1989)	25	% of poor who are kids (1985)	11
What is Social Security tax rate (1979)	25	What is thalidomide (1979)	10
Amount of current gasoline taxes (1984)	23	% gas cost go to oil company profits (1984)	10
% U.S. workers in unions (1944)	23	% poor who are women (1985)	9
What is Watergate about (1972)	22	Average yearly dollars to treat AIDS patient (1987)	9
Define no-fault insurance (1969)	22	% population that is Jewish (1990)	8
What happened at Love Canal (1979)	22	% population that is black (1990)	8
% of federal budget to military (1984)	21	% federal budget to Social Security (1984)	8
Helms trying to buy CBS (1985)	21	Effect of tax law on scholarships (1987)	8
Income tax on $25,000 (1944)	19	% federal spending increased since 1980 (1988)	6
Government regulates radio ownership (1945)	18	Size of federal budget (1951)	6
% of population below poverty line (1989)	18		

An additional 26 percent (86 items) of the survey questions could be correctly answered by one-half to three-quarters of those asked. These included knowledge of public policy: that the government does not establish specific quotas for the time devoted to religious and educational broadcasting; that voting rights and excise tax legislation was passed in 1965; the general thrust of Nixon's economic program; that President Bush vetoed the plant-closing bill passed by Congress in 1990; that school curricula and graduation requirements vary by state; and so forth. More than half of those asked could describe the basic facts surrounding Watergate in 1973 or Three Mile Island in 1980. The day after the 1987 stock market crash, more than half of those asked could say how many points the Dow Jones index lost. Other facts about the domestic scene known by one-half to just under three-quarters of those asked included awareness that farmers were in economic distress in the mid 1970s, that food preservatives and birth control pills had been linked to health problems, the general causes of acid rain, the definition of "the greenhouse effect," and some details of the Social Security system.

More than 60 percent of the items tapping knowledge of domestic politics could not be answered by as many as half of those asked. Of these, a little under half (89 items, or 27 percent of the total) were known by over a quarter of the public. These included awareness of the likely effects of the Taft-Hartley legislation, the purpose of the Hoover Commission (set up by Truman to recommend changes in the structure of the federal bureaucracy), and that immigration legislation was passed by Congress in 1965. Several details of the Social Security system (for example, that the Social Security program was paying more than it collected in 1984 but was collecting more than it paid by 1989) were known by less than half those asked. Less than half (but at least a quarter) of those asked knew that taxes in the United States are generally lower than in Western Europe, what the minimum wage is, and that black unemployment is higher than white unemployment in the United States.[11] Similar numbers knew that the blood of blacks and whites is the same (asked during the 1940s).

The remaining 35 percent of our questions could be correctly answered by fewer than a quarter of those asked. These little-known facts included being able to describe the Wagner Labor Act, knowing what percent of the federal budget went to health care or Social Security, knowing the size of the federal budget deficit, or knowing what the Superfund is. Less than a quarter of the public also knew what Watergate was about in 1972 or about the environmental disaster that occurred at Love Canal. General facts relevant to domestic politics that were largely unknown included the corporate income tax rate, the percentage of U.S. workers that are in unions, the percentage of energy used in the United States that comes from nuclear power, the percentage of gross income tax revenue provided by the top 25 percent of wage earners, or the percent of the poor in the United States who are black or children.

The Substance of Politics: Knowledge about Foreign Affairs

Of the more than 500 questions asked about foreign affairs (see table 2.5), 14 percent were answered correctly by at least three-quarters of survey respondents. These facts included knowing that the Soviet Union (until recently), Cuba, and China are communist nations. Most citizens were also aware of some of the more dramatic or publicized issues of the day: for example, three-quarters or more of the public could name at least one of the nations occupying Germany during the Truman administration, knew that Khrushchev was going to visit the United States during Eisenhower's administration, knew Nixon's reaction to the Mai Lai–related conviction of Lieutenant William Calley, and knew that the United States had a trade deficit in the 1980s and 1990s. As public attention turned to the increasing U.S. dependence on foreign goods during and after the Carter administration, most citizens were aware of whether many large corporations were domestic or foreign and what goods the United States did or did not import.

Table 2.5 Knowledge of Foreign Affairs (Percentage Correct)

Survey Item	%	Survey Item	%
Ozone damage affects whole world (1988)	94	Japan not known for oil reserves (1988)	72
Name one country with nuclear weapons (1988)	93	Who does U.S. government support in Nicaragua (1988)	69
Americans held hostage in Middle East (1989)	91	North Korea is communist (1978)	66
U.S. has trade deficit with Japan (1988)	88	Did rebellion in Romania succeed (1990)	66
Volkswagen is a foreign company (1978)	87	Can Soviets make A-bomb (1949)	63
U.S. has military base in Phillipines (1985)	85	What is Marshall Plan (1950)	63
U.S. provides economic aid to South Korea (1985)	83	Countries signing Camp David accord (1979)	62
Cuba is communist (1988)	82	U.S. is a member of NATO (1964)	61
Name a country occupying Germany (1950)	82	What is the Kremlin (1957)	61
Who brought Berlin dispute to U.N. (1948)	81	Where are Contras and Sandinistas (1988)	60
Nixon reaction to Calley decision (1971)	80	Mineral used in A-bomb (1952)	59
Soviet Union is communist (1948)	78	Most Western European countries are democracies (1948)	59
U.S. imports oil (1984)	78	% South Africans who are black (1985)	59
Mainland China is communist (1985)	77	Size of Japan GNP relative to U.S. (1986)	59
Describe Soviet pressure on Lithuania (1990)	77	Describe unrest in Middle East (1967)	58
Reagan administration to deploy MX missile (1985)	76	Describe goals of SALT treaty (1979)	58
Iran demand for return of U.S. hostages (1980)	74	Where is Persian Gulf (1987)	58
Way fallout from Chernobyl was spread (1988)	73	Describe current problem in Iran (1951)	57
Not all Indians are Hindus (1978)	72	Japan has free elections (1982)	57
England deployed troops in Saudi Arabia (1990)	72	Apartheid is policy in South Africa (1988)	55
		Palestine not independent country (1946)	55
		East Germany is communist (1954)	55
		U.S. will still defend Panama Canal (1978)	54
		Taxes higher in Western Europe than U.S. (1989)	53

Table 2.5 Knowledge of Foreign Affairs (*continued*)

Survey Item	%	Survey Item	%
Spain not a democracy (1948)	52	Where are most immigrants coming from (1993)	35
What is hydrogen bomb (1950)	52	Does Japan have a military draft (1986)	34
Describe situation in Poland (1981)	52	Japan imports U.S. agricultural products (1986)	33
Relation of England to India (1942)	51	Women can vote in India (1978)	33
Black South Africans can't vote (1985)	51	Poland is in Warsaw Pact (1988)	32
Relation of England to Canada (1942)	50	Serbians conquered much of Bosnia (1994)	27
Israel gained ground since 1948 (1973)	50	Two countries in SALT Treaty (1979)	30
West Germany a member of NATO (1989)	50	Argentina ruled by a dictator (1948)	29
Cease-fire in Middle East (1948)	49	# of U.S. soldiers in Vietnam (1967)	29
Only nation to use nuclear weapons (1986)	49	% of oil in U.S. that's imported (1977)	29
What is foreign aid spent on (1958)	48	Country attacking USS *Stark* (1987)	29
No Jordan troops in Saudi Arabia (1990)	48	Describe Panama's government (1988)	28
Not all Soviets in Communist party (1986)	48	% world population: malnourished (1979)	28
Has U.S. recognized Lithuania (1990)	47	Reebok a foreign company (1987)	28
Sweden is a democracy (1948)	46	East Germany in Warsaw Pact (1988)	27
U.S. supports El Salvador government (1983)	46	Describe Saudi Arabia's government (1990)	25
Has U.S. approved SALT treaty (1984)	45	Describe neutron bomb (1977)	24
England rules Palestine (1946)	45	% world population: underdeveloped nations (1972)	22
% U.S. oil from Arab nations (1973)	42	% aliens in U.S. (1940)	20
Who struck first in Arab-Israel war (1973)	42	Shell Oil a foreign company (1986)	19
Kuwait not a democracy (1991)	42	Israel gets largest % U.S. aid (1986)	18
Who controls Formosa (1954)	41	Describe government of El Salvador (1988)	17
Soviets not in NATO (1964)	41	% world population that controls most of money (1979)	17
U.S. has no "no first strike" policy (1988)	40	# of U.S. soldiers killed in Vietnam (1965)	17
Yugoslavia is communist (1948)	39	Size of U.S. trade deficit (1984)	16
France is a member of NATO (1988)	39	Describe the Baruch Plan (1948)	15
No collective bargaining in Russia (1945)	38	Describe the McCarran Act (1955)	14
U.S. in International Court of Justice (1946)	37	What is the Bricker amendment (1954)	13
U.S. has military base on Cuba (1977)	37	Describe Glasnost (1987)	11
Soviets are in Warsaw Pact (1988)	37	U.S.'s largest trading partner (1991)	8
Allies took land from Germany (1944)	36	# of U.S. soldiers killed in Vietnam (1967)	6
When will Panama control the canal (1990)	36	% U.S. real estate foreign owned (1989)	4
England has nuclear weapons (1988)	35	Is U.S. a member of UNESCO (1947)	1
Issues in Israel withdrawal from Egypt (1957)	35		
Describe aspect of U.S. immigration policy (1965)	35		

The largest range and number of questions on foreign affairs were asked during the Reagan and Bush administrations (almost 60 percent of the total), and these items reveal a reasonably rich range of public knowledge. For example, three-quarters or more of the public knew that damage to the ozone layer would affect the whole earth; that Americans were being held hostage in the Middle East; that the United States had a trade deficit with Japan; that there was a pro-Soviet government in Central America; that defense spending was one of the two largest pieces of the federal budget; and that President Reagan planned to deploy the MX missile.

An additional 28 percent of the items were correctly answered by between half and three-quarters of those asked. These items include some issues—such as the trade deficit, U.S.-Soviet relations, and tensions in the Middle East—that were not as prominent as they had been or would become or that asked for more detail than some of the questions discussed above. They also include questions about nations that are neither as prominent in the media nor as central to U.S. policy and politics as such countries as the Soviet Union, China, Israel, or Japan. Nonetheless, the scope of information known by at least half the public is fairly impressive. During the Roosevelt and Truman administrations, half or more of the public could describe the Marshall Plan and the unrest in Iran or could explain the political relations between England, Canada, and India. During the Eisenhower administration over half those surveyed could explain what the Kremlin was and knew that East Germany was allied with the Soviets. During the Kennedy and Johnson years over half those surveyed knew that the United States was a member of the North Atlantic Treaty Organization (NATO) and were aware of the rising unrest in the Middle East, and during the Nixon-Ford years similar percentages knew that Israel had gained, rather than lost, territory since its creation. During the Carter administration, between 50 and 74 percent of the public could, among other things, name the two countries that signed the Camp David Accords, knew that the United States would retain the right to defend the Panama Canal even after it shifted to Panamanian control, and could identify North Korea as communist and South Korea as noncommunist. And during the Reagan and Bush administrations, more than half the public knew, for example, that England sent troops to Saudi Arabia during the Persian Gulf war or whom the U.S. government supported in Nicaragua.

As with the other areas of politics examined, however, more than half of the 553 foreign affairs items could be answered by less than half the general public. Thirty-six percent of the questions were known by only one-quarter to one-half of those asked. In the 1940s, this included knowledge about the forms of government in Sweden and Yugoslavia, that there was a short-lived cease-fire between Jews and Arabs in the Middle East, and that the United States was sending military aid to Greece. In the 1950s, similar numbers were aware that Formosa was controlled by the Nationalist Chinese and could describe some of the things U.S. foreign aid was spent on. In the 1960s, a quarter to half of the public knew about how many U.S. soldiers were stationed in Vietnam or that the Soviet Union was not a member of NATO, and in the 1970s these percentages knew who launched the first attack in the Arab-Israeli war, about what percent of U.S. oil comes from the Middle East, and that the United States has a military base on Cuba. And in the 1980s and 1990s, a quarter to a half of the population knew that adults in the Soviet Union did not have to join the Communist party, about how many nations had nuclear weapons, that Japan is a democracy, that Jordan did not send troops to Saudi Arabia during the Persian Gulf crisis, and that Serbians were the ethnic group that had conquered much of Bosnia.

Finally, nearly a quarter of the items could be answered by fewer than one-fourth of those asked. These little-known facts included knowing that the United States was sharing information about the atomic bomb with England and Canada in the 1940s, being able to describe the McCarran Act or the Bricker Amendment in the 1950s, knowing about how many U.S. soldiers had been killed in Vietnam in the 1960s, knowing how much of the federal budget goes to defense or to foreign aid in the 1970s, knowing that Czechoslovakia was in the Warsaw Pact and Canada was in NATO in the 1980s, and knowing that Canada was the United States' largest trading partner in the 1990s.

Politically Relevant Knowledge: Geography and History

In addition to the rules, people, and substance of politics, other kinds of information can aid a citizen in thinking about and acting in the political world. Two such areas for which we were able to find survey items are geography (147 items) and history (111 items). Ten percent of the geography questions were answered correctly by three-quarters or more of those asked, including the ability to locate the United States, the Soviet Union, or Texas on a map (see table 2.6). An additional 31 percent of the items were known by half or more of those asked. These included the ability to locate Italy, Brazil, or Pennsylvania on a map, as well as knowing that Japan is an island or that California is the most populous state in the

United States. Only a quarter to a half of those questioned could correctly answer 31 percent of the items, including the location of Iran, South Africa, or Missouri or knowing what percent of the world's population lives in Europe, South America, or Africa. The 29 percent of questions known by fewer than a quarter of those asked included locating Hungary or El Salvador on a map and estimating the population of China, Japan, or the United States.

Table 2.6 Knowledge of Geography (Percentage Correct)

Survey Item	%	Survey Item	%
Locate Texas on a map (1988)	91	Locate Chile on a map (1988)	45
Ocean between U.S. and England (1952)	90	Locate Missouri on a map (1988)	45
Locate California on a map (1988)	89	Locate New Jersey on a map (1988)	42
Locate Canada on a map (1988)	86	Locate Massachusetts on a map (1988)	39
Locate U.S. on a map (1988)	86	% of world population in Latin America (1979)	37
Locate Mexico on a map (1988)	81	Where is Panama (1988)	36
Locate Pacific Ocean on a map (1988)	80	% of world population in Africa (1979)	33
Locate Soviet Union on a map (1988)	76	Where is Nicaragua (1988)	36
Locate Italy on a map (1988)	74	Locate Vietnam on a map (1988)	32
Where is Grenada (1983)	63	Locate West Germany on a map (1988)	29
Locate Pennsylvania on a map (1988)	62	Locate Egypt on a map (1988)	28
Locate Peru on a map (1988)	61	% of world population in Asia (1979)	28
Oceans in order west from Hawaii (1988)	59	Locate Poland on a map (1988)	28
State with largest population (1988)	59	Locate Persian Gulf on a map (1988)	25
Japan is an island (1982)	57	Locate Sweden on a map (1988)	23
Where is Nicaragua (1986)	56	Locate Peru on a map (1988)	23
Locate N.Y. on a map (1988)	55	Where is El Salvador (1988)	20
Locate Central America on a map (1988)	55	Locate Colombia on a map (1988)	19
Name one Central American country (1988)	55	Locate Czechoslavakia on a map (1988)	19
Locate France on a map (1988)	54	Locate Bolivia on a map (1988)	17
Locate Illinois on a map (1988)	52	Where is Costa Rica (1988)	15
Locate Ohio on a map (1988)	50	Locate Yugoslavia on a map (1988)	14
Locate Spain on a map (1988)	50	Where is Guatemala (1988)	14
Locate South Africa on a map (1988)	49	Locate Hungary on a map (1988)	14
% of world population in Europe (1979)	47	Locate Paraguay on a map (1988)	13
Locate England on a map (1988)	47	Locate Romania on a map (1988)	11
Locate Argentina on a map (1988)	47	% of world population in U.S. and Canada (1979)	6
Locate Japan on a map (1988)	46	Where is Belize (1988)	4

Table 2.7 Knowledge of Social and Political History (Percentage Correct)

Survey Item	%	Survey Item	%
First president of U.S. (1989)	93	Women could not always vote in U.S. (1989)	90
Reagan never vice president (1987)	92	What happened in 1776 (1989)	88
Who was Christopher Columbus (1975)	92	Lincoln was assassinated (1965)	88
U.S. used A-bomb against Japan (1990)	91		

Table 2.7 Knowledge of Social and Political History (Percentage Correct) (*continued*)

Survey Item	%	Survey Item	%
Why Pearl Harbor is important (1981)	84	Only nation to use nuclear bomb (1986)	49
Who became president after JFK killed (1987)	83	Where was Columbus going (1988)	48
Who is Lee Harvey Oswald (1983)	81	Two nations in SALT talks (1986)	47
Who is Martin Luther King (1985)	81	Two nations at Camp David (1982)	45
What happened in 1492 (1975)	81	More Soviets or U.S. died in World War II (1985)	42
Who was Andrew Jackson (1955)	81	Who was Karl Marx (1975)	41
Who "discovered" America (1990)	78	U.S. war costing most U.S. lives (1990)	38
Nixon's party ID (1989)	78	"The only thing we have to fear . . ." (1958)	37
Who gave U.S. the Statue of Liberty (1986)	74	McKinley was assassinated (1965)	37
What was the Holocaust (1985)	69	War Waterloo fought in (1957)	36
Origin of most early twentieth-century immigrants (1988)	69	What is Mt. Vernon (1957)	35
U.S. and Soviets were allies in World War II (1986)	67	Plato (1953)	34
Which side did U.S. support in Vietnam (1990)	67	"Speak softly and carry a big stick" (1958)	33
FDR's party ID (1989)	63	"With malice toward none . . ." (1958)	32
Truman's party ID (1989)	58	# of times Nixon ran for president (1987)	30
Who was Napoléon Bonaparte (1975)	58	Garfield was assassinated (1965)	29
Who was Eli Whitney (1957)	58	Date of New Deal (1989)	29
Were Philippines ever a U.S. colony (1985)	56	What was the Parthenon (1957)	26
Who was Sigmund Freud (1976)	55	Who was Johannes Guttenberg (1975)	24
War Battle of Bulge fought in (1957)	54	Who was Benjamin Disraeli (1976)	23
Author of Declaration of Independence (1989)	53	Bosnia and Serbia were in Yugoslavia (1992)	21
U.S. occupied Japan after World War II (1985)	50	Name a memorable political slogan (1987)	20
		"I came, I saw, I conquered" (1958)	19
		What was New Deal (1989)	15
		"I have not begun to fight" (1958)	14
		"World must be made safe for . . ." (1958)	14
		What happened in 1066 (1975)	10

The history questions asked on national surveys were often rather eclectic, but they nonetheless offer a glimpse of levels of knowledge in this area (see table 2.7). Of the 111 questions, 28 (25 percent) were correctly answered by three-quarters or more of those asked. These included the ability to identify several historical figures (for example, Christopher Columbus or Andrew Jackson) and historical dates (Columbus's "discovery" of America in 1492 and the American Revolution in 1776). They also included historical facts, such as knowing that Abraham Lincoln was assassinated or that the United States used an atomic bomb against Japan. Another 31 percent of the items were answered by half to three-quarters of those asked, including identifying Napoleon Bonaparte or Sigmund Freud, knowing the party affiliation of Franklin Roosevelt, knowing the war in which the Battle of the Bulge was fought, knowing what the Holocaust was, and knowing which side the United States supported in the Vietnam conflict.

Another 32 percent of the items were correctly answered by only a quarter to a half of those asked. These included identifying Aristotle or Karl Marx, knowing the war in which the battle of Bunker Hill was fought, and that the United States occupied Japan after World War II. It also included the ability to identify the two countries involved in the Camp David Accords four to five years after those accords were signed. Finally, 12 percent of the questions were answered correctly by less than a quarter of the public. These included identifying who said "the world must be made safe for democracy" and knowing what happened in 1066, where the Soviets stood on the German invasion of Czechoslovakia, and when the New Deal occurred and what it was about.

Political Knowledge in Comparative Perspective

How do levels of political knowledge in America compare to those found in other countries? Good comparative data are relatively sparse, especially for knowledge of domestic politics, and existing evidence provides an ambiguous picture. Recent evidence suggests that Americans lag behind residents of many Western nations in their awareness of key political actors and events in foreign affairs (Dimock and Popkin, 1995). Data from surveys in eight nations conducted by the Times Mirror Center in 1994 show that in terms of the percentage able to answer the current events questions correctly, Americans placed third on one item, sixth on two, and came in seventh and eighth on two others (see table 2.8). Of seven nations for which summary tabulations were made, Americans had the second-lowest mean number correct (only Spain fell behind; Mexico was not tabulated). Thirty-seven percent of Americans missed all of the questions, the highest percentage among the seven nations.

Research by Baker et al. (1994) that compared knowledge of national legislatures in the United States, Canada, and Great Britain also suggests that Americans are less informed than citizens of other nations. U.S. citizens averaged less than three correct answers on a ten-item scale measuring knowledge of the U.S. Congress, compared to Great Britains, who averaged over six correct out of ten questions about their parliament, and Canadians, who averaged a remarkable 9.8 correct out eleven questions about their parliament.[12]

Table 2.8 Knowledge of Foreign Affairs in Comparative Perspective (Percentage Correct)

	Canada	France	Germany	Italy	Mexico	Spain	United Kingdom	United States
President of Russia?	59	61	94	76	42	65	63	50
Country threatening to withdraw from nonproliferation treaty	12	7	45	26	6	5	11	22
Who is Boutros Boutros Ghali	26	32	58	43	14	15	22	13
Ethnic group that has conquered much of Bosnia	42	55	77	51	12	24	46	28
Name of group with whom Israelis recently reached peace accord	51	60	79	56	21	29	59	40
Answered four or five correctly	19	25	58	34	—	10	18	15
Answered none correctly	27	23	3	18	—	32	22	37
Mean number correct	1.92	2.13	3.55	2.49	—	1.35	2.01	1.53

A somewhat less grim picture emerges from a 1986 cross-national survey that asked about world leaders (see table 2.9). Americans equalled or exceeded respondents from the other four nations in their ability to name their own head of state (99 percent for Americans, 99 percent for the French, 96 percent for the British, 95 percent for West Germans, and 89 percent for the Italians). Americans were about as likely as the others to know the prime minister of Japan, but they were considerably less able to identify the heads of state of Western European nations. And the five-nation survey that formed the basis for Gabriel Almond's and Sidney Verba's *The Civic Culture* found a considerably higher percentage of Americans and Germans able to name four or more party leaders when compared with the English, Italians, or Mexicans. Americans were behind the Germans, but comparable to the British, in the ability to name four or more cabinet offices.

Table 2.9 Knowledge of Political Leaders in Comparative Perspective (Percentage Correct)

	West Germans	French	British	Italians	Americans
President of U.S.	94	94	93	95	99
Prime Minister of United Kingdom	80	89	96	77	74
President of France	64	99	55	76	34
Chancellor of West Germany	95	59	17	37	16
Prime Minister of Italy	39	18	2	89	6
Prime Minister of Japan	19	17	4	23	19

Finally, a 1988 National Geographic survey asked representative samples of adult citizens from nine countries to locate sixteen places on a map of the world (fourteen countries and two bodies of water). Overall Americans correctly located an average of 8.6 places, putting them sixth (see figure 2.1). Opportunity and motivation clearly play a role in explaining this pattern. Americans are above average in locating places relatively close to them (Canada, Mexico, Central America, the Pacific Ocean, and the United States itself), but they are below average in identifying geographically distant areas (the United Kingdom, France, West Germany, Sweden, Egypt, and the Persian Gulf).

Exploring the Depth of Political Knowledge and Ignorance

Thus far we have treated factual knowledge as a simple matter of right or wrong. This works for some facts (for example, naming the vice president), but for most facts of import there are degrees of knowledge. And the value of even simple information, such as the name of an officeholder, is seldom in the fact itself, but rather in its ability to lead to (or indicate) other, more substantively useful information. How deep is the public's knowledge of politics? Our review of the aggregate survey data provides circumstantial evidence that as the standards for correct answers become stricter or as the details requested increase, the percentage correct declines. But there are limits to the conclusions we can draw from these marginal percentages.

Sixteen questions on our Survey of Political Knowledge allow us to distinguish degrees of correctness. The responses to them confirm the notion that political knowledge often does not run very deep (see table

Figure 2.1 Knowledge of Geography in Comparative Perspective

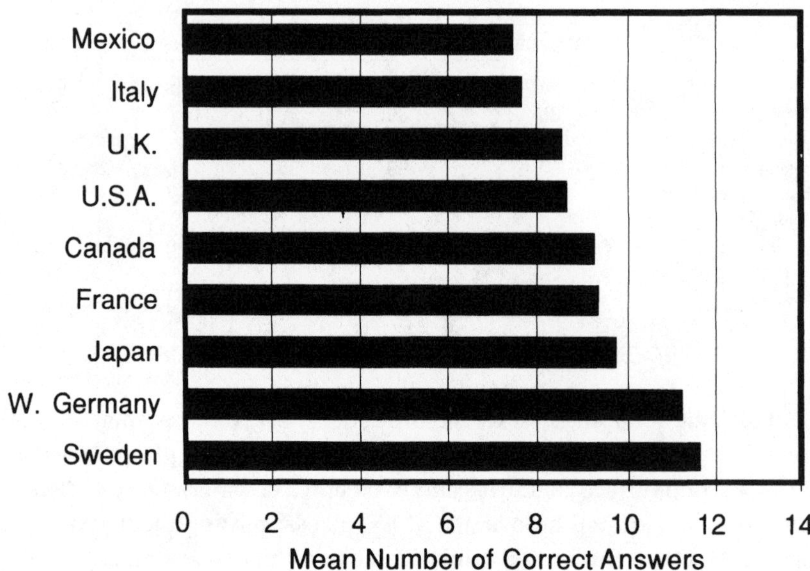

Note: Data were gathered when Germany was still divided.

2.10). For example, 35 percent of our sample could correctly identify a right guaranteed by the First Amendment, but only 20 percent could identify two such rights, and only 9 percent could identify three. More dramatically, 50 percent could identify one right guaranteed by the Fifth Amendment (almost always the right against self-incrimination), but only 2 percent could identify a second. Seventy-one percent of the sample knew that the Reagan administration had supported the rebels in Nicaragua, but only 44 percent knew this while also knowing that the Contras were the rebels and the Sandinistas were in control of the government. When the answers were coded for levels of knowledge, the average percent correct for "surface knowledge" was 41, but for "deep knowledge," it plummeted to 16 percent.

Table 2.10 Levels of Knowledge within Selected Variables

Subject	%	Subject	%
Fifth Amendment		Senators	
Know one or two	50	Know one or two	55
Know two	2	Know both	25
First Amendment		Representative	
Know one, two, or three	35	Claims to know	45
Know two or three	20	Correct or close	34
Know three	9	Correct	29

Table 2.10 Levels of Knowledge within Selected Variables (*continued*)

Subject	%	Subject	%
Rhenquist's ideology		Federal budget: Social Security	
Conservative or moderate	39	Within 10%	30
Conservative	30	Within 5%	14
Arms control agreement		Within 2%	5
Claims has heard of	61	Federal budget: Defense	
Nuclear weapons involved	48	Within 10%	30
Nuclear missiles involved	34	Within 5%	18
Medium-range missiles involved	18	Within 2%	8
In Europe only	4	Percent Poor	
Nicaraguan policy		Within 10%	37
Knows U.S. supports rebels	71	Within 5%	22
Knows U.S. supports Contras	66	Within 2%	18
Also knows Contras = rebels	54	Percent unemployed	
Also knows Sandinistas =		Within 3%	40
government	44	Within 2%	34
Superfund		Within 1%	27
Claims heard of	23	Percent no health insurance	
General knowledge	14	Within 10%	21
Cleans up toxic sites	11	Within 5%	10
New Deal		Within 2%	4
Claims to know	53	Percent black	
Sophisticated, adequate, or vague	30	Within 10%	27
Sophisticated or adequate	15	Within 5%	15
Sophisticated only	4	Within 2%	13
Federal budget: Education			
Within 10%	41		
Within 5%	24		
Within 2%	19		

Patterns of Political Ignorance

The pattern of political ignorance is as revealing as the pattern of political knowledge (see table 2.11). The responses to a range of factual questions on our 1989 national survey indicate that in most cases, people willingly admitted if they did not know the answer to one of our questions (we call these responses *uninformed*).[13] Just under a third of the responses to the questions on our survey were "don't knows" (the median "don't know" response was 26 percent).[14] The percentage of these uninformed answers varied greatly by question format and topic, from the 2 percent who said they didn't know who declared war to the 96 percent who acknowledged they could not name three rights protected by the First Amendment.

Table 2.11 Levels of Knowledge and Ignorance

Subject	Know (%)	Said Don't Know (%)	Gave Wrong Answer (%)	Specific Wrong Answer (%)	Subject	Know (%)	Said Don't Know (%)	Gave Wrong Answer (%)	Specific Wrong Answer (%)
Length of presidential term (o)	96	3	1	*	Size of federal budget (3)	49	7	44	22
Right to counsel (2)	91	4	5	5	Sandinistas govern (2)	48	32	20	20
Women's suffrage (2)	90	6	5	5	Arms treaty (o)	48	49	4	*
Define veto (o)	89	6	5	*	Bill of Rights (o)	46	49	5	*
Can override veto (2)	82	10	8	8	U.S. aids El Salvador's government (2)	43	38	19	19
U.S. has trade deficit (3)	82	8	11	6	First Amendment right (o)	35	58	7	*
U.S. has budget deficit (3)	78	8	14	9	% veto override (o)	35	47	18	6
Nixon's party ID (2)	78	8	14	14	Who declares war (3)	34	2	64	59
Can't require pledge (2)	75	6	18	18	Rhenquist ideology (3)	30	50	20	11
Vice president (o)	74	24	2	*	Both senators (o)	30	63	7	*
Governor (o)	73	21	5	*	House member (o)	29	55	16	*
State can't prohibit abortion (2)	72	13	15	15	Date of New Deal (o)	29	59	12	10
Party control: House (2)	68	15	17	16	% Unemployed (o)	27	19	54	8
U.S. supports Contras (2)	66	25	9	8	Date: women's vote (o)	21	40	39	10
Decides constitutionality (3)	66	10	24	17	Two First Amendment rights (o)	20	79	2	*
FDR's party ID (2)	63	26	11	11	Federal budget: education (o)	19	29	52	15
Truman's party ID (2)	58	26	16	16	% poor (o)	18	27	55	9
Law before *Roe v. Wade* (2)	58	27	15	15	What is New Deal (o)	15	65	20	*
Appoints federal judges (3)	58	13	29	17	% blacks (o)	13	17	70	13
Define recession (o)	57	22	25	*	Superfund (o)	11	86	2	*
Party control: Senate (2)	55	27	18	17	Three First Amendment rights (o)	9	89	2	*
Name one of two senators (o)	55	43	7	*	Federal budget: defense (o)	8	23	69	9
Tariff's effect (o)	52	29	19	*	Federal budget: Social Security (o)	5	26	69	11
Communist can run for president (2)	50	5	45	45	% no health insurance (o)	4	25	55	10
Fifth Amendment right (o)	50	44	6	6	Two Fifth Amendment rights (o)	2	96	2	*

Note: (o) = open-ended; (2) = two choices; (3) = three choices; * = not ascertained.

On average, fewer citizens gave wrong answers (mean = 21 percent, median = 15 percent) than said outright that they did not know the answer. As with both correct and uninformed responses, these *misinformed* answers varied significantly by question format and topic: only 1 percent of our participants gave a wrong answer for the length of a presidential term, but fully 70 percent gave a wrong answer for the percentage of the U.S. population that is black.[15] For just under half (47 percent) of the questions, a *specific* wrong answer was given by at least 10 percent of those asked.[16] And for just over 10 percent of the questions, the percentage misinformed actually exceeded the percentage giving the correct answer.[17] Some of this misinformation undoubtedly reflects guessing, a conclusion bolstered by the fact that the percentage giving a wrong answer was generally higher on the multiple choice than on open-ended questions.[18] Nonetheless the substantive patterns of misinformation, especially for fairly common mistakes, are revealing. There were two broad categories of incorrect answers—found in both the Roper Center data and our Survey of Political Knowledge—that appear to go beyond random guessing or pure ignorance. The first suggests that in some instances citizens are closer to the truth than the simple, static patterns of right or wrong indicate. The second suggests that misinformation can result from the projection of values or from biases in the information provided to citizens.

The Silver Lining: Contested Truths, Close Calls, and Lagged Attention

Just as there are degrees of correctness that distinguish surface knowledge from more deep-seated understanding, so too there are degrees of error. Many of the wrong answers suggest that, for some topics at least, a portion of the uninformed public is more in the shadows than in the dark. Some answers, which we call *contested truths,* are arguably less a matter of misinformation than of interpretation. Even in the realm of facts, "right" and "wrong" is sometimes open to negotiation. This is especially true for questions that deal with complex issues or that are worded ambiguously. Whereas Mexico was democratic in 1948, its hegemonic party system makes answering a question about the nature of this nation's political system less than straightforward. Argentina was officially neutral during World War II, but there is ample evidence that it unofficially aided the Nazis in a variety of ways. Answering the question, "Is India a strong military power?" depends in part on whether one means regionally or internationally and how one factors in the country's nuclear capability. Whether one claims that states or the federal government determine voter eligibility depends on whether one means the broad parameters set by the amended U.S. Constitution or the more specific regulations found within those parameters.

Another variation on this theme is the *close call.* Many of the survey items required establishing cut-off points as to when an answer was too far from the preferred answer to accept. For example, at what point has a citizen demonstrated she knows what a tariff is? Or at what point does a person's estimate of the inflation rate become unacceptably high or low? These, of course, are judgments on which reasonable people might disagree, and they introduce a fair amount of imprecision for estimating knowledge levels. A perusal of the answers to questions that introduce degrees of correctness (table 2.10) suggests that citizens often approach the correct answer even if they do not demonstrate full command of it. Consider, for example, the distribution of responses to three open-ended questions asking respondents what percent of the federal budget was devoted to defense, Social Security, or education (see figure 2.2). There is a very wide spread to the answers, suggesting a disturbing amount of ignorance. Nonetheless, the distributions are hardly random. In each case the answers cluster—even if not always very tightly—around the correct answer.[19]

Many political facts require that citizens be reasonably vigilant surveyors of the changing political landscape: party control of Congress changes, elected and appointed officials are replaced, political alliances form and disintegrate, and so forth. The patterns of knowledge and ignorance about these types of facts suggest that many citizens neither ignore nor fully grasp these changes. For example, in 1980, 71 percent of those surveyed said that the Democrats controlled the House of Representatives before the election (the highest percentage correct in the nine presidential election years in which NES asked this question). But a majority of those surveyed after the election mistakenly thought the Republicans took control of the House. Public awareness before the election may have been a by-product of the highly charged political climate, which led to Reagan's victory and the Republican control of the Senate. Publicity surrounding the latter no doubt confused some citizens regarding what had happened in the House.

On several occasions, survey questions were asked close enough to changes in the political environment to reveal differences in the degree to which citizens are attentive to such occurrences. Many of the wrong answers reflected ignorance less than *lagged attention*. For example, in 1944, 46 percent of those asked thought that John L. Lewis was president of the Congress of Industrial Organizations (CIO), when in fact Philip

Figure 2.2 Distribution of Responses: Allocation of Federal Budget

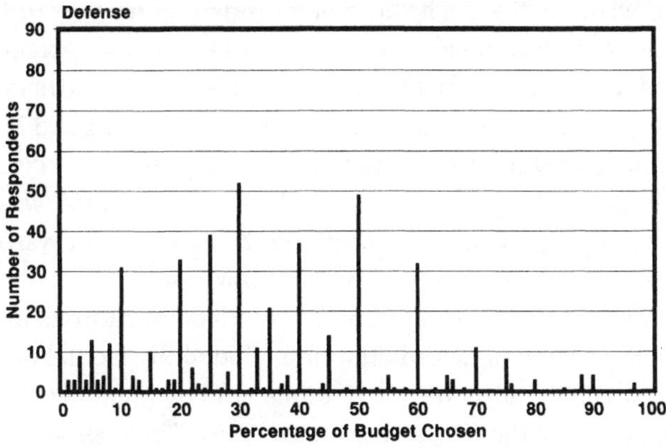

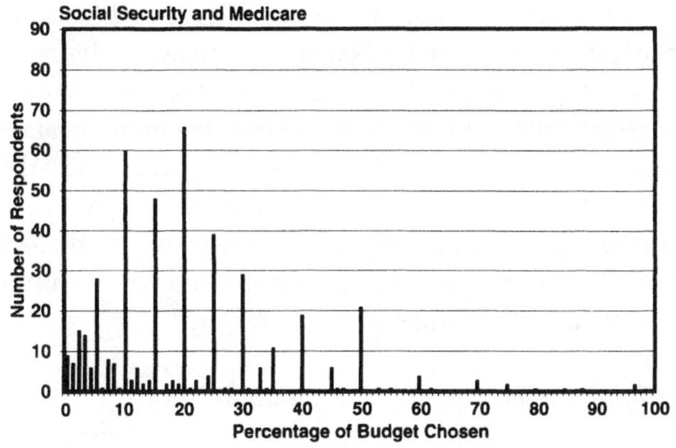

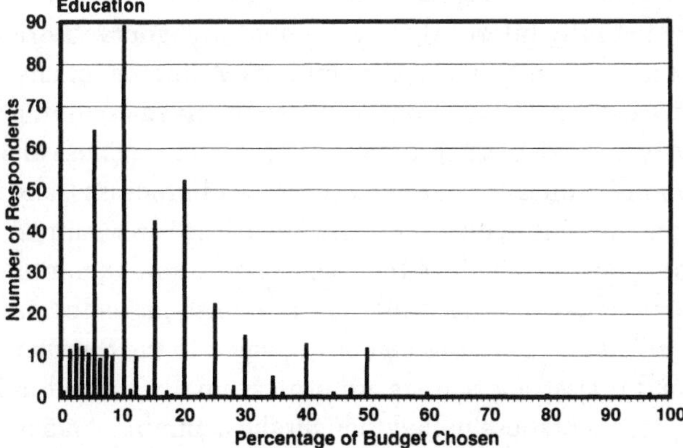

Note: The correct percentages in 1989 were as follows: percent of the budget devoted to defense (26%); Social Security and Medicare (30%); education (3%).

Murray was. However, Lewis had been president of the CIO until 1940. After a power struggle with Murray in 1942, Lewis pulled the United Mine Workers (UMW) out of the CIO; he became president of the UMW in 1944. Similarly, in late January and early February of 1949, only 36 percent of those asked could name the newly appointed secretary of state, Dean Acheson. Another 24 percent, however, were aware that a change had been made, although they could not name the new secretary. And in 1986, although only 43 percent of the public knew that William Rehnquist was the chief justice of the Supreme Court, an additional 29 percent said Warren Burger, who had recently stepped down from that position.

The timing of the 1990 NES survey provided a fortuitous opportunity to examine the notion of lagged attention. One of the factual questions on that survey was to identify the job or office held by Margaret Thatcher. On November 22, while the survey was in the field, Thatcher announced her resignation as prime minister. Just under half the interviews (49 percent) were completed after this announcement, with most of those (38 percent) taking place after Thatcher left office on November 29. Before Thatcher's announcement 47 percent of those asked could identify her as the prime minister of Great Britain. In the week between her announcement and her actual resignation, 49 percent of those asked still identified her as the prime minister, but 43 percent of those people (21 percent overall) noted that she was stepping down. And in the interviews conducted after she actually left office, 12 percent still identified her as prime minister, while 41 percent called her the former prime minister.[20]

The Dark Cloud: Projection and Manipulation

Contested truths, close calls, and lagged attention suggest that although citizens are not fully informed, they are not fully ignorant. Another broad category of misinformation is more ominous. A number of answers took a form that we call *projection*. Some of these involved assuming the best of the U.S. system, if not of the individuals operating it. These answers were most common for questions on institutions and processes, and especially for questions dealing with rights and liberties. For example, large percentages of Americans believe that the Constitution guarantees a job (29 percent), health care (42 percent), and a high school education (75 percent); that all state court cases can be appealed to the Supreme Court (85 percent); and that all journalists are professionally trained (50 percent). Forty-five percent of those polled thought the communist tenet "from each according to his abilities, to each according to his needs," was found in the Constitution.

Not all the examples of projection involved an expansion of rights and liberties. To the contrary, many believe that a person can be tried twice for the same crime (29 percent), that a member of the Communist party cannot run for president (45 percent), that revolutionary speech is not protected by the Constitution (51 percent), and that an accused person must prove his innocence (50 percent). There is also a willingness to extend powers to the president, even if they are contrary to the basic principles of checks and balances. Besides the example of war powers discussed below, many Americans believe the president has the power to adjourn Congress at his will (35 percent), to suspend the Constitution (49 percent), and to appoint judges to the federal courts without the approval of the Senate (60 percent). Citizens often appeared confused about the relation of the Bill of Rights to the states. Many often assumed that states had powers that they knew were denied the national government: for example, establishing a state prayer (45 percent), giving public money to religious schools (46 percent), and allowing silent prayer in schools (50 percent); on this topic, see Brigham (1990).

Equally disconcerting were answers indicating that citizens came to wrong conclusions based on information—often provided by government officials and the media—that was misleading. For example, more people answered that the president had the power to declare war (59 percent) than that Congress did (34 percent). Although this answer is technically wrong, one can see—given presidential actions over the past forty years—why citizens would think this was the president's responsibility. Similarly, during the Watergate revelations most Americans knew that being impeached by the House was only the first of two steps in a president's removal from office, but about a third of those questioned equated impeachment with removal—a conclusion easily reached given the nonspecific way the term was used in the media. In 1985, when the Cold War was still part of the political vocabulary, a quarter of Americans believed that the United States and the Soviet Union fought on opposite sides during World War II. And in 1989, between 21 and 38 percent of Americans (amounting to a plurality in one survey) wrongly believed that U.S. citizens were taxed more than the inhabitants of most West European countries, a conclusion consistent with the dominant political rhetoric and commentary of the 1980s.

Evidence of a *manipulated* public was found by the University of Massachusetts's Center for the Study of Communication (Jhally, Lewis, and Morgan, 1991; Lewis and Morgan, 1992). In a survey about public opinion and political knowledge regarding the then-ongoing Persian Gulf war, the center discovered that knowledge about the politics and history of the region was skewed in a way that benefited the administration's policy of intervention. For example, only 13 percent of those interviewed knew that, shortly before Iraq's invasion of Kuwait, the State Department had indicated to Saddam Hussein that it would take no action if Iraq used force in its territorial dispute with Kuwait, and fully 65 percent said the administration had threatened *at that point* to use force to defend Kuwait. And whereas 53 percent of those interviewed supported the use of U.S. military force to restore the sovereignty of any illegally occupied country, only 31 percent knew that Israel was occupying land in the Middle East and only 3 percent were aware of Syria's occupation of Lebanon. Eighty percent of those interviewed knew Hussein had used chemical weapons against some of his own people, but only 2 percent knew of Kuwait's insistence on lowering oil prices and of the strain this decision was putting on the Iraqi economy. Significantly, the study found that the more accurately informed people were, the less supportive they were of the war. The center concluded: "In short, people knew those facts that fit well with the Administration's war policy, and did not know those facts that might be seen to undermine it. One interesting feature of this selective perception involved those questions where most people gave the incorrect answer. In these instances, a majority would usually choose responses that endorsed the Administration's moral position, even when those responses directly contradicted the facts themselves. In other words, faced with a choice between truth or propaganda, most people chose propaganda" (1992: 2).

The center found similar evidence for a manipulated public during the 1992 presidential election, and again the administration seemed to benefit. For example, respondents were asked, "Of the 4 candidates for president and vice president, who has been accused of using family influence to avoid being sent to Vietnam?" Although both Dan Quayle and Bill Clinton fit this description, 41 percent named only Clinton, 15 percent named only Quayle, and 23 percent named both. Similarly, 73 percent of those asked thought that the Democrat-controlled Congress had passed a budget that was larger than the one proposed by President Bush, while in fact it was smaller.

Our own research also suggests misinformation disproportionately benefits those in political and economic power, but there are more than a few counterexamples. Americans grossly overestimate the average profit made by American corporations, the percentage of the U.S. population that is poor or homeless, and the percentage of the world population that is malnourished. And, despite twelve years of antiabortion administrations, Americans substantially underestimate the number of abortions performed every year.

In the Introduction we argued for the importance of political information as a resource. How resourceful is the American public, as gauged by survey items asked over the past fifty years? Any assessment of the degree to which the citizenry is adequately informed requires a point of comparison. In subsequent chapters we will compare levels of knowledge over time and across groups within the population, but here we will review the evidence mainly from the perspective of Converse's "informed observer."

The popular and scholarly literature on civic knowledge might lead one to conclude, along with Neuman, that "even the most vivid concepts of political life . . . are recognized by only a little over half the electorate" (1986: 16). The survey data examined in this chapter reinforce this conclusion. The most commonly known fact about George Bush's opinions while he was president was that he hated broccoli. During the 1992 presidential campaign 89 percent of the public knew that Vice President Quayle was feuding with the television character Murphy Brown, but only 19 percent could characterize Bill Clinton's record on the environment. Also during that campaign, 86 percent of the public knew that the Bushes' dog was named Millie, yet only 15 percent knew that both presidential candidates supported the death penalty. Judge Wapner (host of the television series "The People's Court") was identified by more people than were Chief Justices Burger or Rehnquist. More people know John Lennon than Karl Marx, or know Bill Cosby than either of their U.S. senators. More people know who said "What's up Doc," "Hi yo Silver," or "Come up and see me sometime" than "Give me liberty or give me death," "The only thing we have to fear is fear itself," or "Speak softly and carry a big stick." More people knew that Pete Rose was accused of gambling than could name any of the five U.S. senators accused of unethical conduct in the savings and loan scandal. And so on.

Less anecdotal evidence provides equally disturbing patterns. Only 13 percent of the more than 2,000 political questions examined could be answered correctly by 75 percent or more of those asked, and only 41 percent could be answered correctly by more than half the public. Many of the facts known by relatively small percentages of the public seem critical to understanding—let alone effectively acting in—the political world: fundamental rules of the game; classic civil liberties; key concepts of political economy; the names of key political representatives; many important policy positions of presidential candidates or the political parties; basic social indicators and significant public policies. And for at least some measure of political knowledge, Americans appear significantly less informed than citizens of most other comparably developed nations. Hardly the stuff of informed consent, let alone of a working representative democracy.

The picture presented in this chapter is more subtle and complex than these simple characterizations suggest, however. In spite of tendencies to look longingly at the level of civic involvement found in many Western European nations, evidence that Americans are less informed is mixed.[21] And for all the insidious comparisons between knowledge of popular and political culture, the former is also filled with facts that are known by remarkably small numbers of people (see table 2.12). Furthermore, there is a wide range of facts about which substantial percentages of the public are aware: institutions and processes, such as the meaning of a veto or party platform; civil liberties, such as the right to counsel and to a trial by jury; political economy terms like *recession* and *foreign trade deficit;* political leaders, such as the president, vice president, governor, and Speaker of the House; policy positions of officeholders, candidates and parties, such as where Truman stood on domestic communism or Michael Dukakis's stand on abortion; social indicators, such as the minimum wage or the U.S. dependence on foreign oil; and public policies, such as Clinton's health care proposal or whether the United States has a budget deficit or surplus. Furthermore, the patterns of partially correct and incorrect answers suggest that many uninformed citizens are struggling at the edge of knowledge, trying at some level to make sense of the political world. Even the *New York Times* article cited at the beginning of this chapter suggests that many uninformed citizens are attempting to act as engaged citizens at the same time their limited knowledge makes effective participation less likely.

Table 2.12 Knowledge of Nonpolitical Facts (Percentage Correct)

Knowledge of popular culture	%		%
Who is Bill Cosby (1988)	93	Who is Floyd Patterson (1957)	44
Who is Chris Evert Lloyd (1984)	83	Name group played at Woodstock (1989)	30
"Hi yo Silver, away" (1958)	71	Slogan "His master's voice" (1977)	28
"Come up and see me sometime" (1958)	61	Woman caught with Gary Hart (1989)	19
Judge on "People's Court" (1989)	54	N.Y. Giants won Superbowl in 1980s (1989)	16

Table 2.12 Knowledge of Nonpolitical Facts (*continued*)

Knowledge of high culture	%		%
Who is Shakespeare (1975)	89	Who wrote *Huck Finn* (1990)	51
Who is Beethoven (1975)	84	Describe Dali's style (1982)	23
Da Vinci was a painter (1982)	70	Name Nobel Prize winner in 1980s (1989)	20
Who is Robert Frost (1964)	69	Who wrote *Great Expectations* (1957)	9
Who is Pavarotti (1984)	57	Jackson Pollock was a painter (1982)	6
Knowledge of religion	**%**		**%**
Mother of Jesus (1954)	95	Holy Trinity (1954)	40
Name one Commandment (1977)	88	Founder of non-Christian religion (1954)	30
Name one of first four books of Bible (1990)	87	What Jesus said to Nicodemus (1977)	29
		Old Testament prophet (1954)	19
Day of week Jews go to service (1964)	56	What IHS stands for (1954)	1
Name five of Ten Commandments (1977)	42		
Miscellaneous knowledge	**%**		**%**
How many inches in a yard (1951)	91	What is saccharin (1979)	46
How many 3-cent stamps for 75 cents (1951)	79	What is metric system (1974)	29
		What is subscription TV (1955)	22
Name an effect of marijuana (1969)	72	% of Americans who smoke (1980)	11
Air conditioners vary in energy use (1978)	54	How many liters in a gallon (1977)	2
What is a prefab house (1946)	54		

Consider some of the information citizens have at their disposal in a single presidential campaign. In 1992, the names of the two presidential candidates were almost universally known. In addition, however, majorities of the public could place the candidates relative to one another regarding their positions on abortion (61 percent), jobs programs (57 percent), defense (56 percent), general government spending (54 percent), and overall ideology (64 percent).[22] Similar percentages could place the two parties relative to each other (53 percent for jobs programs; 57 percent for defense; 59 percent for general government spending; and 59 percent for overall ideology). In addition, 52 percent knew which party controlled the Senate, and 60 percent knew which party controlled the House. True, substantial minorities could not correctly identify where the candidates and parties stood on these issues, and there were other important issues about which the electorate was even less informed, but the picture that emerges is not as black or white as is often assumed.

In the end, what people know is driven not only by what is most important, but also by what is most readily available. For example, one would be hard pressed to argue that the right to counsel is more important than the right of free speech or freedom of the press—and yet knowledge of the former far outstrips the latter. We can not say with certainty why this is the case, but we suspect it is a reflection of the common reference to the right to counsel found on television crime dramas. Similarly, the vice president is arguably a less important official than the secretary of state or one's senators or representative, yet the vice president is far better known to the public. Again, this is a simple matter of opportunity—the vice president is found more often on the news or in the papers. Based on public exposure, it is hardly surprising that more people know who Judge Wapner is than William Rehnquist. Indeed, the only political figures able to compete for air time with the likes of Bill Cosby, Madonna, and other popular entertainers—the president, vice president, and governors—are known by comparable percentages of the American public. None of this relieves citizens of their individual responsibility to be informed, but it suggests that an informed citizenry requires not only will, but also opportunity.

CHAPTER THREE

Stability and Change in Political Knowledge

All thoughtful men agree that the present aspect of society is portentous of great changes. The only question is, whether they will be for the better or the worse.—EDWARD BELLAMY, *Looking Backward*

I don't think about politics. . . . That's one of my goddam precious American Rights, not to think about politics.—JOHN UPDIKE, *Rabbit Redux*

In his novel about the angst of the twenty-something generation, Douglas Coupland coins the term *now denial,* which he defines as "to tell oneself that the only time worth living in is in the past and that the only time that may ever be interesting again is in the future" (1991: 41). There is more than a little now denial in theories about the political impact of changes that have occurred in the United States since World War II. The coming of postindustrial society has been heralded as "a time for the application of [great] means to great ends" (Inglehart, 1977: 392); it has also been vilified as "the closing of the American mind" (Bloom, 1987). Much of this looking to the past or the future is rooted in the philosophic underpinnings of American political thought. The belief that social and political order tends toward entropy is a central tenet of classical republicanism. Constant vigilance—civic virtue—can slow this decay, but in the end it is inexorable. Thus, the present always pales in comparison to the past. But the U.S. political system is also deeply rooted in the Enlightenment's faith in social progress. Rather than the backward longing of republicans, progressives look to the future. Human ingenuity coupled with the knowledge unleashed by the scientific method assures that tomorrow's world will be better than today's.

The inherent tension between these two philosophies is readily apparent in assessments of the current state of American politics. In turn, these assessments lead to competing expectations as to whether Americans should be either more or less informed about politics than they were half a century ago. In this chapter we will test these expectations against the available evidence. We find that in spite of numerous changes in their political, social, economic, and technological environments, Americans are essentially no more nor less informed about politics than they were fifty years ago. This suggests that positive and negative environmental changes have cancelled each other out. It also demonstrates how difficult it is for society to raise its aggregate level of political knowledge. Viewed most pessimistically, it may indicate inherent limits to how informed the general public is willing and able to be. Despite this, we conclude that political ignorance is not intractable. Beneath the overarching pattern of stability are several telling examples of aggregate learning about specific facts. Although what Americans know about politics has changed very little, there is some evidence that it is *changeable,* and although Americans appear less politically educated than one might hope, there is evidence that they are *educable.*

Progress and Peril: Theorizing about the State of Contemporary American Politics

There are reasons for expecting citizens to be differently informed about politics today than they were forty or fifty years ago. These expectations stem largely from societal changes in post–World War II America, which have affected the three determinants of political knowledge: ability, opportunity, and motivation. Consistent with the twin traditions of republicanism and progressivism, observers differ in their views of the impact of these changes.

Civic Ability

Learning about politics requires the ability, motivation, and opportunity to do so. *Ability* covers a fairly wide range of skills, talents, and attributes, from the physical (the ability to see and hear, for example) to the cognitive (the ability to process and retain information) to the social (the ability to read and write).[1] Native intelligence—the innate cognitive ability to process and retain information—undoubtedly plays some role in explaining differences in political knowledge. The ability to obtain, retain, and use political information is also a skill that is learned, and thus refinable, however. Further, although there is little reason to expect the aggregate genetic and physical influences on intelligence to change over time—especially over so short a period as half a century[2]—there are several compelling reasons to suspect that changes in public education have had an impact on what Americans know about politics.

A central purpose of public education in America has always been to teach the requisites of citizenship. Among these requisites has traditionally been political knowledge. The influential progressives Horace Mann,

John Dewey, Henry Adams, and Charles Merriam regarded public education, broadly defined, as the keystone to democracy. For Mann, education, "beyond all other devices of human origin, is the great equalizer of the conditions of men—the balance wheel of the social machinery" (1848: 87). It helped to prevent the dramatic disparities of wealth that prove anathema to democratic politics. According to Dewey, the aim of public schools was "the development of social power and insight" (1900: 18) in citizens who have "a personal interest in social relationships and control, and the habits of mind which secure social changes without introducing disorder" (1966: 99). People educated to these habits and armed with these skills help insure the "commonplace" that "education should not cease when one leaves school," thus providing a citizenry capable of performing its civic duty (1916: 51). The importance of an informed, skilled citizenry remains a guiding principle in educational philosophy (Engle and Ochoa, 1988: 10).

It would seem, therefore, that the expansion of public schooling following World War II and the greater availability of public funds for students attending both public and private institutions of higher learning would bode well for contemporary America's aggregate level of political knowledge. In 1940 the median number of years of education was 8.6, three-fourths of the public had not finished high school, and only 10 percent had some college experience. By the early 1990s the median number of years of education had risen to 12.7, with less than one-fourth not having finished high school and 43 percent having had college experience.

Much of the theorizing regarding purported gains in the public's cognitive mobilization, political skills, levels of conceptualization, or political sophistication explicitly build on these increasing levels of formal education. Acknowledging that "changes have been more substantial than one would expect from the slower and steadier change in educational attainment during the same years," Norman Nie, Sidney Verba, and John Petrocik speculate that "in terms of both magnitude and timing, it seems possible that the rise in conceptual level within the mass public is the consequence of an increasingly educated and thus more knowledgeable and sophisticated public" (1979: 119–20). And according to Ronald Inglehart: "Two basic changes are taking place among Western publics. One is cognitive, the other evaluative. . . . This change does not imply that mass publics will simply show higher rates of participation in traditional activities such as voting but that they may intervene in the political process on a qualitatively different level. Increasingly, they are likely to demand participation in *making* major decisions. . . . The source of these changes is a shift in the balance of political skills between elites and mass. Educational statistics probably furnish the clearest indicator of these changes, although education is merely one aspect of a broader underlying process" (1977: 293).

Not all students of contemporary politics see increases in formal education as inevitably translating into a more informed citizenry. Samuel Popkin writes that "the hoped-for *deepening* of the electorate has not occurred, because an increase in education is not synonymous with an increase in civics knowledge" (1991: 36). Concerns about the quality of contemporary mass education have led others to suggest that although it may be reaching more people, it is teaching them less. These critiques take many forms. For Neil Postman, the dominance of television as the central form of public discourse has reduced teaching to "an amusing activity," as children and young adults increasingly demand to be entertained rather than educated (1985: 142–54; see also his *Teaching as a Conserving Activity,* 1979). Allan Bloom expands this assault on popular culture to include almost every facet of the 1960s, arguing that the simplification and popularization of relativist and nihilist philosophies has reduced the university to "anarchy" in which "there are no recognized rules for citizenship and no legitimate titles to rule. In short there is no vision, nor is there a set of competing visions, of what an educated human being is. . . . Out of chaos emerges dispiritedness, because it is impossible to make a reasonable choice. Better to give up on liberal education and get on with a specialty in which there is at least a prescribed curriculum and a prospective career. . . . The student gets no intimation that . . . new and higher motives of action might be discovered within him" (1987: 337).

This indictment of modern education is fairly broad-based, but it speaks pointedly to the topics of central concern in this book—civic education and factual knowledge. According to Morris Janowitz, the civics curricula of secondary schools has undergone dramatic and harmful changes over the past four decades and has lost much of its emphasis on citizenship as a collective responsibility (1983). For E. D. Hirsch, the decline in public education originated with the concept of "content-neutral curricula" that emphasized personal development over factual learning (1988: xv). Hirsch traces this rejection of factual learning to the philosophy of Jean Jacques Rousseau but, ironically, blames Rousseau's popularization in American educational philosophy on Dewey: "The first chapter of [*Schools of Tomorrow*] carries the telling title 'Education as Natural Development' and is sprinkled with quotations from Rousseau. In it Dewey strongly seconds Rousseau's opposition to the mere accumulation of information. . . . Believing that a few direct experiences would suffice to develop the skills that children require, Dewey assumed that early education need not be tied to specific content. He mistook a half truth for the whole. He placed too much faith in children's ability to learn general skills from a few typical experiences and too hastily rejected 'the piling up of information'" (xv).

Although Hirsch exaggerates the extent to which Dewey (and Rousseau) rejected substantive learning, he is not alone in linking the decline of American education with the progressive reform movement. For Diane Ravitch, this decline resulted less from Dewey's progressive ideals than from the twisting and institutionalizing of them in the public school bureaucracy:

> The progressive education movement, however, took on a new life even as the larger movement subsided. As it separated from the social and political reform movement of which it had been a vital part, the progressive education movement was itself transformed. In its new phase, the progressive education movement became institutionalized and professionalized, and its major themes accordingly changed. Shorn of its roots in politics and society, pedagogical progressivism came to be identified with the child-centered school; with a pretentious scientism; with social efficiency and social utility rather than social reform; and with a vigorous suspicion of "bookish" learning. . . . It was a long while before it was recognized, even by Dewey himself, that the form of progressive education seized upon by the emerging profession was a bastard version, and in important ways, a betrayal, of the new education he had called for. (1983: 46–47)

Significantly and despite their differences, Postman, Bloom, Janowitz, Hirsch, and Ravitch all trace the major decline in American education to changes rooted in the years immediately following World War II—the very point at which education became more readily accessible to the bulk of the American population.

Criticisms of American public education are not limited to republicans. Marxist scholars see the underlying purpose of schooling in capitalist societies as antithetical to meaningful democracy. Samuel Bowles and Herbert Gintis assert that "in promoting what John Dewey once called the 'social continuity of life,' by integrating new generations into the social order, the schools are constrained to justify and reproduce inequality rather than correct it" (1976: 103). The real, if unstated, purpose of public education is twofold: "On the one hand, by imparting technical and social skills and appropriate motivations, education increases the productive capacity of workers. On the other hand, education helps defuse and depoliticize the potentially explosive class relations to the production process, and thus serves to perpetuate the social, political, and economic conditions through which a portion of the product of labor is expropriated in the form of profits" (11).

Even among Marxist scholars there is no simple consensus on the role of public education. George Wood, for example, while agreeing with much of Bowles's and Gintis's critique, argues that children and young adults are "organic intellectuals" capable of critical thinking but largely unaware of their condition (1982). Teachers, therefore, are in a position to make students critically aware even if this is not the intended goal of the education system itself.

In sum, the impact of fifty years of an expanding public education system on the ability of citizens to obtain and retain information about the processes, people, and content of national politics is not easily predicted. In theory, public education in the United States has as one of its central goals the training of citizens in basic civic skills. There are reasons to suspect, however, that in practice this goal has not been given the attention accorded it in theory.

Opportunity

"A popular government," wrote James Madison, "without popular information, *or the means of acquiring it,* is but a prologue to a farce or a tragedy, or perhaps both" (1832: 276, emphasis added). The *opportunity* to acquire information depends on several things: the state of knowledge about the topic in question (in 1900 one could not know the public health risks associated with secondhand tobacco smoke, whereas today this is more firmly established as fact); the frequency with which information is made available (nearly every Japanese citizen—but very few American citizens—can name the prime minister of Japan); the communications technology available (in 1963 it was a matter of hours for almost all Americans to learn that President Kennedy had been assassinated, whereas news of Lincoln's assassination took weeks to reach the same proportion of citizens).

In many ways formal education is a key provider of this opportunity because it not only teaches the skills required for obtaining information, but it also provides the substantive information. This is especially true for information about the rules of the game, which are the mainstay of civics curricula. It is also true for certain kinds of politically relevant information like history and geography. In theory, gains in the level of formal education attained by U.S. citizens should mean greater opportunity to learn, and thus greater levels of knowledge. But for many of the reasons discussed above, in practice a more educated citizenry might not lead to higher aggregate levels of knowledge.

The workplace is also a potential source of political and politically relevant information. In part this is a result of simple conversations with coworkers: "did you hear the news about the unemployment rate?" or "what did you think of the president's speech last night?" It can also result more directly from the requirements of the job. This is especially true in jobs that are directly associated with the government or conditioned on government policies—what Robert Luskin calls "politically impinged occupations." According to Luskin, "more politically impinged occupations provide more political information. Information about what the government is doing or is likely to do, at least in certain policy domains, and about what effects its actions are likely to have, marches even unbidden across the desks of many corporate executives, for example" (1990: 336).

Compared to a few decades ago, more workers hold jobs that are likely to be politically impinged—lawyers, corporate executives, social workers, teachers, and others. In 1940 approximately 15 percent of the workforce (and 8 percent of the adult population) held managerial, professional, and technical jobs of this sort. By 1989, 27 percent of the workforce and 14 percent of the adult population held such jobs. Other post–World War II changes in the labor force also provide reasons to expect changes in the aggregate level of political knowledge. For example, in 1950, 34 percent of adult women were part of the nonhousehold workforce; by 1992 this number was 58 percent. As a result of this trend, the percentage of adults working outside the home (or seeking to do so) increased from 53 percent in 1940 to 66 percent in 1992.

As with education, however, changes in the workforce do not point unequivocally to a more informed public. Verba and Nie, among others, demonstrate that union membership is an important predictor of political involvement (1972: 180). Declines in union membership over the past several decades (from a peak of 26 percent of the labor force in 1953 to about 16 percent currently) may have countered some of the gains in political knowledge derived elsewhere. Similarly, the movement of women into the workforce has been disproportionately to less prestigious, and presumably less politically impinged, jobs, muting the impact of this trend on levels of knowledge. In addition, the opportunity to work outside the home has often come in addition to—rather than in place of—home and child-rearing responsibilities for women, suggesting that some of the advantages associated with working outside the home (for example, a greater incentive to read about politics in one's spare time) might be lost for women.

Perhaps the greatest opportunity to learn about politics is provided by the mass media. The first citizens viewed a free press as a critical component of a working democratic republic. Thomas Jefferson's retort that, given a choice between a government without a free press or a free press without a government, he would select the latter, while hyperbolic, also shows the import placed on the opportunity for citizens to acquire public information.

Technological advances in electronic communications are thought to have created an information explosion with direct implications for creating a more informed citizenry. By shrinking time and space, the telegraph, radio, television, and computer seemed capable of turning a nation of disparate individuals, groups, and communities into an "electronic commonwealth" (Abramson, Arterton, and Orren, 1988). It also seemed to provide an information environment so rich that the costs of learning about politics would be reduced significantly for most citizens. Although aware of potential risks, writers of quite diverse stripes have been quick to point out the potential political benefits from this communications revolution (Toffler, 1980; Barber, 1984; Hollander, 1985). For example, Abramson et al. note: "The great contribution of electronic media to democracy should occur in the widespread distribution of public-affairs information to citizens. In a sense, most of the provisions under which media operate in democratic societies are intended to achieve this fundamental goal. . . . We can, however, point to some specific measures designed to ensure that radio and television promote public political education" (1988: 210–11). And Barber argues that "the capabilities of the new technology can be used to strengthen civic education, guarantee equal access to information, and tie individuals and institutions into networks that will make real participatory discussion and debate possible across great distances" (1984: 274).

As with most aspects of American politics, however, the rise of electronic media in general and television in particular has been viewed by some as evidence of decay rather than progress. For some critics, the ability to communicate almost instantaneously across great distances simply means citizens become inundated with irrelevant information that competes for their attention with information that is more politically relevant. Neil Postman, making this argument, quotes approvingly from Henry David Thoreau's *Walden:* "We are in great haste to construct a magnetic telegraph from Maine to Texas; but Maine and Texas, it may be, have nothing important to communicate. . . . We are eager to tunnel under the Atlantic and bring the old world some weeks nearer to the new; but perchance the first news that will leak through into the broad flapping American ear will be that Princess Adelaide has the whooping cough" (1985: 65). Postman and others also argue that electronic media are unsuited for the kind of rational argumentation and deliberation required in democratic discourse. He puts his case quite starkly, claiming: "a major new medium changes the structure of discourse; it does so by encouraging certain uses of the intellect, by favoring certain definitions of intelligence and wisdom, and by demanding a certain kind of content—in a phrase, by creating new forms of truth-telling. I will say once again that I am no relativist in this matter, and that I believe the epistemology created by television not only is inferior to a print-based epistemology but is dangerous and absurdist"[3] (1985: 27).

A related concern is that the seductive nature of television—the ease with which it can be watched, its entertaining and visually arresting format—is driving citizens away from newspapers and magazines, while at the same time forcing the print media to compete by turning to shorter, less demanding stories and the use of such techniques as color graphics. Indeed, newspaper readership has declined precipitously over the last several decades. In 1945 the ratio of total newspapers in circulation to households stood at over 1.3. Since that time it has steadily declined to its current ratio of less than .7 newspapers per household. Between 1970 and 1987 the percentage of adults who had read a newspaper on any given day declined from 78 percent to 65 percent, with the greatest drop-off found among younger citizens. Over the same period the number of people reading more than one newspaper a day was cut nearly in half. And between 1967 and 1982 the number of people saying they read a newspaper every day dropped from 73 percent to 54 percent (Bogart, 1989: 16; 78–82).

Other observers of the American media are concerned less with the domination of electronic over print media than with the domination of both by a small and ever shrinking number of owners: "At the end of World War II, for example, 80 percent of the daily newspapers in the United States were independently owned, but by 1989 the proportion was reversed, with 80 percent owned by corporate chains. In 1981 twenty corporations controlled most of the country's 11,000 magazines, but only seven years later that number had shrunk to three corporations" (Bagdikian, 1992: 4). According to this argument, the information explosion provides only the illusion of greater choice. While there are approximately 25,000 media outlets in the United States (individual newspapers, magazines, broadcast stations, and so on), over half are controlled by twenty corporations (Bagdikian, 1992: ix).

Of course critics of the media environment would agree that, given the motivation and ability, citizens have access to a wider range of information than ever before. But this raises yet another concern. Because of the overwhelming amount of contextless information available to citizens, sorting through it requires skills and, on occasion, technology not equally distributed among citizens.[4] The result, according to some, is a population increasingly divided into the information-rich and the information-poor (Bell, 1973; Burnham, 1978; Delli Carpini and Singh, 1987).

Motivation

Rabbit's indignant protest highlights the third factor determining what Americans know, and don't know, about the political world. The *motivation* to learn can derive from practical concerns, as with a senior citizen who needs to understand the federal rules regarding Social Security benefits. It can also stem from a less instrumental interest in politics: for example, a Vietnam veteran who continues to follow any news regarding United States–Vietnamese relations or a political junkie who enjoys the latest intrigue from Washington. And the motivation to learn about politics can be rooted in a sense of obligation, as it is with Rousseau's voter, who "instructs himself in public affairs, *however little influence his voice may have*" (Rousseau, 1968: 49, emphasis added). In short, the motivation to follow politics, and thus to learn about it, comes from several places. It results from interest—both a general interest in national and international affairs, and a more focused interest based on personal needs or concerns. It results from a sense of efficacy, the belief that one's involvement in politics is a good investment of one's time, that it will produce either psychic, solidary, or substantive rewards. And it results from a sense of civic duty, the belief that one should be involved in politics regardless of one's personal interests or the likelihood of an identifiable payoff.

There are many reasons to expect citizens to be increasingly motivated to follow national politics over the past half century. Since the New Deal, the federal government has greatly increased the scope of its authority, becoming involved in a wider variety of issues that directly affect individual citizens (Hanson, 1985; Stokes, 1967). Issues that are central to contemporary national politics—social welfare, managing the economy, occupational health and safety, worker-owner relations, civil rights, the environment, abortion—have become part of the national agenda over the past sixty years. The emergence of the United States as one of the two poles in a bipolar world following World War II and the increasing internationalization of economic issues further raised the stakes of Washington's actions.

Many of the societal changes discussed earlier should have increased the public's motivation to follow national politics. Formal education is designed not only to teach skills and information, but also to instill a sense of interest in and obligation toward the political system. Higher education also exposes individuals to ideas and people that are likely to make one's outlook less parochial. Popkin sees this as the central political role played by formal education: "education affects politics . . . by increasing the number of issues that citizens see as politically relevant, and by increasing the number of connections they make between their own lives and national and international events" (1991: 36).

As the economy becomes more regulated at the national level and increasingly international in scope, many jobs require greater knowledge of national and international politics. The rise of electronic media; the creation of national networks and chains; the increased use of satellite, computer, and laser technology; and the availability of cable news networks have brought political events and issues into people's homes at an unparalleled rate and pace.

Again, however, these trends have an alternative interpretation. Many scholars have argued that the conflictual, ambiguous, and unresolved nature of recent national issues has led people away from rather than into the political arena (Converse, 1976; Gilmour and Lamb, 1975; Hirschman, 1982). One can point to a myriad of reasons for people to doubt the efficacy of political involvement: the race riots of 1965 and 1992; the Vietnam war and its surrounding domestic turmoil; the seemingly constant struggle between environmental and economic concerns; Watergate, Koreagate, Abscam, the savings and loan scandal, and the Iran-Contra affair. If more widespread public education has come at the expense of notions of citizenship and civic responsibility—as Janowitz and others suggest—then there is little reason to expect this trend to lead to greater political involvement. The increasingly long economic downturns of the 1970s, 1980s, and 1990s are as likely to lead citizens to focus on personal, immediate goals as public, political ones. And the mass media, with its mind-numbing, rapid-fire presentation of national and international events; its "and now . . . this" format that decontextualizes issues; its cynical, negative presentation of politics, and its constant enticement of alternative entertainment is as likely to turn people away from politics as toward it (Robinson, 1976; Miller, Goldenberg, and Erbring, 1979; Patterson, 1993).

Public opinion data are inconclusive regarding the impact of these events and trends on the political engagement of citizens. Over the last thirty to forty years, internal political efficacy appears to have risen somewhat; public interest in politics and support for civic responsibility has remained relatively steady; and trust in government officials, external political efficacy, and voter turnout has declined significantly (Abramson,

1983; Gilmour and Lamb, 1975; Bennett, 1986; Erikson, Luttbeg, and Tedin, 1991; Flanigan and Zingale, 1987; Teixeira, 1992). Are these the best or worst of times?

Stability and Change in Political Knowledge: Uncovering General Patterns

Although there is a surprisingly rich and varied collection of survey items cataloguing the public's knowledge of politics, these data are of limited use for studying change because the specific facts asked about differ from survey to survey. Despite these constraints, a consensus has emerged concerning contemporary levels of political knowledge. Studies by Russell Neuman (1986), Stephen Bennett (1988; 1989) and Eric Smith (1989) suggest that knowledge is at best no greater than it was two to four decades ago, and it may have declined on some measures.

Our research generally confirms these findings, although we found some evidence of greater knowledge today. Our Survey of Political Knowledge was designed, in part, to replicate knowledge items asked on surveys in the 1940s and 1950s. Figure 3.1 plots the change—or lack thereof—in several of the items. On the basis of fifteen comparisons (not all of which are shown on the figure), the public today appears slightly more knowledgeable than it was in the 1940s and 1950s. On nine of the items, the percentage answering correctly in 1989 was higher than in the earlier surveys (by 1 to 15 points). Of the remaining items, two were down 1 percent, and four others declined by 2, 5, 9, and 10 percent.

The overall similarity is more striking than the differences. Only three items show increases greater than 10 percentage points (there were fifteen-point increases in those knowing what the first ten amendments are called and that Congress can override a presidential veto, and a twelve-point increase in ability to define "presidential veto"). Given a relatively small median increase across all fifteen items (4.5 percent), it appears that over fifty years, the level of public knowledge has remained remarkably stable.

Analyses drawing on a larger set of items lead to a similar conclusion. We found 227 questions that were asked more than once in identical or near-identical form.[5] Table 3.1 summarizes these items (the questions and the marginal percent correct for each can be found in appendix 3). They are evenly distributed among institutions and processes (52 items), public figures and political parties (57 items), and foreign affairs (54 items). There are fewer items about domestic politics (24 items). In addition to

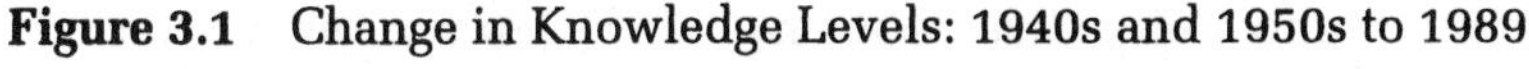
Figure 3.1 Change in Knowledge Levels: 1940s and 1950s to 1989

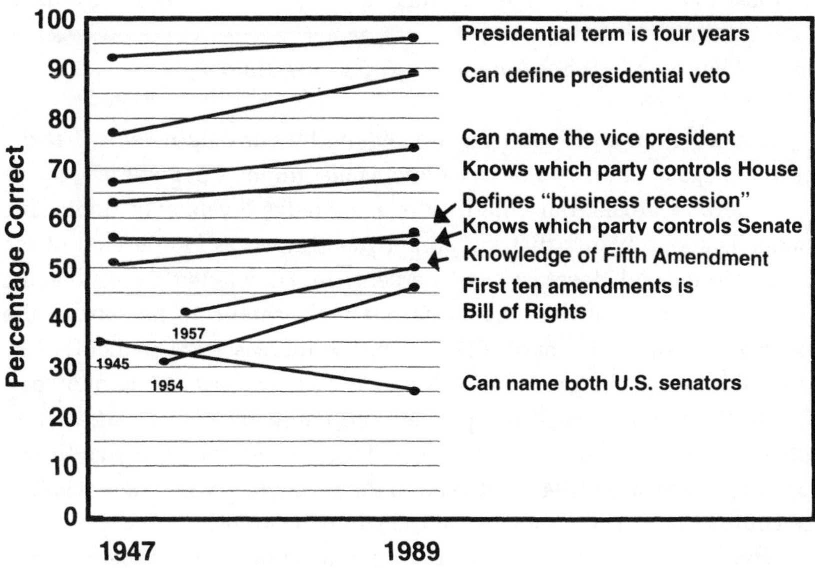

Table 3.1 Summary of Over-Time Data

	Institutions and Processes	Public Figures and Political Parties	Foreign Affairs	Domestic Affairs	Geography	History
Number of items	52	57	54	24	31	9
Percentage of items	23	25	24	11	14	5

Note: Total questions, 227; total time points, 586; total observations, 749; items repeated once, 7090; items repeated two times, 1990; items repeated three times, 590; items repeated more than three times, 690; mean length of time between observations, 11 years; median length of time between observations, 7 years.

these directly political items, we included 31 items related to knowledge of geography and 9 about history.

Most of the items (158, or nearly 70 percent) were repeated only once; 44 items (19 percent) were repeated twice; 12 (5 percent) were repeated three times; and 13 were repeated more than three times. All told, the 227 items were asked 586 different times. These, in turn, provided 749 observations of (potential) change.[6] The mean length of time between observations was just under eleven years; the median length was seven years. We use these observations as the units of analysis in the research to follow.

General Patterns in What Americans Know over Time

A simple cut at the patterns uncovered by our data reveals that the mean change over all 749 observations is just under 1 percent (see figure 3.2). There is substantial volatility in knowledge levels over time. This change is about evenly distributed between increases (50 percent of the observations) and decreases (46 percent) in knowledge about specific facts. While most of this change is relatively small, 38 percent of the observations show decreases (17 percent) or increases (21 percent) of 10 percent or more. The greatest decline in knowledge was a drop of 66 percent in the percentage of the public who could recall the secretary of defense in 1977 compared with 1953. The greatest increase was the 56 percent gain between 1945 and 1985 in the percentage who knew whether the United States was a member of the United Nations.

The information in figure 3.2 does not take into account the length of time between observations—change over forty years is treated the same as change over a few months. When the distribution is based on the average yearly change, levels of knowledge appear a good deal less volatile (see figure 3.3). Nearly a third of the observations averaged less than a percentage point increase or decrease per year, and fully 60 percent averaged a percentage point or less yearly change. Only 9 percent of the items averaged yearly changes of 10 percent or more, with 2 percent of the observations registering declines and 7 percent registering increases. Overall, the mean yearly change was slightly under 1 percent. The maximum yearly decline was 39 percent, the result of an unusually large difference between the percentage of the public who could identify Nelson Mandela in two surveys conducted during 1990.[7] The largest average yearly gain in aggregate knowledge was 44 percent and reflected increased knowledge about the United States' status in the United Nations between 1945 and 1946.

What accounts for these patterns? Do they result from the coincidental combinations of factors affecting the opportunity and motivations to learn about politics, or are there more structural explanations? Are Americans generally any more or less informed about politics today than they were twenty years ago? Fifty years ago? If environmental changes are at work, one would expect the length of time between comparisons to be an important predictor of change. The longer the period between the first measurement of aggregate levels of knowledge and the second measurement, the more time for systemic changes (for example, in the media envi-

Figure 3.2 Distribution of Percentage Change per Observation

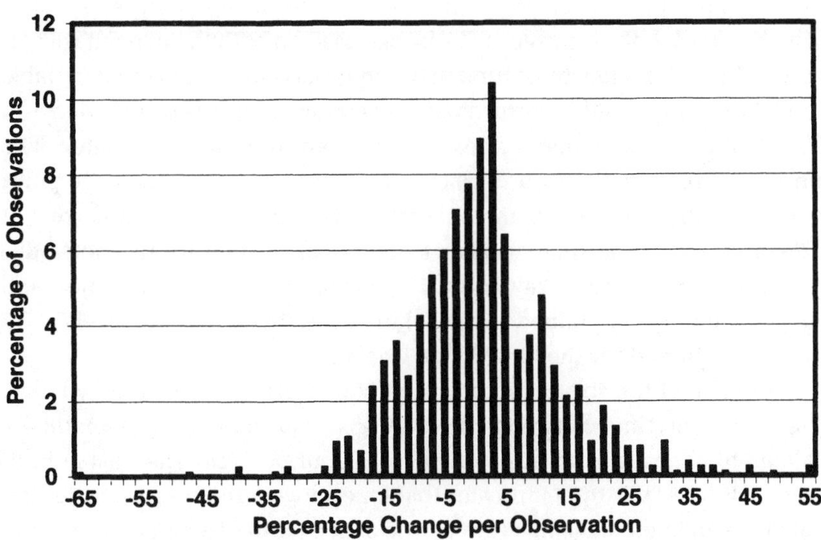

Figure 3.3 Distribution of Average Percentage Change per Year

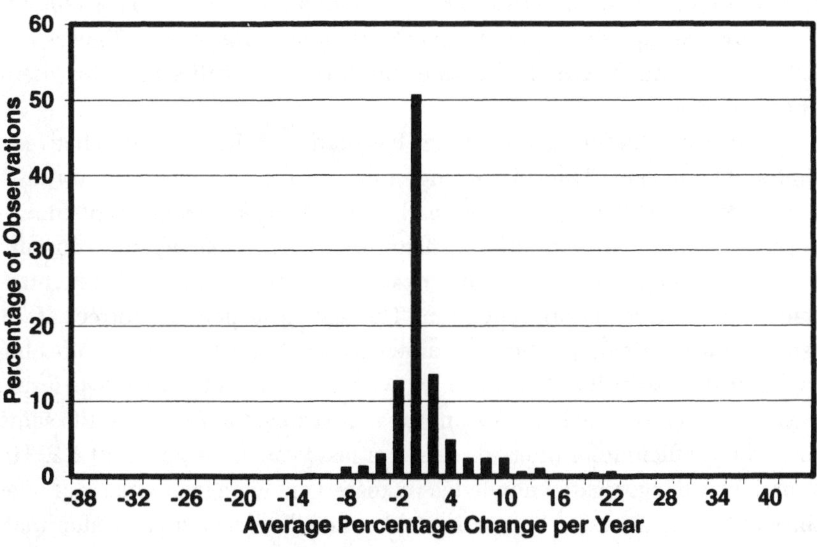

ronment or educational policy) to occur. More specifically, if knowledge levels increase with time, then the progressive vision discussed earlier in this chapter would be supported, but if they decrease with time the more pessimistic republican view would seem more accurate.

We have 749 specific observations in which the percent correct at some initial point in time (T1) can be compared to the percentage correct at some later point (T2). We begin our analysis with a simple model in which the percentage correct at T2 is regressed on both the percentage correct at T1 and the length of time between observations. This two variable model explains about two-thirds of the variance in levels of knowledge at T2. Most of this explanatory power is derived from the T1 variable. The unstandardized *b* of .94 ($p < .001$) means that for each percentage point correct at T1, there is a commensurate 0.94 percentage point correct at T2—a very close fit that suggests a good deal of stability in knowledge over time.[8] Put another way, about 67 percent of the overall variance (and 88 percent of the explained variance) in aggregate knowledge levels at T2 can be accounted for the knowledge levels at T1.

In spite of the strong predictive power of prior levels of knowledge, the length of time between observations also appears systematically related to changes in what people know about politics. The unstandardized *b* of -0.13 ($p < .001$) indicates that for each year that passes, the aggregate level of knowledge declines a little over a tenth of a percentage point. At first blush this analysis implies that the cumulative effect of environmental changes over the past fifty years has led to a modest decline in levels of knowledge of between 6 and 7 percentage points. This conclusion, however, appears to contradict the evidence presented in figures 3.1, 3.2, and 3.3, all of which indicates slightly more gains than losses in knowledge.

The answer to this small paradox lies in the nonlinear relation between time and knowledge.[9] Most "learning" appears to occur over the short run—five years or less—followed by a small decline in aggregate levels of knowledge over time. This underlying pattern becomes clear when a dummy variable for the interval of five or fewer years between T1 and T2 is introduced into the regression equation. The aggregate percent correct at T1 remains the dominant predictor of knowledge at T2 ($b = 0.94$), again attesting to the relative stability of political knowledge. Length of time between surveys, however, is now insignificant (unstandardized $b = -.01$). At the same time, the coefficient for intervals of five or less years is a significant 4.2.[10] In sum, levels of aggregate knowledge increased an average of 4 percent over the short run but tended to remain stable or decline very slightly after that. Conceivably, this small, initial burst of "learning" reflects the combination of increased motivation and opportunity that coincide with the emergence of new issues, personalities, and so forth.[11]

Thus far we have treated different types of political knowledge as interchangeable, and we have ignored the possible impact of different political periods on the motivation or opportunity to learn about politics.

The results of a slightly more complex regression model that attempts to control for these factors are found in table 3.2. In addition to the three independent variables used above, we included two dummy variables for types of knowledge (public figures and substance of politics) and three for the decade in which the T2 observation took place (the 1960s, 1970s, or 1980s and early 90s).[12] This model explained just over 70 percent of the variance in the T2 levels of political knowledge. The impact of the three variables included in our earlier model remain about the same: the percentage correct at T1 continues to dominate the model, short-term "learning" still occurs, and there is little evidence of aggregate changes in knowledge after five years (although, consistent with the data presented in figures 3.1, 3.2, and 3.3 this coefficient is now positive).

Table 3.2 Regression Analysis Predicting Knowledge Levels at T2

	b	se *b*	beta	*t*	*p*
Percent correct at T1 (coded in percentages)	0.92	0.02	.81	40.10	.0000
Five-year or less interval (coded 0–1)	3.26	1.24	.07	2.63	.0087
Length of time between T1 and T2 (coded in years)	0.07	0.05	.04	1.21	.2243
Facts about the substance of politics (coded 1 = foreign or domestic affairs; 0 = other)	7.04	1.39	.14	5.05	.0000
Facts about public figures and political parties (coded 1–0)	−0.47	1.15	−.01	−0.41	.6808
The 1960s (coded 1 if T2 occurred in 1960s; 0 if not)	4.02	1.75	.06	2.30	.0218
The 1970s (coded 1 if T2 occurred in the 1970s; 0 if not)	−4.99	1.65	−.10	−3.03	.0026
The 1980s (coded 1 if T2 occurred in 1980 to 1991; 0 if not)	−1.65	1.60	−.037	−1.03	.3045
Constant term	1.77	2.09		.849	.3963
		adjusted r^2 = .71 (significance of model: .0000)			

Note: *b* is the unstandardized regression coefficient; se *b* is the standard error of *b*; beta is the standardized regression coefficient; *t* is the *t*-value of beta; *p* is the *p*-value of beta.

The new variables help flesh out our understanding of how aggregate levels of knowledge have changed over the past half century. Levels of knowledge during the 1960s average about 4 percentage points higher than those of the two prior decades, which we attribute to the politicized atmosphere of that era. Consistent with the view that the 1970s marked a retreat from public involvement (Hirschman, 1982), knowledge levels during the 1970s were 5 percentage points lower than the 1940s and 1950s and 9 percentage points less than the 1960s. The impact of the 1980s and early 1990s on levels of knowledge was also negative relative to the 1940s and 1950s, although this coefficient is statistically insignificant. Change in levels of knowledge also varied depending on the type of information involved: all things being equal, knowledge about substantive political issues increased about 7 percentage points more than did knowledge about other types of politics.[13]

These patterns are revelatory regarding the dynamic underlying aggregate changes in political knowledge, but in the end, the dominant pattern remains one of remarkable stability, especially given the political, social, and technological changes that have occurred in post–World War II America. This point is graphically illustrated in table 3.3. Using the results presented in table 3.2, we calculated predicted levels of aggregate knowledge about civics, public figures, and substantive policy, assuming a starting percentage correct of 50 percent in 1959. For all three types of information, knowledge peaks in 1964, declines through 1979, and then rebounds slightly by 1991. In the end, while aggregate knowledge of substantive politics appears slightly greater than it was thirty-two years earlier and knowledge of civics or of public figures is slightly less, both changes are quite marginal. This conclusion is reinforced by comparing only those questions first asked before 1960, and then asked again after 1980. For these ninety-one observations (with an average length of time of thirty-seven years between them), the mean change was an increase of less than 1 percent, and the median "change" was a remarkably steady zero.

Table 3.3 Estimated Changes in Political Knowledge for Three Hypothetical Facts

	1959	1964	1969	1979	1991
			Percentage Correct		
Civics	50	56	53	44	48
People and parties	50	55	52	44	48
Substance of politics	50	63	60	51	55

Exceptions to the Rule: Case Studies of Change in Aggregate Political Knowledge

The analyses above show that levels of knowledge for most aspects of politics have not changed dramatically over the last fifty years. But what about exceptions to the rule? Political learning results not only from incremental changes in skills, opportunities, and motivations over the decades, nor only from periods of unusually heightened politics. Often the causes of learning are more idiosyncratic and dependent on unique combinations of events, personalities, and conditions. Such change might have little systematic impact on long-term levels of knowledge, yet it can still be informative regarding the factors that lead to political learning.

The residuals from the regression analysis described above provide one way of selecting exceptions to the rule. Thirty-three of the 749 cases had standardized residuals that exceeded 2.0. These cases involved 18 specific facts (if the same question was asked more than twice, it produced several observations). As significant deviations from the expected norm, these cases serve as potentially informative instances of unusual "learning" and "forgetting." Interestingly, of the 33 observations (and 18 facts), 25 (12) involved cases where increases in knowledge exceeded expectations, while only 8 observations (involving 6 specific facts) were cases of unusually great decline. Do these exceptions from the norm represent idiosyncratic facts, or do they have more substantive explanations?

Aggregate Declines in Political Knowledge

Of the eight cases in which knowledge declined at unexpectedly great rates, three involved the public's ability to name the persons who held key cabinet positions (defense, state, and labor) in the Carter as compared to the Eisenhower administrations. Both questions were open ended and both were asked early in the presidents' first term (February 9–18, 1953, for Eisenhower and January 7–13, 1977, for Carter). The differences appear to result from how well known each person was before being appointed and from the relative controversy generated by (and thus media attention to) the nominations themselves. Pre-nomination notoriety also underlies the drop in recognition of the secretary of state in 1970 (William Rogers) and 1985 (George Shultz) as compared to 1958 (John Foster Dulles) (see table 3.4).

John Foster Dulles, Eisenhower's nominee for secretary of state, had nearly half a century of highly visible diplomatic experience, dating to The Hague Convention of 1907. Dulles also served as a member of the American delegation to the Versailles Peace Conference in 1919, negotiated the peace treaty with Japan following World War II, was the central member of the U.S. delegation to the organizational conference for the United Nations in 1945, and served for many years as the U.S. delegate to the United Nations. His counterparts in 1970, 1977, and 1985, although not novices to public life, were figures of much less public stature. William Rogers, President Nixon's first secretary of state, had served as attorney general during Eisenhower's second term but spent most of his life as a corporate lawyer and had been out of the public spotlight for nearly a decade before becoming secretary of state.[14] In addition, Rogers had very little foreign policy experience. Cyrus Vance, President Carter's nominee, had a more extensive public résumé, but except for a brief stint as President Kennedy's secretary of the army some fifteen years earlier, most of these positions were unlikely to put him in the public eye: legal counsel for several Senate committees, general counsel for the Department of Defense, deputy secretary of defense under President Johnson, and deputy chief delegate to the Paris peace talks. Vance was described in the 1977 *Current Biography* as "a quiet, self-effacing team player who believes the secretary of state should delegate key responsibilities." George Shultz, President Reagan's secretary of state in 1985, had held several cabinet positions in the late 1960s and early 1970s, but none of them were particularly visible ones (secretary of labor, secretary of the treasury, and OMB director). In addition, Shultz had spent the decade before his appointment as secretary of state in private business and academia.

The relative public familiarity with Eisenhower's nominees for secretaries of defense and labor, compared to that of President Carter's nominees, seems to result from the attention given to the nominations themselves. Charles Wilson, Eisenhower's nominee for defense secretary, had developed public recognition during his tenure as president of Delco Electronics and of General Motors, where he introduced the notion of tying cost-of-living raises for employees to the Consumer Price Index. Nonetheless, and despite his reputation for quotable if controversial public statements, he was a relatively obscure figure until his nomination in late 1952. His nomination and subsequent confirmation hearings became newsworthy when he initially refused to sell his $2.5 million worth of stock in General Motors. This controversy led to the often misquoted statement, "What's good for our country is good for General Motors, and vice versa."[15] Harold Brown, President Carter's nominee for this office, had a long history of involvement in U.S. national security policy, but like many of Carter's appointments, he was a low-keyed pragmatist with little visibility.[16] His nomination and appointment generated little controversy and little media attention.

Martin Durkin's nomination for secretary of labor was more controversial than Wilson's, in part because he was the first trade unionist to hold the post in twenty years (Durkin had been president of the AFL-affiliated United Association of Journeymen and Apprentices of the Plumbing and Pipe Fitting Industry). More newsworthy, however, was the fact that Durkin was a Democrat who had opposed the Republican-initiated Taft-Hartley Labor Act and had endorsed and actively campaigned for Adlai

Stevenson—Eisenhower's opponent in the 1952 presidential campaign! Senator Taft called his nomination "incredible" and "an affront to millions of union members and officers who had the courage to defy the edict of officials like Mr. Durkin that they vote for Stevenson," and it was reported in the press as the most surprising and controversial of Eisenhower's appointments. Compare this to Jimmy Carter's selection of Ray Marshall, a well-liked but obscure economics professor from the University of Texas with no national political experience or exposure.

Table 3.4 Large Declines in Political Knowledge

Topic	Percentage Correct T1	Percentage Correct T2	Percentage Change
Secretary of defense	68 (1953)	2 (1977)	–66
Secretary of state	59 (1953)	12 (1977)	–47
Nelson Mandela	56 (2/90)	17 (11/90)	–39
Secretary of state	57 (1958)	18 (1970)	–39
Secretary of state	57 (1958)	25 (1985)	–32
Secretary of labor	32 (1953)	1 (1977)	–31
Democratic vice presidential candidate	80 (1964)	55 (1968)	–25
Survivors' benefits (part of Social Security)	87 (1979)	63 (1981)	–24

Data on the percent of Americans correctly identifying the Democratic nominee for vice president in 1964 versus 1968 provide additional evidence for the role specific circumstances play in determining the opportunity and motivation to learn about politics. Again the likely reason for this fairly substantial difference lies in the prior visibility of the two candidates. In 1964 Hubert Humphrey was a prominent member of the Senate who had received international attention as a result of his 1958 meeting with Nikita Khrushchev. That same year, after the Democrats' resounding victory in the congressional elections, his portrait appeared on the cover of *Time* magazine. In 1960 he was the first and most visible challenger to John Kennedy in the battle for the Democratic party's nomination for president. He also undoubtedly benefited from the unusual circumstances of his nomination (Johnson had served as president for a full year without a sitting vice president). Muskie, in 1968, was a much less well known public figure who had never actively sought the nomination for president and who was nominated under much less compelling circumstances.

Certain kinds of knowledge require citizens to carefully survey the political landscape for changes. Wrong answers occasionally reflected less ignorance than lagged attention. At the aggregate level, this lagged attention can appear as a kind of temporary national amnesia. Knowledge about the process of presidential succession provides an interesting example of how the public reacts to changes in the rules of the game (see table 3.5). The 24 percent decline in knowledge about who would succeed President Truman should he die in office appears to be a result of the fact that the procedure for presidential succession changed between the asking of the two questions. In March 1947, when the first question was asked, 46 percent correctly said the secretary of state would become president (there was no sitting vice president at this time). By August, however, the law had changed and the Speaker of the House was next in line. Note that the percentage of those naming *either* the secretary of state or the Speaker is about the same as the percentage correct in March. Note also that in 1985, when a similar question was asked, the percentage correct had rebounded to the level of March 1947 (an additional 27 percent still believed or misremembered that the secretary of state was next in line). Clearly what we are seeing are a series of snapshots in which the population "learns" a new fact through a kind of slow motion surveillance of the political world.[17]

Table 3.5 Knowledge of Presidential Succession (Percentage Correct)

Who is in line for presidency after the vice president	March 1947	August 1947	1985
Secretary of state	46*	19	27
Speaker of the House	—	22*	47*

Note: * = correct answer.

Only one case of dramatic decline in knowledge appears to be forgetting in the traditional sense. In February 1990, 56 percent of the public could identify Nelson Mandela, the longtime leader of the African National Congress. At this time Mandela was receiving an unusually large amount of media attention because of his anticipated release from a South African jail after over twenty years of political imprisonment (he was released about a week after the survey was completed). Slightly less than ten months later, however, South African politics were no longer at the center of U.S. media attention, and only 17 percent of the public could recall who Mandela was.[18]

Aggregate Increases in Political Knowledge

Examples of unusually large gains in knowledge are more common than examples of decline, and they are especially instructive regarding how opportunity and motivation can combine to increase knowledge at the aggregate level. As with declines in knowledge, many of the most dramatic changes involve public figures (see table 3.6). Knowledge of who Harry Truman was jumped 30 percent between the time of his nomination as the Democratic vice presidential candidate in 1944 and when—due to Franklin Roosevelt's death in office—he became president. Two months before his first nomination for president Adlai Stevenson was known by 34 percent of the public. Four years and one failed presidential campaign later, and on the verge of a second nomination, 88 percent of the public knew who he was. Averell Harriman received a similar if less impressive boost as a result of his failed attempts to secure the Democratic nomination for president in the 1950s.

Table 3.6 Large Increases in Political Knowledge

Topic	Percentage Correct T1	T2	Percentage Change
Adlai Stevenson	34 (1952)	88 (1956)	+54
Define fallout	17 (1957)	57 (1961)	+40
How is Medicare funded	41 (1962)	75 (1974)	+34
Marion Barry	7 (1989)	40 (1990)	+33
Harry Truman	68 (1944)	98 (1947)	+30
Averell Harriman	25	55	+30
Lee Iacocca	31 (1980)	61 (1984)	+30
Balance of trade	53 (1977)	83 (1989)	+30
How is Medicare funded	41 (1962)	69 (1979)	+28

Ten of the twenty-four outliers that demonstrated unusually large increases in knowledge involved being able to identify the Democratic or Republican nominee for vice president (see table 3.7). As with the instances of aggregate declines in knowledge, these increases seem the result of differences in the prior visibility of the candidates: John Sparkman's relative obscurity in 1952 as compared to Lyndon Johnson in 1960, Hubert Humphrey in 1964, or Walter Mondale in 1976; Richard Nixon's low profile in 1952 as compared to Robert Dole's in 1976; or George Bush's recognition in 1980 (based on his political experience and his early success in the presidential primaries) relative to Nixon in 1952, Henry Cabot Lodge in 1960, William Miller in 1964, or Spiro Agnew in 1968.

Table 3.7 Patterns of Knowledge about Vice Presidential Candidates (Percentage Correct)

Party of Candidate	1948	1952	1960	1964	1968	1976	1980
Republican	58	45	60	62	62	72	84
Democrat	49	32	69	80	55	66	—

The religious affiliations of the candidates was a central issue in press coverage of the 1960 presidential race (see table 3.8). Questions about John Kennedy's Catholicism and its potential impact on his loyalties and judgment were key to this concern. Much of the general public learned of these facts through the course of the election. While the public learned the religious affiliations of both men, more people learned about Kennedy. This is not surprising, given the emphasis on his Catholicism. Certainly Kennedy's religious affiliation was not the most important issue in 1960 for most voters. Nonetheless, the patterns of aggregate learning that occurred are informative regarding the media's potential impact on other, arguably more significant issues.

Table 3.8 Patterns of Knowledge about the Religious Affiliations of John Kennedy and Richard Nixon (Percentage Correct)

	4/59	7/59	2/60	7/60
John Kennedy	48	46	69	84
Richard Nixon	36	39	59	56

Local public officials and corporate executives seldom gain national notoriety, but there are easy explanations for two exceptions to this rule. Marion Barry, mayor of Washington, D.C. for a dozen years, went from being known by 7 percent of the public to 40 percent in the space of ten months as a result of his videotaped arrest for drug use. And Chrysler President Lee Iacocca's regular appearance on television commercials—rather than his business acumen—undoubtedly explains the unusual increase in his level of recognition.

Other large gains in knowledge of public figures, while not among the outliers in our regression analysis, also reflect this combination of motivation and opportunity. The prime minister of Japan, usually recognized by fewer than 5 percent of the public, could be identified by almost a fifth of those asked as a result of a series of scandals rocking the Japanese government in 1986. And the percentage able to identify at least one member of the Keating Five—the senators associated with the savings and loan scandal—doubled between May 1990 and January 1991.

Not all increases in knowledge resulted from revelations about the seamier side of politics. Many involved the emergence of local and state public figures or less visible national officeholders onto the scene of presidential politics. Knowledge of Estes Kefauver jumped 16 percent when he was nominated as the Democratic vice presidential candidate in 1956. And awareness of Earl Warren was 24 percentage points higher for his role as chief justice of the Supreme Court than as governor of California. Foreign and international leaders can become better known in the United States without taking a bribe or sleeping around. Awareness that Kurt Waldheim was secretary general of the United Nations increased 25 percentage points during his tenure.[19] And knowledge that Mikhail Gorbachev was the leader of the Soviet Union increased 21 percent between 1985 and 1986. Most examples of aggregate gains and losses discussed thus far appear tied to coincidental combinations of opportunity and motivation, but some increases in knowledge are more clearly tied to larger political cycles. For example, the largest gains in knowing the name of one's U.S. representative or the challenger in a House race occur between surveys taken in off-years and those taken in presidential election years.

Gains in political knowledge are not limited to information about public figures. Four of the largest increases in aggregate knowledge involved comparisons with the 1945 level of awareness regarding U.S. membership in the United Nations (see table 3.9). In March 1945, when the question was first asked, the United States was on the verge of officially joining the fledgling international organization but had not yet done so. Within a year the percent correctly answering this question had risen to three-quarters of the population and increased until, by 1985, this fact was nearly universally known.

Table 3.9 Patterns of Knowledge about U.S. Membership in the United Nations (Percentage Correct)

	3/45	3/46	5/46	1976	1985
Is U.S. a member of U.N.	40	75	84	85	96

The explosive increase in knowledge about what the term *fallout* means is also instructive (see table 3.6). The question was first asked in 1957—well into the nuclear age but not during a period of exceptional tensions between the United States and Soviet Union by cold war standards. The question was repeated in December of 1961, however, immediately following the Cuban missile crisis, when both the motivation and the opportunity to learn the meaning of the term increased dramatically. Not surprisingly, knowledge of this term increased from 17 percent to 57 percent of the public.[20]

The final two cases of unusually large gains in aggregate knowledge involve substantive issues: funding for Medicare and the balance of trade. In 1962, when Medicare was first proposed and debated, 41 percent of the public knew that it was to be funded through the Social Security program. By the mid-to-late-1970s, over a dozen years after the program became policy, this number had increased to as much as 75 percent. In both 1977 and 1989 the United States suffered from a trade deficit. In 1977 the balance of trade did not draw much media, and thus much public, attention. By 1989 the twin deficits—the federal budget and the balance of trade—were of central concern. Not surprisingly, public knowledge of the trade deficit increased 30 percent over this period.

Although not among the regression outliers, the well-documented pattern of learning about U.S. policy in Nicaragua provides ample evidence of both the difficulty and the possibilities of educating the public about political issues (see table 3.10). In August 1983, 29 percent of the public knew that the Reagan administration was supporting rebels who opposed the government of Nicaragua. As the issue of aid to the rebels was debated in Congress and through the media, this percentage increased slowly over the next two years, so that by March 1986 59 percent of the public was aware of this fact. Thereafter, however, and despite the continued prominence of aid to the Contras throughout the debates over the Iran-contra scandal, the percent of the public that could correctly answer this question showed little systematic change of any kind.

Table 3.10 Patterns of Knowledge about U.S. Policy in Nicaragua (Percentage Correct)

	8/83	5/84	3/85	6/85	3/86	3/86	4/87	6/87	8/87	1/88
Does administration support rebels or government	29	33	37	46	50	59	45	52	54	55

Surveying Party Politics: The Impact of Distinct Stands on Political Learning

The political parties are critical actors in determining what citizens know and don't know about politics. As final evidence of the public's capacity to learn about politics and the role played by the political environment in that process, we turn to an examination of changes in public knowledge about the issue stands of the national parties. In most years for which the NES provides data, majorities of the public were correctly able to place the Democratic party and its presidential candidates to the left of their Republican counterparts on such issues as women's role in society, aid to minorities, jobs, education, and school desegregation (Stimson, 1990: 352–53). Although the stands of the Democratic and Republican parties usually diverge on these issues, in many years the differences are subtle at best, making it more difficult for citizens to learn where the parties stand relative to each other. When the party positions become more distinct, substantial portions of the public appear to learn.

For example, in 1956 and 1960 about 20 percent of those surveyed saw the Democratic party as more liberal on federal aid to minorities than the Republican party, about the same percentage as saw Republicans as the more liberal party (see table 3.11). The two parties were rated similarly on their stands regarding school desegregation. This balance is reflective of the actual stands of the two parties during this period. While Truman led the way to desegregating the military, the initial efforts to pass civil rights legislation in the 1940s and 1950s were often championed by Republicans. Moreover, the ruling in *Brown v. Board of Education* was handed down during Eisenhower's presidency, and it was Eisenhower who issued the executive order to desegregate the schools in Little Rock, Arkansas. By 1968, however, both civil rights and federal aid to blacks had become strong planks in the Democratic party platform, and the Republican party had moved away from its long-term emphasis on the former and often actively opposed the latter. This shift was not lost on a significant portion of the American public: in 1964 and 1968 between 50 and 60 percent of those surveyed saw the Democrats as the more liberal party on aid to minorities, while only 7 to 11 percent saw the Republican party as the more liberal. And 50 to 56 percent saw the Democrats as more liberal on school desegregation, compared to 7 to 9 percent who saw the Republicans in this light.

Table 3.11 Change in Knowledge of Party Stands

Issue	Year	Percentage Selecting Party as More Liberal	
		Democratic Party	Republican Party
Aid to minorities			
	1956	20	22
	1960	23	21
	1964	60	7
	1968	51	11
School desegregation			
	1956	23	25
	1960	16	20
	1964	56	7
	1968	52	9
Women's roles			
	1972	30	10
	1976	34	8
	1980	60	9
	1984	59	13

Source: Stimson, 1990: 352.

A similar example of the public's ability to survey the changing political terrain is provided by the stands on the role of women developed by the parties. In 1972 and 1976, about a third of the public saw the Democratic party as more liberal on this issue. In contrast, only about 10 percent of the public saw the Republican party as more liberal. Again, these modest differences fairly accurately reflected the small differences between the two parties in the early 1970s (for example, while the Democratic party and candidates were somewhat more committed to feminist issues, both parties supported the ERA and all four presidential candidates were nominally pro-choice). By 1980, however, the Republican party had become firmly captured by social conservatives who aggressively expounded more conservative rhetoric on such issues as the role of women. (For example, in 1980 the Republican party removed support for the ERA from its platform and added planks advocating a constitutional amendment outlawing abortion and supporting legislation "protecting and defending the traditional American family.") At the same time, the Democratic party strengthened its commitment to feminist concerns, including "support for the ERA, opposition to reversals of past ratification of the ERA, a pledge to hold no national or regional party meetings in unratified states, endorsement of the 1973 Supreme Court decision allowing abortion, support for increased federal funds for child-care programs, and commitment to the principle of equal pay for equal work" (Klein, 1984: 157). As a result of this more sharply defined difference between the two parties, the percentage of the public knowing that the Democratic party was the more liberal on women's roles in society increased to around 60 percent in 1980 and 1984, and the percentage seeing the Republicans as the more liberal party held about constant.

Is the Glass Half Empty or Half Full?

There are several yardsticks for measuring the American public's knowledge of politics. In chapter 2 we assessed levels of knowledge from the perspective of an informed observer. In this chapter we have compared levels of knowledge over time and used past performance as a standard against which to measure current performance. Again we find good news and bad news.

The good news is that in spite of concerns over the quality of education, the decline in newspaper readership, the rise of sound-bite journalism, the explosion in national political issues, and the waning commitment to civic engagement, citizens appear no less informed about politics today than they were half a century ago. The bad news is that in spite of an unprecedented expansion in public education, a communications revolution that has shattered national and international boundaries, and the increasing relevance of national and international events and policies to the daily lives of Americans, citizens appear no more informed about politics.

The stability of political knowledge in the face of seemingly momentous changes in the ability, opportunity, and motivation to be informed might be interpreted as evidence that the problem is intractable—that current levels of knowledge represent a natural ceiling above which it is unreasonable to expect a polity to rise. From this perspective, our only comfort is that the more negative structural trends of the second half of the twentieth century have not eroded what the public knows about politics.

An alternative view is that this stability results from the neutralization of potential gains promised by the expansion of public education and the communications revolution. This stasis results from the countertrends discussed earlier in this chapter; from the relatively poor civic use to which contemporary education and communications have been put; and from the failure to supplement advances in education and communication with parallel advances in the structure and uses of the public sphere and, more specifically, the political sphere.

Our analysis cannot prove that this interpretation is more accurate, but it does provide evidence consistent with this viewpoint. Certainly the overall stability of levels of political knowledge in the face of profound structural change is puzzling. The case studies of aggregate gains and losses in knowledge about particular facts, however, suggest that levels of public knowledge are not always immutable. And although the specific information learned and the reasons for learning it might not always be what an informed observer would deem the most appropriate, they are consistent with the kinds of information most emphasized by political leaders, the media, and a public weaned on the politics of personality and crisis management. Further, much of what is learned (for example, information about the issue stands of the two parties) is of clear relevance to acting as competent citizens in a representative democracy. Perhaps most important, while the conclusions drawn from our examination of specific cases—for example, that aggregate levels of knowledge increase as public officials become more prominent or as issues and processes become more relevant and visible—may seem obvious, these are precisely the kinds of relations that are assumed away in arguments suggesting that given levels of knowledge are intractable. The fact that learning occurs provides reason for believing that given the appropriate ability, motivation, and opportunity, more learning—about more civically relevant things—is possible.

CHAPTER FOUR

Who's Informed? Individual, Group, and Collective Patterns of Political Knowledge

"Why, may we ask, do you take in three dailies, and three weeklies?" "Because," she replies, "I am interested in politics and wish to know the facts."—VIRGINIA WOOLF, *Three Guineas*

His ignorance was as remarkable as his knowledge. . . . That any civilized human being in this nineteenth century should not be aware that the earth travelled round the sun appeared to me to be such an extraordinary fact that I could hardly realize it. "You appear astonished," he said, smiling at my expression of surprise. "Now that I do know it I shall do my best to forget it. . . . You see," he explained, "I consider that a man's brain is like a little empty attic, and you have to stock it with such furniture as you choose. A fool takes in all the lumber of every sort that he comes across, so that the knowledge which might be useful to him gets crowded out, or at best is jumbled up with a lot of other things, so that he has difficulty in laying his hands upon it. Now the skillful workman is very careful indeed as to what he takes into his brain-attic. He will have nothing but the tools which may help him in doing his work, but of these he has a large assortment, and all in the most perfect order. It is a mistake to think that little room has elastic walls and can distend to any extent. Depend upon it there comes a time when for every addition of knowledge you forget something that you knew before. It is of highest importance, therefore, not to have useless facts elbowing out the useful ones." "But the Solar System!" I protested. "What the deuce is it to me?" he interrupted impatiently: "you say that we go round the sun. If we went round the moon it would not make a pennyworth of difference to me or my work."—SIR ARTHUR CONAN DOYLE, *A Study in Scarlet*

Early in one of our group discussions with residents of the Richmond, Virginia, area, Tom, a forty-two-year-old office worker, eagerly entered the conversation to criticize U.S. foreign policy in the Middle East and Central America.[1] He displayed a wealth of knowledge about the history of U.S. involvement in those areas and great skepticism about the means and motives of the CIA and other agencies. When the subject of the discussion shifted to domestic politics, and later to state and local matters,

Tom fell silent, occasionally admitting when probed that he paid no attention to those other realms of politics. Tom was an *information specialist,* and his domain of expertise was foreign policy.

Our group discussions also included people like Charles, a forty-seven-year-old lab technician and Nancy, a thirty-one-year-old manager. Nancy had well-informed opinions on nearly every topic we discussed and was as comfortable with international politics as she was with local zoning issues. By contrast, Charles's views across the range of topics were moralistic and personal, based largely on his own experiences and those of others he knew. "I remember feelings more than facts," he said, acknowledging his lack of awareness of issues.

How common are information specialists like Tom? In our group discussions, they were the exception rather than the rule. Most people we spoke with were like Charles and Nancy: it was relatively easy to characterize them as highly, moderately, or poorly informed about politics. This could simply reflect the idiosyncracies of the twenty-one people with whom we spoke. Generalizing to the U.S. public requires more systematic evidence.

The patterns of knowledge referred to in the chapter title have two meanings. One is a micro-level phenomenon and pertains to how individual citizens organize and access political information—that is, how it is structured in the mind. The other meaning is systemic and refers to the pattern of information holding across the citizenry. The two notions are related—how citizens collect and store political information has implications for the range of knowledge they will have, which in turn affects how knowledge is distributed among citizens.

Understanding the patterns in what citizens learn and retain is important for several reasons. For researchers, the patterns are a key to developing a reliable and valid measure of political knowledge. A common criticism of attempts to gauge what citizens know is that there is no particular set of facts that an appropriately informed citizen need know. As we noted earlier, knowledge is relative, and thus more knowledge of politics is better than less, regardless of its specific content. Knowledge is also situational, meaning that the importance of any particular fact depends on the use to which it is put. Finally, within these general rules, knowledge of the institutions and processes of politics, of substantive issues, and of political leaders and parties is of central import in acting as an effective citizen.

No single test could include all the facts that might be deemed politically relevant. Thus, the reliability and validity of any scale purporting to measure general political knowledge depend in part on how well it captures the larger pattern of what people know.[2] On one hand, if citizens tend to specialize a great deal, a single index of knowledge is apt to lack validity—not knowing the particular facts on which one is tested would be little indication of what else he or she may know about politics. On the other hand, if citizens who know about one area of politics also tend to know about others (or if the degree of specialization is limited to a few identifiable areas), a small but carefully crafted set of questions can serve as a good indicator of what citizens know more broadly.

There is another, more theoretical reason for determining whether citizens tend to be specialists or generalists. It is possible that while most citizens find it irrational to be broadly informed about politics, they may learn about issues of relevance to them. This pluralist model describes a rational division of labor among the public and ensures that the collective interests of citizens will be protected by the potential actions of specialists.[3] As noted in chapter 1, there are reasons for doubting whether the aggregation of the opinions of issue specialists would produce the same determination of the public good as would the deliberation of generalists. Nonetheless, if the pluralist model is an accurate description of how information is distributed among citizens, then low aggregate levels of political knowledge may be less problematic to the functioning of democracy than is often implied. If, however, citizens are generalists, the questions of how informed the public is and who is more or less informed become critical.

Related to this are questions about the *variability* in knowledge across citizens and the *shape* of that distribution. Whereas the low mean level of political knowledge is the "fact" most widely cited in characterizations of the mass public, the level of variability is at least as politically consequential. As Philip Converse has speculated: "it is my belief that most of us rather underestimate just how great the differences [among citizens in their level of political knowledge] actually are. They are not just 'differences.' They are orders of magnitudes of differences and conceivably in a real way, orders of magnitudes of orders of magnitudes" (1990: 373).

The data in chapter 2 showed considerable variation in knowledge about specific facts. Yet variation in individual items drawn from different surveys tells us little about how knowledge, once aggregated into broader domains, is distributed among citizens at a particular time. The shape of this distribution—whether there are concentrations at high, medium, or low points on a continuum of knowledge—has significant political implications.[4] In particular, given the centrality of political knowledge to effective citizenship, it is important to consider how the distribution of knowledge is related to the distribution of other politically relevant resources in the society. The political equality of all citizens depends fundamentally on the ability of citizens to discern their individual and collective interests and to act effectively on them. Although inequality in other kinds of resources (such as money for contributing to interest groups or campaigns) renders some citizens more effective than others, the system still provides a substantial measure of political power through such tools as the vote. But inequalities in political knowledge that correspond with those of more tangible resources can result in corresponding inequalities in the effectiveness of even relatively simple or easy means of participation.

In this chapter we will explore the patterns of political knowledge at three levels—individual, collective, and group. Beginning with a systematic test of whether citizens are best described as generalists or specialists, we conclude that while there is some evidence for modest specialization, citizens tend to be more or less informed about all aspects of national politics. We will then examine the distribution of general political knowledge in the U.S. public, showing that citizens vary dramatically in how much they know. The public as a whole cannot accurately be described as ignorant (or, for that matter, well informed). Finally, we will explore group differences in political knowledge, documenting that those groups most disadvantaged economically and socially—and who, not coincidentally, have been historically restricted in their civic involvement—are also the least likely to be informed about politics and thus continue to be politically disadvantaged as well.

Patterns of Knowledge about Different Political Topics

Imagine that someone knows that the Reagan administration supported the Contras in their effort to overthrow the government of Nicaragua. Does this indicate that he or she is also likely to be knowledgeable about other aspects of the administration's Nicaragua policy? About foreign policy more generally? And how does this knowledge relate to a different area of politics, such as a citizen's awareness of basic civil liberties guaranteed by the Constitution? To answer these questions, let us first consider two alternative models.

One model views political knowledge as a "general trait" (Zaller, 1986).[5] Although some people may be more informed than others, those who are well informed about one aspect of politics are likely to be well informed about others—exemplified by Nancy in our group discussions. By the same token, citizens like Charles who are uninformed in one area are likely to be uninformed in others. This unidimensional model of political knowledge implies that sources of information (mainly formal education and the mass media) regularly address a broad range of topics and that citizens vary in their attention to these sources. In addition, the nationalization of both education and the news media—especially television—means that most citizens are exposed to the same pool of information. Finally, citizens are motivated to learn about politics not by narrow interests (or self-interest), but by a more general political interest and sense of civic duty. As a result, this learning tends to cut across specific domains of politics. Evidence for this model has been offered by Neuman (1986) and Smith (1989), both of whom used factor analysis of several NES data sets from 1956 to 1980 to argue that a variety of direct and indirect knowledge measures formed an acceptable single factor model.

The alternative view is that political knowledge is "domain specific." That is, much like Tom, citizens are specialists who are knowledgeable only in particular areas. Unlike the unidimensional model, the multidimensional model assumes that sources of information vary significantly in the topics they address, and that people have varying access to these sources and different motivations for learning about politics. Thus the pattern of knowledge reflects group differences in experiences, interest, and access to information (Owen and Stewart, 1987; Bennett, 1990). The result is a citizenry divided into numerous "issue publics" (Almond, 1950; Miller, Suchner, and Voelker, 1980; Miller, 1983).[6]

A concerted effort to find evidence of issue publics in the 1985 NES pilot survey yielded weak and mixed results. The survey included a battery of twenty-seven factual knowledge items with several questions in each of three distinct domains of politics: economics, foreign affairs, and race. It is illustrative of the somewhat subjective nature of the inquiries that different conclusions were reached by the two principal investigators, Shanto Iyengar and John Zaller. Iyengar (1990) concluded that, while the evidence is equivocal, what people know about politics is at least partially "subject-matter specific" (166). Zaller (1986) conceded that there is some evidence for domain-specific, as opposed to general, political knowledge but concluded that differences in the performance of the domain-specific and the general knowledge scales were small enough and rare enough to suggest that knowledge is "a highly general trait" (1).

A theoretically based argument and related evidence for the existence of a multidimensional knowledge structure is found in the work of many cognitive psychologists, whose concept of the *schema* has influenced many political scientists in their efforts to understand how citizens organize their cognitions about politics. According to one widely used cognitive psychology text, a schema "is a cognitive structure that represents organized knowledge about a given concept or type of stimulus. A schema contains both the attributes of the concept and the relationships among the attributes" (Fiske and Taylor, 1984: 140).[7] Schemata are by definition domain specific, though the breadth of the domain can vary widely. Further, although a given political schema is considered to be domain specific, it is also hypothesized that such schemata are likely to be connected with others. Under most circumstances, this linkage is thought to increase the speed and efficiency of information processing by facilitating the activation of relevant contextual information and attitudes when new information is received or a judgment is required. If knowledge schemata exist, we would expect them to be manifested by the appearance of fairly high intercorrelations among bits of information within a domain—in other words, by the appearance of factors or clusters of knowledge variables. And to the extent that the political schemata are linked with one another, we would expect the factors to be intercorrelated.

Given the potentially distinct mix of interest, ability, and opportunity that people bring to politics, individuals are likely to develop numerous, often idiosyncratic schemata.[8] Nonetheless, there are enough regularities to the structures and processes of American politics to anticipate that certain schema will be more common than others. For example, Richard Lau and David Sears argue that "it is safe to assume that most adults will have some sort of party schema" (1985: 360–61), and a variety of studies have attempted to test or employ this notion (Lodge and Hamill, 1986; Hamill, Lodge, and Blake, 1985; Conover and Feldman, 1984; Rahn, 1989). Ruth Hamill and Milton Lodge believe that it is plausible that some citizens would manifest multiple schemata, with the ability "to apply an ideological, partisan, racial, class, or other schema to the interpretation of political events" (1985: 92).

Stephen Bennett's (1990) analysis of the 1988 National Election Survey provides support for the existence of partisan schemas, although it also tends to reinforce the view that purely factual knowledge is more or less one-dimensional. His maximum likelihood factor analysis included both knowledge measures and evaluations of the candidates and parties and revealed three distinct factors: a "GOP-ideology-information" factor (facts and opinions that reflect positively on Republicans and negatively on Democrats); a "Democratic-issues-information" factor (facts and opinions that reflect positively on the Democrats and negatively on the Republicans); and a "specific information" factor (nonpartisan information such as having an opinion about important governmental institutions).

Our focus on objective, factual information is different from most mainstream research on political cognitions. Nonetheless, two key questions we ask in this chapter—"How are political facts organized in the minds of individual citizens?" and "What do these individual-level structures tell us about the division of 'civic labor' within the body politic more generally?"—parallel those asked by researchers interested in more valenced information and beliefs. Thus, throughout this chapter we draw, both implicitly and explicitly, on schema theory as a way of framing our analysis and interpreting patterns in the data.

Data and Methods

To obtain data that cover a wide range of factual topics, we use several different surveys. Most important is our 1989 Survey of Political Knowledge, which was designed in part to probe the dimensionality of knowledge about national politics. We also utilize several surveys that measure knowledge about more specific substantive topics (for example, knowledge of foreign affairs, gender-specific issues, or race-specific issues) and several others that measure knowledge about political arenas other than national politics (for example, state politics and local politics).

Our statistical analysis involves two steps. The first step employs confirmatory factor analysis (LISREL) to ascertain whether certain predicted patterns (or factors) exist in the data—that is, are citizens specialists or generalists and if specialists, about what kinds of topics? With LISREL, the actual interrelationships among a set of selected variables (based upon a covariance or correlation matrix) are compared to an hypothesized set of interrelationships. If the difference between the hypothesized model and actual data is small, the model is considered a plausible simplification of the latent structure underlying the data. If, in contrast, the differences are great, the model is deemed less plausible or implausible. More specifically, we compare the relative fits of a unidimensional model, which assumes that political knowledge is a general trait, with several multidimensional models that assume political knowledge is made up of relatively independent domains. An overview of dimensional analysis with LISREL is provided in Appendix 4.

The pattern of inter-item correlations is not, in and of itself, enough to determine what latent variable (for example, "general political knowledge") or variables are being tapped (Piazza, 1980; Zeller and Carmines, 1980; Smith, 1989). One must further examine the relation of the hypothesized factor(s) with other, theoretically related variables—a process known as construct validation. For example, if knowledge of partisan facts (such as, which party controls various legislative bodies) is a distinct dimension, we would expect that individuals with strong party identification are more likely than others to know such facts. The second step of the analysis uses multiple regression to compare and contrast how knowledge about different political topics correlates with variables (for example, political interest, formal education, media use) that are hypothesized to be linked to political learning. In addition to providing evidence for the presence or absence of substantively distinct knowledge factors, this analysis also helps in determining the practical utility of these distinctions, for example, by helping us to understand how citizens learn about certain topics or how they use different kinds of information in forming political opinions or making political decisions.

The analyses to follow present an often complex picture of how knowledge is structured individually and across groups of citizens. Nonetheless, they also provide a picture that is consistent and interpretable. To the general question of whether the U.S. public is composed of information specialists, the answer is no. Knowing, for example, that a citizen is informed about foreign affairs is a strong indicator that he or she is also informed about domestic affairs, about the institutions and processes of government, and about other aspects of politics. Although for several categories of knowledge (information about racial and gender issues, about partisan politics, and about local politics) we find some evidence of separate factors, these factors are still quite highly correlated with one another, indicating that most people who are knowledgeable in one area are also knowledgeable in others. We also find some distinctiveness in the patterns of relations between these domains of knowledge and key demographic, attitudinal, and behavioral variables. While not sufficient to make the case for separate issue publics, these exceptions to the rule are illuminating regarding the way individuals and groups become informed about politics and the consequences of these different pathways to political knowledge.

Knowledge of National Politics

The 1989 Survey of Political Knowledge included fifty-one questions intended to tap knowledge about three broad political domains: rules of the game, people and parties, and the substance of politics. These three domains encompassed seven more specific ones: institutions and processes, civil rights and liberties, public figures, party politics, domestic affairs, foreign affairs, and political history. After determining the extent to which the three broad domains were themselves unidimensional in nature, we used LISREL to explore different hypothetical structural models. We compared three models: a unidimensional model; a three-dimensional model based on the originally hypothesized domains; and a five-dimensional model that builds on the findings of our analyses of dimensionality within domains. Tables presenting the LISREL analysis can be found in Appendix 4.[9] A strong case for a unidimensional model can be made (see model A4.1a in table A4.1), with all the indicators of fit being quite strong. The three-dimensional model makes only modest improvements in the indicators (model A4.1b). The only hint of possible multidimensionality is in the interfactor correlations between the people-and-parties dimension and both the rules of the game (.83) and the substance of politics (.80).[10] The five-factor model, which treated knowledge of gender issues, partisan issues, and public leaders as separate dimensions, found somewhat stronger evidence of meaningful multiple dimensions, although these dimensions are still strongly correlated (model A4.1c). The lowest interfactor correlations were between gender and party (.52), between gender and civil rights and liberties (.70), and between party and issues (.72). In sum, the LISREL analyses support the view that political knowledge tends to form a single dimension, although certain evidence is consistent with the existence of correlated but partially distinct subdomains.

A wide range of variables correlate with political knowledge. Among these are interest in politics, education, media use, and demographic characteristics like gender. If political knowledge is at least partially multidimensional, we would expect the patterns of association between knowledge and these independent variables to vary, depending on the particular domain of knowledge that is being measured. We would expect, for example, knowledge about people and parties to require greater surveillance of the immediate political environment and to be more strongly correlated with media use. Knowledge of parties and partisan-related facts should be greater among strong partisans than among other citizens. And knowledge of substantive issues should be more strongly related to citizens' attention to politics than would knowledge of rules of the game. In contrast, if the hypothesized dimensions of knowledge are not very distinct, we would expect to see a consistent pattern of relations between the scales and the predictor variables.

As a test of construct validity, six knowledge scales were regressed on a set of sixteen independent variables. These scales included the three domains of knowledge initially hypothesized and the three subdomains of gender-related rights, party knowledge, and public leaders that emerged from the LISREL analyses.[11] The independent variables included five measures of motivation, four of political behavior, five of demographic characteristics, and two of educational attainment. (For a brief description of each of these variables see table A4.2 in Appendix 4.)

The results of the regression analyses are presented in table 4.1 (both unstandardized "*b*s" and standardized betas are reported).[12] The sixteen variables explain between 42 and 50 percent of the variance in each of the scales based on the three general factors. In addition to this overall consistency in the percentage of variance explained, education, income, and race had fairly similar effects across all three scales as measured by the standardized regression coefficients. The remaining variables demonstrated patterns of association that suggest slightly different pathways to political knowledge. Although generally small, most of these variations are consistent with the logic of differential learning outlined above. For example, following and talking about politics were positively correlated with all three domains of knowledge, but they were most strongly associated with knowledge of substantive political issues—the type of information requiring the greatest self-motivation to learn. Self-reports of having studied civics in high school proves a weak predictor of political knowledge, but it most closely approaches statistical significance on the domain of knowledge most likely to be taught in such classes—the rules of the game. Newspaper readership is not associated with knowledge about rules of the game (which consists of information not often or directly explained in the press), but it is positively associated with knowledge about people and parties.[13] Other sources of information (including radio or magazines that are more likely to run the gamut of political information) are positively associated with all kinds of knowledge. And television viewing, once other measures of media use are controlled for, is weakly or negatively associated with all three types of information.

Table 4.1 Regression Analyses of Knowledge Domains

Variable	Rules of the Game	Substance	People and Parties	Gender	Party	People
(scale)	(0–22)	(0–18)	(0–11)	(0–4)	(0–5)	(0–6)
Follow politics	0.44	0.53	0.27	0.01	0.14	0.13
	.11*	.15***	.08*	.01	.07	.07
Education	0.86	0.72	0.63	0.14	0.33	0.30
	.29****	.28****	.28****	.20****	.26****	.23****
Internal efficacy	0.40	0.27	−0.04	0.09	−0.02	−0.01
	.13***	.10**	−.02	.11*	−.02	−.01
Discuss politics	0.37	0.41	0.24	−0.00	0.13	0.11
	.11**	.14***	.09*	−.00	.09*	.08
Income	0.24	0.20	0.13	0.04	0.06	0.07
	.07*	.07*	.05	.06	.04	.05
Other source:	0.69	0.63	0.38	0.04	0.08	0.30
newsmagazines	.08*	.08*	.06	.02	.02	.08*
Read news in	−0.00	−0.01	0.05	−0.01	0.01	0.04
newspaper	−.00	−.02	.14****	−.02	.05	.19****
Sex (female)	−1.22	−1.76	−0.76	−0.04	−0.29	−0.47
	−.16****	−.27****	−.13****	−.02	−.09**	−.14****

Table 4.1 Regression Analyses of Knowledge Domains (*continued*)

Variable	Rules of the Game	Substance	People and Parties	Gender	Party	People
(scale)	(0–22)	(0–18)	(0–11)	(0–4)	(0–5)	(0–6)
Other source: radio	0.89	0.23	0.79	0.11	0.30	0.50
	.09**	.03	.11***	.05	.07*	.12***
Party ID strength	−0.37	−0.09	−0.25	−0.04	0.20	0.04
	−.10**	−.03	−.09**	−.04	.12***	.03
Region (South)	−0.23	−0.01	−0.35	−0.02	−0.04	−0.31
	−.03	−.02	−.06	−.01	−.01	−.09**
Watch TV news	−0.01	−0.01	−0.00	−0.01	−0.00	−0.00
	−.02	−.02	−.01	−.05	−.00	−.01
Race (black)	−2.28	−2.10	−1.48	−0.08	−0.89	−0.59
	−.18****	−.19****	−.15****	−.03	−.16****	−.11**
Trust	−0.06	−0.29	−0.27	−0.02	−0.11	−0.16
	−.01	−.04	−.05	−.01	−.03	−.05
Age	0.02	0.02	0.07	0.00	0.04	0.02
	.07	.12***	.39****	.05	.45****	.24****
Civics instruction	0.23	0.01	−0.01	0.01	−0.05	0.05
	.05	.00	−.00	.01	−.02	.02
r^2	.42	.48	.50	.08	.41	.38
Standard error of the regression	2.89	2.33	2.04	.88	1.27	1.30

Source: 1989 Survey of Political Knowledge
Note: Top entry in each cell is the unstandardized regression coefficient (*b*). Bottom entry is the standardized coefficient (beta).
*$p<.05$. **$p<.01$. ***$p<.001$. ****$p<.0001$.

Strength of partisanship is positively and significantly associated with only one domain of knowledge: people and parties. Disaggregating this domain into separate "people" and "party" scales further clarifies this relation and reveals a potentially important schema through which citizens filter political information. The party scale—knowledge of party control of the House and Senate and the party identification of Nixon, Truman, and Franklin Roosevelt—was significantly associated with strength of party identification, while the people scale—chiefly the identification of current public officials—was not. This is consistent with the notion that partisanship is a concept around which many citizens organize their knowledge of the political world. Notably, education remained a strong predictor of both scales.

Several other suggestive patterns also emerge from the demographic measures. Males are generally more informed than are females, but this association is especially strong regarding substantive issues. Further, the association between sex and rules of the game (beta = -.16) is due more to gender differences in knowledge of political processes (.20) than political rights (.10), a finding consistent with a motivational basis for some of our demographic relations (that is, given the history of women's struggle for inclusion into the political sphere, issues of political rights are likely to be more salient to women than are national political processes). Significantly, a knowledge scale based only on gender-relevant information (information about suffrage and abortion rights) is the only one of our scales for which gender did not have a significant impact. Younger citizens are only a little less likely than older ones to know about the kinds of political facts taught in schools (in which they have been recent captive audiences), but are much less likely to know about current public figures and the political parties.[14]

Corroboration for the findings of the Survey of Political Knowledge is provided by two pilot surveys of the National Election Studies. Although neither survey was as broad as our 1989 study, each had particular strengths. One facilitated a search for issue publics, and the other provided a more extensive measurement of partisan knowledge for comparison with other domains.

The 1985 NES pilot survey probed domain-specific knowledge in three areas: five questions dealt with racial issues and leaders, nine with foreign affairs, and seven with economic matters. A LISREL analysis showed that a unidimensional model performed well.[15] A three-dimensional model (based on the different substantive topics tapped by the questions) made marginal improvements in the fit of the data. The interfactor correlations, while not as large as those found in the 1989 survey, were substantial and consistent across the three factors (.79 to .85). A test of construct validity provided little additional support for the existence of distinct issue publics. The one statistically and substantively interesting difference across the three domains was the impact of race. Blacks were significantly less knowledgeable than nonblacks on foreign policy, economic policy, and general political knowledge, but there were no substantive or statistically significant differences on race-relevant issues.[16]

The 1991 NES pilot included four of the civics knowledge items we had developed for the 1989 survey, along with a wide range of questions on party-related issues and about the identity of domestic and foreign leaders. The results of our LISREL analyses closely matched those described above: a single factor model yielded an acceptable fit, while a three-factor model with intercorrelated dimensions (interfactor correlations ranging from .70 to .86) improved the fit slightly. The lowest interfactor correlation was between rules of the game and partisan knowledge (.70), providing further evidence for the partial distinctiveness of information about the parties. The construct validation told the same general story.

The results of our analyses of the 1985 and 1991 NES data provide additional evidence for some domain-specificity of political knowledge, but they also suggest that even with substantively distinct topics like international relations, economics, and race, the subdomains of knowledge are strongly intercorrelated. Put more concretely, we continue to find that, for example, while knowledge about the United Nations is a good predictor of knowledge about other aspects of international relations, it is almost as good a predictor of knowledge about racial issues, economic issues, and, ultimately, of general knowledge about national politics itself. Finally, it is quite notable that knowledge about the institutions and processes of government—information which the mass media rarely stress—is highly intercorrelated with knowledge about current issues and people in politics. People who retain knowledge of current issues also tend to have knowledge of both the means by which issues are dealt with by the political system and the political elites who deal with them.

Knowledge about State and Local Politics

A strong theoretical argument can be made for the existence of distinct dimensions of political knowledge across different levels of government. The extent of political participation varies across national, state, and local levels, as do the types of people who participate in these arenas (Milbrath and Goel, 1977; Verba and Nie, 1972). Many theorists and practitioners argue that state and local politics involve issues that are more tangible, immediate, and personal and so are more likely to engage citizens (Boyte, 1980). High rates of mobility among the populace suggest that many citizens will have lived in their communities for too short a time to know much about them. Furthermore, information about state and local politics is much less likely to be taught in schools, and the array of media covering these issues is different from that covering national issues. All of this suggests not only that citizens may differ in how knowledgeable they are from level-to-level of government, but also that the sorts of people who are informed about each level may vary.

We conducted a statewide Virginia survey in 1990 to examine the dimensionality of state versus national political knowledge. This survey included several items measuring knowledge about state-level politics, as well as a small set of national knowledge items. In 1991 we conducted another survey in Richmond, Virginia. This was designed to gauge the dimensionality of local knowledge, and it included five national and four local knowledge items. For the results of several LISREL analyses using these two surveys see tables A4.3 and A4.4. In the statewide survey, a single-factor model (model A4.3a in table A4.3) produced a poor statistical fit, and a model distinguishing between knowledge of national politics and knowledge of state politics (model A4.3b in table A4.3) did little to improve this fit. But a three-factor model (model A4.3c in table A4.3), which separated partisan knowledge from knowledge of both national and state politics, performed well. In addition, the interfactor correlations were consistent with the notion of partially distinct factors (.74 between national and state knowledge). The fact that state and national partisan knowledge loaded together, along with the lower interfactor correlation between party knowledge and the other two factors (.66 for each), is further evidence of the existence of a somewhat distinct partisan schema among citizens, a schema that cuts across different levels of government.

Our data indicate that local politics is even more distinct from national politics. A one-factor model (model A4.4a in table A4.4) that combined knowledge of national and local politics had an unacceptable statistical fit, but a two-dimensional model in which these two levels were treated as distinct fit the data well (model A4.4b in table A4.4). The interfactor correlation (.69) was sufficiently small to support the notion of partially separate domains.

Regressing the local, state, party, and national knowledge scales from the two surveys on a set of independent variables adds to the evidence that these domains are somewhat distinct (see tables 4.2 and 4.3). This is especially true for the local versus national comparison (table 4.3). Knowledge of national politics is significantly related both to gender (men are more knowledgeable) and to having children living at home (those with children are less knowledgeable), but no such relations exist for knowledge of local politics. These patterns are consistent with the argument that women remain most closely tied to private and semiprivate spheres (which intersect with local politics in such institutions as the public schools), while men continue to dominate the public and, especially, national spheres (Elshtain, 1981; Darcy, Welch, and Clark, 1987). They also suggest that although having children at home serves as a distraction from national politics, this is more than counteracted by the special relevance of local politics to those with children. Also telling is the finding that although blacks in our sample were less knowledgeable than whites about national politics, they were significantly more knowledgeable than whites (controlling for socioeconomic characteristics) about the aspects of local politics tapped in the 1991 Richmond city survey. This result strongly suggests that the context of politics is critically important for what citizens learn. The population of Richmond is more than one-half African American, and the city government is biracial in its makeup. At the time of the survey, both the city manager and superintendent of schools were black, and black respondents were more likely than white ones to be able to name them. However, the benefits of black empowerment go beyond the ability to name important black leaders. Black respondents were as knowledgeable as whites about the rules of the game in Richmond politics, including about the existence of a ward system for elections and the appointment process for selecting the mayor.

Table 4.2 Construct Validity of National and State Scales

Variable	National	Party	State	Overall
(Scale)	(0–4)	(0–5)	(0–7)	(0–16)
Employment status	0.04	−0.04	−0.19	−0.19
	.03	−.02	−.08*	−0.4
Marital status	0.03	−0.04	0.01	−0.01
	.01	−.01	.00	−.00
Race	0.34	0.79	−0.04	1.1
	.11***	.17***	−.01	.10***
Gender	0.30	0.64	0.58	1.5
	.12***	0.18***	.13***	.18***
Education	0.44	0.41	0.66	1.5
	.42***	.27***	.33***	.41***
Age	−0.01	0.03	0.03	0.05
	−.11***	.24***	.20***	.17***
Income	0.09	0.08	0.25	0.42
	.10**	.06	.15***	.14***
Party strength	−0.07	0.31	−0.12	0.11
	−.05	.14***	−.04	.02
Follow politics	0.17	0.42	0.65	1.2
	.13***	.21***	.26***	.26***
Adjusted r^2	.37	.30	.34	.45

Source: 1990 statewide Virginia survey.
Note: Top entry in each cell is the unstandardized regression coefficient (*b*). Bottom entry is the standardized coefficient (beta).
$^{*}p<.05$. $^{**}p<.01$. $^{***}p<.001$.

Table 4.3 Construct Validity of National and Local Scales

Variable	National	Local	Overall
(Scale)	(0–4)	(0–5)	(0–9)
Employment status	−0.05	0.29	0.24
	−.02	.09**	.05
Marital status	0.04	0.16	0.20
	.01	.05	.04
Race	0.63	−0.31	0.33
	.22***	−.10**	.07*

Table 4.3 Construct Validity of National and Local Scales (*continued*)

Variable	National	Local	Overall
(Scale)	(0–4)	(0–5)	(0–9)
Gender	0.61	0.06	0.66
	.21***	.02	.13***
Children	−0.11	0.02	−0.10
	−.08**	0.01	−.04
Education	0.55	0.50	1.06
	.43***	.38***	.47***
Age	0.01	0.27	0.28
	.01	.27***	.17***
Income	−0.02	0.09	0.08
	−.01	.06	.03
Newspapers	0.00	0.05	0.05
	.00	.16***	.10***
Television	−0.23	−0.03	−0.26
	−.06*	−.01	−.04
Radio	0.14	0.05	0.19
	.04	.01	.03
Follow politics	0.07	0.09	0.16
	.09**	.11***	.12***
Vote presidential race	0.17	0.27	0.44
	.05	.08*	.08**
Adjusted r^2	.43	.32	.41

Source: 1991 Richmond city survey.
Note: Top entry in each cell is the unstandardized regression coefficient (*b*). Bottom entry is the standardized coefficient (beta).
*$p<.05$. **$p<.01$. ***$p<.001$.

Three conclusions emerge from our examination of the structure of political knowledge. First, in all but two of the analyses (the comparison of state and national and the comparison of local and national data), a single-factor model provided a statistically acceptable simplification of how political knowledge is structured among individual citizens. In the national surveys, knowledge about the substance of politics, about political actors, and about the institutions and processes of politics were all highly intercorrelated.

Second, in spite of the general unidimensionality of knowledge, the statistical performance of the model usually was improved by increasing the number of factors in substantively meaningful ways. This improvement was most dramatic in distinguishing local and state politics from national politics (where a unidimensional model was not a statistically acceptable representation of patterns in the data) and in separating partisan knowledge from other types. Distinguishing among different substantive issue areas (most notably gender and race) also made appreciable, though modest, improvements in some models.

Third, in spite of this evidence of domain specificity, the individual factors in all of the models were correlated with one another (see table 4.4). The median interfactor correlation across the five data sets was .78, and it ranged from .97 (rules of the game with substance of politics) to .52 (gender issues with partisan knowledge). Even issue areas that are conceptually quite distinct displayed high intercorrelations (for example, .85 between knowledge of racial issues and foreign policy).

Table 4.4 Summary of Interfactor Correlations

Domains	Correlation	Data Source	Number of Dimensions in Model Tested
Rules of the game X substance of politics	.97	1989 SPK	3
Gender issues X substance of politics	.89	1989 SPK	5
Rules of the game X people	.86	1991 NES	3
Racial issues X foreign policy	.85	1985 NES	3
Rules of the game X people and parties	.83	1989 SPK	3
Economic issues X foreign policy	.82	1985 NES	3
Substance of politics X people and parties	.80	1989 SPK	3
Party X people	.80	1989 SPK	5
Party X people	.79	1991 NES	3
Racial issues X economic issues	.79	1985 NES	3
Gender issues X people	.77	1989 SPK	5
Party X rules of the game	.75	1989 SPK	5
State politics X national politics	.74	1990 VA	3
Party X substance of politics	.72	1989 SPK	5
Party X rules of the game	.70	1991 NES	5
Gender X rules of the game	.70	1989 SPK	5
Local politics X national politics	.69	1991 RICH	2
Party X state politics	.66	1990 VA	3
Party X national politics	.66	1990 VA	3
Party X gender issues	.52	1989 SPK	5

Note: Entries (correlations) are the interfactor correlation coefficients from confirmatory factor analyses using LISREL. SPK = 1989 Survey of Political Knowledge; VA = statewide Virginia surveys; RICH = Richmond city survey; NES = National Election Study.

The Collective Distribution of Political Knowledge

The analysis thus far demonstrates that, with some important but limited exceptions, people who know a lot about one aspect of national politics also know a lot about others. The fact that most citizens are generalists is important both methodologically and substantively. Methodologically, it allows us to assume that a scale with a limited number of factual items, if carefully constructed, can be used to approximate what citizens know more generally about national politics (see Appendix 2 for a more detailed discussion of these measurement issues).

Substantively, it suggests that the pluralist model of democracy, at least as it applies to information about politics, is wrong.[17] What citizens know about politics is consistent with our notion that the requisites of contemporary democracy include being broadly informed about the rules, players, and substance of politics.

These findings raise additional questions. The fact that citizens are generalists also means that citizens who are uninformed about one area of politics are likely to be uninformed about most areas. Thus, how informed the citizenry is and who is informed become important considerations in understanding the civic competence of the general public and the distribution of political power among specific groups.

Recall that we consider knowledge of politics a resource that can benefit both the individual and the polity. Like any resource, it can be distributed in more or less equitable ways. Three hypothetical patterns of the dispersion of knowledge across the public, each of which is consistent with our finding that most citizens are generalists, are shown in table 4.5. Each asterisk represents 1 percent of the public. In the first, labeled *managerial democracy,* knowledge is distributed among the populace in the shape of a pyramid, with a wide base and narrow peak. In this model, a few individuals are very knowledgeable about politics, but most citizens are uninformed. We call this model "managerial" because it implies that only a few individuals are in a position to make effective use of their democratic rights and thus to exercise disproportionate influence over the making of public policy. Gross characterizations of the public as inert, apathetic, and ignorant imply this type of distribution.

Table 4.5 Three Hypothetical Distributions of Political Knowledge

	Managerial Democracy	Pragmatic Democracy	Strong Democracy
High Knowledge	*	**	*******************
	***	*****	*****************
	*****	*********	***************
	*******	**************	*************
	*********	********************	***********
	***********	********************	*********
	*************	**************	*******
	***************	*********	*****
Low	*****************	*****	***
Knowledge	*******************	**	*

Note: The figures display hypothetical distributions of respondents, with the highest scores at the top of the figure and the lowest scores at the bottom. Each asterisk represents 1 percent of respondents.

At the opposite extreme is *strong democracy.* Here the pyramid is inverted, implying that most citizens are highly informed and only a few are underinformed or uninformed. This model conforms most closely with the civic assumptions of democracy in which citizens are able to play an active, even direct, role in governing themselves. Between the two models is a third alternative, in which the distribution of knowledge is diamond-shaped. Here the population is divided into a few very informed people, a few totally uninformed people, and most people who cluster in the middle ranges of knowledge (if plotted as a graph it would take the form of the normal distribution—the familiar bell curve). This distribution, which we call *pragmatic democracy,* would be the product of a political culture in which the acquisition of political information was a civic norm, political information was reasonably accessible through the schools and the mass media, and most citizens had enough motivation and cognitive skill to gather and retain at least a moderate amount of factual knowledge (Neuman, 1986: 170–78).

How does the actual distribution of knowledge compare to these hypothetical ones? One answer to this question, based on a simple additive scale composed of all the knowledge items in our 1989 Survey of Political Knowledge (see Appendix 2 for a description of the validity and reliability of this scale) is shown in table 4.6. We divided the scale (which ranged from 0 to 51) into ten equal segments (0 to 5, 6 to 10, and so on, through 46 to 51) and then plotted the percentage of respondents falling within each segment.[18]

Table 4.6 Actual Distribution of Political Knowledge

Level of Knowledge (% correct on scale)	Political Knowledge (by score deciles)
90–100	
80–89	**
70–79	*******
60–69	***************
50–59	*********************
40–49	********************
30–39	*****************
20–29	************
10–19	*****
0–9	*
	median = 49%

Note: Each asterisk represents 1 percent of respondents.

The shape of the distribution comes a good deal closer to the model of pragmatic democracy than to either the strong or managerial models. This suggests, as did our analyses of individual items in chapter 3, a somewhat more informed public than many observers assume. Whether or not this level of information is enough for most citizens to engage the political system effectively is an issue we explore in chapter 6. At a minimum, however, it provides some initial evidence in support of our argument that if theories of collective rationality, heuristic decision making, and on-line processing are accurate descriptions of how most citizens make sense of the political world, it is because most citizens have a base of knowledge from which to do so.

At the same time, the finding that most citizens are at least modestly informed about politics should not obscure the fact that there is still substantial inequality in how much people know. Even this fairly normal distribution of information results in large differences across knowledge classes—the mean percent correct for the most-informed 30 percent of our sample was nearly three times greater than that for the least-informed third (see table 4.7). To the extent that political knowledge has an impact on one's ability to engage the system effectively, these differences suggest that a large segment of the population is disadvantaged politically. This is reason for concern in a democracy. It is especially troubling, however, if variations in knowledge levels mirror variations in other political resources.

Table 4.7 Knowledge Classes

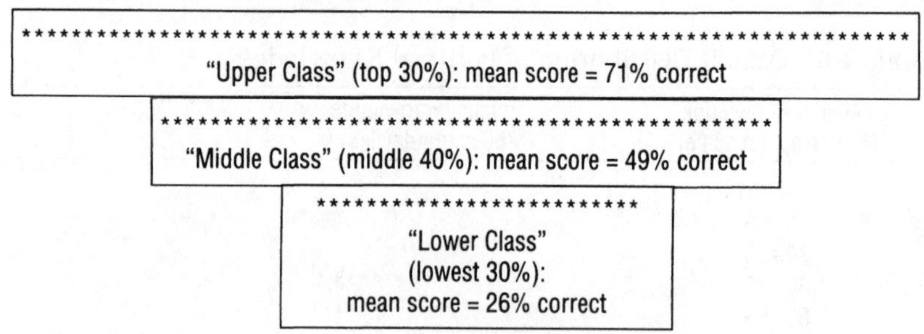

Note: Each asterisk represents 1 percent correct.

Group Differences in Political Knowledge

In studies of citizenship "the public" is often treated as a single, undifferentiated collection of people. There are, of course, good reasons for doing this. People differ in a host of ways, but as citizens each adult is granted the same status. In theory, at least, each citizen's voice, whether heard directly through the vote or indirectly through a public opinion survey, is weighed equally. In addition, much of "the public good" and "the public will" is consensual, rising above cultural and economic differences (Mansbridge, 1983). To the extent that citizens' politically relevant interests are similar or compatible, the question of *how* informed the public is would outweigh the question of *who* is informed: a rising tide lifts all ships equally when they are anchored in the same port.

But as theorists from Rousseau to Mansbridge also argue, much of politics is about the determination of the public good, a process that benefits from the input of citizens with diverse interests. In some cases, broad-based input facilitates consensus building: citizens are forced to take the needs of others into account in constructing a vision of the public good. This is true whether one envisions the general will as the simple aggregation of individual and group interests or as a more distinct phenomenon in which the whole is more than the sum of its parts. Thus, even when politics deals with consensual issues, democracy is furthered as the range of informed opinions upon which a consensus is built increases.

In addition, not all politics is consensual. Individual, group, and class interests differ on many issues. Much of politics inevitably involves conflict over the allocation of scarce goods and services. Indeed, many of the things we value as a society derive their worth directly from their relative scarcity, a characteristic of what Fred Hirsch (1976) calls "positional" goods and services.

Because much of politics is conflictual, the study of politics often centers on issues of power. And information is a central form of political power. Further, in the battle for "who gets what, when, and how" (Lasswell, 1958), it is the relative power wielded by competing political interests that is important. In the realm of adversarial politics, the question of who is informed becomes paramount.

As we will demonstrate in chapter 6, less informed segments of the public are—in part because of their lack of knowledge—less able to discern their political interests, less likely to participate in politics, and, most important, less likely to connect their political interests effectively to their political participation. Democracy requires not only an arena for the management of conflict, but also citizens who are equally capable of representing their often disparate interests in that arena. Without this relative equality, politics becomes little more than the institutionalization of economic and social inequities—a kind of political caste system.

Documenting Group Differences in Political Knowledge

Although there is no shortage of important, often idiosyncratic conflicts in American politics, much of this nation's enduring political history has been defined by four critical struggles: between the economically advantaged and the economically disadvantaged; between whites and blacks; between men and women; and (in a somewhat different way) between the generation in power and the generations that precede and follow it. In part these struggles result from differences in how each group defines both its own interest and the public interest. They also result from the historical exclusion of the poor, blacks, women, and young adults from many aspects of the public sphere. Indeed, the two sources of conflict are closely related. The political limits placed on members of these groups were often justified by assuming that they lacked the civic capacity to know what was in their own or the public interest. Differences in opinion were thought to reflect ignorance rather than objective conditions or the contestable nature of politics. Even when these differences were granted as legitimate, political theorists and practitioners tended to conflate the interests of socioeconomic elites with the public good, and so privilege their views over those of less advantaged citizens. Restricting the public life of members of these groups, however, made it unlikely that they would have the opportunity, or would develop the necessary motivation and ability, for competent citizenship. As a result, the fears of political theorists become a self-fulfilling prophesy: members of these groups are often less likely to discern their interests, tie them to the public interest, or translate them into effective political action.

Legal restrictions on political participation based on class, race, gender, and age have all but disappeared in the United States, but the full integration of these groups into public life has yet to be achieved. Many of the ways citizens become politically informed involve social and economic circumstances (for example, formal education and politically impinged occupations) that are still less accessible to members of these groups. The legacy of past exclusion also has created norms and expectations that continue to serve as subtle barriers to political engagement. Thus, there is reason to believe that members of these traditionally excluded groups continue to be less politically informed than their more advantaged counterparts.

Comparisons of how well members of these groups were able to answer the individual questions about national politics contained in our 1989 survey and the 1988 NES survey are revealing (see tables 4.8 and 4.9). The size of the knowledge gaps vary from item to item, but the overall pattern is compelling: men are more informed than women; whites are more informed than blacks; those with higher incomes are more informed than those with lower incomes; and older citizens are more informed than younger ones.

The extent of these differences can be summarized in several ways. Of the sixty-eight questions asked across the two surveys, the percentage correct for women was as high or higher than that for men in only five cases, and in no case was the percentage correct for blacks as high as for whites or for low-income citizens as high as that for upper-income ones. The comparison across age cohorts reveals a somewhat more variable pattern, although fifty-five of the sixty-eight questions were answered correctly by a greater percentage of pre–baby boomers than post–baby boomers.

The sizes of these gaps in knowledge are substantial. The median percent correct across all the items in the 1989 survey (see table 4.8) for men was 1.35 times that for women; for pre–baby boomers, 1.38 times that for post–baby boomers; for more affluent citizens, 1.59 times that of relatively poor citizens; and for whites, more than twice that for blacks.

The cumulative effect of these question-by-question differences can be gauged by summing across all the items to make a knowledge index. A summary of the distribution of scores on the 1989 knowledge index arranged by group is shown in figure 4.1. These "box plots" graphically illustrate the disparity in knowledge across gender, race, income, and age cohorts. Fully three-quarters of the women in our survey scored below the median for men. Substantially more than three-quarters of those from families earning under $20,000 a year scored below the median for those earning more than $50,000, as was the case for post–baby boomers when compared to pre–baby boomers. And three-quarters of black Americans scored below three-quarters of white Americans, a knowledge gap of dramatic proportions. Similar patterns were found in the 1988 NES data.[19]

As a final demonstration of the extent of group differences in political knowledge, we compared the average scores on the two knowledge scales (measured as the percent of the questions answered correctly) for members of different segments of the population (figure 4.2). The average score for the total 1989 sample was 47 percent and for the 1988 NES sample it was 50 percent, meaning the typical citizen could answer about half the questions correctly. This average masks substantial differences across different segments of the population. These differences are especially dramatic when considered for groups of citizens that combine the advantages and disadvantages associated with age, class, race, and gender. The most informed citizens were older males whose family income exceeded $50,000 (65 percent correct on the 1989 scale and 76 percent correct on the 1988 scale). These scores were over two and a half times higher than

Table 4.8 Group Differences in Knowledge of National Politics (Percentage Correct)

Survey Item	Men	Women	White	Black	Upper[a]	Middle[a]	Lower[a]	Pre–Baby Boom[b]	Baby Boom[b]	Post–Baby Boom[b]
Length of presidential term	96	95	97	89	97	97	93	96	97	93
What is a veto	94	85	93	61	96	92	81	91	88	83
Does U.S. have a trade deficit	91	73	86	58	95	89	68	82	83	85
Is there a right to counsel	90	92	91	89	92	89	94	89	91	97
Can veto be overridden	90	75	85	60	85	85	76	86	79	78
Did women always have suffrage	89	90	94	71	95	95	81	91	91	77
Does U.S. have a budget deficit	82	74	84	45	88	87	66	80	78	71
Name governor	81	66	76	62	82	79	67	78	71	62
Did U.S. support Contras	76	57	71	33	88	69	59	65	69	59
Name vice president	79	69	80	38	91	83	58	79	71	67
Must students pledge allegiance	78	74	79	55	84	80	69	74	77	75
Nixon's party	79	76	80	65	86	81	73	88	74	74
Can states prohibit abortion	75	71	76	54	84	74	69	68	77	74
Party control of House	73	64	72	44	85	72	63	77	68	31
Who reviews law's constitutionality	72	60	69	49	85	70	55	69	67	45
Contras are rebels	68	42	58	30	79	56	47	54	56	49
FDR's party	67	59	67	44	72	64	56	85	46	36
Define recession	65	50	62	25	72	60	44	62	54	49
Status of abortion before *Roe*	63	54	59	64	57	61	54	60	56	62
Truman's party	63	54	62	37	65	61	50	80	40	36
Who appoints judges	60	56	62	32	72	64	46	67	52	41
Name one of your U.S. senators	61	50	59	33	75	57	49	66	50	28
Can communist run for president	59	41	51	48	63	55	38	50	50	47
Party control of Senate	58	52	59	31	77	59	46	64	50	36
Describe recent arms agreement	57	39	53	12	65	52	34	48	48	41
Define effects of a tariff	56	48	56	28	60	59	42	51	52	54
Describe one Fifth Amendment right	56	45	55	27	61	55	40	51	53	37

Table 4.8 Group Differences in Knowledge of National Politics (Percentage Correct) (*continued*)

Survey Item	Men	Women	White	Black	Upper[a]	Middle[a]	Lower[a]	Pre–Baby Boom[b]	Baby Boom[b]	Post–Baby Boom[b]
Size of federal budget	56	42	53	26	57	54	41	46	51	51
What are first ten amendments called	53	39	50	13	66	48	37	41	49	53
% required to override veto	50	21	37	22	54	37	26	37	32	32
U.S. supports El Salvadoran government	50	37	44	33	47	45	39	41	47	36
Describe one First Amendment right	42	32	40	15	46	40	31	29	42	47
Percent unemployed	41	14	29	7	46	26	22	33	23	13
Who declares war	40	29	36	10	48	36	25	33	36	32
Rehnquist's ideology	37	24	30	28	44	30	26	29	31	36
Name U.S. representative	31	27	32	16	41	27	29	39	21	17
Name both U.S. senators	31	19	28	13	44	28	13	32	21	10
Federal budget: education	24	14	19	11	29	18	19	15	24	17
What is the Superfund	24	5	16	3	34	13	9	13	17	4
% poor in U.S.	23	15	22	2	29	24	8	18	21	12
Describe two First Amendment rights	22	16	20	5	23	21	15	15	21	25
Define the New Deal	20	11	17	3	29	14	13	21	11	5
% black in U.S.	19	7	13	5	26	14	5	12	13	12
Date of New Deal	11	13	14	0	17	13	9	18	7	9
% with health insurance	11	7	9	7	11	9	8	9	10	3
Date of women's suffrage	10	9	10	5	14	10	8	11	10	4
Federal budget: defense	10	6	7	15	9	8	6	10	6	6
Describe three First Amendment rights	9	7	8	2	11	8	6	3	10	19
Federal budget: Social Security	4	6	5	4	10	5	4	5	5	4
Describe two Fifth Amendment rights	2	2	3	0	4	3	1	2	2	2
Median % correct	56.5	42	54	26.5	65	56	41	50.5	50	36.5

Source: 1989 Survey of Political Knowledge

[a] Upper = $50,000 and above; middle = $20,000–49,999; lower = $19,999 or less.

[b] Pre–baby boom = born before 1946; baby boom = born 1946–64; post–baby boom = born after 1964.

Table 4.9 Group Differences in Knowledge of National Politics (Percentage Correct)

Survey Item	Men	Women	White	Black	Upper[a]	Middle[a]	Lower[a]	Pre–Baby Boom[b]	Baby Boom[b]	Post–Baby Boom[b]
Mikhail Gorbachev	82	63	75	47	88	78	57	70	73	62
Ted Kennedy	77	63	72	53	88	73	57	73	70	37
Party control of House	71	51	63	41	79	65	46	69	56	29
Parties' positions on defense spending	68	49	59	51	76	63	47	51	63	56
Margaret Thatcher	67	55	64	37	83	66	46	57	64	47
Ideological placement of candidates	66	48	59	38	79	62	42	52	60	50
Party control of Senate	65	46	57	38	73	58	42	65	49	26
Ideological placement of parties	63	48	57	39	79	60	40	52	58	44
Parties' positions on government spending	60	45	52	49	72	56	40	48	56	36
Parties' positions on guaranteed jobs	57	38	47	45	67	51	35	42	51	43
Yasser Arafat	55	23	40	20	57	41	25	42	36	16
Parties' positions on health insurance	54	37	46	37	65	47	35	42	48	34
George Shultz	53	28	42	19	60	40	29	48	34	20
Above average information (interviewer rating)	50	30	41	25	65	44	22	39	41	19
House candidate and his/her party	34	24	30	13	35	29	23	36	24	17
Jim Wright	22	8	15	7	26	14	10	19	12	4
William Rehnquist	5	3	4	9	10	4	9	3	4	1
Median % correct	60	45	52	38	72	56	40	48	56	34

Source: 1988 National Election Study.

[a] Upper = \$50,000 and above; middle = \$20,000–49,999; lower = \$19,999 or less.

[b] Pre–baby boom = born before 1946; baby boom = born 1946–64; post–baby boom = born after 1964.

Figure 4.1 Distribution of Political Knowledge by Demographic Groups

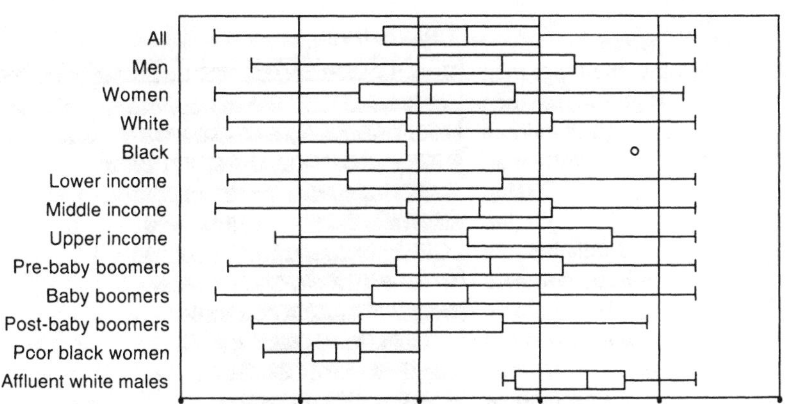

Note: Each "box" represents the people who scored from the twenty-fifth to the seventy-fifth percentile on the political knowledge index (the middle 50 percent for each of the groups in question). The "branches" extending to the left and right of each box show the range of scores achieved by the remaining most- and least-informed 25 percent. The vertical line inside each box represents the median score for each group. The "o" represents outliers that fall between 1.5 and 3.0 standard deviations above or below the middle 50 percent.

those achieved by the least informed group in our sample: black women whose family income was less than $20,000 a year (the full extent of this difference is captured in the last box plot in figure 4.1). More generally, the patterns demonstrated in both samples show the exceptionally close fit between political knowledge and socioeconomic status.

Stability and Change in Knowledge Gaps

Aggregate levels of political knowledge have remained remarkably stable over the past half century. Many of the societal changes that occurred in that time have particular relevance to the groups we are examining here. For example, changes in the economic, social, and political status of women and blacks should have narrowed the knowledge gaps with men and whites. The greater availability (and thus lowered cost) of information provided by the electronic media should have especially benefited lower-income citizens. The shifting political agenda in the 1960s and 1970s, which brought increased national attention to many social issues of special interest to younger citizens, should have raised their motivation to follow—and so learn about—politics. But did they?

Over-time data with which to examine group trends in political knowledge are relatively scarce, but the NES surveys provide some evi-

Figure 4.2 Relative Knowledge across Selected Groups

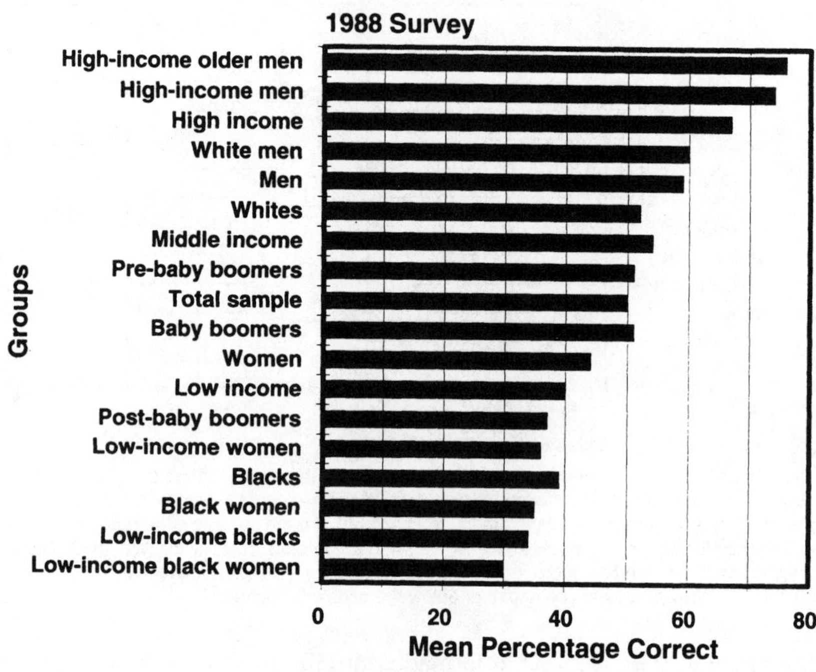

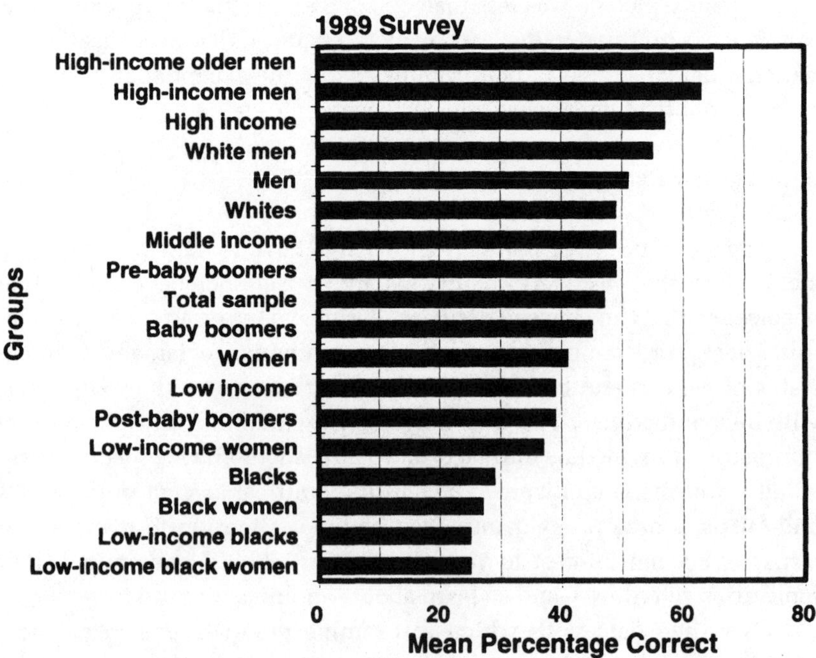

dence. Based on four knowledge items—knowing which party is more conservative, which party controlled the House of Representatives, the number of likes and dislikes mentioned about the political parties, and the number of likes and dislikes mentioned about the candidates for president—we can trace the knowledge gaps between men and women, between whites and blacks, between lower-, middle-, and upper-income citizens, and between pre–baby boomers, baby boomers, and post–baby boomers (see figures 4.3 through 4.6).[20]

The over-time patterns, with few exceptions, suggest that relative gaps in knowledge have not declined over the past thirty to forty years. Gender and class gaps in knowledge are the most consistent over time (figures 4.3 and 4.5). The knowledge levels of women and of low-income citizens—in both absolute terms and relative to men and higher-income citizens—are about the same today as they were in the 1950s and 1960s. In a way that echoes the rise and fall of the civil rights movement in the United States, the knowledge gap between blacks and whites did close between the 1950s and early 1970s, but it reemerged thereafter (figure 4.4). By 1988, the racial gap in knowledge is only slightly smaller than it was three to four decades earlier (see Rosenstone and Hansen, 1993, for parallel data on political participation). The over-time pattern among the three age cohorts is the most complicated, which is not surprising given that age is less clearly tied to social and economic advantages and that our simple analysis distinguishes poorly between generational and life cycle effects (figure 4.6). In general, pre–baby boomers and baby boomers are about equally informed, although there was a slight tendency for the latter cohort to have been less informed than the former when they first entered the electorate in the mid-1960s. By the mid-to-late 1980s, however, baby boomers were equally or more informed than the older cohort. Post–baby boomers, in contrast, were less informed when they entered the electorate, and—at least for the short time line and few questions for which we have data—there is little indication that this gap is shrinking as they grow older.[21]

Because part of our 1989 national survey was devoted to the replication of several questions asked by the Gallup Organization during the 1940s and 1950s, we were able to compare group differences in knowledge across this somewhat longer time span and for a wider range of information (though for only two time points in each case). The conclusions drawn from these comparisons generally support those drawn from the NES data, with the knowledge gaps remaining relatively stable over time. The ten questions for which gender comparisons could be made showed a reasonable amount of fluctuation, with the gap declining by as much as 10 percentage points on one question (knowing which party controls the

Figure 4.3 Over-Time Trends in the Knowledge Gap, by Sex

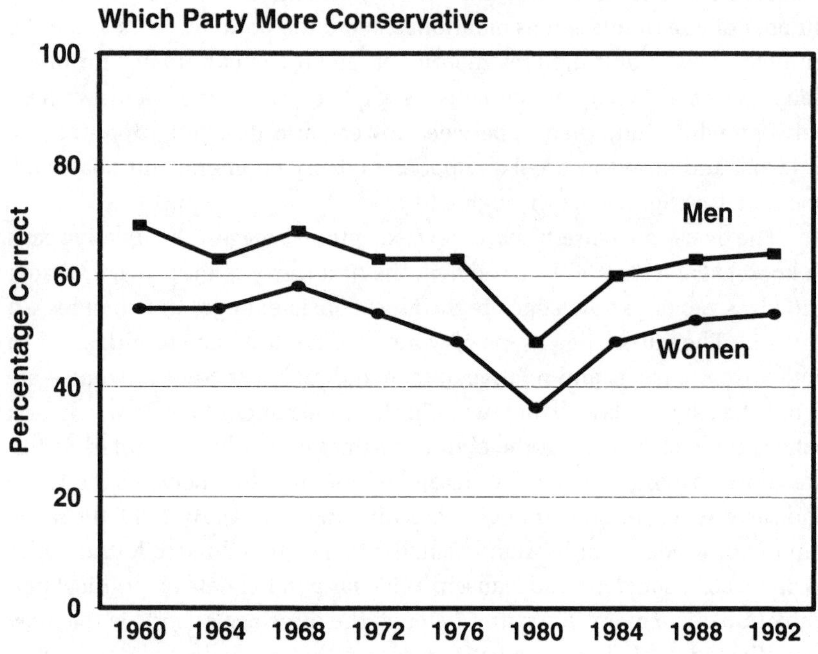

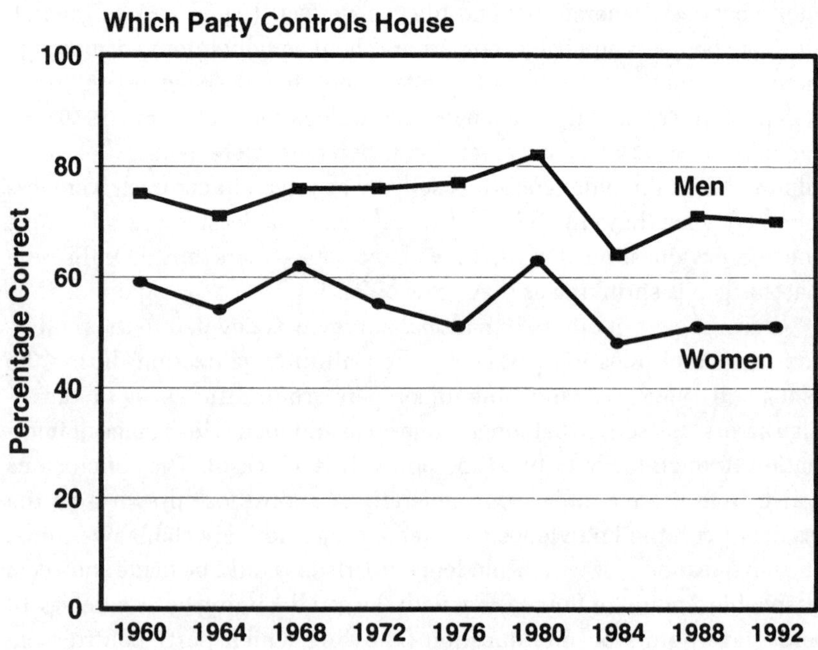

Figure 4.3 Over-Time Trends in the Knowledge Gap, by Sex (*continued*)

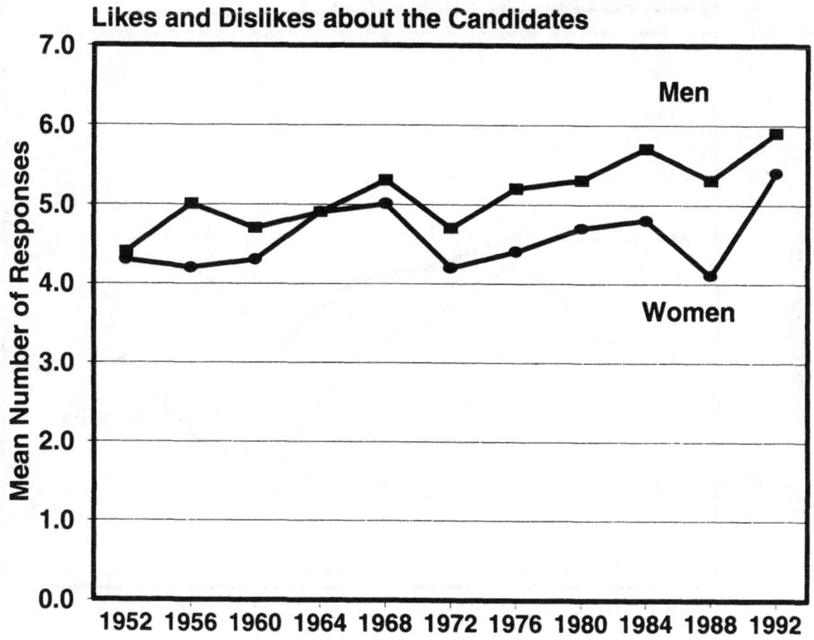

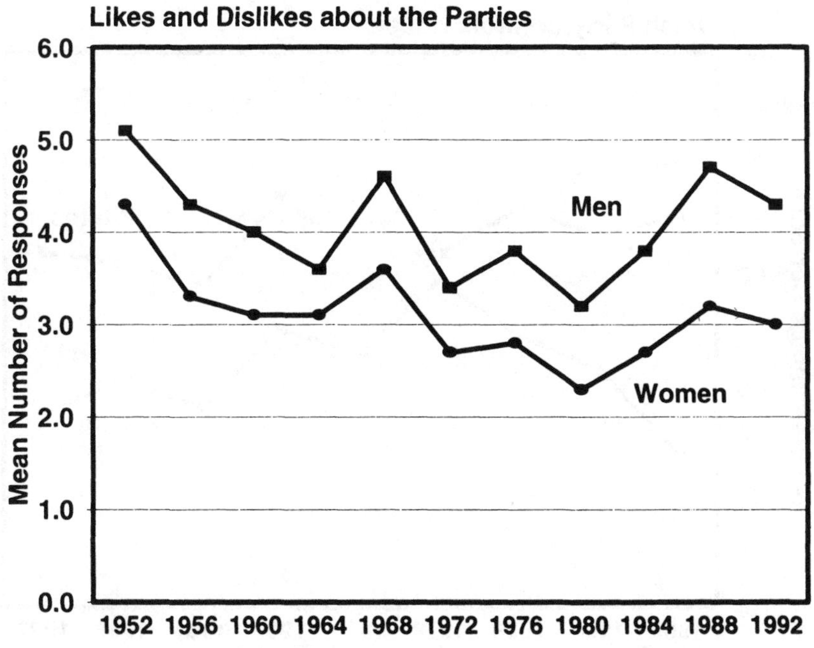

Figure 4.4 Over-Time Trends in the Knowledge Gap, by Race

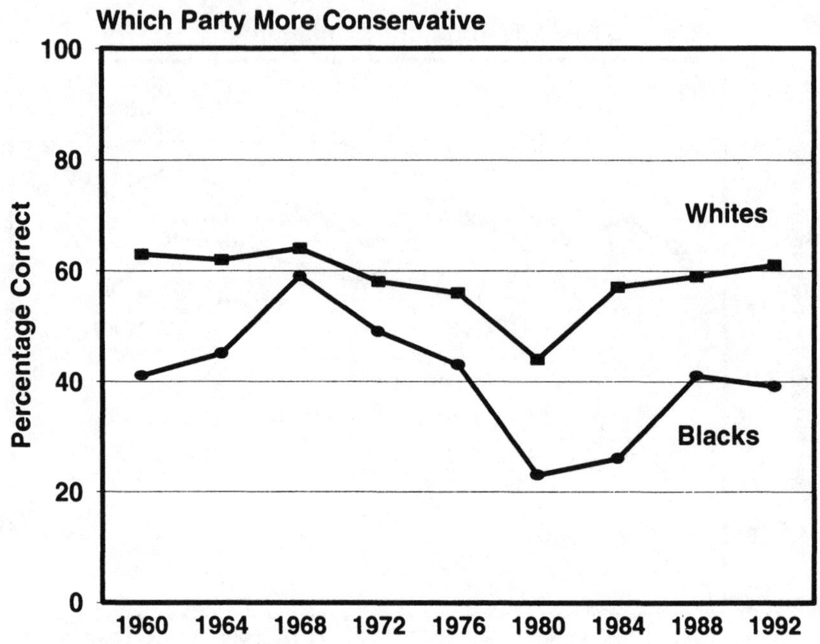

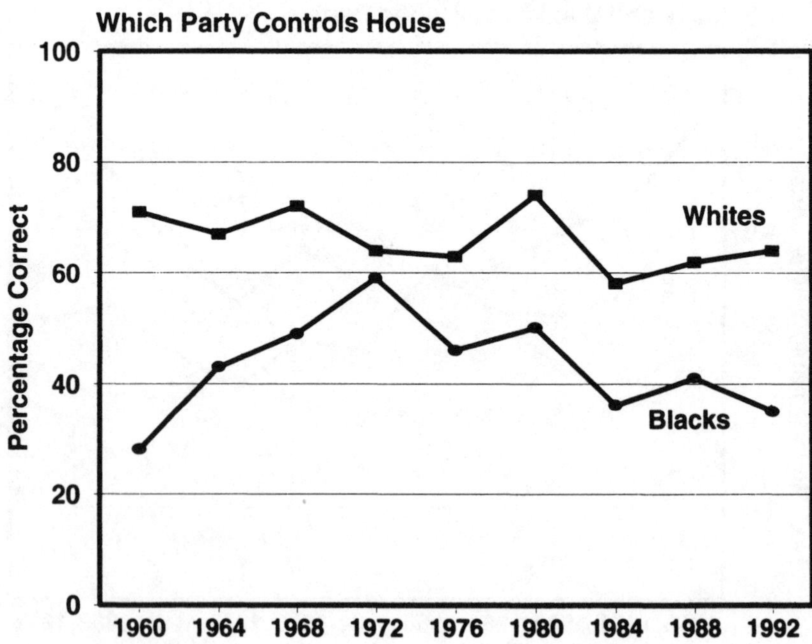

Figure 4.4 Over-Time Trends in the Knowledge Gap, by Race (*continued*)

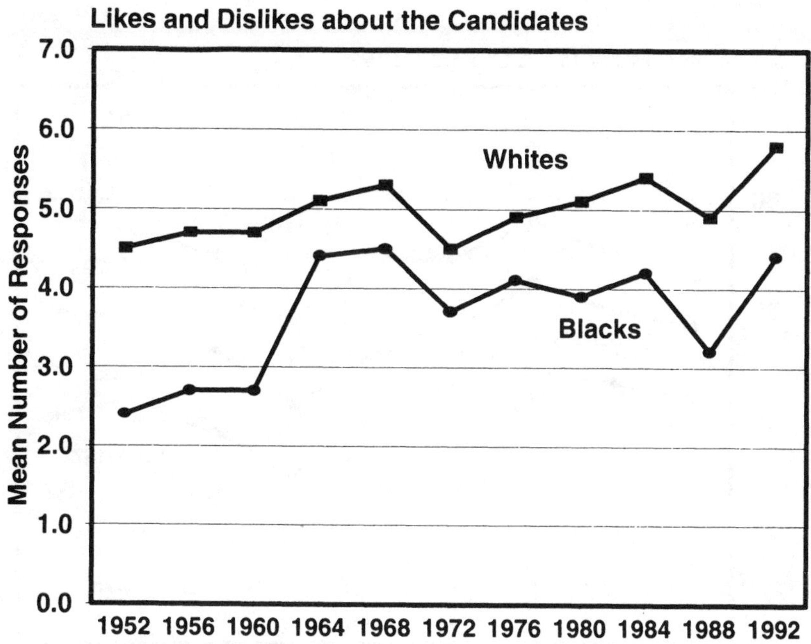

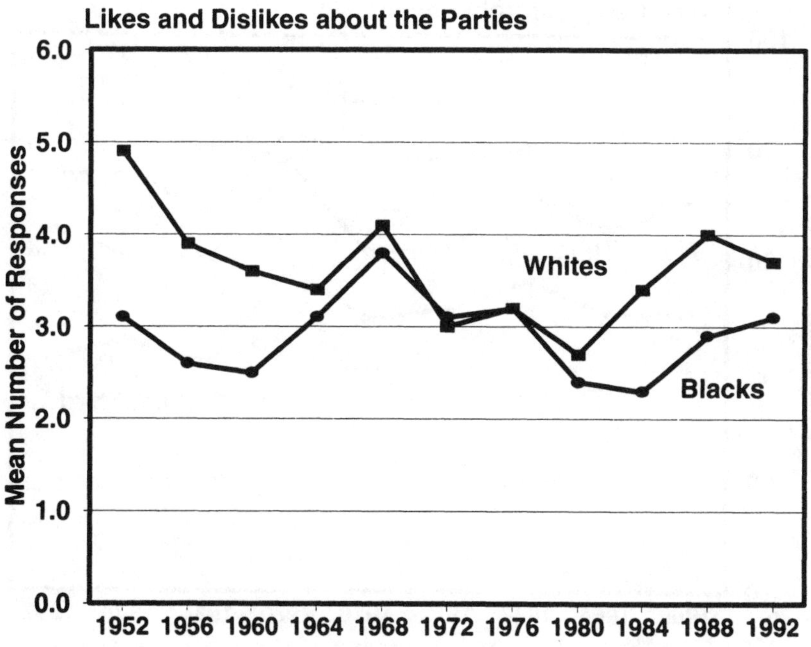

Figure 4.5 Over-Time Trends in the Knowledge Gap, by Family Income

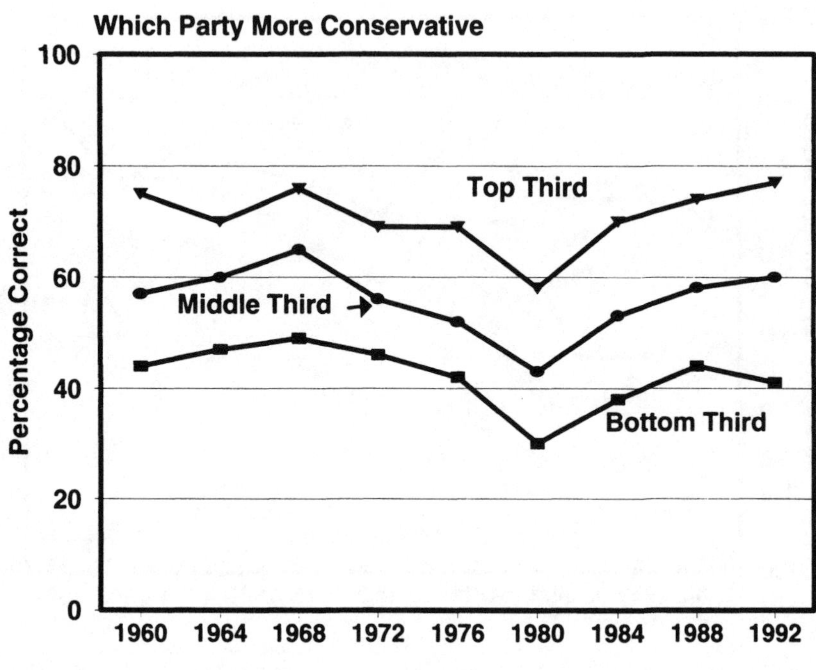

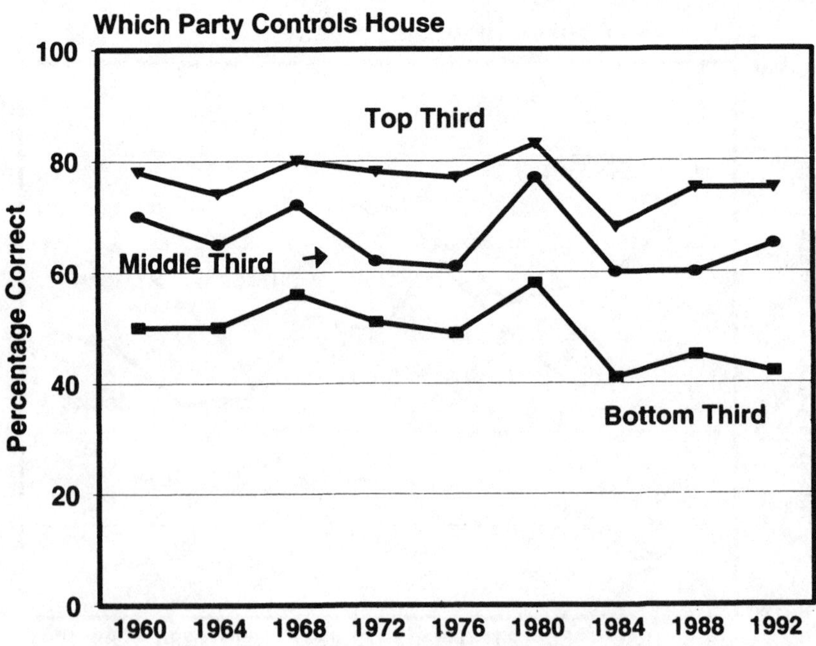

Figure 4.5 Over-Time Trends in the Knowledge Gap, by Family Income (*continued*)

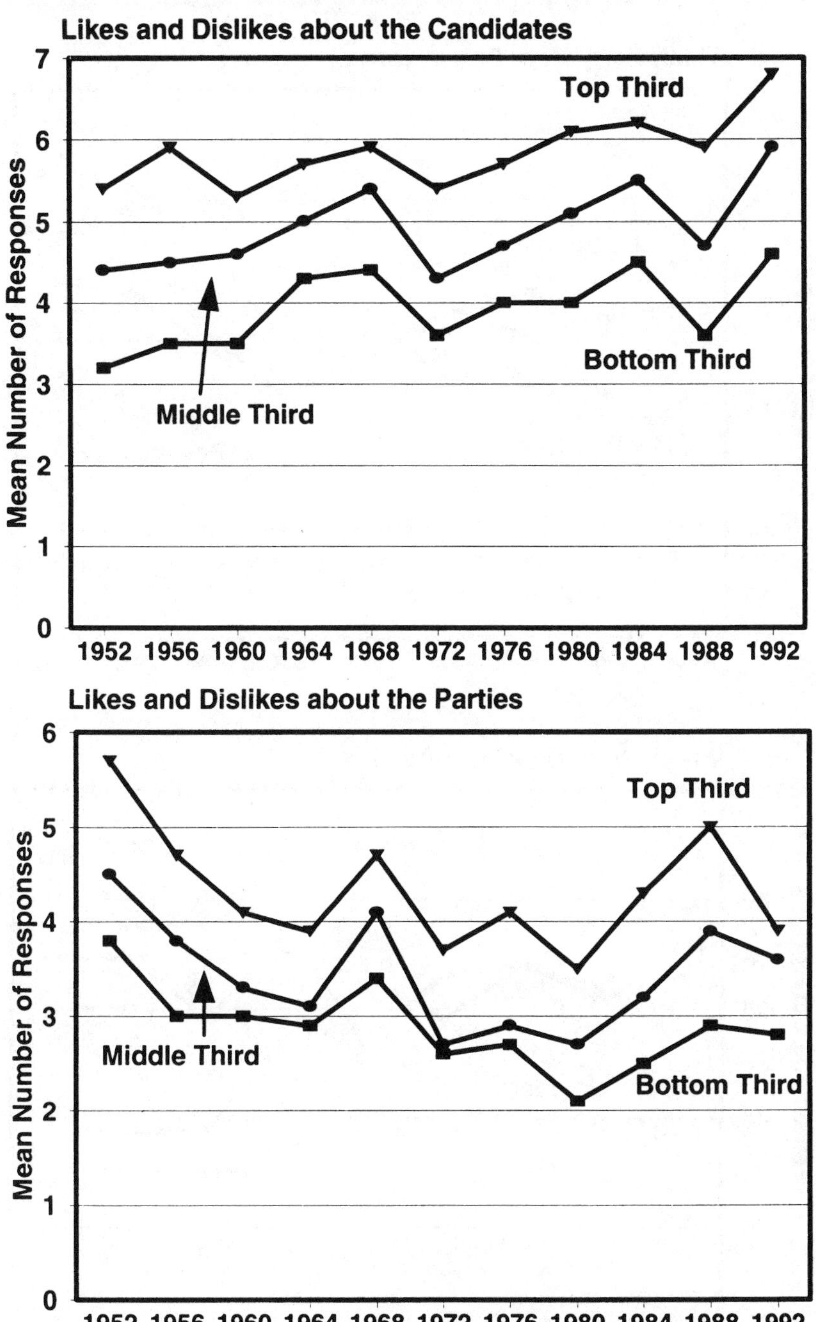

Figure 4.6 Over-Time Trends in the Knowledge Gap, by Age Cohorts

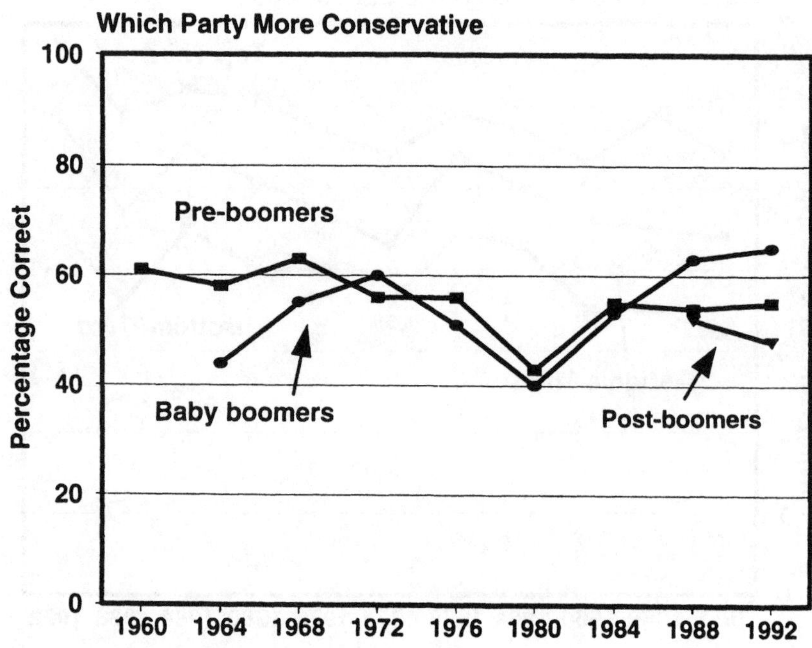

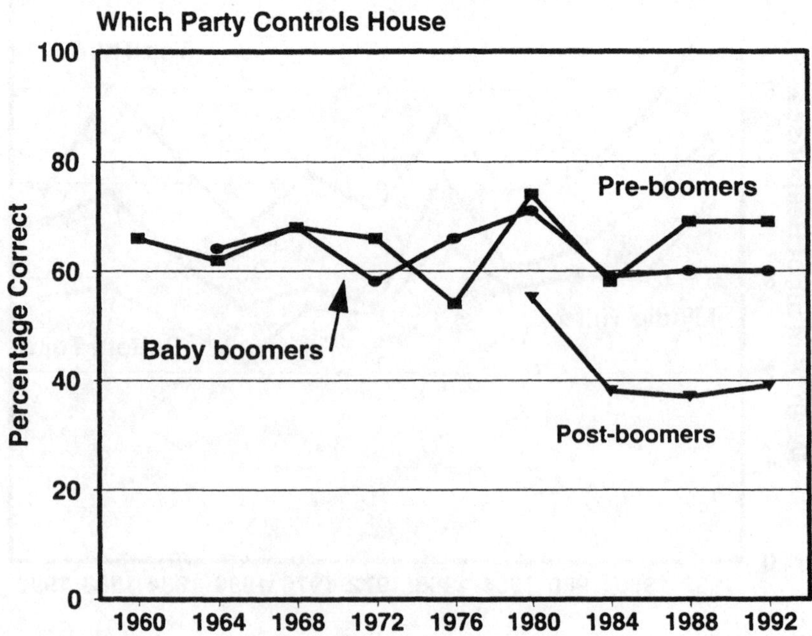

Figure 4.6 Over-Time Trends in the Knowledge Gap, by Age Cohorts (*continued*)

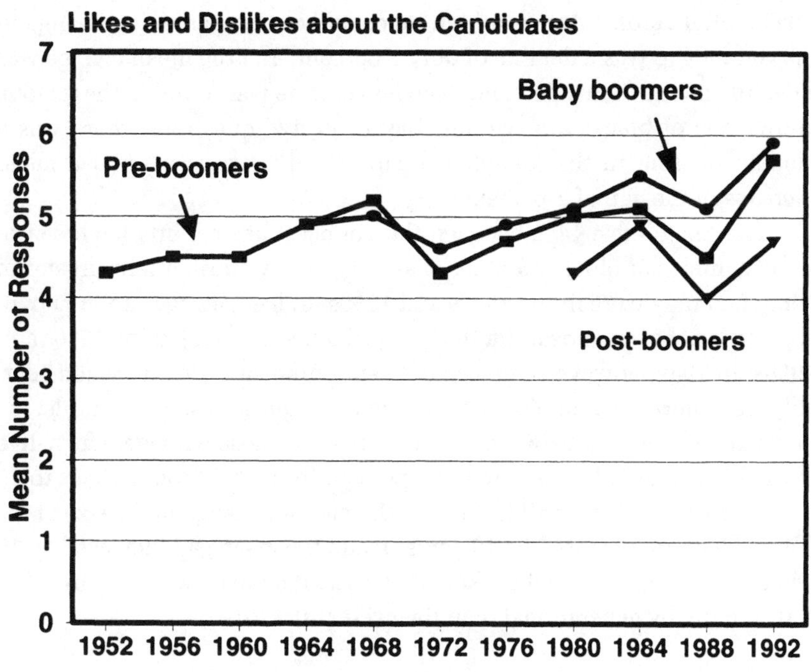

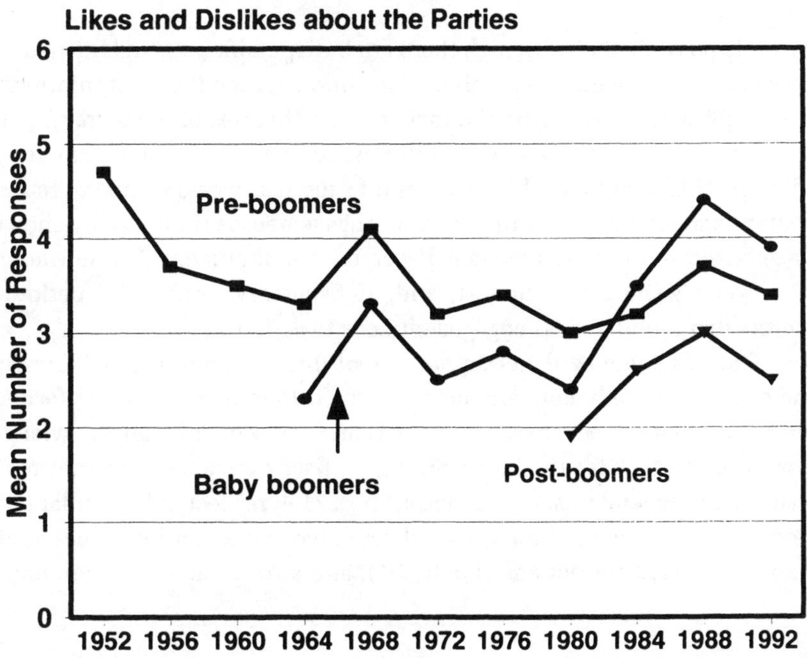

Senate in 1989 versus knowing this in 1947) but increasing by 8 percentage points on another (knowing—again in 1989 as compared to 1947—that it takes a two-thirds majority in both Houses to override a presidential veto).[22] Across all ten items, however, the median change in the gender gap was a decline of only 5 percent, and the mean change was a decline of less than 2 percent. Even less change was found in the relative knowledge of blacks and whites. Based on five questions, there was a median decline in the knowledge gap of only 1 percent, and a mean *increase* in the gap of 2 percent.[23]

The knowledge gaps between the youngest age cohorts (eighteen to twenty-nine year olds) and older ones are actually substantially greater in 1989 than they were in the 1940s and 1950s. Indeed, an age gap in knowledge does not even appear (for the five questions we have) in the 1940s and 1950s. In 1989, however, eighteen to twenty-nine year olds were considerably less informed than older citizens on these questions. For example, the mean knowledge gap between young adults and those who were forty-five to fifty-four years old went from 2.5 percent in the 1940s and 1950s to 19 percent in 1989. Across all five items, the median change in the size of the knowledge gap increased by 10 percent, and the mean gap increased by 16 percent. This suggests that the knowledge gap demonstrated in figure 4.6 is driven more by generational than life cycle processes.

Testing the Elite Theory of Democracy

It is possible that, although there are indisputable gaps in knowledge, these gaps mask a more equitable distribution among the most informed, active citizens. Drawing on the logic of elite theories of democracy, perhaps our focus on the general public, while well intentioned, is overly idealistic. According to this argument, in the real world of liberal representative democracy, meaningful civic engagement is limited—by choice or necessity—to a relatively small percentage of citizens. These watchdogs keep government honest, and, if necessary, sound the periodic alarms that mobilize less engaged citizens to action.

There is some evidence in defense of this notion of limited democracy. For example, voters are more informed than nonvoters, the former averaging 25.4 correct answers on our 1989 Survey of Political Knowledge compared to 19.3 for the latter. Strong partisans are also more informed than true independents, averaging 24.1 and 21.4, respectively. Similar patterns are found using the 1988 NES data: voters were more informed than nonvoters (12.2 correct answers to 7.1), and strong partisans were more informed than independents (11.7 to 7.2). These findings, however, conceal important differences among groups whose political views are likely to differ. For example, whereas partisans are more informed than nonpartisans, strong Republicans are significantly more informed (26.1 in the 1989 survey and 13.3 in the 1988 survey) than are strong Democrats (22.7 and 10.3). Further, voters and partisans are not random subsets of the general population: the very groups most likely to be politically uninformed are often the most likely to be underrepresented among these more activist citizens. Finally, politics in the United States extends well beyond partisan politics and voting in periodic elections.

A more direct test of the elite model is to examine the demographic makeup of the most informed segment of society. If women, blacks, the poor, and the young are fairly represented within this "guardian class," then discrepancies in the larger population, while perhaps still a matter of concern, become less serious. The demographic makeup of the 1989 sample, along with the percentage of various demographic groups found in the most informed fifth of the sample—the information elite, if you will—is presented in table 4.10. The underrepresentation of women, blacks, the poor, the young, and their various combinations, coupled with the overrepresentation of men, whites, the affluent, and older citizens is profound and in some instances rivals the demographic distortions found in comparisons of the general public with elected officials. To the extent that the real world of politics occurs in the exchanges between elected officials, administrative officials, and a small-but-informed elite citizenry, this conversation is one in which the voices of a large segment of the American public are very faint.

Table 4.10 Groups as a Percentage of Most-Informed and Least-Informed Quintiles

	Group as a Percentage of . . .			
Group	Information Rich (top 20%)[a]	Information Poor (bottom 20%)[b]	Total Sample[c]	Percent Misrepresentation[d]
White males	65	15	39	+50
Men	71	31	47	+40
Whites	93	56	82	+37
High income	31	6	15	+25
High-income males	23	3	9	+20
Pre–Baby boomers	57	37	46	+20
Middle income	53	35	52	+18
Post–Baby boomers	4	13	10	− 9
Baby boomers	39	50	44	−11

Table 4.10 Groups as a Percentage of Most-Informed and Least Informed Quintiles (*continued*)

Group	Group as a Percentage of . . . Information Rich (top 20%)[a]	Information Poor (bottom 20%)[b]	Total Sample[c]	Percent Misrepresentation[d]
Poor black women	<1	17	4	−17
Black women	<1	21	6	−21
Poor blacks	<1	23	6	−23
Blacks	3	33	11	−30
Poor women	5	42	20	−37
Women	29	69	53	−40
Low income	16	60	32	−44

Source: 1989 Survey of Political Knowledge.
[a] Percentage of the most-informed quintile of the sample that is made up of the group in question.
[b] Percentage of the least-informed quintile of the sample that is made up of the group in question.
[c] Percentage of the sample that is made up of the group in question.
[d] Percent represented in top quintile minus percent represented in bottom quintile.

Political Power and the Structure of Political Knowledge

In this chapter we have explored the way knowledge of specific political facts can be viewed in terms of broader patterns of what individuals, groups, and the collective public know more generally about politics. We find that citizens tend to be generalists in their knowledge of politics, though there are important exceptions to this pattern, especially when considering different levels of government. There is great variability in what Americans know about politics, making it nearly impossible to characterize the public as informed or uninformed. There is, however, a disconcerting correspondence between the distribution of political knowledge across the public and the distribution of other valuable resources that are both the source of political power and a consequence of it.

These findings have a number of practical and theoretical implications. First of all, the unidimensional nature of knowledge suggests that researchers developing national or general political knowledge scales need not be overly concerned with the mix of specific topics covered by individual items. Scales made up of items tapping only knowledge of institutions and processes, substantive issues, or public figures are likely to serve as reasonable measures of the overarching construct. There is, however, enough evidence of dimensionality that researchers constructing surveys should select items that cut across the subdomains. The distinctiveness of partisan knowledge demonstrated in several of our analyses, coupled with the fact that such items often dominate surveys used by political scientists, suggest that care be taken to not create scales exclusively dependent on these types of questions (nor to exclude them). Moreover, researchers interested in particular populations or special issues should remain aware that the conclusions drawn about the sources and consequences of knowledge can be affected by the substantive items included in their analysis.

Second, the patterns of public knowledge about politics that we observed provide clues about the importance of several determinants of learning about politics: general interest in politics, the perceived relevance of specific types of information, the value of prior knowledge, and the nature of the information environment. Reported interest and engagement in politics was a significant predictor of nearly every type of political knowledge we examined.[24] People who say they follow politics are likely to know more about any aspect of politics than those who claim not to pay attention. This is an unsurprising finding, but it reinforces the important point that self-motivation is a key element in building an informed citizenry and that most of those interested in politics are broadly interested. Relevance, however, remains an important factor in explaining knowledge differences. Although less informed than whites on most political topics, blacks were more informed on racial issues. A significant gender gap was seen for most types of political knowledge, but not for gender-relevant items or for local politics. Strong partisans were more likely than others to have party-related knowledge. The perceived relevance of certain types of information can overcome one's lack of general interest in politics.

The patterns of inter-item and interfactor correlations we found are consistent with schema, knowledge gap, and associative memory network theories (Lodge and Hamill, 1986; Graber, 1988; Tichenor, Donahue, and Olien, 1970; Rahn, 1989; Krosnick and Kinder, 1990). At the heart of each of these theories is the notion that new information is processed in relation to old: that what one learns and remembers depends on what one already knows (Price and Zaller, 1993; Bennett, 1994). Once a particular fact is learned, this knowledge serves as a context for new information—the hook upon which additional facts become caught. The holding of this fact also signals past (and so likely future) exposure to additional information. Although at some level the holding of any particular piece of information increases the probability of learning additional facts of all kinds, similarities between new information and what is already known increase the likelihood of exposure to the former and, more important, the likelihood of a meaningful context within which to understand it. This should increase the likelihood of retaining the new information. In turn, the greater the number of facts learned, the more (and more varied) are the hooks that are available for additional learning.

Of course, our ability to demonstrate this process is limited by the cross-sectional nature of our data. But what might a snapshot (perhaps a CAT scan is the better analogy) of the public mind look like if this is how citizens learn about politics? Certainly not unequivocally unidimensional, because individuals come to their knowledge through distinct paths and so should have areas of politics about which they are more fully informed than others. Neither, however, should it be unequivocally multidimensional, because political knowledge of one kind increases the likelihood of learning about other aspects of politics, although it does so with less potency the less similar the new information is to the old. We should, instead, expect patterns very much like the ones we found: webs of highly intercorrelated subdomains of knowledge, each made up of substantively related facts.

Political learning is affected not only by individual factors, such as one's interest in politics, but also—and often profoundly—by forces external to the individual: the information environment and, more generally, the political context in which learning occurs. The distinctive patterns observed with knowledge of local, state, and national politics suggest that differences in the availability of political information at the three levels of politics interact with variations in individual interest and motivation.

Interpreting the interactions among political interest, stored knowledge, and the availability of information as a dynamic process is useful in bridging the gap between the psychology and the sociology of political learning. Whether by choice or circumstance, interest in and exposure to different pieces of political information vary from group to group and from class to class in the United States. Evidence of these differences is found in the muted but distinct relations we uncovered between gender, race, age, and partisanship, on the one hand, and the various domains of political knowledge, on the other. These domain-specific differences are ultimately dwarfed by a larger, more consistent pattern in which the same groups of citizens (whites, men, the more educated, the more generally politically interested and engaged) are relatively better informed about virtually all aspects of politics. The resolution between a theory of learning that is domain specific and an observed pattern of information holding that is only modestly so can be found in the resource advantages of those who are more informed. Individuals whose socialization experiences are most likely to encourage political engagement (a norm only imperfectly measured by standard survey items) are most likely to seek out information. These individuals are also likely to be in environments where their exposure to political information is greatest. As a result, they develop more hooks of the sort described above, develop them earlier and at a greater pace, and are in environments where these hooks are most likely to catch new pieces of information. Although individuals may initially learn about politics for disparate reasons and so learn disparate things, in the long run, resource-rich individuals and groups develop a more general political knowledge.

The consequences of this process for larger issues of democratic governance are profound. Certainly one can take comfort in the fact that citizens tend to be generalists and thus, to the extent that they are informed, are able to draw on a wide range of knowledge in fulfilling their civic responsibilities. Also comforting is our finding that, contrary to elite, managerial, and rational choice theories, most citizens are at least modestly informed about national politics, and that this is especially true among those who vote or participate in other ways. Our analysis also finds, however, that political ignorance is not randomly distributed but is most likely to be found among those who arguably have the most to gain from effective political participation: women, blacks, the poor, and the young. These gaps show little evidence of declining over time. To the extent that political knowledge is both a central component and an indicator of civic competence, the patterns of knowledge presented in this chapter provide reason for concern about the state of democracy in contemporary America: to paraphrase Orwell, while all citizens are equal, some citizens are more equal than others. Schattschneider is correct in saying that "the flaw in the pluralist heaven is that the heavenly choir sings with a strong upper-class accent" (1960: 35). To this observation we would add that it sings with an accent that is decidedly older, white, and male as well.

CHAPTER FIVE

Explaining Political Knowledge

Not that it is solely, or chiefly, to form great thinkers that freedom of thinking is required. On the contrary, it is as much and even more indispensable to enable average human beings to attain the mental stature which they are capable of.—JOHN STUART MILL, *On Liberty*

A more intelligent state of social affairs, one more informed with knowledge, more directed by intelligence, would not improve original endowments one whit, but it would raise the level upon which the intelligence of all operates. The height of this level is much more important for judgement of public concerns than are differences in intelligence quotients.—JOHN DEWEY, *The Phantom Public*

Why are some citizens very knowledgeable about politics, yet others are almost totally uninformed? Understanding how and why citizens learn about politics is an important step in any attempt to increase the aggregate level of political knowledge in the United States. It is also a necessary precursor to identifying the roots of political inequality and for determining ways to remedy this situation.

Political learning is a lifelong activity, one that is shaped by many important social, economic, cultural—and idiosyncratic—influences. No simple model can succinctly capture all the pathways by which citizens come to be informed. But the fact that citizens differ in their levels of political knowledge in systematic, predictable ways suggests that there are a number of identifiable regularities to the process of political learning.

In this chapter, we will explore a variety of individual and systemic factors that influence what citizens know about politics. Although we draw on a number of different surveys for evidence, our principal method of analysis continues to be cross-sectional—that is, an analysis of factors that explain differences in political knowledge among respondents in surveys taken at one point in time.[1] We will outline a simple model of influence and then estimate the actual linkages statistically. Following this, we will take a closer look at the operation of specific components in the model. Throughout our analyses, we devote special attention to understanding the roots of the significant group disparities in knowledge.

Influences on Political Knowledge

People learn about a subject if they have the ability, motivation, and opportunity to do so (Luskin, 1990). Ability—the possession of adequate cognitive skills—should make any type of learning easier. Motivation—the desire to learn—affects the extent to which individuals seek out information and how much attention they pay to that which comes their way. And opportunity—the availability of information and how it is packaged—affects how easily a citizen can learn, given his or her ability and motivation. Each of these elements is a necessary but not a sufficient condition for learning about politics. Greater amounts of one requisite of knowledge can, however, compensate for shortcomings in another area.

The value of the ability-motivation-opportunity triad is primarily conceptual, as the three elements seldom correspond in one-to-one fashion with individual characteristics or institutional sources of political information. For example, formal education affects the ability to learn about politics by teaching cognitive skills, but it also exposes students to specific facts about the political world (thus providing the opportunity to learn), and it generates interest in the social and political world in a variety of ways that affect a citizen's motivation to learn. We will use the ability-motivation-opportunity triad both as a way of organizing our discussion of factors, and as a way of assessing how a given, measurable factor influences the acquisition and retention of political knowledge.

A number of studies have examined the correlates of political knowledge (Neuman, 1986; Bennett, 1988; Luskin, 1990; Smith, 1989; Lambert et al., 1988). Because of this, one can, as Stephen Bennett has put it, begin the search for explanatory factors by "rounding up the usual suspects"—age, sex, race, education, political interest, and so forth (1988).[2] We drew on prior research in this area and on the results of our analyses in chapter 4 to round up a number of different variables that are plausibly linked to political knowledge.[3] Based on the finding that most people are generalists in what they know about politics, we use additive indexes composed of nearly all available factual items in each survey as our measures of political knowledge, omitting only those of questionable reliability or validity (see the Appendix 2 for a description). Where appropriate, however, we disaggregate our knowledge scales to examine the impact of demographic, structural, attitudinal, and behavioral variables on particular domains of knowledge.

A Simple Model

A simplified path model with three major elements thought to influence political learning is shown in figure 5.1. Furthest from knowledge (on the left) are demographic characteristics. Race, sex, region (living in the South), and age are related to knowledge levels, but we assume that this is because of their relation with other, more proximate factors, such as educational level or interest in politics. Next in the pathway is a cluster of variables labeled "structural": these include formal education, income, and politically impinged occupations. The demographic characteristics on the left are partial determinants of all three of these (for example, because blacks have less easy access than whites to higher education and many high-status jobs and earn less on average, race helps determine how structurally advantaged or disadvantaged one will be). Whereas two of the structural variables (education and occupation) may also capture variations in the opportunity to learn about politics and so could have a direct effect on knowledge, all three should affect learning primarily via their influence on the third cluster of variables, labeled "behavioral." These reflect, in large part, the motivation element of the triad and include interest in politics, attention to political news and information in the media, discussion of politics with friends and others, political efficacy and trust, and sense of civic duty.[4] Composite indexes of the structural and attitudinal variables were created, and the parameters of the model estimated using ordinary least squares regression.[5]

From a statistical point of view, the simplified model performs quite well with all three surveys we examined; it explains between 56 and 59 percent of the variance in knowledge levels. Standardized path coefficients for the model using the 1988 NES data are shown in figure 5.1 (paths with coefficients less than .10 are not shown). The behavioral variables constitute the strongest single correlate of political knowledge, with a direct path of .49. The cluster of structural factors, however, has a strong direct effect (path coefficient = .30), as well as substantial indirect effects through their influence on behaviors. Gender affects knowledge directly as well as indirectly through structural and behavioral characteristics.[6] Age is related to political knowledge through its impact on both structural and behavioral factors. Finally, race and region of residence matter principally because of their influence on the structural variables.

Figure 5.1 A Simplified Path Model of Political Knowledge

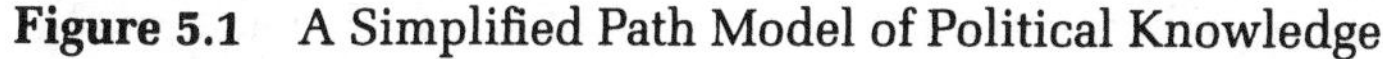

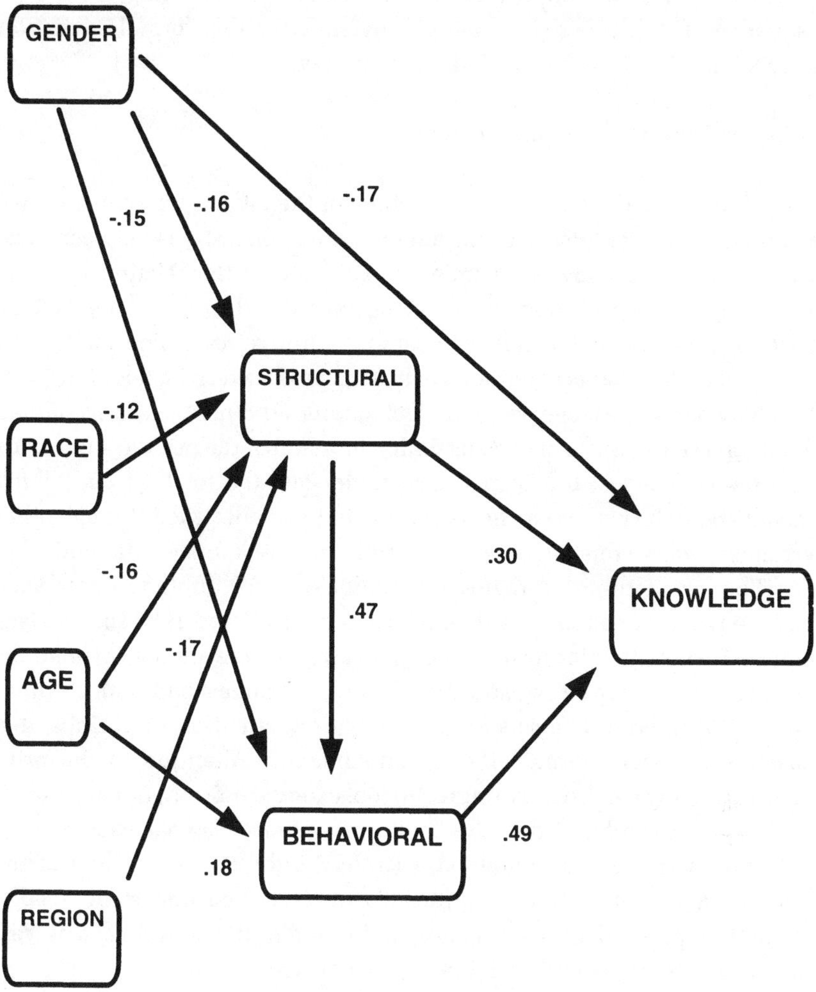

Note: Entries are standardized regression coefficients (path coefficients).
Paths smaller than .10 are not shown.

This model is quite powerful in accounting for differences in levels of political knowledge. The consistency of the results from the 1988, 1989, and 1992 surveys (conducted by two organizations using different modes of data collection) adds to our confidence that the patterns are not the result of idiosyncratic factors (such as different knowledge measures) or the vagaries of the sampling process. Although this simplified path model obscures a great deal because it combines variables into clusters, it helps in grasping the full impact of specific factors by situating them in a sequence of influences (for example, by showing that formal education affects knowledge both directly and indirectly).

A Closer Look at Individual Factors

To examine the component variables in the model, we prepared two kinds of evidence. First, we computed simple correlations between each variable and the knowledge indexes. This shows the relation between knowledge and a particular factor without regard to the role of other factors. Second, we estimated a simple linear and additive regression model that included all the factors simultaneously. This produced estimates of the relation between knowledge and each factor, with all other factors accounted for. In one sense, this provides us with a measure of the net effect of a variable on knowledge, but it may also understate the total effects (which include both the net direct effects and the indirect effects felt through other variables); where this might occur, we will refer back to the path model.

The correlation and regression coefficients for political knowledge and the twenty-one individual variables in the 1988 and 1989 surveys (see table 5.1) show that for nearly all of the variables, the simple correlations with knowledge are strong and significant.[7] The largest correlations (from .38 to .60) in both data sets are for education, attention to politics, discussing politics, internal efficacy, and income. Attention to the print media, holding a politically impinged job, external efficacy, having a sense of civic duty, gender, and (in the 1989 survey) race also have sizable correlations with political knowledge (from .26 to .35). And many of the remaining variables (for example, attention to the electronic media, strength of party identification, age, and living in the South) have at least modest correlations with what people know about politics.

Table 5.1 Relation between Political Knowledge and Various Predictors, 1988 and 1989

Variable	1988 National Election Study		1989 Survey of Political Knowledge	
	Simple *r*	*b* and beta	Simple *r*	*b* and beta
Follow politics (+ interest in campaigns in 1988 survey)	.60	0.40 .25****	.44	0.96 .12**
Education	.55	0.80 .26****	.54	1.90 .33****

Table 5.1 Relation between Political Knowledge and Various Predictors, 1988 and 1989 (*continued*)

Variable	1988 National Election Study		1989 Survey of Political Knowledge	
	Simple *r*	*b* and beta	Simple *r*	*b* and beta
Internal efficacy	.51	0.77 .15****	.38	0.53 .09**
Discuss politics	.44	0.15 .07***	.46	0.83 .13***
Income	.42	0.07 .09****	.39	0.59 .10**
Other source: newsmagazines	.35	0.08 .02	.31	1.41 .08**
Politically relevant employment	.35	0.32 .03		
Read news in newspaper	.32	0.11 .07***	.35	0.03 .03
Sex (female)	−.31	−1.73 −.17****	−.27	−3.00 −.21****
External efficacy	.28	0.01 .00		
Sense of civic duty	.26	0.24 .07***		
Other source: radio	.20	0.15 .02	.24	1.83 .10***
Party ID strength	.19	0.49 .10****	.08	−0.03 −.00
Region (South)	−.19	−0.69 −.07***	−.12	−0.41 −.03
Watch TV news	.18	0.01 .01	.18	−0.00 −.00
Race (black)	−.18	−1.00 −.06***	−.33	−5.00 −.21****
Attitude on women's rights	−.13	−0.16 −.06**		
Children under six in home	−.10	−0.33 −.04*		
Trust	.08	−0.07 −.06**	−.03	−0.55 −.04
Age	.06	.02 .08***	.12	0.10 .23****
Civics instruction			.09	0.22 .02
r^2		.59		.56
Standard error of the regression		3.24		4.87

Notes: Top entry in the cell is the unstandardized regression coefficient (*b*). Bottom entry is the standardized coefficient (beta).

*$p<.05$. **$p<.01$. ***$p<.001$ ****$p<.0001$.

When their joint effects are considered in the multivariate analysis, most of the variables remain as significant predictors of knowledge levels. Education and attention to politics emerged as the most important factors, followed by gender. Internal efficacy and income remained statistically significant, although the size of their impact declined substantially. Holding a politically relevant job bore no significant relation with knowledge once other factors were controlled. Although race remained a significant predictor in both data sets, much of its initial correlation vanished in the multivariate analysis using the 1988 survey.[8] The relation between age and knowledge actually strengthened, due in part to the fact that the lower educational level of older cohorts makes it appear that knowledge does not increase very much with age.Taken as a whole, the pattern of both simple correlations and betas supports the notion that political knowledge is the product of many different experiences, traits, and influences (see Nadeau and Niemi, 1992, for a similar argument).

Civic Motivation: Attitudinal and Behavioral Sources of Political Knowledge

The effect of motivation on political knowledge is manifested in several ways. Most directly, it is seen in the strong relation between knowledge levels and survey respondents' reported interest in and attention to politics. But it is also seen indirectly in the amount and types of knowledge held by different groups in the population.

The cluster of variables including interest, media attention, discussion of politics, and political efficacy has a substantial and positive impact on learning and yielded the largest direct path coefficient to political knowledge of any of the variables in our model (.49 in the 1988 NES data; see figure 5.1). Even when disaggregated, however, the component variables each display significant independent relations with knowledge (table 5.1). The standardized regression coefficient (using the 1988 NES data) was .25 for attention and interest, .15 for internal efficacy, and .07 each for discussing politics, reading news in the newspapers, and having a sense of civic duty. Results from the 1989 Survey of Political Knowledge were similar, although in this study attention to news on radio and in newsmagazines was also significant, and reading newspapers (controlling for other forms of media use) was not. These findings are consistent with those of other researchers (for example, Bennett, 1989, 1990). Indeed, Luskin (1990) finds motivation to be the strongest predictor of political knowledge.[9]

Although interest—the feeling of curiosity or attraction—might seem to be a necessary condition for learning about any topic, there is a unique influence on political learning that sometimes provides motivation unaccompanied by interest: a citizen's sense that paying attention to politics is an obligation or duty. Many citizens see politics as distasteful or intrinsically uninteresting but nevertheless pay attention because they believe they should. In a 1991 Virginia survey, we asked respondents who followed politics "most of the time" (47 percent of the sample) if they did so because they enjoyed it or because they felt they should. This attentive group of respondents was split nearly evenly, with 46 percent saying they enjoyed politics, and 47 percent saying they kept up with it out of a sense of duty. The groups differed relatively little on a 6-point political knowledge scale.[10]

Another potential source of psychological engagement is anxiety. The commonsense notion (tied in part to the protectionist theory of democracy) that individuals would be motivated to learn by fear of the consequences of ignorance is nicely supported by George Marcus's and Michael MacKuen's work on learning during presidential election campaigns (1993). Examining panel data from the 1980 election, they show that anxiety—citizen response to the candidates including anger, unease, fear, and disgust—was a significant independent predictor of how much citizens learned about the candidates' issue positions over the course of the campaign (678–80).[11] The authors conclude that "emotion is a catalyst for political learning" (672).

Surprisingly, reported attention to the mass media is a relatively weak predictor of an individual's level of political knowledge—even for observed knowledge that could not have been learned in school. Reported attention to the print media is a significant predictor (for the NES data), but watching television news is not (see table 5.1).[12] Other studies have come to the same conclusion, although many of them also find little evidence of newspapers' impact (see, for example, Robinson and Levy, 1986; Drew and Weaver, 1991).[13]

This finding is unsatisfying, given that much of one's observed knowledge about politics must come, at least initially, from the mass media.[14] Similarly, the finding that television is a completely ineffective teacher is somewhat implausible. Television news is rightly criticized, but it seems unlikely that viewers learn nothing from it that is detectable in well-designed surveys. At least two recent studies have cast doubt on the conventional wisdom that citizens learn nothing from television. Vincent Price and John Zaller (1993) examined the extent to which citizens recalled various stories that had recently appeared in the news. They concluded that self-reported attention to the mass media was, indeed, a poor predictor of recall of news stories. But, notably, after controlling for an array of potentially confounding factors (including the most important one—prior levels of political knowledge), they found that exposure to television news was more strongly related to recall than was newspaper reading.[15]

Russell Neuman's, Marion Just's, and Ann Crigler's study reaches much the same conclusion (1992). Although it was true that individuals who preferred television news had lower initial levels of political knowledge than those who preferred newspapers or magazines, this difference was almost entirely a result of the fact that users of the print media had higher levels of cognitive skill. When this confounding variable was controlled, the knowledge advantage of those preferring print media vanishes: "The entire relationship between knowledge of the issues and media surveillance habits washes out when we control for cognitive skill" (Neuman, Just, and Crigler 1992: 99). Furthermore, in their experimental studies, they found that newspapers were less effective than television and magazines in transmitting information to citizens with average levels of cognitive ability. They argue that the style of presentation of television and magazines provides essential context for remembering factual information and increases the likelihood that an individual will understand and retain it. By comparison, newspaper stories, with their "inverted pyramid" format, are apparently much less comprehensible to citizens with weak to average cognitive skills (106–9; see also Weaver, 1975).[16]

Beyond one's psychological engagement and attention through the media is actual participation in political affairs. Theoretically, participation and knowledge should be closely linked. Citizens should learn about politics as they take part in it, and because of the activity they should be more attentive to political information outside the context of participation as well. Moreover, knowledge should stimulate participation by lowering the costs of doing so and by making the benefits of participation more apparent. Two studies involving political knowledge and participation found strong reciprocal effects between the two variables. Jane Junn's 1991 study reached three important conclusions for our purposes. First, using a measure of electoral participation in the 1980 NES panel study, she found a strong, independent impact of participation on knowledge. Second, she found a sizable effect of other kinds of participation on knowledge in the 1987 General Social Survey (the participation measure included working to solve community problems and contacting public officials, in addition to campaign activities). Third, in both analyses she found substantial reciprocal effects, with knowledge affecting participation, as well as vice versa. Junn's findings are corroborated by an analysis of the 1976 NES survey by Jan Leighley (1991), who found that a variety of types of participation boosted knowledge (205–7; see also Tan, 1980). Other researchers have described this mutual relationship as a spiral in which knowledge and participation each feed upon the other (Neuman, 1986: 128–31; Graber, 1988: 140). The existence of a strong interdependence between knowledge and participation has an important practical implication: efforts made to boost one of these will, in all likelihood, benefit the other.

Motivation and the Relevance of Information

Although they lack a more general interest in and understanding of the political world, some citizens may find particular aspects of politics especially relevant and so pay closer attention to them. The concept of specific issue publics is intended to describe this type of particularized engagement in politics.

There is relatively little evidence for a strong version of this notion—one that describes the citizenry as composed of many small issue publics, each concerned with and knowledgeable about specific issues. In the process of assessing the construct validity of various subdomains of knowledge, however, we did find evidence that certain issues were more familiar to individuals for whom the topics were arguably of special relevance. Women and African American citizens are less knowledgeable than men and whites about much of national politics. But there are no significant gender differences on knowledge about abortion issues, and black citizens are actually more knowledgeable than whites in their knowledge of racial issues and black political figures. Moreover, evidence from one of our state surveys in Virginia suggests that the greater relevance of certain information for African Americans is not simply a matter of black citizens paying attention to black politicians or issues that are explicitly racial. In comparing white and black respondents with similar levels of education, income, political interest, national political knowledge, and tenure in the state, we found that black Virginians were nearly 20 percentage points more likely than whites to know the state has a death penalty for murder. Although we do not have direct evidence, we surmise that African Americans are acutely aware that blacks constitute a disproportionate percentage of the death row population. Given that there is strong public support among whites for the death penalty (68 percent in Virginia) and that executions in the state are generally well publicized, this racial difference in awareness is a striking example of how the relevance of a political fact can affect the likelihood that it will be known.

The Central Role of Formal Education

The finding that, collectively, political attitudes and behaviors are the most powerful predictors of knowledge levels suggests that individual citizens bear much of the responsibility for what they know and don't know about politics. Psychological and behavioral engagement in politics, however, is at least partially determined by systemic factors. In our model, about half of the direct path between these variables and political knowledge is accounted for by structural conditions, such as education, income, and occupational status, in that they are themselves influenced by the structural variables (figure 5.1). In addition, these structural variables have a strong and independent impact on knowledge (a direct path coefficient of .30). Of these variables, the most powerful predictor of political knowledge is formal education (table 5.1). This impact can be seen in the direct relation between education and knowledge, but it is also found in the indirect effect of education both on political engagement and on such other structural variables as income and occupational status. This robust relation is documented in numerous studies of knowledge and political sophistication, and it also holds across every subdomain of political knowledge we examined. Indeed, of all the individual demographic, structural, attitudinal, and behavioral variables we examined in the 1988, 1989, and 1992 surveys, education was the strongest single predictor of political knowledge.

A breakdown of twenty-five items[17] from our 1989 survey by level of education shows that political knowledge increases with education (table 5.2), as does a similar analysis of the 1988 NES data (table 5.3). The items are sorted according to the size of the differences between the least (no high school diploma) and most (college graduates) educated groups. The differences average nearly 36 percentage points in the 1989 data and 43 points in 1988. In the 1989 study, an average of nearly three-fourths of the college graduates could answer the questions correctly, compared with an average of less than 40 percent for those who did not finish high school and just over half for the high school graduates. Most of the differences among educational groups in these two surveys are even larger when looking at individuals in similar age groups.[18]

Table 5.2 Knowledge by Education (Percentage Correct)

Survey Item	No High School Diploma	High School Diploma	Some College	College Graduate	Difference, High Minus Low Education
What are first ten amendments called	18	44	58	79	61
Describe recent arms agreement	21	48	61	73	52
Who appoints judges	39	55	62	87	48
Name vice president	49	75	86	97	48
Who reviews constitutionality of laws	47	66	68	92	45
Did U.S. support Contras	46	64	78	91	45
Define recession	37	58	62	81	44
Party control of Senate	36	54	65	78	42
% vote required for veto override	18	31	43	58	40
Party control of House	52	71	67	90	38
Describe one Fifth Amendment right	30	51	65	67	37
Does U.S. have a budget deficit	57	83	83	94	37
Describe one First Amendment right	15	37	43	51	36
Must students say pledge of allegiance	54	82	82	88	34
Can communist run for president	40	43	59	72	32
Name both U.S. Senators	15	21	27	47	32
Truman's party	48	56	60	77	29
Name governor	55	78	83	83	28
Define the New Deal	7	11	17	35	28
Nixon's party	66	75	85	93	27
What is the Superfund	4	8	16	30	26
% unemployed	18	18	27	44	26
FDR's party	58	55	65	84	26
Does U.S. have a trade deficit	67	83	91	91	24
Did women always have suffrage	73	95	94	97	24
Name U.S. representative	22	25	37	41	19
Averages (means)	38	53	61	74	36
N	75	193	167	171	

Source: 1989 Survey of Political Knowledge.

Table 5.3 Knowledge by Education (Percentage Correct)

Survey Item	No High School Diploma	High School Diploma	Some College	College Graduate	Difference, High Minus Low Education
Interviewer rating of respondent's information level (above average)	14	26	46	73	59
Ideological placement of the parties	27	44	68	84	57

Table 5.3 Knowledge by Education (Percentage Correct) (*continued*)

Survey Item	No High School Diploma	High School Diploma	Some College	College Graduate	Difference, High Minus Low Education
Ideological placement of the candidates	29	48	68	81	52
Identify Margaret Thatcher	31	56	71	83	52
Identify Yasser Arafat	14	29	45	65	51
Parties' positions on government guarantee of jobs	23	37	58	72	49
Which party controls U.S. House	38	52	69	84	46
Identify George Shultz	20	30	44	66	46
Parties' positions on defense spending	31	52	73	76	45
Identify Mikhail Gorbachev	47	68	79	92	45
Which party controls U.S. Senate	34	48	61	77	43
Parties' position on government services and spending	33	42	60	75	42
Identify Ted Kennedy	48	64	77	90	42
Parties' positions on health insurance	26	34	56	67	41
Name one House candidate and his/her party	15	25	32	43	28
Identify Jim Wright	4	9	17	30	26
Identify William Rehnquist	1	1	4	10	9
Averages (means)	26	39	55	69	43
N	369	610	398	368	

Source: 1988 National Election Study.

The Impact of Formal Education: Structural Patterns of "Taught" and "Observed" Knowledge

The primacy of formal education as a facilitator of political knowledge lies in its relevance to all the components of the opportunity-motivation-ability triad: it promotes the opportunity to learn about politics by transmitting specific information and influencing career paths and social networks; it increases the motivation by socializing students to the political world and stimulating their interest in it; and it develops the cognitive ability necessary for effective learning.

Primary and secondary schools tend to teach particular aspects of politics, most notably the institutions and processes of government—so-called civics. To the extent formal education boosts levels of knowledge by providing the opportunity to learn specific facts, knowledge of civics should be more strongly associated with primary and secondary education than are other domains of knowledge. Recent research by Richard Niemi and Jane Junn (1993), in which they find a measurable and statistically significant boost in civics knowledge associated with studying civics, provides just such evidence.[19] Our Survey of Political Knowledge also turned up some tantalizing if equivocal evidence—among adults—for the efficacy of civics instruction; survey respondents who recalled having a civics course in high school scored higher on our measure of knowledge of rules of the game than those who did not recall such a course. At the same time, having had a civics course was not correlated with other types of political knowledge.[20] More generally, we found that although younger people were significantly less knowledgeable about the substance of politics (beta for age = .12) and people and parties (.39), there was a statistically insignificant relation between age and knowledge of the kinds of political facts taught in schools (.07).

In recent years there has been an increasing emphasis in the secondary schools on teaching about political rights (Janowitz, 1983). If schools help transmit specific information, this shifting emphasis should be reflected in the patterns of knowledge demonstrated by different age groups. We found such evidence in one of our Virginia surveys (table 5.4). At each educational level (above that of high school dropouts), the youngest cohort of respondents was equally or more knowledgeable about the Bill of Rights than most of the older cohorts, a pattern not seen with most other types of political knowledge—including general knowledge of the Supreme Court. Indeed, for the latter post-secondary education makes the difference. Among the youngest cohort, less than a third of those whose formal education is limited to a high school diploma could correctly state who nominates Supreme Court justices or which branch of government rules on the constitutionality of laws. Among those who finished college, eight in ten knew these facts. Further evidence of the impact of this shift in emphasis (and thus of the importance of schools in transmitting particular facts) is found by disaggregating the relation between age and knowledge of the rules of the game in our national Survey of Political Knowledge. Although younger citizens are significantly less knowledgeable than older ones about political processes (beta = .14), there is no substantive or statistical relation between age and knowledge of specific political rights.

Table 5.4 Education, Age, and Knowledge of Judicial Politics and the Bill of Rights (Percentage Correct)

	No High School Diploma	High School Diploma	Some College	College Graduate
Does the Bill of Rights include consumers' rights				
Age 18–29	*	62% (56)	68% (67)	69% (54)
Age 30–44	15 (31)	42 (82)	63 (70)	77 (100)
Age 45–64	20 (36)	43 (53)	65 (58)	75 (56)
Age 65 and older	14 (47)	15 (32)	44 (21)	49 (19)
Does the Bill of Rights include rights to government benefits				
Age 18–29	*	71 (56)	81 (67)	81 (54)
Age 30–44	33 (31)	60 (82)	77 (70)	85 (100)
Age 45–64	36 (36)	58 (53)	87 (58)	91 (56)
Age 65 and older	29 (47)	42 (32)	73 (21)	64 (19)
Supreme Court determines the constitutionality of laws				
Age 18–29	19 (53)	32 (183)	51 (135)	80 (70))
Age 30–44	39 (72)	43 (230)	62 (202)	87 (233)
Age 45–64	36 (100)	54 (189)	71 (100)	89 (137)
Age 65 and older	44 (133)	62 (103)	72 (55)	87 (52)
President nominates justices to the Supreme Court				
Age 18–29	15 (53)	30 (183)	53 (135)	79 (70)
Age 30–44	25 (72)	42 (230)	59 (202)	85 (233)
Age 45–64	28 (100)	65 (189)	77 (100)	90 (137)
Age 65 and older	46 (133)	70 (103)	73 (55)	88 (52)

Sources: 1991 statewide Virginia survey conducted by the authors (first two items) and 1992 National Election Study (last two items).
Notes: *N* of cases in parentheses. * = sample size too small for reliable estimate.

Evidence that the schools teach particular kinds of facts about the political system should not obscure the broader impact of education: knowledge differences by education extend to all types of political information. The number of years of school completed is as strongly associated with *observed knowledge* of current issues and leaders as it is with knowledge of the institutions and processes of government. The multifaceted nature of education's effects is seen in the pattern of items in table 5.2. Five of the top ten items (in the magnitude of differences between the better and lesser educated) involve observed knowledge rather than facts taught in school. Several of the items in the bottom half of the table (in other words, those with the smallest differences by education) are hybrids; they would constitute observed knowledge for some respondents (for example, Truman's party identification) but taught knowledge for others.

All education, but especially college, has a powerful effect on political knowledge through the development of skills and orientations that make it easier for the well schooled to comprehend and retain political information. This view is consistent with the finding by Herbert Hyman, Charles Wright, and John Shelton Reed (1975) that the effect of a college education was just as strong for political interest and information seeking as it was for factual knowledge. It is also consistent with data from the 1989 Survey of Political Knowledge, which showed that among respondents who attended college, political knowledge (and political interest) varied very little according to undergraduate major. Those who studied subjects far afield of politics or social sciences had average scores on indexes of political knowledge, political interest, and media use that were only slightly lower than those who majored in these disciplines. Of course, this does not indicate that courses in politics, history, or social sciences make no contribution to the college effect—general education requirements still exist in most colleges, guaranteeing that students have some exposure to this material. But the fact that concentration in these areas does not leave a distinctive mark on most citizens is consistent with the notion that higher education promotes the acquisition of political knowledge through the stimulation of political interest and the development of cognitive skills.

Clearly, then, differences in educational attainment capture much more than just the specific information imparted by the schools. Cognitive skills are learned in school, and schools teach contextual knowledge about politics, history, economics, geography, and other subjects that make subsequent learning about politics easier.[21] Educational attainment—independent of other characteristics—is a strong predictor of recall of recent stories in the news media (Price and Zaller, 1993). Schools also attempt to inculcate an interest in politics and a desire to remain informed throughout life. And, of course, there are social and economic differences associated with greater and lesser levels of schooling that may affect the types and amount of political information to which individuals are exposed before, during, and after their formal education. Education is associated with many relevant characteristics: the holding of a professional or managerial job that entails exposure to political information; the extent of free time available for attending to politics; whether one travels and is consequently exposed to the workings of politics in other states and nations; and the likelihood that, as a woman, one will live within a traditional milieu that discourages political engagement.

Skepticism about Education's Effects

The importance of schooling's role in promoting political knowledge has been seriously challenged in recent years. Robert Luskin's analysis of the influences on political sophistication concluded—after controlling for intelligence and other characteristics that are correlated with schooling—that formal education per se makes no measurable contribution to one's level of political sophistication (1990). Eric Smith, citing M. Kent Jennings's and Richard Niemi's work and his own reanalysis of their panel data, found that students' levels of factual political knowledge do not increase greatly as they go through high school and college. He concludes that "education is not the key to the public's understanding of politics" (1989:219).

The skepticism expressed by Smith and others is based in part on the belief that much of the observed relation between schooling and knowledge is spurious—largely a consequence of selection effects in which socially or cognitively advantaged individuals are more likely to achieve higher levels of education. Discussing the Jennings and Niemi data, Smith argues, "those who went on to higher education were more knowledgeable in the beginning" (1989: 216). According to this view, preexisting cognitive and social differences both determine the amount of schooling a person gets and explain most or all of the subsequent variation in political knowledge associated with education. Because of the faith American society has placed in education as the key vehicle for developing a competent and politically equal citizenry (Dewey, 1916), this matter warrants close attention.

The Role of Intelligence

Better-educated individuals know more about politics, in part, because education has provided them with valuable cognitive skills. But it is also true that individuals with greater cognitive skills are likely to do better and go farther in school than those with lesser skills. The relevant issue for the dispute over the role of education—as an institution in society—is the question of how much of one's cognitive ability is a product of schooling and how much is innate or developed through other means (such as a stimulating and supportive home environment), subsequently affecting how much schooling one gets. This vexatious issue is manifested in the continuing debate over intelligence and intelligence testing. Some of what is commonly called intelligence is no doubt genetic and to some extent heritable. But many scientists believe that the heritability of intelligence is substantially overestimated. Among others, Stephen Jay Gould (1981) has mounted a strong case against the notion of intelligence as a single, measurable, and heritable entity.[22]

We lack a clear resolution of this matter as it pertains to political knowledge, both because of disagreements about the immutability of intelligence and because of the lack of good measures of cognitive ability in most surveys that contain valid measures of political knowledge. The clearest point of view to date is Luskin's (1990). His analysis used the 1976 NES survey, which (like subsequent surveys) includes an interviewer rating of the respondent's "apparent intelligence" (very high, above average, average, below average, or very low). In Luskin's model, intelligence turns out to be the second strongest predictor of political sophistication (behind political interest), while education has no independent effect. Luskin offers many caveats, acknowledging the weakness of the intelligence measure, but he nevertheless concludes that schooling itself is inconsequential.[23]

The NES intelligence measure is, in our view, highly sensitive to the context of the survey. Interviewers—who, of course, are not psychologists trained in the measurement of cognitive ability—must rely on the available observed behavior of respondents to make judgments about intelligence. Because this behavior involves discussions about politics, the resulting rating is not independent of the phenomenon the model is trying to explain—sophistication about politics. Telling evidence of this fact is found in the lower average rating of intelligence given to female respondents, 36 percent of whom (in 1988) were rated "above average" or "very high" on intelligence, compared with 49 percent of males. Because there is little reason to believe the samples of males and females differ in intelligence and because women are less knowledgeable about the political topics discussed, it seems clear that interviewers are basing judgments of intelligence at least in part on the political sophistication of respondents.[24] Such a phenomenon would lead to exactly the result seen in Luskin's model: interviewer-rated intelligence is highly correlated with measures of political sophistication. Thus, as a more direct measure of performance in the interview, and one that is correlated with education, the intelligence variable may rob education of some of its impact in the model, leading to the conclusion that education is unrelated to political knowledge.

In surveys containing better measures of cognitive ability, such ability is an important factor in explaining individual variation in political knowledge. These measures typically capture skills or contextual knowledge of the sort that schooling develops. Neuman's analysis of a 1972–73 Bay Area study (1986: 117–20) found that scores on a brief vocabulary test were correlated with political sophistication at the same level as education (.33). When used in a multiple regression equation, the vocabulary score's impact was reduced but not eliminated (it declined to a beta of .19). Education's impact changed little (beta = .30). Large-scale experimental research by Neuman, Just, and Crigler (1992: 97) concluded that cognitive ability was one of the two strongest predictors of baseline levels of knowledge (knowledge levels of the experimental subjects when they were tested before the experiments). In this multivariate analysis, educational level was a much weaker predictor (beta = .11 compared with cognitive ability's .28). Neuman, Just, and Crigler's measurement of cognitive ability was much stronger than that typically available in sample surveys.[25] Again, however, their finding that education's independent effect was much smaller than that of cognitive ability is less a demonstration that schooling is not important than a specification of how it matters. Cognitive ability as measured by their tests is strongly influenced by formal education. Their results indicate that, for the particular knowledge measures they employed, education promotes the acquisition and retention of political knowledge in part through the development of important intellectual tools.

Education Effects over Time

The availability of surveys of political knowledge from forty to fifty years ago makes it possible to compare the effects of education on knowledge today and in the past: in essence, to see the effects of education over a period when the selectivity of those receiving more education declined. Higher education (or even completion of high school) was largely reserved for a social and intellectual elite earlier in this century; consequently, selection biases should be much more important among older cohorts and in earlier surveys as explanations for knowledge differences between the better and lesser educated. If, however, political knowledge differences by education are similar in magnitude among older and younger cohorts, and in earlier and later surveys, we could reasonably conclude that selection biases were relatively unimportant as an influence on knowledge or, alternatively, that such biases were important in the past but now have been supplanted by stronger effects of schooling. Either way, we would have evidence that education matters.

Twelve factual items in our 1989 Survey of Political Knowledge replicate Gallup items from the 1940s and 1950s and allow a comparison to be made. The knowledge differences between specific education groups (for example, between those finishing high school and those attending college) were of comparable magnitude in 1989 and in the 1940s and 1950s. This suggests that the relative effectiveness of different levels of schooling is about the same today as in the past.

This inference—based on the average differences among groups—is bolstered by a more systematic analysis using multiple logistic regression to estimate the impact of schooling on three knowledge items while controlling for gender and age. To aid interpretation of the results, we used the regression coefficients to estimate the probability that a forty-year-old male or female respondent at different educational levels would correctly answer the knowledge items.[26] These data indicate that the boost in the probability of a correct answer associated with a given step on the educational ladder is very similar today to what it was forty to fifty years ago (see table 5.5).

Table 5.5 Logistic Regression Analysis of the Effects of Education over Time

Knowledge that two-thirds vote is needed to override presidential veto

	Probability of Correct Answer 1947	Change in Probability from One Education Group to the Next		Probability of Correct Answer 1989
		1947	1989	
Males				
No high school diploma	.43			.26
High school diploma	.69	.26	.20	.46
Some college	.83	.14	.14	.60
College graduate	.88	.05	.12	.72
Females				
No high school diploma	.22			.08
High school diploma	.45	.23	.09	.17
Some college	.65	.20	.10	.27
College graduate	.74	.09	.11	.38

Knowledge that the first ten amendments are called the Bill of Rights

	Probability of Correct Answer 1954	Change in Probability from One Education Group to the Next		Probability of Correct Answer 1989
		1954	1989	
Males				
No high school diploma	.21			.23
High school diploma	.50	.29	.29	.52
Some college	.65	.15	.13	.65
College graduate	.81	.16	.18	.83
Females				
No high school diploma	.14			.15
High school diploma	.38	.24	.25	.38
Some college	.53	.15	.14	.52
College graduate	.72	.19	.22	.74

Table 5.5 Logistic Regression Analysis of the Effects of Education over Time (*continued*)

Ability to name both U.S. senators				
	Probability of Correct Answer 1954	Change in Probability from One Education Group to the Next 1954	1989	Probability of Correct Answer 1989
Males				
No high school diploma	.24			.14
High school diploma	.47	.23	.10	.24
Some college	.51	.04	.09	.33
College graduate	.68	.17	.19	.52
Females				
No high school diploma	.12			.07
High school diploma	.28	.16	.06	.13
Some college	.30	.02	.06	.19
College graduate	.47	.17	.15	.34

Sources: For 1989, Survey of Political Knowledge; for veto questions (1947), Gallup study # USAIPO 47–0396; for Bill of Rights and senators (1954), Gallup study # USAIPO 54–0526. Both Gallup data sets obtained from the Roper Center for Public Opinion Research.

These data may not, by themselves, put to rest the objections of those who believe that educational differences are a result of selection effects rather than anything the schools do. Consider, however, the pattern we would expect if selection were the primary force operating here. Advanced schooling is far more common today than in the past—a much greater proportion of the public now graduates from high school, attends or graduates from college, and proceeds to graduate education. Thus, citizens at a given educational level above that of high school dropout—especially the highest levels—are a much less selective group than in the past. If the higher knowledge levels of the better educated were once largely the result of cognitive or social advantages enjoyed by those able to move up educationally, that is far less likely to be true today.[27] Because the knowledge differences between educational levels today are as large as they were in the past, it is reasonable to conclude that the schools and the abilities and habits they develop in students are largely responsible.

This argument is strongly supported by the massive secondary analysis of survey data presented in Herbert Hyman's, Charles Wright's, and John Shelton Reed's *The Enduring Effects of Education*. On the basis of comparisons involving 54 surveys, approximately 80,000 respondents, and 250 knowledge measures—most of which dealt with public affairs or politically relevant topics—the authors conclude that "education produces large, pervasive, and enduring effects on knowledge and receptivity to knowledge" (1975: 109). Their findings survive numerous controls for the demographic characteristics, social origins, and cognitive ability of respondents (which address the issue of self-selection) and extend over a wide span of time and range of birth cohorts.

Although evidence for the various impacts of education on political knowledge is strong, one aspect remains troubling. In spite of significant increases in educational attainment, aggregate levels of political knowledge are about the same today as they were forty to fifty years ago, raising the possibility that the schools today are less effective at transmitting political information or stimulating political engagement. Why, given dramatically increasing educational opportunities, higher average levels of educational attainment, and the strong relation between education and political knowledge at the individual level, have aggregate political knowledge levels remained relatively stable over the past half century? Although no definitive answer exists, it is clear that during the past forty years, a substantial decline in overall political engagement among the public has occurred. This change is manifested in lower levels of interest in campaigns, weakened psychological attachment to political parties, and sharp declines in the belief that government is responsive to the citizenry.[28] According to Ruy Teixeira's analysis, these changes in engagement explain much of the decline in voter turnout over the period—even as education and other demographic changes were working in the opposite direction (1992: chap. 2). Driving much of the decline in engagement and participation was a decline in political mobilization from such sources as the political parties and social movements (Rosenstone and Hansen, 1993: chap. 6). These forces would certainly affect political knowledge levels as well, given the strong link between knowledge and political engagement. In the face of these changes, knowledge levels might well have declined dramatically if education levels had not increased during the past forty years.

Explaining Group Differences in Political Knowledge

Our analysis in chapter 4 documented substantial group differences in political knowledge. Much of this can be accounted for by the structural disadvantages faced by women, blacks, the young, and the economically less affluent (see figure 5.1 and table 5.1). This is most strongly and consistently the case for the last of these four groups. Nearly 80 percent of the simple correlation between income (which is included as part of the structural variable in figure 5.1) and political knowledge (.44 in the 1988 NES survey and .46 in the 1989 Survey of Political Knowledge) is explained by the relations between income and the other structural and behavioral variables. Put another way, less affluent citizens are less knowledgeable largely because income is related to holding a politically impinged job and being more formally educated, and because these structural conditions increase the likelihood that one will have the opportunity, ability, and motivation to learn about politics. The relations between political knowledge and the remaining three groups are more complex.

Age and Political Knowledge

The simple correlation between age and measures of general political knowledge is relatively low (.06 in the 1988 NES and .12 in the 1989 Survey of Political Knowledge).[29] But age represents two very different types of influence, and these tend to work against each other in affecting knowledge levels. Age is a measure of one's position in the life cycle—a notion that captures both the amount of time one has been exposed to the political world, as well as changing aspects of one's social and economic circumstances. Political knowledge is likely to increase with lengthier exposure to politics because repetition increases learning. In addition, interest (and thus knowledge) may grow as one encounters certain events, such as sending children to school, buying a house, or dealing with laws involving inheritance. Age also denotes one's generational position, which reflects events and circumstances unique to the time that members of a particular cohort were growing up and being socialized to politics. The likely impact of generational differences is complex. On the one hand, there are substantial generational differences in the opportunity for formal education. Older cohorts in the United States had a much lower likelihood of graduating from high school and attending college than does the current generation of young people, thus advantaging the latter in their ability and opportunity to learn about politics. On the other hand, more recent generations have shown a large and persistent disengagement from politics, evidenced by lower levels of following politics in the media, interest in politics, and certain political behaviors like voting (Delli Carpini, 1986). This should substantially depress the motivation to learn about politics. Beyond this, generational differences in issue salience are likely to have less systematic—yet potentially important—effects on what is learned. The consequence of these offsetting influences is a relatively weak correlation between age and knowledge.

As can be seen in figure 5.1, the actual impact of age on political knowledge is substantially stronger than indicated by the simple correlations. Much of this impact is about equally split between the indirect effects of age on knowledge through both structural circumstances (beta = -.16) and the cluster of motivational factors labeled "behavioral" (+.18).[30] The negative sign of the relation between age and structural circumstances means that younger citizens are more likely to be educated, to earn (or be in families that earn) more money, and to hold politically impinged jobs, suggesting that this path is capturing the generational rather than the life cycle impact of age. The positive relation between age and attitudes means that older citizens are more likely to be politically engaged. This is likely to be the result of both generational and life cycle effects.

Not all of the relation between age and political knowledge is accounted for by structural and behavioral variables. Indeed, when all of the demographic, structural, and behavioral variables are held constant in a multivariate analysis (table 5.1), the direct effect of age is actually larger than the simple correlations (.08 in the 1988 data and .23 in the 1989 data).[31] We suspect that this direct path represents both life cycle and generational differences in circumstances, attitudes, and behaviors that are not adequately captured by our measures. This is supported by a closer examination of the types of knowledge on which older and younger citizens differ. For example, age appears to boost knowledge of political leaders and of partisan matters more than other domains of knowledge—a finding consistent with the fact that younger citizens are less likely to follow politics or to develop strong partisan attachments. Partial correlation coefficients (with education held constant) between age and several knowledge items show that the strongest positive correlations are, not surprisingly, for historical facts that many older citizens would know through experience—for example, the partisanship of former presidents (see table 5.6). Awareness of current leaders and partisan majorities, however, is also positively correlated with age.

A more general comparison of age differences over time suggests a sharp generational break in political engagement, with recent cohorts of young people evidencing substantially lower levels of knowledge about current public figures and issues than did younger cohorts in previous years. According to analyses of Gallup and Roper surveys by the Times Mirror Center for the People and the Press, age differences in knowledge for many types of issues today are greater than they were during the period from 1941 to 1975 (Times Mirror, 1990). In surveys taken during the 1940s, 1950s, and 1960s, young people were about as knowledgeable

Table 5.6 Partial Correlations between Age and Knowledge (Controlling for Education)

FDR's party	.48	What is the Superfund	.06
Truman's party	.43	What arms limited by IMF treaty	.05
Nixon's party	.30	Who does U.S. support in Nicaragua	.04
Which party has majority in House	.25	Percent black in U.S.	.03
Knowledge about New Deal	.23	Can students be required to say pledge of allegiance	.03
Percent unemployed in U.S.	.23	Can communist run for president	.03
Which party has majority in Senate	.22	Does U.S. have trade deficit	.02
Name of U.S. senators	.21	Rehnquist's ideology	.02
Name of U.S. representative	.21	Who does U.S. support in El Salvador	.02
Name of state attorney general (state survey)	.21	Percent poor in U.S.	.01
Who appoints judges	.20	Who declares war	.01
Which party has majority in state senate (state survey)	.19	Effect of tariff on U.S. trade	.00
Name vice president	.18	Provision of Fifth Amendment	–.00
Date of the New Deal	.16	Size of U.S. budget	–.04
State legislature is in session (state survey)	.16	Knowledge of *Rust* decision (state survey)	–.04
What is a recession	.14	Which party opposes abortion (state survey)	–.04
Which party has majority in state house	.13	Spending on defense	–.05
(state survey)	.13		
Women's suffrage	.12	First ten amendments are Bill of Rights	–.07
Name of governor	.12	Can states prohibit abortion	–.07
Judicial review	.12	Spending on education	–.08
Date of suffrage	.09	Provisions of First Amendment	–.15
Does U.S. have budget deficit	.09	Does Constitution include right to government benefits (state survey)	–.16
Name of lieutenant governor (state survey)	.07	Does Constitution include freedom of speech and press (state survey)	–.17
Veto override majority	.07	Does Constitution include consumers' rights (state survey)	–.20
Length of president's term	.06		

Sources: Items labeled "state survey" are from two statewide Virginia surveys. Other items are from the 1989 Survey of Political Knowledge.

as older people on questions about political issues and public figures. Beginning in the mid-1970s, reported attentiveness to the news fell among young respondents, and their knowledge levels about things in the news lagged behind that of older respondents. This conclusion is supported by our finding of an emerging generation gap in political knowledge in NES surveys conducted over the past thirty years (chapter 4).

Although the net effect of both life cycle and generational forces appears to produce lower knowledge levels for younger citizens, this relation is not immutable. For several contemporary issues—the intermediate range nuclear missile treaty, the Superfund, U.S. involvement in Central America, abortion—younger citizens are only slightly less knowledgeable than their elders. And for many questions bearing on constitutional rights, younger citizens are more knowledgeable than older ones. Taken as a whole, these patterns suggest that individuals become increasingly attentive to politics and to political leaders as they grow older, but that despite structural advantages, recent generations are less politically engaged (and thus less politically knowledgeable) than were past generations. Perhaps most significantly, the opportunity and the perceived relevance of certain issues to younger generations can mitigate this relation, while the lack of opportunity or the perceived irrelevance of issues can intensify it.

Race and Political Knowledge

The simple correlation between race and political knowledge is strong and negative (-.18 in the NES data and -.33 in the Survey of Political Knowledge). In the NES data, about two-thirds of this relation is accounted for by structural and behavioral differences (table 5.1), with most explained by the single path from race, through structure and behaviors, to knowledge (figure 5.1). Findings based on the Survey of Political Knowledge are similar, though somewhat more complex. Only about a third of the simple correlation is accounted for by structural and behavioral differences, again with most of this explained by the single path from race, through structure and behaviors, to knowledge.[32]

As with age, we suspect that the direct path from race to knowledge (-.06 and -.21 in the 1988 and 1989 surveys, respectively) results from structural and attitudinal differences not well captured in our analyses. Evidence regarding the relation between race and knowledge of racially relevant facts from the 1985 NES pilot study (see chapter 4) and from our state and local surveys provides support for this. So too does our finding that blacks are less knowledgeable than whites about the kinds of facts taught in schools (rules of the game) even when levels of education are controlled for. This indicates that measures of years of schooling can miss differences in the quality of education—an issue especially relevant to blacks who are more likely than whites to be educated in schools that are resource-poor (Kozol, 1991).

Gender and Political Knowledge

The impact of gender on political knowledge is perhaps the most complex and problematic. The existence of at least some gender difference in political knowledge is not surprising, given the history of women's exclusion from national politics and the continuing inequality between women and men in many of the resources that contribute to political integration. The size of gender differences (see tables 4.8 and 4.9) and their apparent persistence over a period when other indicators showed increased political engagement by women (see figure 4.3) raise questions about the genesis of the gap and the factors that contribute to its maintenance. Although much of this gap results from circumstances unique to women, answers to these questions may help us to understand more about the influences on political learning for groups with similar experiences (for example, blacks), as well as for the dynamics of political learning in general.

Most theories regarding gender differences in political orientations are rooted in structural and situational explanations: females know less about politics than males because of differences in how the sexes are socialized and because of the different opportunities afforded them to engage the political world. But how, specifically, do structural and situational inequities translate into differences in political knowledge? The simplest argument is that they act as a barrier, preventing women who have the motivation to learn about politics from having the opportunity or ability to do so. In most age cohorts, women have less formal education than men (and education is related to political knowledge). A smaller percentage of women is in the labor force (and employment outside the home provides politically relevant experiences). Women are also likely to work in less politically impinged jobs (Luskin, 1990). Unmarried women have lower incomes than unmarried men (and income is associated with political knowledge). Because of child-care responsibilities, women have less time for political activity and spend less time in contact with adults—who are more likely than children to talk about politics.[33] According to this argument, if women had the same incomes, educational attainment, types of employment, free time, and social and work-related contacts as men, their levels of political knowledge would be similar. If these factors do not constitute barriers in the strict sense of the word, they may nevertheless provide negative reinforcement, discouraging women from learning about politics. Socioeconomic disadvantages simply make it more difficult for women to be psychologically engaged in politics.

The simple bivariate relation between knowledge (as measured by the fifty-one-item and twenty-one-item scales in the two national surveys) and gender is -.27 and -.31, respectively (see table 5.1). To the extent that gender differences in levels of political knowledge result from structural, situational, and attitudinal differences, controlling for such differences should reduce this bivariate relation. In both data sets the betas (showing the net impact) are smaller than the bivariate correlations, dropping from −.31 to −.17 using the 1988 data and from −.27 to −.21 using the 1989 data. Put another way, these data suggest that roughly one-quarter to one-half of the relation between gender and political knowledge is explained by structural, situational, and attitudinal variables.

The role played by specific structural and situational factors differs by gender and by position in the life cycle. We estimated the full model (in other words, including all variables) separately for older (age forty-five and up) and younger (age eighteen to forty-four) women and men in the 1988 NES survey. Having young children in the home depresses the political knowledge levels of younger women: a coefficient of -.58 indicates that having two young children "costs" a woman over one point on the twenty-one-point scale.[34] Living in the South was associated with lower levels of political knowledge for both younger and older women (coefficients of −.97 and −1.19, respectively) but had a much weaker effect on men. Beyond these factors, other personal characteristics had about the same effect on men as they did on women.

The path model (figure 5.1) allows us to decompose the simple bivariate relation between gender and knowledge into four specific pathways. Consistent with the notion of structural barriers, about 16 percent of the original relation (1988 data) is explained by the path from gender through structure to knowledge. A slightly smaller percentage (13 percent) is explained by the negative reinforcement argument, defined here as the path from gender through structure and attitudes to knowledge. Taken together, the two structure-based arguments account for about 30 percent of the original relation.

The path model also provides some insight into what is missed by the structural arguments. An additional 23 percent of the original relation is accounted for by the path from gender through attitudes to knowledge, suggesting that even while in nominally equal socioeconomic circumstances, women are less psychologically engaged in politics and thus less likely to be politically informed. And the direct path from gender to knowledge remains large and significant; it accounts for more than 50 percent of the original relation.

Undoubtedly some of the strength of these two pathways results from measurement error and a failure to account for all the relevant structural and situational factors that depress women's knowledge of politics.[35] It also seems likely, however, that some is due to more deep-seated differences in socialization. Most obviously relevant here is explicitly political socialization, which may be different for many females as a result of the legacy of de jure gender discrimination and attendant societal views of the "proper" (in other words, nonpolitical) role of women. Although few women alive today were prohibited by law from voting or taking part in politics, many were socialized to politics by mothers who were (and by fathers who directly experienced the presuffrage period). Traditional views of the appropriate role for women in politics have not vanished. Although only a small minority of survey respondents express such views, they are found in younger as well as older cohorts (Bennett and Bennett, 1989). When conservative norms were not explicitly transmitted to the next generation, the example of nonparticipation by mothers would still have a significant impact on daughters (and, in a different way, on sons).[36] Evidence to support a socialization theory of the gender gap in knowledge can be found in the civics knowledge and attitudes of school students. Niemi's and Junn's (1993) analysis of data from the National Assessment of Educational Progress (a large national survey of school-age children) found that males were more likely than females "to say that government is their favorite subject, or that they enjoy civics classes more than their other classes" (6). Male students were significantly more politically knowledgeable than females, even after controlling for a number of background and curriculum variables.

Gender role socialization that is not explicitly political may also have significant political implications. The nature of—even the very existence of—many of these differences between women and men is controversial. As summarized by scholars such as Carol Gilligan (1982) and Deborah Tannen (1990), girls from an early age are less interested in the rules of the game and notions of abstract justice than are boys. Their games tend to be less conflictual and more likely to founder if disputes arise (Lever, 1976: 483; Lever, 1978: 476). In addition, girls (and women) are more interested in and more likely to talk about personal, immediate, consensual issues, whereas boys and men turn to more conflictual, abstract, and less personal topics. To the extent that these generalizations apply to the political world, we would expect women to be less knowledgeable and concerned about much of mainstream national politics, given its conflictual, rules-driven, abstract, and physically and psychologically distant nature.

These socialization explanations are difficult to assess directly with the data we have available, although the path in figure 5.1 from gender through attitudes to knowledge provides some circumstantial support for the political socialization argument, and the direct path from gender to knowledge is consistent with a gender socialization explanation. Beyond this, testing the socialization explanations necessarily consists of deriving plausible propositions that follow from them, and then looking for data that support or contradict them.

One such proposition is that socialization away from mainstream politics would affect the motivation to learn about politics, rather than the ability or opportunity to do so. If this is the case, we would expect women to exhibit greater levels of knowledge on issues perceived as more relevant to them. This was precisely the pattern we observed in a range of different surveys: topics of potentially special relevance to women showed smaller or nonexistent gender gaps. For example, a 1994 Times Mirror national survey found women to be 22 percentage points less able than men to name Boris Yeltsin as the president of Russia, and 18 points less able to name the Serbs as the group besieging Sarajevo; however, on the issue of health care, which is a central concern in the private sphere, women were only 4 points less likely than men to know that President Clinton's proposed reform program mandated employers to provide coverage to their workers. And there were trivial or nonexistent gender gaps on knowledge of presidential candidate positions on abortion in the 1992 National Election Study and gubernatorial candidate positions in two 1989 Virginia election surveys we conducted.[37]

An important implication of both the structural and socialization arguments is that women opt out of national politics because of some combination of their exclusion from it and its perceived irrelevance to them, relative to the costs of engagement. Thus, within more hospitable arenas for women's political activities, gender differences in knowledge should be smaller or nonexistent. Local politics may provide one such setting. Issues that directly affect family, schooling, and community are most often and most tangibly debated in the local arena. Given this physical and symbolic closeness to the private sphere of women, their participation in local politics has always been viewed as more acceptable, and so this arena has been more accessible. This access is reflected in the relatively high percentage of female representation in city and county leadership positions as compared to that in state and national legislative or executive positions (Darcy, Welch, and Clark, 1987). If historical exclusion and a sense of issue irrelevance are partly responsible for women's relatively lower levels of knowledge about national politics, then gender differences in knowledge should be muted at the local level.

Several surveys confirmed this expectation. Women in the Richmond, Virginia, metropolitan area were at least as knowledgeable as men on such topics as how the mayor and city council are selected, which party controlled the county board of supervisors, and the names of elected and appointed officials (table 5.7). Women were quite a bit more likely than men to know the name of the head of the local school system, a finding confirmed nationally by the General Social Survey.[38]

Table 5.7 Knowledge of Local Politics, by Gender

Survey and Subject	Males % Correct	Females % Correct	% Difference	Odds Ratio
Richmond city survey (1991), *N*=800				
Who is Boris Yeltsin	43	23	–20	2.5
% needed to override a veto	45	26	–19	2.3
Party control of U.S. House	60	41	–19	2.2
Who reviews constitutionality of laws	72	61	–11	1.6
How is city council elected	60	53	–7	1.3
How is mayor selected	62	59	–3	1.1
Name the city manager	60	60	0	1.0
Name the school superintendent	11	18	+7	0.6
Richmond city survey (1990), *N*=409				
Who is the current mayor	31	28	–3	1.2
How is mayor selected	62	59	–3	1.1
Heard or read about historic designation controversy	81	84	+3	0.8
Chesterfield County survey (1991), *N*=329				
National unemployment rate	55	31	–24	2.7
Does U.S. have a trade deficit	92	81	–11	2.7
First ten amendments are the Bill of Rights	74	63	–11	1.7
Is there a county impact fee	34	26	–8	1.5
Harry Truman's party affiliation	65	60	–5	1.2
Name the local U.S. representative	35	31	–4	1.2
Which party has most seats on county Board of Supervisors	33	32	–1	1.1
Name the school superintendent	30	40	+10	0.6
General Social Survey (1987), *N*=1819				
Name governor	82	71	–11	1.9
Name U.S. representative	38	31	–7	1.4
Name head of local school system	28	33	+5	0.8

Sources: Richmond city and Chesterfield County surveys conducted by the authors. General Social Survey conducted by the National Opinion Research Center at the University of Chicago.
Note: Shaded rows contain national or state knowledge items for comparison.

Two local surveys also included questions on national politics and provided a basis of comparison. The gender differences were much more pronounced for national politics. For all of the questions examined, the median gender difference on local politics items was –3 percentage points; for national and state items it was –11 points. Taking account of structural and situational differences between the women and the men (via multiple regression analyses), the gender gap in knowledge of local politics is actually one with a small (though statistically nonsignificant) female advantage.

Our exploration of the sources of the gender gap in political knowledge highlights the complex, interactive effects of structural, attitudinal, and environmental factors, as well as the difficulty in capturing these processes with standard measures of political engagement and structural opportunity. Given the similarities between women and African Americans in the obstacles each faced in achieving full rights of citizenship, much of what we have found about the gender gap in political knowledge may also apply to the race gap. The absence of legal barriers to participation in politics for women and blacks is no guarantee that the opportunities are, in fact, the same as for men and whites.

The lack of a gender gap on gender-relevant issues and matters of local politics also provides a vivid example of the situational nature of political knowledge and reinforces our earlier caveat regarding the dimensionality of knowledge. Political knowledge is mostly—but not entirely—unidimensional. Some types of issues are of special relevance to certain groups, and some arenas of politics are more accessible to them. Where this is true, the groups will be more motivated to learn and better able to do so.

The Impact of the Information and Political Environments

A wide variety of personal and group characteristics, attitudes, and behaviors are statistically associated with political knowledge. Our model, however, has a significant limitation: it is a closed system based entirely on factors specific to the individual and does not take account of external factors critical to political learning. Two omitted factors are noteworthy. First is the *information environment*, which varies enormously, and with great consequence for how well the public is able to comprehend the political world. Second is the effect of the *political environment* on individual engagement in politics. Citizens vary in their interest not only according to personal characteristics and socialization experiences, but also with how the political environment acts upon them (Rosenstone and Hansen, 1993).[39] Although these two external factors are difficult—and in some ways impossible—to include in a static model like figure 5.1, we have tried to take account of them as we explored the specific influences within the motivation-ability-opportunity triad. We now examine these impacts more directly.

Citizens occupy a world of considerable variation in the opportunity to learn about politics. This variation is manifested in many ways: in the political information available through their jobs; in their political, social, and cultural settings (for example, the kinds of people they interact with on a regular basis); and of course through the mass media. Although how citizens choose to attend to available information will differ, the amount and type of information available also affects how much they learn.

One reason effects of the mass media have been difficult to detect is that most research in this area assumes the opportunity to learn is constant—that is, adequate information is available through the modern news media, regardless of where an individual lives. Consequently, variability in knowledge among individuals is usually attributed to individual differences in motivation and ability. In fact, however, there is considerable evidence that the media environment is important. This evidence comes from a variety of settings and typically bears on only a small portion of the range of political knowledge. Yet the accumulated weight of the evidence indicates that what is available to citizens is a more important factor in their learning than has generally been acknowledged.

Steven Chaffee and Donna Wilson (1977) found that survey respondents in communities with more newspapers (that is, a media-rich environment) were able to name more problems facing their state than respondents in media-poor communities. Similarly, Peter Clarke and Eric Fredin (1978) found that citizens in communities with highly competitive newspapers had greater knowledge about their U.S. Senate races than respondents in less competitive or monopoly communities. Studies utilizing the Philadelphia-New Jersey-New York media environment have demonstrated strong effects related to the opportunity to learn. Scott Keeter and Harry Wilson (1986) and Keeter and Cliff Zukin (1983) demonstrated how media coverage of presidential primary campaigns occurring in states adjacent to New Jersey—and thus not of direct relevance to New Jersey citizens, whose own primary was later in the process—produced greater learning among citizens exposed via the local media than among those who saw the same events only through the national media. The extent of such "passive learning" was impressive (see also Zukin and Snyder, 1984).

A number of studies have demonstrated the effects of highly contested campaigns for seats in the House of Representatives. When both candidates spend more on advertising and generate more local news coverage, citizens learn more. Peter Clarke and Susan Evans combined citizen survey data from the 1978 National Election Study, content analyses of the news, and surveys of journalists in congressional districts for which NES data were available. They found large variations in levels of voter knowledge about the candidates and were able to explain much of this variation by the extent of campaign coverage in the media. "Even in the face of campaign spending, press attention is strongly related to the public's understanding about both incumbents and challengers in tight races, and about challengers in lopsided contests" (1983: 98). In addition, they found that campaign expenditures were strongly correlated with what voters knew about both candidates in races for open seats and about challengers in close races (99).

The Case of State Politics

State government and politics provides a natural setting for exploring the impact of the media environment on levels of political knowledge. Media coverage of state government and politics varies considerably. Media located in or near state capitals are likely to pay greater attention to state news than are those in distant areas. There are several reasons why, once one leaves the media environment of a state capital, coverage of state politics declines. Despite the intrinsic importance of state news, journalists historically have paid relatively little attention to state government and politics.[40] The lack of visual appeal dampens television news' interest in covering such stories (Gormley, 1978). Many state capitals are small cities far from the population centers, so coverage is expensive and usually understaffed for the task. A 1984 survey found that 38 percent of newspapers' state bureaus had just one reporter during legislative sessions, and 58 percent had only one reporter between sessions (Brooks and Gassaway, 1985: 29–31). Finally, media located in markets that cross state boundaries must divide air time and news space across two or more jurisdictions, further reducing coverage of state politics.

As a result of these different media environments, individuals living near state capitals are likely to have a greater opportunity to learn about state politics and government, whereas individuals in multistate markets may have considerably less opportunity. Our 1990 and 1991 surveys on state political knowledge in Virginia enabled us to test this notion. Residents of Richmond (the state capital) should know more than residents of other parts of the state; residents of the northern Virginia suburbs of Washington, D.C. (a multistate metropolitan area) should be the least knowledgeable. To test this hypothesis, respondents to the surveys were sorted according to their residence in these three geographic areas (Richmond, northern Virginia, and the rest of the state).

The Richmond area media, which have easy access to the state legislature and state executive officials, devote much greater attention to news of state politics than do the media elsewhere in the state, as a content analysis of the *Richmond Times-Dispatch, Washington Post,* and *Fairfax Journal* (the largest northern Virginia daily) confirmed. The northern Virginia area has no in-state VHF network affiliate television stations, and local newspaper readership is dominated by the out-of-state *Washington Post.*[41]

A direct comparison of knowledge levels across the regions would be misleading, owing to demographic differences between the residents. In particular, three variables would confound this simple comparison: length of residence in Virginia, education, and levels of knowledge about national politics. Longer-term residents know more about state politics than those who have spent less time in the state, but northern Virginians (on average) have lived in the state for shorter periods than their fellow citizens (mean of 14.5 years since age eighteen for northern Virginia residents, compared with 24.0 elsewhere). Similarly, residents of northern Virginia are much better educated: nearly half of our northern Virginia survey respondents (46 percent) report having a four-year college degree, compared with 23 percent in Richmond and 19 percent elsewhere. Because the goal of our analysis is to determine the impact of the media environment on learning about state politics, we need to control for variations in knowledge about national politics that might reflect differences in motivation or ability more generally.[42]

To control for these confounding variables and produce estimates of the effect of living in different regions of the state, we employed multiple logistic regression analysis to compute the probability that a typical Virginia respondent (based on the modal or average category in each of our independent variables) living in Richmond, northern Virginia, and elsewhere would correctly answer each of the items.[43] The estimated probabilities for the state items in the winter 1990 survey (plus knowledge of the death penalty from a survey one year later) show dramatic differences in several of the items, especially when comparing the Richmond and northern Virginia areas with each other (table 5.8). For example, the predicted probability that a resident of northern Virginia would be able to name the state's attorney general was .15; the probability for an individual with the same characteristics in Richmond would be .58. Similarly, the probability that a Richmond resident would know that the general assembly was in session was .75; a demographically comparable northern Virginia resident's probability would be .27.[44]

Table 5.8 Predicted Probability of Correct Answers to Selected Items (Based on Logistic Regression Analysis)

	Richmond Area	Northern Virginia	Rest of State	Difference Richmond-Rest	Difference Northern Virginia-Rest
Name governor	.92	.67	.82	.10	–.15
Name lieutenant governor	.29	.19	.14	.15	.05
Name attorney general	.58	.15	.32	.26	–.17
General Assembly in session	.75	.27	.45	.30	–.18
Party control of House of Delegates	.51	.47	.54	–.03	–.07
Party control of state senate	.38	.25	.33	.05	–.08
Name both U.S. senators	.15	.05	.09	.06	–.04
Name U.S. House member	.25	.33	.33	–.08	.00
Knows Virginia has the death penalty	.89	.52	.68	.21	–.16

Source: 1990 statewide Virginia survey conducted by the authors; death penalty item is from a 1991 statewide Virginia survey.
Note: Entries are predicted probability of a correct answer to the indicated question. Logistic regression was used to estimate the coefficients. These probabilities are for a Virginia resident who is average on the independent variables: a female with some college education who has resided in Virginia at least ten years since age eighteen, has a family income of $35,000 to $50,000 annually, reports following politics "some of the time," and gave three correct answers on the index of national political knowledge (one correct answer in the poll that contained the death penalty item).

All in all, the regional differences in knowledge of state politics provide impressive evidence that differences in the information environment can be very important in affecting what citizens will learn about politics. The magnitude of the differences reveals not only that the media can have an effect, but that the effect can determine whether a minority or a majority of citizens will be aware of a particular leader, event, or policy. The Virginia example for state political news is not an isolated one. There are numerous places in the United States where large urban populations are likely to be exposed to far less state news coverage than in other parts of the state (see Keeter and Wilson, 1986). But the more general point is that what citizens learn is not just a function of their motivation and capability.

The Dog That Didn't Bark: A Missing Ingredient for Promoting Political Knowledge

As Steven Rosenstone and John Mark Hansen demonstrate, variations in political participation across individuals and over time are related not only to characteristics of individuals, but to the efforts of political leaders to mobilize citizens. Indeed, much of the decline in electoral participation since the 1960s can be accounted for by decreases in mobilization, especially mobilization aimed at less affluent citizens (Rosenstone and Hansen, 1993: chap. 7). It stands to reason that political knowledge, too, is affected by mobilization or its absence.

Using the approach employed by Rosenstone and Hansen, we looked for evidence that citizens contacted by the parties or candidates in election campaigns would display greater knowledge about the election (controlling for personal characteristics and other variables). Being contacted was not a statistically significant predictor of knowledge, independent of other factors in the model (suggesting that information provided in the contact itself does not measurably affect a person's knowledge level, at least for the questions in our index). But Rosenstone's and Hansen's analysis suggests that being contacted boosts a person's engagement, an effect we found as well. Since engagement boosts knowledge, contacting may have a reasonably strong indirect effect on knowledge. Supporting this contention, we found that when measures of political engagement are omitted from the regression analysis, reported contact by candidates or parties is a statistically significant predictor of knowledge. The unstandardized regression coefficient suggests that being contacted adds one point, on average, to an individual's knowledge score.[45]

Although this evidence suggests that political organizations have the potential to boost knowledge levels through mobilization, there is not much evidence that they are taking full advantage of this. For example, only about a quarter of the 1992 NES sample reported having been contacted by a party or candidate in an attempt to garner their vote, with 18 percent of those earning less than $15,000 a year reporting such a contact, compared to 31 percent of those earning more than $50,000 a year. Similarly, only 28 percent of those earning less than $15,000 a year reported being contacted to register to vote, compared to 40 percent of those earning more than $50,000.[46]

There is intriguing, if circumstantial, evidence for this relative lack of mobilization in the pattern of relations between income and knowledge. Across all knowledge items in the 1988 National Election Study survey, the median gap between the highest (more than $50,000) and lowest (less than $10,000) income groups is 40 percentage points (see table 5.9). The gaps for recognizing Mikhail Gorbachev or George Shultz are 42 and 41 points, respectively. Significantly, the gaps in knowledge about facts that are arguably of more immediate relevance to the economically disadvantaged are about as large (for example, the gap in identifying Ted Kennedy is 39 points, and the gap for correctly placing the political parties relative to one another on the issue of government services and spending is 43 points). Thus, low-income citizens are as far behind the more affluent in knowledge of people and parties committed to the problems of the disadvantaged as they are in knowledge of presumably less relevant facts.

Table 5.9 Knowledge by Income (Percentage Correct)

	Under $10,000	$10,000–19,999	$20,000–34,999	$35,000–49,999	$50,000 and Above	Difference, Highest Minus Lowest
Interviewer rating of respondent's information level (above average)	15	28	44	45	64	49
Identify Margaret Thatcher	36	53	65	68	83	47
Ideological placement of the parties	36	44	57	66	79	43
Parties' position on government services and spending	36	44	54	68	79	43
Identify Mikhail Gorbachev	46	66	76	80	88	42
Which party controls U.S. House	37	53	60	72	79	42
Ideological placement of the candidates	37	46	59	68	79	42
Identify George Shultz	19	37	39	43	60	41
Identify Yasser Arafat	16	32	40	44	57	41
Identify Ted Kennedy	48	64	72	75	87	39
Which party controls U.S. Senate	34	49	54	64	73	39
Parties' positions on defense spending	40	52	63	62	76	36
Parties' positions on health insurance	30	39	46	49	65	35
Parties' positions on government guarantee of jobs	33	37	49	54	67	34
Identify Jim Wright	6	12	14	15	26	20
Name one House candidate and his/her party	17	28	28	31	35	18
Identify William Rehnquist	0	2	5	3	10	10
Averages (mean)	29	40	49	53	65	37
N	293	363	443	274	266	

Source: 1988 National Election Study.

This is damning evidence of the absence of effective institutions to organize and mobilize the interests of working-class and poor citizens. Under any rational scheme of political mobilization, the political party of the lower social stratum would work to ensure that its likely supporters were aware of its positions. For a variety of reasons identified by such writers as Thomas Byrne Edsall (1984) and Walter Dean Burnham (1982), the Democratic party, labor unions, and other groups are presumably less effective at these tasks than they were in the past, and nothing has taken their place. Whereas the relevance of information for certain groups sometimes overrides other forces (for example, the higher awareness of blacks about the death penalty or women's knowledge about abortion issues), these examples tend to pertain to highly concrete issues about which group mobilization has occurred. More abstract knowledge, useful for ongoing surveillance of the political system as it deals with one's political interests, is still the province of those fortunate enough to advance educationally and financially.

Political learning is affected by the attention citizens pay to politics, their ability to comprehend and absorb what they are exposed to, and the amount and kind of information made available to them. Of these three factors, greatest attention is typically paid to motivation.[47] Motivation is certainly critical to the development of an informed citizenry. Interest, engagement, and a sense of civic duty, however, are not fixed characteristics of individuals. They are influenced both by personal attributes, such as education and income (which are somewhat beyond the control of the individual), and by systemic factors, such as the nature of the information and political environments. They are also influenced by the perceived relevance of politics to individuals and groups and by the legacy of historical patterns of political inclusion and exclusion.

The ability of citizens to learn about politics is as important as their motivation. Education is the key determinant of ability. Both direct and indirect effects of formal education on political knowledge are powerful. Large majorities of the college educated could correctly answer most of the knowledge items in our surveys, but fewer than half of those with high school diplomas or less could do so. Moreover, educated individuals are better positioned to participate in politics, which boosts knowledge, and are more likely to be the target of efforts to inform and mobilize them. Again, however, access to education (and to other circumstances likely to develop one's ability to learn) is often limited by social and economic considerations, leading to systematic differences in who is and who is not informed.

Finally, what citizens learn about politics is dependent on the opportunities presented to them, and these opportunities vary depending on personal and group circumstances. They also vary by the larger information and political environments in which citizens live.[48] Conclusions from our study of knowledge of state politics undoubtedly hold for other arenas as well. Coverage of news about Congress is quite small compared with that for the president, and attention to a typical member of Congress by his or her local press is minuscule, due to many of the same factors that constrain coverage of state politics. It is little wonder that less than half the public—even among the college educated—can name their House member or volunteer the name of any candidate running for Congress. And despite the significance of the Supreme Court in U.S. politics, its composition and operations are highly obscure, as evidenced by the almost complete lack of recognition of the chief justice's name and low levels of awareness that he is a conservative.[49]

Clearly, all the elements of the motivation-ability-opportunity triad have significant impacts on political knowledge levels, both independently and in combination with each other. Just as clearly, all three elements are influenced by a variety of individual, group, and systemic factors. These factors are not randomly distributed among citizens, however, which helps explain why groups that are economically, socially, and politically disadvantaged are also the most likely to be politically uninformed. Although this finding is reason for concern, it also points the way to possible remedies. Since motivation, ability, and opportunity are tied to objective conditions that are somewhat manipulable, it should be possible to change these conditions to produce a more informed and more equitably informed citizenry. For example, making information more easily accessible is likely to increase what people know, especially for the individuals and groups least able to become informed through motivation or ability alone. In the end, there is nothing natural about certain levels of interest, ability, or opportunity. If current levels of these requisites to good citizenship are unable to provide a public that is adequately and equitably informed we should—rather than simply lamenting this state of affairs, blaming those who are underinformed, or arguing that an informed citizenry is unnecessary—work toward creating a political environment more capable of informing the public's discretion.

CHAPTER SIX

The Consequences of Political Knowledge and Ignorance

That men if freed from . . . intellectual error . . . would live together harmoniously . . . cannot be proved or disproved except by trial. But such a proposition is basic to any demand for or justification of a democratic society.—C. B. MACPHERSON, *Democratic Theory: Essays in Retrieval*

Say first, of God above or man below,
What can we reason but from what we know.
—ALEXANDER POPE, *An Essay on Man*

Faith
Faith is an island in the setting sun
But proof, yes
Proof is the bottom line for everyone.
—PAUL SIMON, "Proof"

Why be concerned if Americans know less about politics than an informed observer would deem appropriate? If the information explosion and growth of public education have done little to increase aggregate levels of knowledge? If some citizens are significantly less informed than others? One answer, inspired by the views of Rousseau, Pateman, and others who write from the tradition of communitarian democracy, is that being informed about the workings of government is something to be valued for its own sake, a civic equivalent to Socrates' belief that the unexamined life is not worth living and his entreaty to "know thyself." Thus, uncovering the patterns of what citizens know and don't know is important in its own right, and the individual and group differences in knowledge documented in this book constitute prima facie evidence of systematic failures at this fundamental level of democratic politics.

Knowledge is also an instrumental good that helps to enlighten one's self-interest and to translate it into effective political action. A broadly and equitably informed citizenry assures that the public will is determined fairly and that government action is viewed as legitimate. If more knowledgeable citizens are better equipped to articulate their interests and better able to reward and punish political leaders for their actions, then when interests clash, less informed citizens are at a decided disadvantage.

Is there tangible evidence in support of these propositions? Many of the individual and collective effects of an informed citizenry are likely to be too subtle to be easily measured with the kinds of survey data available. In particular, because most surveys focus on opinions and behaviors tied to electoral politics, the impact of knowledge for civic roles outside of this arena is not well documented. Nonetheless, in this chapter we will demonstrate a number of ways political knowledge contributes to good citizenship and thus to the polity more broadly. First, political knowledge promotes civic virtues like political tolerance. Second, political knowledge promotes active participation in politics. Third, political knowledge helps citizens construct stable, consistent opinions on a broad array of topics. Fourth, political knowledge helps citizens identify their true interests and connect these with their political attitudes. And fifth, political knowledge helps citizens link their attitudes with their participation so that their participation serves their interests. On all five of these dimensions, the differences between the best- and least-informed citizens in the United States are substantial and often dramatic.

The value of political knowledge is situational, relative, and collective. First, although the wide variety of political choices citizens are asked to make and the numerous activities they can engage in suggest that an effective citizen needs to be broadly informed about politics, the instrumental benefits of knowledge usually derive from specific information relevant to a particular situation. For example, knowledge of civil liberties and judicial processes promotes political tolerance, and knowledge of where candidates stand on abortion is necessary if a voter is to use this issue to choose among candidates.

Second, the value of political knowledge is relative in that, for most manifestations of citizenship, additional increments of knowledge produce measurable improvements in the performance of those roles. All things being equal, the more informed people are, the better able they are to perform as citizens. Moreover, the most knowledgeable group in several of our analyses—the top quartile—is not composed of superhumans who have been required, in Walter Lippmann's skeptical words, "to yield an unlimited quantity of public spirit, interest, curiosity, and effort" (1925:2). And yet they arguably meet high standards of citizenship.

Third, the benefits to individuals are also consequential for the system as a whole—that is, the value of political knowledge is collective. All interests in society benefit from a greater consensus on democratic values and an accompanying tolerance for divergent viewpoints. Broader participation increases the legitimacy of the government and provides it with greater authority to act on behalf of society's interests. A better-informed citizenry allows for a more subtle and sophisticated public discourse about the issues of the day. And a better-informed citizenry places important limitations on the ability of public officials, interest groups, and other elites to manipulate public opinion and act in ways contrary to the public interest.

Citizens with greater or lesser amounts of knowledge differ in many ways other than in what they know, and these differences can confound the search for knowledge's effects. In most of our analyses we utilize statistical controls and other techniques in an effort to isolate the effects of knowledge. But because knowledge is intimately tied to other characteristics of good citizenship—for example, it is both a cause and an effect of political interest and participation—it is not always possible nor sensible to disentangle it from other related qualities. Indeed, by controlling for other variables in an attempt to isolate the independent contribution of knowledge, we may be underestimating knowledge's impact in some instances. Consequently, raising knowledge levels could have, in addition to the direct benefits we describe, a number of indirect benefits as well.

Promoting Support for Democratic Values

It is axiomatic in a democracy that although conflict over the proper course of public policy may be inevitable, there is consensus on fundamental procedures for resolving conflicts and determining policy. To function well, a democracy needs a consensus among its citizens on a number of specific values, such as majority rule and minority rights, the rule of law, or freedom of the press. Political knowledge entails an awareness of key democratic values. Equally important, political knowledge promotes the acceptance of these values.

One key democratic value is *political tolerance,* "a willingness to permit the expression of ideas or interests one opposes" (Sullivan, Piereson, and Marcus, 1982: 2). Sparked by evidence from a number of surveys conducted since the 1950s, there is considerable debate over the extent of political tolerance among the public. There is nearly unanimous public agreement on the basic principles of free speech and other civil liberties, but their application to specific cases involving feared or despised groups is much more controversial (Prothro and Grigg, 1960; McClosky and Brill, 1983). For example, majorities of the public appear willing to deny members of certain groups the right to run for office, hold public rallies, teach in the public schools, or even belong to such a group (Gibson, 1992: 340).[1]

To test the impact of political knowledge on tolerance, we placed a small module of tolerance items on our Survey of Political Knowledge.

Respondents were asked which of three groups (communists, atheists, or the Ku Klux Klan) they liked the least.[2] They were then asked whether they agreed or disagreed with permitting members of that group to make a speech in the city or town where they lived or to teach in the public schools.[3] Just over one-fourth (27 percent) of the sample said they would permit a member of their chosen group to teach in the public schools, and 58 percent said they would permit them to make a speech.[4] We constructed a simple tolerance index by summing responses to the two items.[5]

Political tolerance increases dramatically as knowledge of civil rights and liberties increases (see figure 6.1). But what is the dynamic driving this relation? The answer may be found in considering the explanations for why education is related to tolerance. Several studies suggest that education is strongly correlated with tolerance (Nunn, Crockett, and Williams, 1978; Bobo and Licari, 1989), but the mechanism by which it does so is not obvious.[6] Three major routes of influence have been hypothesized. First is simply the exposure to diverse ideas that is an inevitable consequence of formal education. As Samuel Stouffer put it: "Schooling puts a person in touch with people whose ideas and values are different from one's own" (1955: 127). This contact with alternative views occurs within the context of an institution that ostensibly values diversity and argument. Second, education promotes cognitive sophistication, which may promote a closer connection between general norms and specific applications (Bobo and Licari, 1989). Third—and most central to our focus here—education may provide specific instruction regarding the norms and procedures of a liberal democracy. Knowledge of these key societal values would seem a necessary, if not sufficient, condition for the development of a tolerant public (McClosky and Brill, 1983).

We fashioned a test of the third explanation—the so-called social learning hypothesis. If the utility of political knowledge is situation-specific, then political tolerance should be especially affected by information that is relevant to this democratic norm. Among the knowledge items in the survey were several that dealt with issues of civil liberties and the principal institution associated with disputes over them, the Supreme Court. An index was created using five of these items (alpha = .63).[7] The remaining knowledge items in the survey were used to form an alternate index. The net impact of civil liberties knowledge on tolerance was estimated using a multiple regression analysis. In addition to knowledge, the model included several variables known to be related to tolerance: education, family income, ideology, age, sex, race, residence in the South, and political engagement.[8] The results of this analysis with and without political knowledge included in the equation show that knowledge of civil lib-

Figure 6.1 Political Tolerance by Knowledge of Courts and Civil Liberties

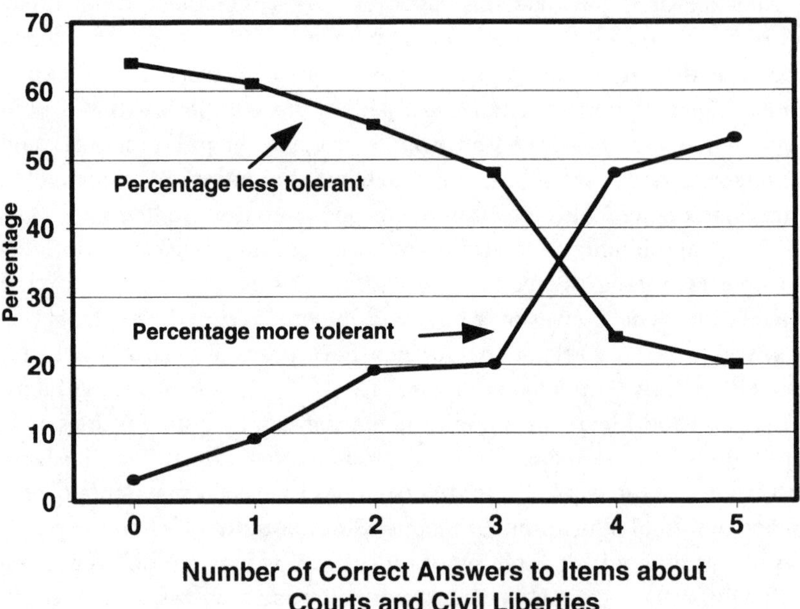

erties was a much stronger predictor than any other factor in the model (table 6.1). Including it in the equation doubled the explained variance of the model (from 8 to 16 percent). In addition, two variables that were significant predictors of tolerance when political knowledge is not included were weakened considerably when knowledge entered the analysis. Most notably, education lost nearly all of its predictive power. Gender was the only other variable with a statistically significant coefficient (though its effect, too, was weakened).

Table 6.1 Multivariate Regression Model of Political Tolerance

	Without Knowledge		With Knowledge	
Variable	Unstandardized *b* and Standard Error	beta (standardized regression coefficient)	Unstandardized *b* and Standard Error	beta (standardized regression coefficient)
Knowledge of Supreme Court and civil liberties			0.299	.35****
			.043	
Education	0.107	.16***	0.030	.04
	.032		.032	
Sex (female)	−0.371	−.14**	−0.262	−.10*
	.118		.114	

Table 6.1 Multivariate Regression Model of Political Tolerance (*continued*)

	Without Knowledge		With Knowledge	
Variable	Unstandardized *b* and Standard Error	beta (standardized regression coefficient)	Unstandardized *b* and Standard Error	beta (standardized regression coefficient)
Income	–0.035 .052	–.03	–0.070 .050	–.06
Age	0.003 .004	.03	0.000 .003	.00
Race (black)	–0.148 .207	–.03	0.024 .200	.01
Region (South)	0.085 .120	.03	0.158 .115	.06
Political engagement	0.116 .035	.15***	0.060 .034	.08
Ideology (conservative)	0.029 .050	.03	–0.002 .048	–.00
Constant	5.78 .588		5.74 .562	
Adjusted r^2	.08		.16	
Standard error of the regression	1.27		1.22	
N	503		503	

Source: 1989 Survey of Political Knowledge.
Note: The top entry in the cell is the unstandardized regression coefficient (*b*). The bottom entry is the standard error.
* = $p<.05$. ** = $p<.01$. *** = $p<.001$. **** = $p<.0001$.

This suggests that political knowledge is a significant influence on political tolerance, independent of education and other factors. But is it the particular type of knowledge—knowledge about civil liberties and the Supreme Court—that matters, as suggested by the social-learning hypothesis? Political knowledge is a very general characteristic. Perhaps the crucial aspect is overall political awareness or general cognitive sophistication and not the specific type of knowledge captured by the civil liberties index. When substituted for the civil liberties index, the alternate index (composed of all other knowledge items) performs about as well in the regression analysis. But this is because individuals who are knowledgeable on the civil liberties index are also likely to be generally knowledgeable about politics (the correlation between the two indexes is .69). When the two indexes are included in the regression together, the coefficient for the alternate index shrinks to insignificance, but the civil liberties measure remains strong. Although this falls short of proving Macpherson's proposition "that men if freed from . . . intellectual error . . . would live together harmoniously," it is striking evidence of the import of an informed citizenry and of the situation-specific utility of political information.

Evidence suggesting that relevant political knowledge promotes other democratic norms and values is provided by James Fishkin's experiment with a "deliberative opinion poll" in Great Britain. In this study, a randomly selected panel of voters who were provided with three days of extensive (and politically balanced) briefings on crime and the criminal justice system became substantially more supportive of measures to ensure the procedural rights of criminal defendants (1994: 28). Although the group remained very concerned about crime and was quite supportive of punitive measures to reduce it, a greater familiarity with the procedures and logic of the system led many to support protecting the rights of those accused of crimes.

Promoting Political Participation

A politically active citizenry is a requisite of any theory of democracy. At a minimum, this means regular participation in the electoral process. Knowledge is a principal correlate of several forms of electoral political participation. In the 1988 presidential election, nearly nine out of ten of the most knowledgeable 10 percent of respondents voted; by comparison, among the least-informed decile, only two in ten did so.[9] In between, we observe a nearly monotonic increase in turnout as knowledge rises (figure 6.2). The same pattern is apparent in other elections (Neuman, 1986: 84–89).[10] Other types of electoral participation are also strongly related to knowledge. In the 1992 election, only 16 percent of the least-knowledgeable decile of citizens reported any type of campaign participation, such as trying to influence the vote of others or working for a candidate; by comparison, 72 percent of the best-informed decile did so. These data, as well as the percentage who contributed money to a candidate, group, or party, are shown in figure 6.2. Knowledge also boosts participation in nonelectoral activities, such as working to solve a local community problem or contacting a public official (see chapter 5; Junn, 1991; Leighley, 1991).

Knowledgeable citizens participate in politics more than less knowledgeable ones. But what accounts for this? Several straightforward explanations exist. Knowledge promotes a number of civic attitudes and behaviors (such as political interest and efficacy) that motivate participation. Political knowledge boosts participation because it promotes an understanding of why politics is relevant. It is noteworthy that in the 1992 National Election Study, political knowledge—compared with such vari-

Figure 6.2 Political Participation and Political Knowledge

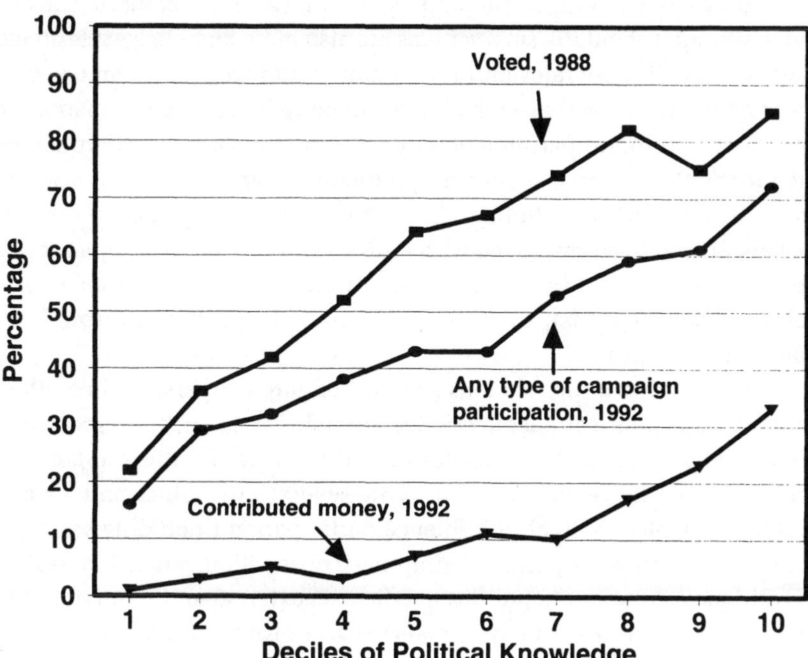

ables as media use, interest in politics, efficacy, or demographic characteristics—was the strongest predictor of whether an individual said she or he cared about the outcome of the election.[11]

But knowledge should also have a more direct impact on participation by providing the specific facts necessary to make citizens aware of opportunities to participate, and of how to participate once aware of these opportunities—so-called mobilizing information (Lemert, 1981). Although it is difficult to avoid being aware of a presidential election, most other elections are less visible. Furthermore, registering to vote often requires an awareness of where and when to do so, and the location of polling places is not always obvious. Other avenues for political participation are more difficult to discover and may require considerable knowledge to find and use. For example, if one wished to be involved in a party's nominating process for a state or local office, one would need to know something about the rules and procedures, and one would need to know them well in advance of the election to which they applied.

We lack the kinds of specific factual questions for a direct test of Lemert's notion of mobilizing information. But our analysis of political tolerance demonstrated that information is used situationally. In addition, because our general knowledge scales are designed to measure what citizens know more broadly about politics, we can assume that those who are more informed about the survey items are also more knowledgeable about facts that are directly relevant to the act of participating. We can use this assumption to indirectly test the impact of knowledge on participation. If knowledge promotes participation by providing mobilizing information, then it should remain a significant predictor of participation even when we control for other attitudinal, behavioral, and demographic variables that are known to be correlated with both knowledge and participation. If, however, knowledge has no impact on participation once these other variables are controlled for, then its impact must be primarily through its effect on motivation.

To determine if the relations shown in figure 6.2 persist when other personal and political characteristics are held constant, we regressed a dichotomous participation variable (0 = didn't vote, 1 = did vote) on the political knowledge index, along with several attitudinal and demographic variables thought to influence participation (including sex, age, race, personal income, politically impinged occupation, education, region of residence, attention to politics, media use, external and internal political efficacy, and trust in government).[12] The results of this analysis for voter turnout in the 1988 NES survey (based on a validated vote) are presented in table 6.2. To ease in interpretation, the predicted probabilities that an otherwise typical individual (that is, someone at the mean or mode on the other independent variables) would vote, given different levels of political knowledge, are included in the table.[13]

Table 6.2 Predictors of Voter Turnout (Logistic Regression Coefficients)

Variable	*b*	Standard Error
Political knowledge	.08****	.02
Sex	.46**	.14
Age	.01*	.005
Black	−.38	.20
Family income	−.01	.01
Politically impinged occupation	.25	.17
Education	.11*	.05
Lives in South	−.95****	.13
Married	.49***	.14
Political engagement	.32***	.09
Internal efficacy	.16*	.08
External efficacy	.15**	.07
Has telephone	1.27****	.31
Tenure in present communitiy	.33****	.07
Strength of party ID	.27***	.07
Constant	−3.77****	.44

Table 6.2 Predictors of Voter Turnout (Logistic Regression Coefficients) (*continued*)

Predicted Probability of Voting for Typical Respondent (all other variables set at their mean or mode)	
Level of Political Knowledge	Probability
1 standard deviation below mean	.50
At the mean	.59
1 standard deviation above mean	.69

Source: 1988 National Election Study.
* = *p* <.05. ** = *p* <.01. *** = *p* <.001. **** = p <.0001.

Most the independent variables were significantly related to voting. Consistent with the notion that knowledge has a direct and independent impact on participation, the knowledge index remained a highly significant predictor of turnout. The predicted probability of voting for a typical respondent who was one standard deviation above the mean on political knowledge was .69, compared with .50 for those who were one standard deviation below the mean (while holding other characteristics and attitudes constant at their means or, where appropriate, their mode). Having more knowledge—regardless of one's social status or reported levels of interest, efficacy, and media use—is a strong predictor of voting. The fact that knowledge has a strong independent impact is notable in that voting, compared with other forms of participation, requires relatively little knowledge.

This analysis suggests that part of knowledge's impact on participation is through the provision of relevant, mobilizing information. Of course, distinguishing knowledge's direct and indirect impact on participation should not obscure the fact that both pathways are important. Political knowledge matters because of the specific information contained within it and because it promotes other civic qualities, such as political interest, media use, or efficacy. In turn, interest, media use, and participation affect knowledge. Given the extent to which these civic requisites are a part of an intertwined, self-supporting structure of orientations, it may be impossible to say exactly how much one influences the other. In the end, however, common sense and everyday experience in other domains of life tell us that knowledge both stimulates and facilitates action.[14]

Political Knowledge and the Quality of Opinions

Although political participation can be seen as a good in and of itself (Pateman, 1970), its primary value is as a means for translating individual and collective interests into public action. Political attitudes are a critical building block of instrumental political behavior. When expressed in the form of opinions in surveys, attitudes can influence political candidates, elected officials, interest groups, and other citizens. To the extent that attitudes guide the choices of citizens in voting and other forms of political participation, they can have a direct impact on public policy. Knowledge, in turn, leads citizens to develop more numerous, stable, and internally consistent attitudes.

What Are Attitudes and How Do They Develop?

Observable political behavior is the raw material social scientists have to work with in studying attitudes and their formation, and its most common form is the expression of opinions in a survey. *Opinions* are considered to be the visible manifestations of *attitudes,* defined as relatively durable orientations toward an object.[15] More fundamental than either attitudes or opinions are *values,* which are enduring standards for what is desirable (Rokeach, 1973). Among other functions, a value serves as "a standard or criterion . . . for developing and maintaining attitudes toward relevant objects and situations" (Rokeach, 1968: 450).

Values are tied to attitudes and opinions through *beliefs* (see, for example, Dawson, 1979: 103–5). Beliefs are distinctly cognitive elements that link an individual's values to her or his attitudes and opinions about a concrete issue and what—if anything—should be done about it. Beliefs do not have to be true, of course. Through this concept, however, political knowledge becomes relevant to a consideration of values, attitudes, and opinions. For example, one's attitude toward the welfare system does not flow directly from relevant core values like individualism or equality, but from the linkage of these values to what is known or believed to be true about the specific program and the environment in which it will operate. Does the welfare system actually weaken individual responsibility and initiative? Is the welfare system rife with clients who could work but simply do not want to? How long do people typically stay on welfare? Similarly, whether one takes the position that U.S. involvement in the Vietnam war was a noble cause or an immoral folly may depend not only on one's feelings about communism as a system of government, but also on such factual knowledge as the historical roots of the war in colonialism and nationalism.

Unlike the more general notion of beliefs, political knowledge, as we define it, is *accurate* information about politics. We assume that the greater the accumulated store of accurate information, the more likely it is that attitudes will be based on realistic beliefs about the political world (though the strength of this relation will vary according to the specific values involved). In addition, the greater the store of information, the more often citizens will be able to connect their values with concrete matters of politics—in other words, the more likely they are to form attitudes about political questions. If these assumptions are correct, the attitudes of the well informed should be significantly different in character from those of the ill informed.

This conceptualization of attitudes is at the heart of recent research aimed at understanding the sometimes anomalous nature of opinions as revealed through survey research. A fundamental question among attitude researchers is what the expression of opinion in a survey actually tells us about the existence of an underlying attitude. It has long been recognized that many survey respondents will provide answers to opinion questions even in the absence of a considered judgment about the topic. Some will even provide an opinion on fictitious or highly obscure issues (Schuman and Presser, 1981: 147–57; Bishop et al., 1980). The nature of the survey interview as a social exchange evidently encourages many respondents to "help" the interviewer by providing answers even when they are unprepared to do so or to answer so as to avoid appearing ignorant or unengaged. Can real opinions be distinguished from pseudo-opinions?

This stark distinction may be inappropriate. Hardly anyone—even a political scientist—walks around armed with specific opinions on every political issue. Research during the past decade or so has seen growing acceptance of the notion that many opinions tend to be constructed on the spot during political conversations or interviews for a public opinion survey. John Zaller and Stanley Feldman have offered the clearest explication of this model: "Most citizens, we argue, simply do not possess preformed attitudes at the level of specificity demanded in surveys. Rather, they carry around in their heads a mix of only partially consistent ideas and considerations. When questioned, they call to mind a sample of these ideas, including an oversample of ideas made salient by the questionnaire and other recent events, and use them to choose among the options offered" (1992: 579–80).[16]

The "mix of only partially consistent ideas and considerations" to which Zaller and Feldman refer is strongly influenced by a citizen's level of political knowledge. Highly knowledgeable citizens will be exposed to and remember more ideas and considerations than will the less aware. They also will be better able to evaluate new information in terms of its consistency with their political values and other information they hold, accepting (and remembering) considerations that are consistent with their values and rejecting those that are not. Consequently, the survey responses of the better-informed citizen will, in all likelihood, be more stable over time and more consistent with responses on related issues.

Zaller develops the implications of this model in his book *The Nature and Origins of Mass Opinion*, which draws on Converse's early work on information flow and partisan stability as a model for how public opinion is formed and changed (Converse, 1962). Although Zaller generally avoids judging opinions as good or bad, his model does have an implicit normative standard: whether or not opinions are consistent with underlying values. A key variable in ensuring this consistency is political knowledge. Knowledge, in the form of contextual information, "enable[s] citizens to perceive relationships between the persuasive messages they receive and their political predispositions" (1992: 42). Thus, political knowledge is critical to the "effective translation of political predispositions into *appropriate* policy preferences" (Zaller, 1991: 129, emphasis added).

If political knowledge is integral to the development of meaningful attitudes, we should be able to observe a number of differences between well-informed and poorly informed citizens. First, better-informed citizens should have more numerous attitudes. That is, compared with the less informed, they should be able to figure out where they stand on more issues. Second, their attitudes should be more stable over time because they are based on values and information that are relatively stable. Third, their attitudes should be more durable; that is, they should be less susceptible to change from irrelevant or specious arguments or information—though perhaps more likely to change when they encounter new information that is relevant. Fourth, if the attitudes of the better informed are more closely tied to basic values and orientations, they should be more internally consistent with one another (in part because many of them stem from the same values) and display a simpler structure. The available evidence strongly confirms all four of these expectations.

Knowledge and Attitudes: Opinion Holding

Political knowledge is a very strong predictor of opinion holding.[17] In the 1988 National Election Study, the knowledge index we constructed was by far the best predictor of levels of *opinionation*—that is, the number of issues on which the respondent provided an opinion rather than a "don't know" response.[18] In a multiple regression analysis with nine demographic and political variables that were, individually, significantly correlated with opinion holding, the knowledge index dwarfed the others (beta = .35, compared with .07 for the runner-up—family income). A composite variable of political interest and several media-use items barely achieved statistical significance in the model ($p = .06$).

Corroborating evidence is provided by Jon Krosnick and Michael Milburn, who examined opinionation levels in NES surveys from 1956 to 1984 and found that "objective political competence" was by far the strongest predictor of opinionation (1990: 61). Political knowledge was one component of objective political competence, and in several of the surveys it was the one most strongly related to levels of opinionation.[19]

A telling exception to this pattern is a tendency for the best-educated survey respondents (and presumably the most knowledgeable ones) to be less likely to offer opinions on highly obscure issues about which almost no one would be aware (Bishop, Tuchfarber, and Oldendick, 1986). Schuman and Presser (1981: chap. 5) report that respondents with more than a high school education were nearly 20 percentage points more likely than those with less than a high school diploma to give a "don't know" response about the Agricultural Trade Act of 1978 (a genuine issue but one that received almost no news coverage). Similarly, Krosnick and Milburn found that although objective political competence was positively related to opinionation, this relation was weakest among the best-educated respondents. They speculate that highly sophisticated individuals may be somewhat more reluctant than others to offer what appear to be simplistic summary responses to complex policy questions (1990: 64). Thus, citizens who are relatively knowledgeable about politics are more likely to have (or construct) opinions on a wide array of subjects, but less likely to offer their views on issues about which they feel underinformed or for which their opinions are not easily categorized into the available choices.

Knowledge and Attitude Stability over Time

To the extent that citizens manifest opinions that are weakly grounded in genuine orientations (or even simply random), we would expect considerable instability in individual-level survey data over time. That is, if the same respondents are asked for their opinions in a subsequent interview, many of them would provide different answers.[20] This pattern of low correlation between answers at two or more time points is familiar to students of public opinion, and it was the principal evidence upon which Philip Converse based his thesis that much of public opinion consisted of *nonattitudes* (1964; 1970). Indeed, the instability of opinions in surveys is a key datum for some observers who doubt the capacity of the public for effective self-government.

Converse's thesis of nonattitudes has had many critics. The clearest alternative view holds that the pattern of low correlations among opinions over time is principally a result of *measurement error* and not an absence of political orientations by respondents (Achen, 1975; Erikson, 1979; Jackson, 1979; Judd and Milburn, 1980). According to this view, most citizens are assumed to have true attitudes on most issues, but the survey process is inherently variable and unreliable. Although repeated expressions of opinion by individuals would tend to center on their true attitude, any given measurement contains errors that contribute to the perception that no true attitude actually exists.

The dispute between the nonattitude and measurement-error camps is somewhat intractable; as Paul Sniderman and his colleagues have suggested, "the root issues are not methodological but ontological" (Sniderman, Brody, and Tetlock, 1991: 17). Both sides have very strong evidence in favor of their views. Citizens don't know much about many issues. And surveys certainly do have a great deal of measurement error in them. Can these two sources of instability be disentangled, and what does this tell us about the value of political knowledge?

Recent work by Stanley Feldman (1989) and Robert Erikson and Kathleen Knight (1993) suggests that political knowledge has a substantial impact on the extent of response variability in panel studies, a finding that favors the nonattitude thesis. Working with a five-wave panel survey from the 1980 presidential election, Feldman found general political knowledge to be a strong predictor of response stability for a wide range of attitudes. Erikson and Knight found that of several possible variables, "ideological literacy" (the ability to place the Democratic party and presidential candidates to the left of the Republicans) was the only consistent and statistically significant predictor of response variance (that is, stability and instability) in one's own self-reported ideological identification. They conclude that "the ideologically illiterate show a pattern closer to that of the classic non-attitude holder than one might think possible in empirical research. Not only do they display evidence of far more error variance, they also show very little true variance" (21–22). The authors uncover a similar, though somewhat weaker, relation between the stability of party identification and knowledge of which party controls Congress. Most of the change in party identification over the course of the panel they examined was error rather than true change, and it was concentrated among respondents who were unaware that the Democrats held a majority in Congress.

The clear relation between levels of political knowledge and opinion stability is evident in panel surveys of the National Election Studies conducted in 1984 and 1990–91–92.[21] Identical versions of three seven-point opinion items (ranging from very liberal to very conservative responses) were asked on both interviews in each panel. To measure consistency, we recoded responses into three categories.[22] Respondents were considered to have a consistent opinion if they chose the same direction (left, right, or middle) as recoded by us, in both waves of interviewing. If they had no opinion in both waves, they were excluded from the analysis so as not to confound the holding of an opinion with the stability of opinions (see figure 6.3).[23]

Figure 6.3 Attitude Crystallization over Two Waves of a Panel Survey, by Knowledge Level

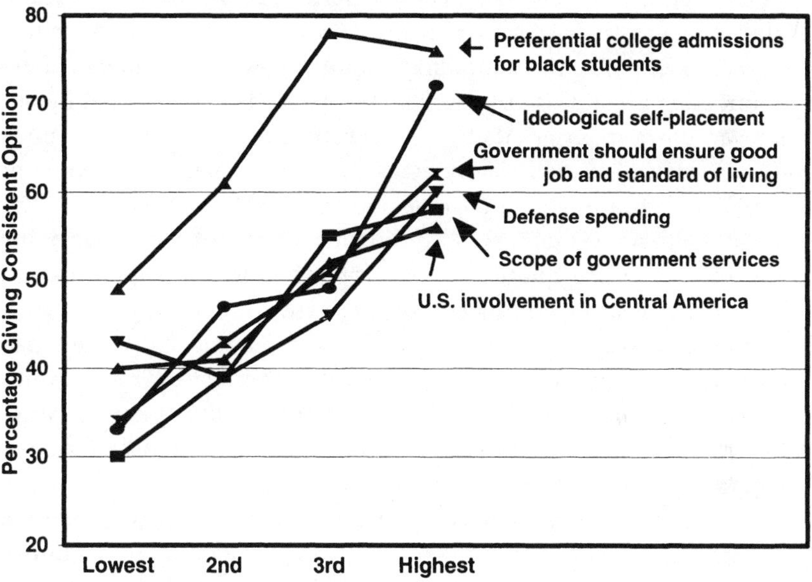

For three of the six items, only about a third of the least-knowledgeable quartile gave the same response in successive waves of interviewing. Among the best informed, an average of over 60 percent did so.[24] Overall stability was greatest, as one might expect, on a racial issue: preferential treatment for black applicants to college.[25] But even with this issue there was a 27-point difference in stability between the best and least informed—about the average for all issues. Compared with education, family income, interest in election campaigns, and general attention to politics, information was by far the strongest predictor of stable opinions.[26]

Response instability, a characteristic that has led many observers to question how meaningful public opinion really is, is strongly related to political knowledge. On a variety of issues, better-informed citizens manifest more stable attitudes.[27]

Knowledge and the Responsiveness of Attitudes

If well-informed citizens are more likely to have stable attitudes, or to have sophisticated heuristics for reasoning their way to more appropriate opinions on subjects about which they have given little or no thought, then it is also likely that they are better able to process new information and incorporate it into their belief systems. If this is true, what are the implications? On the one hand, better-informed citizens should be more likely to change their attitudes in response to certain kinds of critical information. On the other hand, they should be less susceptible to efforts to manipulate them, less vulnerable to propaganda, less affected by particular events or messages that are irrelevant, and less likely to manifest "response effects" in surveys. Evidence for these notions has been found in a variety of studies. Donald Kinder and Lynn Sanders (1990) found that low-information respondents in a national survey were most susceptible to the way in which questions were framed. Acknowledging that the survey setting is artificial, the authors argue that it does mimic political debate in many respects: "The interference and probing that surveys necessarily impose resemble to some extent the way that citizens are provoked by politicians and political events outside the survey context" (1990: 99). Political actors, like survey researchers, have discretion over how public issues are framed.

Studies of presidential debates have also found that susceptibility to influence varies by level of information. In an examination of the impact of the presidential debates of 1980, David Lanoue (1992) found that voters who were in the lower to middle range on a political information scale were more likely than others to be influenced by the content of the debates and by the media interpretation of them. And in a study of voter reaction to the second presidential debate of 1992, we found that better-informed voters were considerably less likely than others to change their opinions of the presidential candidates as a result of viewing the debate. Among a panel of 104 undecided and weakly committed voters from the Richmond area, correlations between panelist's evaluations of the candidates before and after the debate were generally much higher for the best informed than for the least informed.

Of course, greater resistance to persuasion is not a good unto itself. A foolish consistency is more than the hobgoblin of little minds—in politics, it may also be the enemy of progress. Fundamental notions of liberal democracy—the discovery of truth through the exchange of ideas, deliberation, reconsideration—all imply that attitudes should change under certain circumstances. Political knowledge has a positive function in this process. In addition to helping citizens recognize and reject irrelevant information, knowledge should also promote a greater recognition of relevant information and facilitate its incorporation into belief systems. In broad terms, Zaller's model of the dynamics of public opinion supports this notion. One of his clearest examples is public opinion about the Vietnam war. Early in the war when most communication from elites was favorable toward U.S. involvement, public opinion was not very divided, even among the most-informed citizens. Later, when news and elite communication about the war was much more divided, public opinion became highly polarized—but only among those who were knowledgeable. Informed citizens with hawkish values were highly supportive of the war, while those with dovish values were not. Among the less knowledgeable, there was little difference between hawks and doves in terms of support for the war (Zaller, 1992: chap. 9).[28] A similar pattern of assimilation or rejection of elite messages and other information was observed for the issue of U.S. involvement in Central America during the mid-1980s (144–47).

Thus, political knowledge helps citizens make sense of the political world by providing them with a basis for evaluating new information in light of their own values. In many instances, this will mean that the attitudes of the well informed will be more durable. In others, however, it suggests that the knowledgeable citizen will be better able to recognize the relevance of new information and, when appropriate, adjust their attitudes and opinions accordingly.

Knowledge and the Structure of Attitudes

To the extent that attitudes reflect the influence of a core value held by an individual, opinions on different but related issues should be consistent with one another. Conversely, if individuals develop attitudes with little or no guidance from more central political orientations and values, we would have little reason to expect opinions to be consistent with one another (Judd and Downing, 1990). Converse's original formulation of attitude constraint was predicated on the notion that specific attitudes derived from "some superordinate value or posture toward man and society, involving premises about the nature of social justice, social change, 'natural law,' and the like" (1964: 211).[29] If the link between attitudes and values is facilitated by knowledge holding, the attitudes (or opinions) of better-informed citizens should be more internally consistent than those of the less informed.[30]

Consistency is also promoted in another, more socially constructed way. Citizens learn from political elites, interest groups, social movements, citizen activists, and from the political culture more generally, in Converse's words, "what goes with what" (1964: 212). Similarly, political elites take cues from the public in building political coalitions and developing political agendas. This social source of constraint is especially important in promoting consistency between attitudes that fall into disparate domains and for which a number of different core values could be relevant. For example, it is not necessarily obvious why a pro-choice position on abortion and support for gun control are both liberal views since they entail opposite notions of government involvement in the personal decisions of citizens. But interested groups and political leaders draw on a different set of values to forge the linkage (or consistency) between these issue positions. The tendency to aggregate somewhat disconnected opinions into fewer and simpler constructs is the inevitable outcome of the need to build governing coalitions and to provide platforms for political action. This aggregating process is especially important in a two-party system like the United States'. The national conversation through which these coalitions are formed is most likely to occur between political elites and the segment of the population most aware of elite opinion and most influential in shaping it through their participation. Thus, consistency within the public that mirrors the structure of conflict as it appears among activists and elites—whether the public's opinions were cause or effect—is apt to be greater among the better informed.

Previous research on the relation between attitude consistency and political knowledge has used a variety of methods and has produced fairly mixed evidence of a linkage.[31] The most direct approach was taken by James Stimson, who reasoned that if the debate over consistency was fundamentally about the dimensionality of attitudes—the extent to which opinions on the individual issues could be reduced to a simpler set of orientations—it should be possible to compare the consistency of belief systems among citizens of higher or lower knowledge through factor analysis. He divided the 1972 NES survey sample into four groups based on education and political knowledge and factor analyzed ten attitude variables within each group. The simplest structure was observed within the highest knowledge group, for whom only two factors were extracted.[32] By contrast, within the lowest knowledge group, four factors were extracted. Stimson concluded "that roughly the upper half in cognitive ability [knowledge and education] seem to have structured their beliefs, at least on traditional political issues, around the left-right continuum. For the lower half, belief dimensions are more complicated, more issue-specific, less stable and less powerful" (1975: 411).

Using the 1988 NES survey, we replicated Stimson's analysis, making two modifications. First, we used our knowledge index (rather than an index of knowledge and education) to divide the sample into four groups. Second, we limited the items in the factor analysis to questions dealing with the role and scope of government in the socioeconomic sphere (for example, government services and spending, health care, spending on assistance to the unemployed). Consequently, we expected a unidimensional structure to emerge. The results of a principal components analysis of eight items show that among respondents in the lowest quartile of knowledge, three (mostly uninterpretable) factors emerged, while among the second and third quartiles two factors were extracted (see table 6.3). Only among the most knowledgeable quartile was a single factor observed. Clearly, a unidimensional liberal-conservative axis underlies the attitudes of the well informed on these questions, whereas the pattern for the less informed is much more ambiguous.[33]

Table 6.3 Attitude Structure by Level of Political Knowledge

	Knowledge Level			
	Lowest Quartile	2nd Quartile	3rd Quartile	Highest Quartile
Number of factors extracted	3	2	2	1
Variance explained by first factor	30%	31%	37%	44%
Loadings of individual variables on first (unrotated) factor:				
Government services and spending	.27	.60	.68	.72
Spending on the unemployed	.69	.69	.74	.71
Spending on food stamps	.70	.59	.64	.69
Spending on the homeless	.62	.54	.67	.69
Government guaranteed job and good standard of living	.50	.56	.59	.67
Spending on minorities	.67	.63	.58	.66
Government role in health insurance	.30	.40	.49	.62
Spending on the schools	.47	.38	.42	.53

Source: 1988 National Election Study.
Note: Analysis was by method of principal components.

There is ample evidence that political knowledge is an important resource in the development of political opinions. Better-informed citizens hold more opinions, have more stable opinions, that are resistant to irrelevant or biased information (but are responsive to information that matters), and have opinions that are more internally consistent with each other and with the basic ideological alignments that define American politics.

Political Knowledge and Enlightened Self-Interest

A healthy democracy requires a citizenry capable of knowing and expressing its interests and of doing so in the context of the broader public interest. Philosophers and theorists have long wrestled with the question of what is a citizen's political interest. Rightly enough, there is great reluctance to impute interests to individuals. At the same time, citizens clearly differ in the accuracy of their perceptions about the political world and about the likely impact of government policies on them, on important groups to which they belong, and on the polity more generally. Where perceptions on these matters are incomplete or inaccurate, we would question whether a citizen had fully comprehended his or her interest. The lack of sufficient information is one barrier to knowing one's interest. Another is incorrect information. Although political observers may debate the extent of "false consciousness" among the public—and few will offer an operational definition of it—most would agree that some citizens, on some issues, don't know their interest because they have been manipulated by others who, in Hamilton's words, "flatter their prejudices to betray their interests" (Hamilton, Madison, and Jay, 1787–88: #71).

A common theoretical approach to the identification of interests is through the notion of *enlightened preferences.* In this context, "enlightened" refers not to some absolute standard of what is right or just but rather to the conditions under which the individual chooses among available alternatives. For example, Robert Dahl writes, "A person's interest or good is whatever that person would choose with fullest attainable understanding of the experiences resulting from that choice and its most relevant alternatives" (1989:180–81). Similarly, Larry Bartels's (1990) work on interests draws on three theorists across the political spectrum, whose common theme is information: what would an individual choose if she or he had perfect information and could experience the results of choosing each alternative (Mansbridge, 1983; Connolly, 1972) or "saw clearly, thought rationally, [and] acted disinterestedly and benevolently" (Lippmann, 1955).

Greater information does not assure that citizens will reach a consensus on important issues. Each individual brings a unique mix of personal experiences to his or her political calculus. Nonetheless, values, attitudes, and opinions do not develop in a vacuum, but rather are *socially constructed* out of material conditions and cultural norms. While some of these conditions and norms are likely to be similar for all members of a polity, many vary depending on one's particular socioeconomic location. For some issues at least, greater information is likely to lead to clearer and more consistent expressions of group interests.

The combined concepts of enlightened preferences and socially constructed opinions permit an empirical study of interests. If more-informed citizens are better able to discern their interests, and if material interests differ across groups in the population, it should be possible to detect the influence of information by comparing the opinions of better- and lesser-informed members of different groups. Specifically, we may look for three different but related phenomena. First, to what extent and under what conditions does knowledge sharpen the differences between groups, moving their members closer to positions that are arguably consistent with their group norms and material circumstances? Second, to what extent and under what conditions does knowledge encourage consensus building, moving citizens to positions that reflect a greater understanding of the circumstances of groups to which they do not belong? And third, to what extent and under what conditions do shifts in individual opinions collectively affect where the political center lies in the opinion environment? That is, does greater knowledge move the mean opinion a significant amount to the left or right?

We should reiterate that we do not see information or knowledge as the *only* determinant of a citizen's interest. One's views are based on norms and values rooted in belief systems only partially connected to the empirical world. In addition, the foundational issues of politics and society are inherently contestable (Connolly, 1983) and so cannot be solved through the technical appraisal of facts. Nonetheless, as with the other aspects of opinion formation examined in this chapter, factual knowledge can help facilitate the process by which values, attitudes, and beliefs are combined into the expression of political interests. These interests may be defined narrowly (what is in my best interest?) or more broadly (what is in the best interest of people like me? of the polity as a whole?), but to be meaningful, they must be based—at least partially—on an accurate understanding of the processes, people, and substance of politics.

Using data from the 1992 NES survey, we examined the group-level impact of political knowledge by comparing four different types of group differences in opinion: the opinions of those experiencing economic hardship and those who are economically more advantaged, the opinions of blacks and nonblacks, the opinions of men and women, and the opinions of younger and older citizens. We selected these groups because extant theory and research suggests that there are important material and cultural differences among members of different classes, races, genders, and age cohorts that should be and often are reflected in their expressed opinions about certain issues. We also selected them because the poor, minorities, women, and the young have been historically excluded from much of the public sphere and thus collectively have lacked many of the resources (including political knowledge) to effectively construct and articulate either their group interests or their notions of the broader public interest. We are not, of course, arguing that these are the only groups for which political knowledge is likely to be important in the construction of enlightened preferences. As evidence of this, we also compare the opinions of people who differ in their religious views.

In searching for the impact of political knowledge on group-level opinions, it is important to choose issues that are arguably relevant to the group characteristics in question—there is little a priori reason, for example, to expect men and women to differ systematically in their views regarding the trade or budget deficits. In the class and gender analyses, we looked at differences in opinions related to the proper scope of government in the area of social welfare, since theory and prior evidence suggest that economically troubled citizens and women are likely to draw on different values and experiences in evaluating such policies than are economically advantaged citizens or men. We also looked at gender differences in opinions about abortion—an issue of obvious relevance to women. For similar reasons we compared black and nonblack opinions on a racial attitudes scale, and the opinions of different age cohorts on such emerging social issues as gay rights, abortion, and the role of women. And we compared opinions about homosexual rights for three groups of respondents based on their views of the Bible.[34] In each case we reasoned that opinions on these issues are influenced by a number of factors, including an individual's social and demographic characteristics. However, the precise way in which one's social, economic, and political location affects opinions is likely to be mediated by how much one knows about politics. For example, how being African American affects one's views on social welfare is plausibly influenced not only by one's personal circumstances, but also by knowledge of how those circumstances have been affected by prior government policies, of the connection between personal circumstances and the history of blacks in America, of the current plight of other blacks, and so forth. Hence, to the extent that group differences are influential in the construction and articulation of interests, we should be able to see this more clearly among the most knowledgeable individuals.

As a practical matter, the dearth of highly knowledgeable individuals in certain subgroups—for example, the poor and the uneducated—imposes limits on what we can learn simply by looking at those individuals in a typical opinion survey. Further, because opinions are likely to be affected by a variety of personal and demographic factors other than political knowledge, and because these factors vary within groups, it is necessary to control for these potentially confounding effects. For each of the analyses presented in the next section, we used multiple regression to estimate the impact of a set of twenty-two personal characteristics (for example, race, sex, age, income, marital status) and political knowledge on the particular attitudes of interest. The regression model also included interaction terms for political knowledge and each of the personal characteristics. These interactions permit an estimation of how knowledge affects the relation between personal characteristics and attitudes.[35] To simulate what the attitudes would be if all members of a group had a uniform level of knowledge, the regression coefficients from the model are used to compute an estimated attitude for each member of the group in the survey, using each person's actual data for all variables except political knowledge, which is imputed as either "uninformed" or "fully informed."[36]

For example, in the first analysis, two sets of estimates were computed: one assumed that everyone scored zero on the political knowledge scale, and the other assumed that everyone scored 28 (the highest possible score). Individuals were separated into three groups corresponding to the number of financial problems they had experienced in the past year. Each individual's score on each variable was inserted into the equation, along with the appropriate imputed knowledge score (zero or 28, depending on which analysis was being conducted) and the corresponding interaction terms for knowledge with the other variables. This led to an estimated attitude score for each person. These estimates were aggregated (as means) for each group and then plotted on a graph. The opinion scale, arrayed along the vertical axis, is based on factor scores. Thus, the mean score for the sample is zero, and scores are based on their deviation from the sample mean (for example, a score of 1.0 is one standard deviation above the sample mean). The scale for all graphs in this section ranges from -1.5 to +1.5 standard deviations. A fuller discussion of the methodology for this analysis is presented in Appendix 5.

Political Knowledge and the Expression of Economic Interests

Although the utility of class as an analytic concept in U.S. politics has long been debated, it is certainly true that citizens differ in their objective financial condition and in their need for certain types of government assistance. Accordingly, we followed a commonsense notion of group interest and hypothesized that economically distressed citizens, many of whom have direct experience with public assistance, would have different opinions regarding government social welfare programs and an expansive role for government than would citizens whose personal financial circumstances were more favorable. Further, and central to our argument, we anticipated that the opinions of less knowledgeable citizens within each group would be different from those of their more informed counterparts, since the latter should be better able to tie their objective conditions to larger societal and political circumstances and policies. This was precisely what we found.

The relation between opinions on an index of seven domestic issues and political knowledge for three groups of respondents in the 1992 National Election Study—those who had experienced no financial problems (about 16 percent of the sample), those who had experienced six or more problems (about 15 percent), and those in between (one to five problems; the median for the sample was three)—are shown in figure 6.4.[37]

After controlling for other factors, it is clear that group opinions about government's role in promoting social welfare are affected by how much citizens know about politics. Furthermore, the differences between better- and lesser-informed members of each group are substantively interpretable and intuitively plausible: knowledgeable individuals reporting no financial problems are more opposed to government social welfare than are their less knowledgeable counterparts. By contrast, knowledgeable individuals reporting six or more problems are considerably more liberal on these issues than are less knowledgeable individuals in similar economic circumstances. And for those in the middle, knowledge appears unrelated to opinion. The combined effect of knowledge on economically advantaged and disadvantaged citizens results in more polarized opinions among the better informed. Thus, political knowledge appears to facilitate a closer linkage between group interests and political attitudes. If all citizens were "fully informed" in 1992, opinions regarding social welfare policies and the role of government would have been more clearly aggregated into distinct ideological camps that were more closely tied to objective group conditions.[38] Significantly, there are collective consequences for a more broadly informed public. First, the range of opinion (as measured by the mean opinion of the groups) would expand significantly,

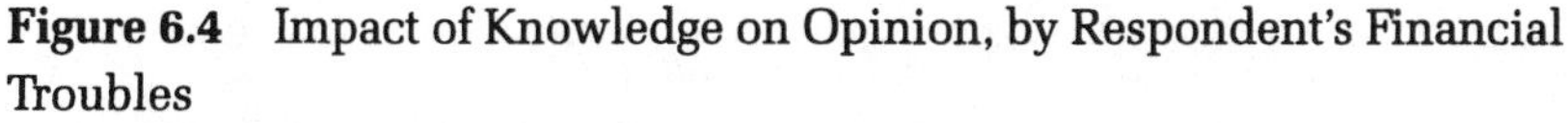

Figure 6.4 Impact of Knowledge on Opinion, by Respondent's Financial Troubles

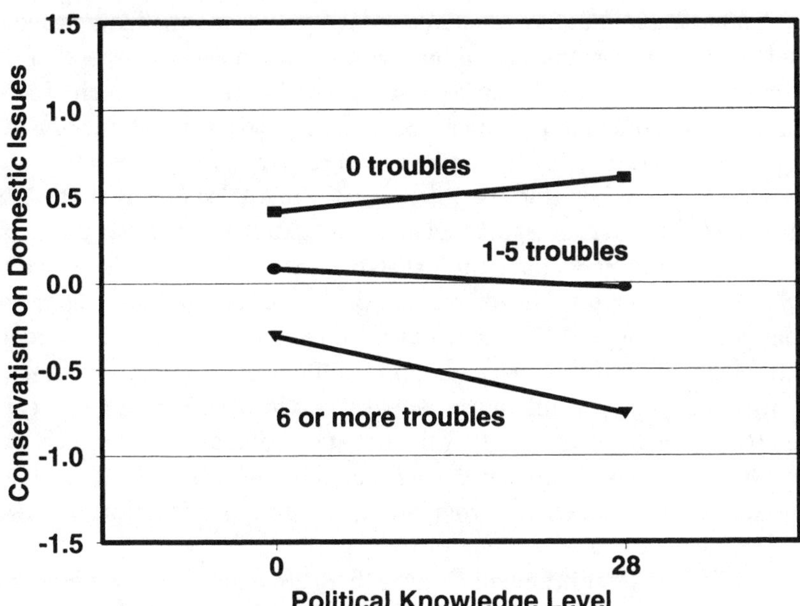

Note: Knowledge scale ranges from 0 (lowest possible score) to 28 (highest possible score).

broadening the public environment within which policy options are debated. And second, the net effect of these individual-level shifts would be to shift the mean opinion of the general public in a liberal direction (from zero to -.05 on the standardized opinion scale).[39]

It is important to note that although our findings are consistent with traditional class-interest and false-consciousness arguments (that is, economically distressed individuals who are politically informed are more supportive of government assistance than either their less informed counterparts or more knowledgeable but financially secure citizens), nothing in the logic of our argument requires this particular pattern. It is certainly plausible, for example, that informed but economically distressed citizens might conclude that government assistance programs contribute to a cycle of dependence and a culture of poverty and thus oppose such programs. Similarly, economically advantaged and politically informed citizens might reasonably conclude that social welfare programs are valuable for the polity even if they themselves would not benefit directly. Enlightened preferences are based on the *conditions* under which opinions are constructed—most centrally the presence of relevant information that is equitably distributed—rather than the particular substance of the opinions that emerge from these conditions.

Political Knowledge and the Expression of Gender-Based Interests

Numerous studies have documented the emergence of a gender gap in public opinion over the past fifteen years, most notably in the area of domestic social welfare policy (Shapiro and Mahajan, 1986). Much of this gap is attributable to the divergent financial and social situations of men and women and the way the parties have responded to issues affecting women.[40] Overlaid on this are differences by marital status, which often reinforce the gender schism (Weisberg, 1987). To the extent that political interests differ by gender and marital status, we would expect to see these differences reflected in the expressed opinions of married men, married women, single men, and single women. And to the extent that knowledge facilitates the connection between political interests and public opinion, we would also expect differences between less and more informed members within each group. Whether the net effect of knowledge is to create greater polarization or greater consensus, however, depends on the specific way informed men and women define their group interests and the public interest more generally.

Among the least-informed citizens there are only modest differences in domestic political opinion among members of the four groups (married men, married women, single men, single women). As knowledge increases, however, both single and married men become slightly more conservative, while married women move slightly in the liberal direction and single women become quite a bit more liberal (see figure 6.5). These changes lead to a clear gender and marriage gap on domestic welfare issues among knowledgeable citizens. As with our economic analysis, a "fully informed" citizenry would have collective consequences, resulting in a public opinion environment that is more ideologically diverse and slightly more liberal (again, a shift of -.05 on the standardized scale).

Knowledge also promoted greater gender differences on the issue of abortion. On a four-issue abortion index, the overall attitudes of men and women were about the same, but as women become more knowledgeable (other factors being equal) they also become more supportive of abortion rights (see figure 6.6). Significantly, knowledge also promotes greater support for abortion rights among men—a pattern that could result from more knowledgeable men believing that a woman's right to choose is also in their interest or believing that the right to choose is legal and just regardless of their own interests. Although the effect for men is quite weak, it highlights the fact that increased knowledge need not always lead to movement in opposite directions among the groups in question. Nonetheless, because of the difference in the rate of change among women and

Figure 6.5 Impact of Knowledge on Opinion, by Sex and Marital Status

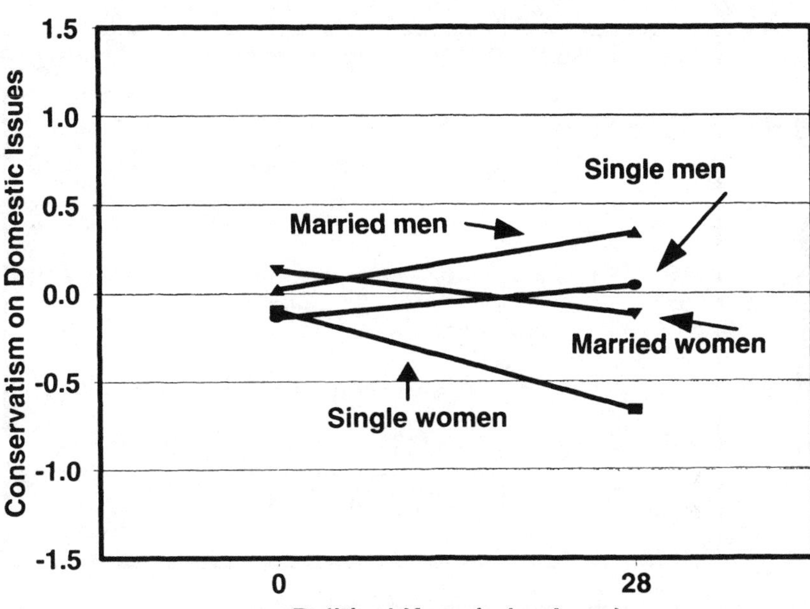

Note: Knowledge scale ranges from 0 (lowest possible score) to 28 (highest possible score).

men as knowledge rises, their relative position changes from one in which women are slightly more conservative than men to one in which women are considerably more liberal. The collective impact of a fully informed citizenry would be to shift the sample mean for attitudes on abortion in a liberal direction (from zero to +.30 on our scale).

Political Knowledge and the Expression of Age-Based Opinions

The political agenda is made up of numerous issues, some of which have endured over the centuries and others that have emerged out of new social and economic conditions. Although changes in the political agenda result from numerous factors, generational replacement is a key component (Delli Carpini, 1986; 1989). Younger citizens enter the political arena with values shaped by conditions and experiences different from those of the cohorts who preceded them. This, in turn, can lead to different notions of what government should do. At the same time, the conditions that produce changes in the political agenda are often experienced by all age cohorts (what are called "period effects"), suggesting the possibility of a more uniform shift in opinion as group members become more informed.

Figure 6.6 Impact of Knowledge on Opinion about Abortion, by Sex

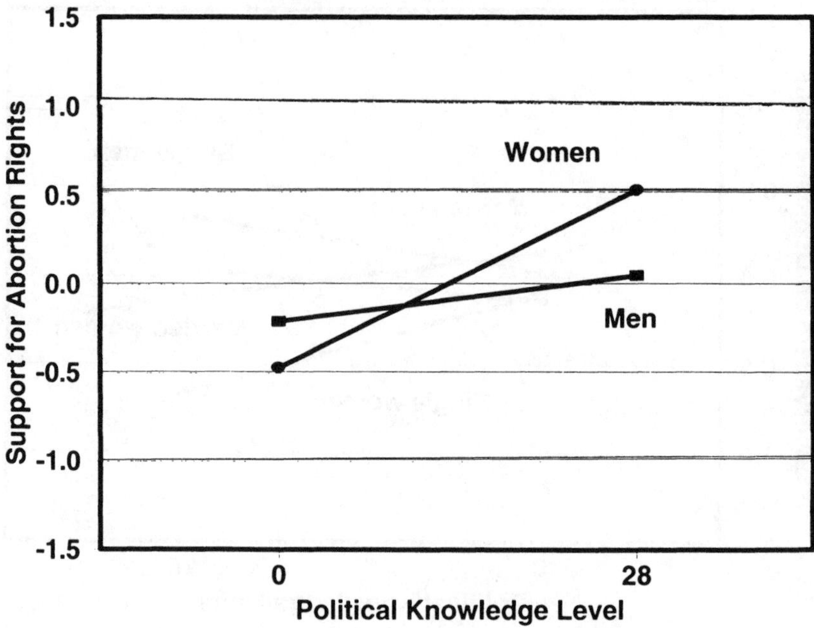

Note: Knowledge scale ranges from 0 (lowest possible score) to 28 (highest possible score).

Three political issues that have emerged over the last two decades and that are arguably driven in part by differences in generational worldviews and in part by more broadly experienced societal changes are abortion, gay rights, and the role of women in society. We created a scale of attitudes on these issues and divided survey respondents into three groups: post-boomers (born 1965 or later), baby boomers (born 1947–64), and pre-boomers (born before 1947). As with our other analyses, we expected opinion differences within each group to emerge as levels of political knowledge increased. Our expectations regarding differences across groups are less clear. To the extent that attitudes are based on age or generation, increased knowledge should lead to wider gaps in opinions across informed members of different age cohorts. To the extent that more broadly experienced conditions are driving the emergence of new issues, however, members of all age groups should move in a similar direction as knowledge increases.

Our analysis reveals that both cohort and period effects appear to be at work (see figure 6.7). Regardless of knowledge levels, the oldest cohort—the pre-boomers—is consistently the most conservative on these new agenda issues while the post-boomers are consistently the most liberal. All three groups, however, become more liberal as they become more knowledgeable. Further, because the knowledge effect is most pronounced for the post-boomers, the gap between them and the other groups is larger among the most knowledgeable segment. The net effect of a fully informed citizenry would be to shift the mean opinion of the public on these issues -.28 points in a liberal direction.

Figure 6.7 Impact of Knowledge on Attitudes about Generational Issues, by Age Cohort

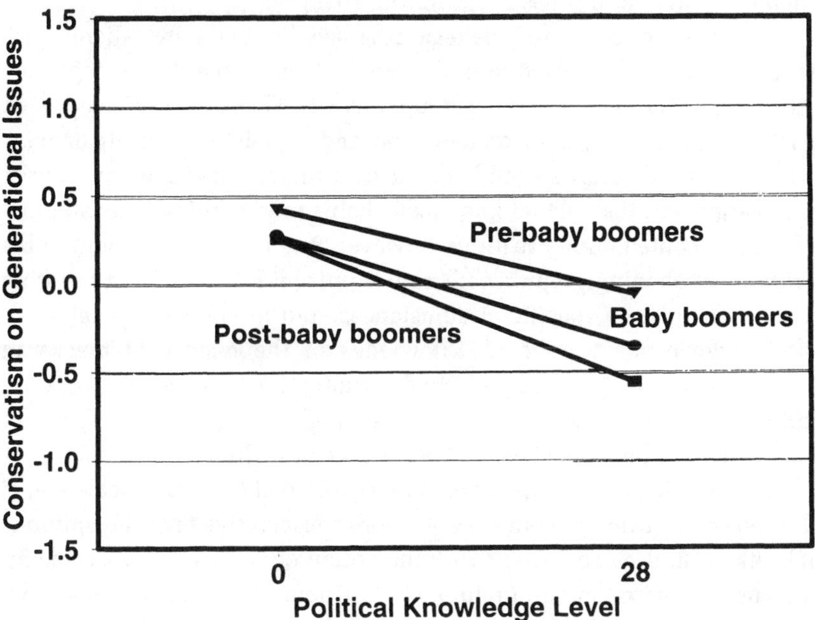

Note: Knowledge scale ranges from 0 (lowest possible score) to 28 (highest possible score).

Political Knowledge and Opinions on Race

Our final two analyses are particularly illuminating regarding the importance and the limits of political knowledge in the development of enlightened opinions. Government programs aimed at redressing the legacy of racial discrimination are among the most salient and divisive in American politics (Edsall and Edsall, 1991). Blacks and nonblacks differ markedly in their views about government's proper role in dealing with present and past racial discrimination and in their views about the reasons for the socioeconomic problems of African Americans. Research suggests several sources of these differences. Support for or opposition to race-based policies appears to be partially based on deep-seated attitudes (and prejudices) regarding the races and from simple calculations of individual or group self-interest (Carmines and Stimson, 1989; Edsall and Edsall, 1991). Opinions regarding such policies are also rooted in a more complex array of values, such as ideological views about the scope of government, ethnocentrism, and notions of fair play (Sniderman and Piazza, 1993). In either event, connecting one's values to one's attitudes and opinions is eased by the obviousness of who benefits (directly, at least) from race-based policies. Indeed, race is often considered an "easy issue" because of its high salience and symbolic quality (Carmines and Stimson, 1989).[41]

To the extent that opinions regarding racial policies are salient, symbolic, and easily connected to underlying values, factual knowledge may play a minimal role in clarifying group interests. The sharp divide between black and nonblack opinion on this issue, and the relative stability of opinions about racial policies would seem to confirm this view. If we are correct in our argument that factual knowledge helps in grounding beliefs in historical and contemporary realities, however, then information should play a role in weakening prejudices based on misguided beliefs, in tailoring broad principles to specific circumstances, and in connecting values to specific government policies. Knowledge of the history of blacks in America, of the de jure and de facto discrimination they faced as a group, and of the current economic and social plight of a large proportion of blacks should affect the views of both blacks and whites.

The opinions of nonblacks on a four-issue racial opinion scale are, at all levels of knowledge, considerably more conservative than the opinions of blacks, a finding consistent with the notion of race as an easy issue for citizens to discern their group interests (see figure 6.8). But greater knowledge—independent of income, age, sex, education, and other factors—produces greater support for government efforts on behalf of blacks. Significantly, while the effect is weaker (though statistically significant) for nonblacks than for blacks, both groups become more liberal as knowledge levels increase.[42] The net effect of these shifts is to create a slightly greater opinion gap between informed blacks and nonblacks but collectively to move opinion in a direction more sympathetic to race-based government policies. (The mean opinion of a fully informed citizenry would be .18 points more liberal on our scale than the mean of the actual sample.)

Political Knowledge, Religious Beliefs, and Support for Gay Rights

Religiosity provides an interesting test of the role of political knowledge in connecting values and opinions in that for many citizens religious beliefs are based more on faith than reason. For these people, political

Figure 6.8 Impact of Knowledge on Racial Attitudes, by Race

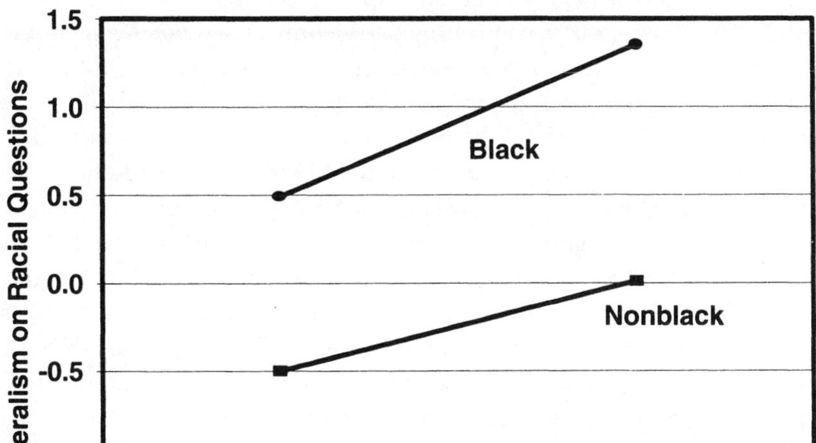

Note: Knowledge scale ranges from 0 (lowest possible score) to 28 (highest possible score).

knowledge is unlikely to affect opinions if those opinions have a religious rather than secular basis. One policy area where this is likely is gay rights. The most visible opponents to gay rights have been Christian conservative groups who see the Bible as the literal word of God, and who use the Bible as the basis of their opposition to homosexuality. Thus, citizens who are biblical literalists would be likely to draw on their religious beliefs (and on cues provided by their religious leaders) in constructing their opinions on this issue. Citizens who are religious but who do not read the Bible literally should be freer to base their political opinions on more secular values and beliefs. In addition, mainstream church organizations (whose followers tend not to be biblical literalists) have been divided over this issue, with some endorsing various rights for homosexuals and others remaining neutral. Thus, the opinions of believers who are not literalists should be more responsive to political information of the sort tapped in our surveys (for example, about civil rights and liberties). Finally, citizens who do not believe the Bible is the word of God (literal or not) should be the most likely to construct their opinions about gay rights on secular values and beliefs and so should be the most responsive to political information.[43]

To gauge the effect of knowledge on patterns of opinion across religious groups, we divided respondents into three groups according to their views on the Bible. We estimated the impact of political knowledge on the opinions of these groups, controlling for the impact of other demographic factors (figure 6.9). As expected, across all levels of knowledge biblical literalists are the most opposed to gay rights, those who do not believe the Bible is the word of God are the most supportive, and those who believe the Bible is the word of God but are not literalists are in the middle. Political knowledge promotes greater support for gay rights among the latter two groups, with the greatest effect occurring for those who do not believe the Bible is the word of God. Political knowledge has no significant impact on the views of the biblical literalists, however. Clearly, biblical literalists are connecting their religious values to their political opinions through beliefs that are less affected by secular concerns (and secular information). The pattern of responses demonstrates the political consequences of the biblical dictate, "Render unto Caesar the things that are Caesar's, and unto God, the things that are God's." More generally, it demonstrates that certain political opinions are based on values and orientations (schemas, if you will) activated by beliefs unlikely to be affected by the type of political information measured in our surveys. Even with the lack of relation between opinions and political information among biblical literalists, the collective impact of a fully informed citizenry would be to increase the mean level of support for gay rights by .10 points.[44]

Taken together, these analyses of class, gender, age, race, and religion demonstrate that the ability of citizens to connect their personal needs and concerns with larger social and economic forces—to see, for example, that one's condition can arise from causes that extend beyond personal abilities and shortcomings—requires information of the sort tapped in our surveys. Such information becomes more necessary if citizens are to connect their individual and group conditions in a meaningful way to government action. The specific nature of the connection between knowledge and opinion is complex. Whereas in most instances more information leads one to support policies that benefit one's own group, there is also evidence that a broader understanding of the substance and dynamics of American politics might lead to consensus building, or at least movement in a similar direction, even on potentially divisive issues. Greater knowledge resulted in more support among older citizens for women's and gay rights, among men for abortion rights, and among whites for race-conscious government programs. It also promoted support for tolerant policies toward homosexuals among broad segments of the public. Indeed, the value of greater information is not only to better understand the political roots of one's own condition, but of the condition of others (see also

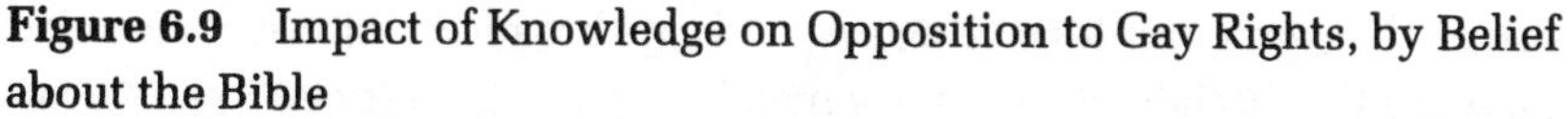

Figure 6.9 Impact of Knowledge on Opposition to Gay Rights, by Belief about the Bible

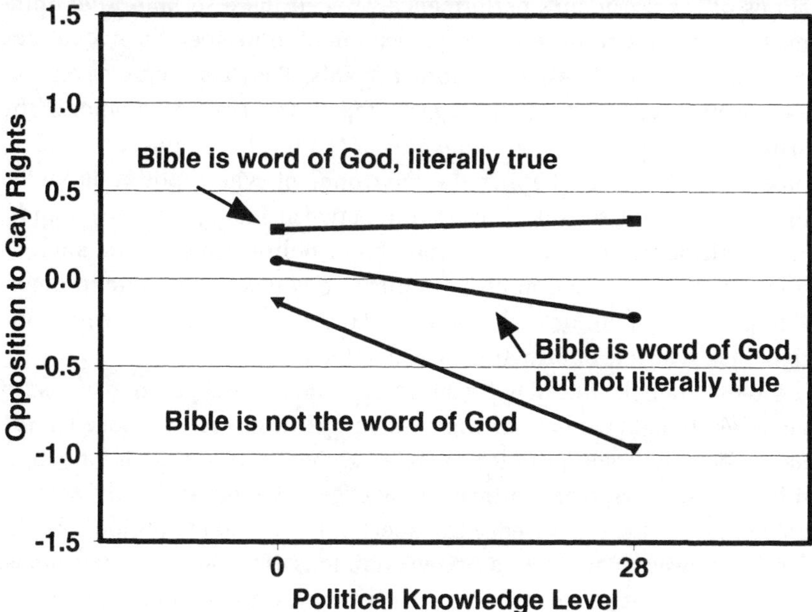

Note: Knowledge scale ranges from 0 (lowest possible score) to 28 (highest possible score).

Popkin and Dimock, 1995). Information's role in the formation of opinions is not deterministic, but it emerges from its interaction with personal, group, and national notions of fairness and responsibility.

The individual-level impact of political knowledge also had tangible impacts on the collective opinion environment in which policy is debated. Were citizens fully informed, group interests would be more clearly articulated. Further, the range of opinions expressed—and thus the ideological and substantive space within which political discussion takes place—would expand significantly. Finally, the political center, as measured by the mean opinion on these issues, would shift in small but measurable ways. In short, the parameters of public discourse are affected by how informed or uninformed the public is.

Political Knowledge and the Translation of Policy Views into Instrumentally Rational Attitudes

Although opinions on specific issues or policy areas can play a direct role in the actions of government, the realities of modern democracies require that such opinions be aggregated into broader coalitions. Two critical ways this broader support is gauged are party identification and evaluations of the president's performance. We call these *second-order* opinions because they represent the aggregation of more specific evaluations about issues, candidates, and public officials. They also serve as an efficient means of articulating these aggregated views because evidence of the partisan makeup of the electorate and of the level of support for officeholders is critical in shaping the environment where policy is made. Finally, they serve an intervening role between *first-order* issue stands, such as those discussed above, and actual political behaviors, such as voting. Party identification in particular is a valuable heuristic in determining who to vote for and where to stand on issues about which one might lack relevant information (see chapter 1).

To illustrate the role of political information in the expression of instrumentally rational presidential approval and partisanship, we looked at the relation between issue attitudes and these second-order opinions for people with different levels of political knowledge.[45] We have already demonstrated that political knowledge can affect the *direction* of opinions; for the present analysis we will take a citizen's opinions as a given. Our question is: how does knowledge affect the relation between attitudes and party identification, or between attitudes and ratings of the president? The relation between party identification and opinions on the domestic issues index is shown in figure 6.10. One line on the graph shows the relation for citizens who are at the mean level of knowledge; the others show the relation for citizens at the midpoint of each of the four quartiles of knowledge.[46]

For the entire sample, mean Republican identification increases (moving up on the y-axis) as opinions become more conservative (moving to the right on the x-axis). But this aggregate relation conceals a great deal. Party identification among the least-knowledgeable quartile of citizens shows little relation with their stands on issues, ranging from a predicted mean of "leaning Democrat" among the most liberal citizens to "independent-independent" among the most conservative. As we move up through the quartiles of knowledge, the connection becomes progressively stronger. Clearly, knowledge is an important factor in forging a link between views on issues and one's choice of a party. This, in turn, suggests that the value of partisanship as a short cut to political decision making is dependent on citizens' ability to base that partisanship on more specific political information.

Presidential approval depends to a greater extent than party identification on short-term and nonideological factors. Still, popular control of public policy requires that presidents (and other elected officials) act on

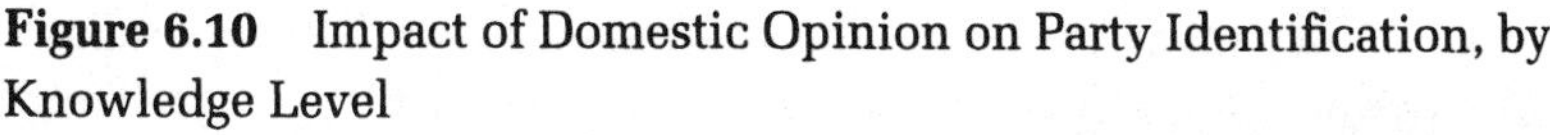

Figure 6.10 Impact of Domestic Opinion on Party Identification, by Knowledge Level

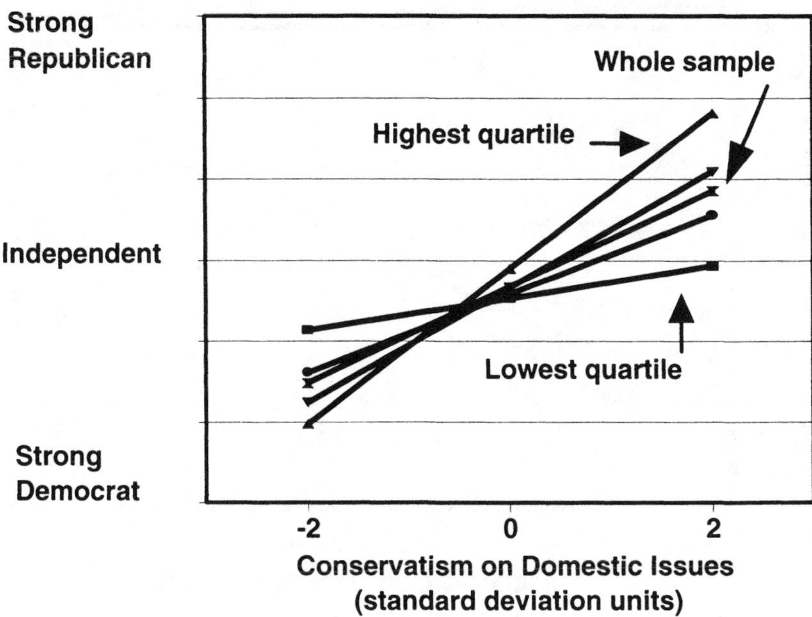

their own issue stands and party platforms. To the extent that they do so, some citizens should like what they are doing while others will not. To be a useful indicator of the public's satisfaction with the substantive performance of a president, approval should depend in part on citizens' views on important issues. The estimated mean approval of President Bush in 1988 shows that for the least-knowledgeable quartile, views on domestic issues were unrelated to opinions of presidential performance, but for the most knowledgeable the relation was very strong (see figure 6.11).[47]

What is the political significance of this finding? Public approval is an important political resource; it strengthens a president's ability to negotiate with Congress as well as with other political elites (Neustadt, 1976; Kernell, 1986). It also serves as an important check on government action (and inaction), giving citizens a political voice during the critical years between elections when policy is actually made and implemented. Political knowledge increases the likelihood that approval ratings are tied to citizens' views on issues, sharpening the communications between the public and elected officials by providing more substantively meaningful cues to political elites.

Figure 6.11 Impact of Domestic Opinion on Approval of George Bush in 1988, by Knowledge Level

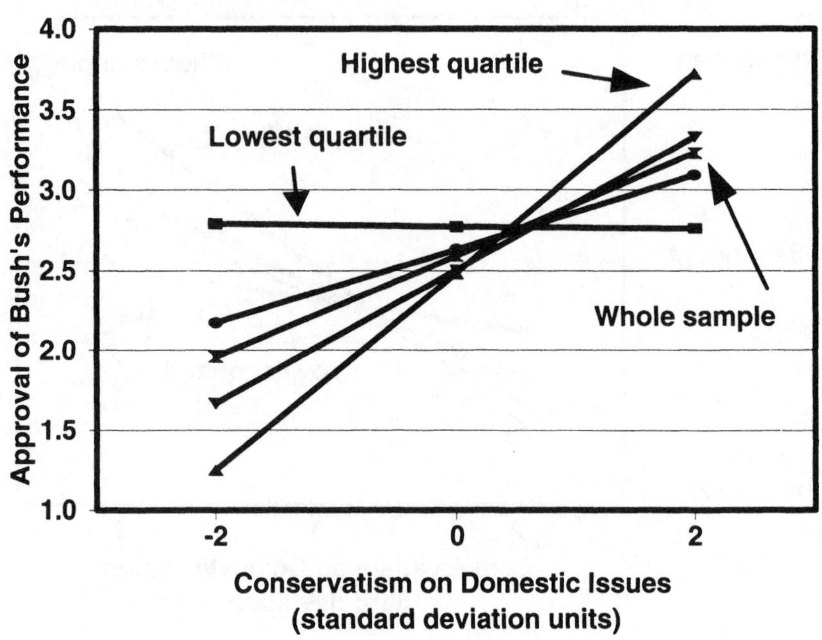

Connecting Attitudes with Participation

Political knowledge is critical to the development of numerous, stable, and consistent political opinions that are tied to objective group conditions and linked in meaningful ways to evaluations of public officials and support for political parties. Although these first- and second-order opinions can be influential in their own right, the keystone to civic power is political participation. Our earlier analysis suggested that more informed citizens are more likely to participate, but to what extent do they participate in ways that connect their opinions to their behavior? At a minimum, our argument would suggest that information should help citizens select candidates who best reflect their views and are most like them in terms of basic values.[48] This implies that better-informed voters will use more information in choosing a candidate, and potentially use different criteria for their choices, than would less-informed voters.[49]

Issue-Consistent Voting

In order to cast a vote that expresses their political views, voters must be aware of both what the candidates (or the parties) stand for and what they themselves want. An instrumentally rational vote requires consistency between citizens' opinions on issues and their vote.[50] Although we do not wish to argue that voting based on candidate qualities is misguided (surely everyone who is rational wants an honest and competent president), what elected officials do while in government ought to be at least as important as their personal qualities if the notion of republican government is to be meaningful.[51] If a citizen favors more government spending to assist the poor, a rational vote is usually for a Democratic candidate.[52] For someone who favors greater defense spending, in most elections that means she should vote for a Republican candidate. More generally, if citizens can meaningfully identify themselves—and the two parties or candidates—as conservative or liberal, what constitutes a rational vote is easy enough to infer.[53]

To explore the role of political knowledge in promoting issue-consistent voting, we built a simple presidential candidate choice model and tested it with data from the 1984, 1988, and 1992 National Election Studies. As we are concerned with determining which voters choose the candidate whose views are most consistent with their own, the only variables in the model are political knowledge and three opinion measures: attitudes on domestic policy (the additive index used earlier), foreign policy (an additive index of military and foreign issues like defense spending), and self-described liberal-conservative ideology.[54] Unlike models designed to explain the full range of factors that determine an individual's vote choice, we included no measures of partisanship, retrospective evaluations of the incumbent president, or perceptions of candidate personal qualities.[55]

We used two approaches to estimate the role of political knowledge in promoting issue-consistent voting. Both methods tell the same story, but they provide slightly different ways of summarizing the effect of information and dealing with alternative explanations. One method involved splitting the sample into groups according to level of political knowledge and estimating the model separately for each level. The other approach included interaction terms for knowledge by each of the three attitudes.[56] If the impact of attitudes is greater for better-informed citizens, we would expect the interaction terms to be positive and significant. In both approaches, the coefficients for the model were estimated using maximum likelihood logistic regression.

The effect of information is dramatic. The effectiveness of the model in explaining variation in presidential votes in 1984, 1988, and 1992 for four groups (quartiles) of voters divided on the basis of their scores on the knowledge index is shown in figure 6.12.[57] The figure plots the pseudo-r^2 of the model at each level of knowledge. The better we can predict how a citizen will vote simply by knowing his or her stands on issues, the higher the pseudo-r^2. Among the least-informed quartile of voters, the pseudo-r^2 for the model was 17, 16, and 13 percent for the three elections. By contrast, among the best informed, it was 81 percent in 1984 and 1988, and 82 percent in 1992.[58]

Figure 6.12 Variance of the Vote Explained by Issues and Ideology, by Information Level, 1984–92

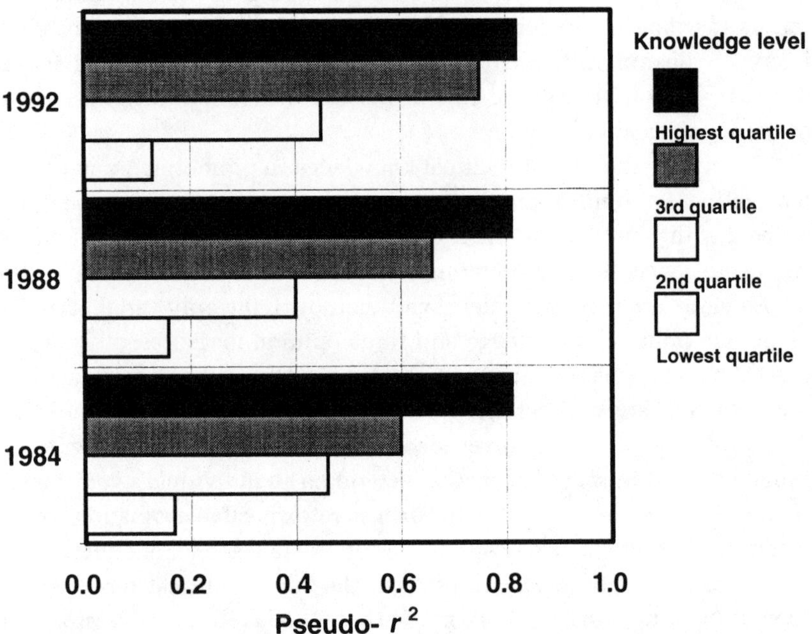

The relative value of political knowledge is clearly evident in figure 6.12. It is also evident in figure 6.13, which shows the strength of the association between the vote and each of the three types of attitudes—domestic and foreign issues, and ideology.[59] Among the least-informed fourth of the voters, only their domestic policy attitudes were a statistically significant predictor of the vote. As knowledge increased, all the coefficients grow and become significant. Each additional increment of knowledge tightens the connection between attitudes and the vote.

An analysis of the relation between the respondents' self-described ideology and the estimated probability of a vote for George Bush in 1988 shows the catalyzing effects of political knowledge on voters' ability to employ ideology in their evaluations (see figure 6.14). The logistic regression models for each of the four knowledge groups were used to produce

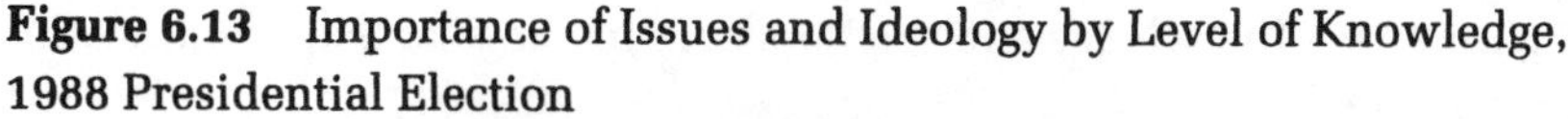

Figure 6.13 Importance of Issues and Ideology by Level of Knowledge, 1988 Presidential Election

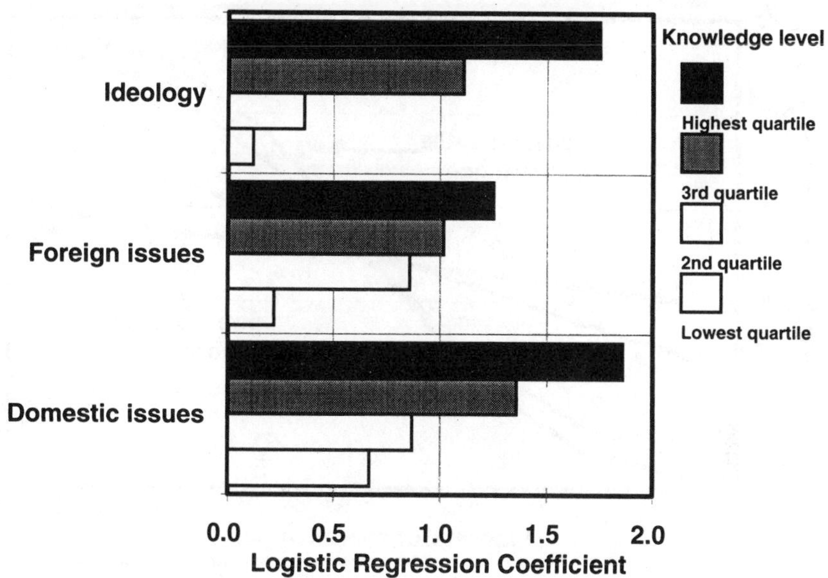

the estimates. To isolate the effects of ideology, the scores for the domestic and foreign policy variables were set at their means. For the least-knowledgeable quartile of voters, the probability of a vote for George Bush rose relatively little as the respondents' self-described conservatism increased. In contrast, for the best informed, the model forecasts an almost certain Bush vote for the most conservative respondents, and an almost certain Dukakis vote for the most liberal.

Results of the other method of estimation—using the interaction terms between knowledge and attitudes—tell the same story but also make possible a test of plausible rival explanations for what appears to be a knowledge effect. Based on these tests, it is clear that the effect we observe is of knowledge and not of cognitive ability or political engagement, both of which are related to but different from knowledge. Cognitive ability is poorly measured in the NES surveys, but possible surrogates include education and interviewer-rated intelligence. Both of these, as well as a summary measure of political engagement (for example, political interest and attention to the media), were tested. When the knowledge index and its interaction terms were not included in the models, intelligence formed a modest interaction with ideology, and engagement did so with foreign attitudes and ideology (significance levels of .06 to .08). But when political knowledge interaction terms were also included in the model—providing

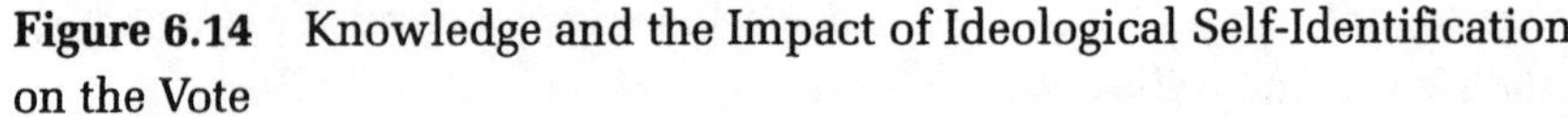

Figure 6.14 Knowledge and the Impact of Ideological Self-Identification on the Vote

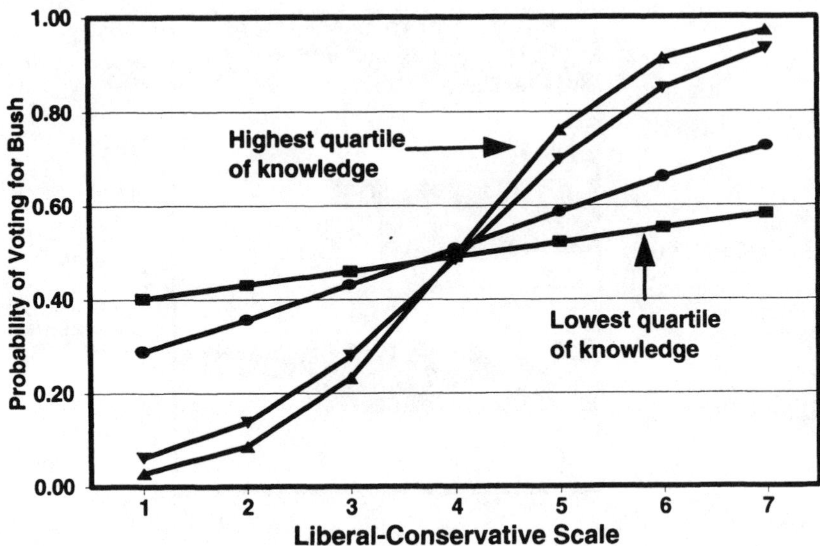

a head-to-head test—the rival interaction terms were nonsignificant and exceedingly weak. It is knowledge, independent of interest or cognitive ability, that makes issue-consistent voting possible.[60]

The fact that we can correctly forecast nine out of ten presidential votes among well-informed citizens (the top quartile) using only simple measures of their opinions on issues, and with no reliance on variables closer to the vote decision (for example, approval of the incumbent, perceptions of the candidates, economic evaluations, or partisanship), strongly suggests that, for this segment of the population, issue voting is alive and well and that the voter's information level is the key factor in determining who engages in it. In the three most recent presidential elections, voting by well-informed citizens—not a tiny elite but those able to answer most of the relatively simple and straightforward knowledge items—was issue consistent and highly predictable. Also encouraging, and consistent with our argument that the value of knowledge is relative, is that even modestly informed voters are able to connect their issue stands to their vote, though not with the same precision as more informed citizens. For the substantial portion of citizens who are poorly informed, however, voting was poorly connected to their views on issue, thus weakening the collective political impact of their participation.

Less Informed Citizens and the Role of Economic Factors in the Vote

Although our model indicates that issues matter even to the less informed, its overall performance for these voters—in terms of votes correctly predicted—was weak. What other factors enter into their decisions? Many studies of vote choice have found evidence that economic concerns influence the vote, either through the voter's perception of the economy's performance, the voter's personal financial condition, or both. The evidence for the role of the economy is strong, both in individual-level analyses and in aggregate data. Vote-forecasting models that rely primarily on changes in economic conditions are often uncannily accurate, rivaling election-eve surveys (Fair, 1988; Tufte, 1978; Rosenstone, 1983; Lewis-Beck and Rice, 1992; Campbell, 1992).

At the individual level a principal question about economic effects is the extent voting is influenced by personal economic circumstances—so-called egocentric voting—as opposed to one's views of the national economy—so-called sociotropic voting (Welch and Hibbing, 1991; Kiewiet, 1983; Kinder, Adams, and Gronke, 1989).[61] This distinction is especially relevant to our concerns for two reasons. First, one's personal economic circumstances, in the absence of considerations of how those circumstances are tied to the performance of the national economy, would seem a relatively poor mechanism for evaluating candidates. Second, sociotropic voting, because it evaluates candidates on the basis of collective rather than individual concerns, is not only arguably more politically relevant, but is also more communally driven: public rather than private interests determine one's political actions.

To examine the way knowledge affects economic influences on presidential voting in 1988, we added two economic measures to our model: perceptions of how the U.S. economy had changed in the past year (a five-point scale from much better to much worse), and changes in the respondent's personal economic circumstances (also a five-point scale). Consistent with the work of other researchers, we found evidence of sociotropic but not egocentric voting for the sample as a whole. But this general pattern masked important differences among those with different levels of political knowledge. Personal financial conditions were significantly associated with the vote for the lowest information quartile, but perceptions of the national economy were not. Moving up through the information quartiles, the independent impact of personal circumstances diminishes to insignificance, while the coefficient for national economic perceptions becomes significant (the role of issues and ideology remains roughly as it was without the economic terms included). Equally telling, among the least-informed voters, adding the economic variables to the model improved the pseudo-r^2 substantially: it rose from 16 percent to 25 percent. The economic terms, however, improve the overall explanatory power of the model very little for voters above the mean in political knowledge.

These results suggest that for many of the least-informed citizens, for whom the substantive positions of the candidates (and indeed, their own views) are indistinct, voting in 1988 was based on simple retrospective evaluations that rewarded or punished the incumbent party depending on personal circumstances—at best a crude and self-centered measure of the quality of representation. Among better-informed voters, personal economic circumstances did not make an independent contribution to the vote. Rather, they tended to use national economic conditions (a heuristic arguably more politically relevant and collectively oriented) as one piece of a more complex decision-making process.[62]

These findings—that changes in personal financial conditions have a greater independent impact on the vote of less knowledgeable citizens than of those with greater knowledge—may appear contradictory to the notion of group interests put forth earlier. In that analysis, we described the impact knowledge had on the relation between personal financial problems and opinions on domestic issues, arguing that knowledge appears to lead to greater congruence between attitudes and objective group interests. We do not believe these results are incompatible. First, unlike the current analysis, which focuses on relatively short-term evaluations of one's financial condition, the economy, and the performance of public officials, our earlier analysis examined more deep-seated notions of both class and politics. Issue attitudes dealing with broad questions of the proper scope of government are more basic and enduring political orientations than is the decision to vote for a particular candidate for president. Similarly, the measures of financial hardship used in our earlier analysis (putting off medical treatment, having to take a second job, receiving federal aid such as food stamps, and so forth) tap more long-term, structural aspects of economic status than do relative evaluations of one's personal financial circumstances.

Second, it is *not* our argument that self-interest—whether defined in class or individual terms—is irrelevant to the political decision making of better-informed citizens. Rather, its primary impact is indirect, interacting with broader considerations of the state of the nation and of the real and preferred actions of government. As evidence for this, consider the relation between our economic troubles scale, evaluations of the condition of the national economy, and the 1992 presidential vote (table 6.4). The data in this table shows the percentage voting for George Bush among four different groups of voters, divided according to whether or not they saw the economy as having gotten worse, and whether or not they had experienced four or more financial problems in the past year. It is clear that both personal circumstances and perceptions of the national economy independently affect the vote. But one pattern is especially noteworthy. Among less knowledgeable citizens who experienced financial problems, Bush received little support (around one-fifth of the vote) regardless of their views of the national economy. But among the more knowledgeable citizens who had financial problems, views of the national economy made a significant difference in the vote. Among those who saw the economy declining, only 14 percent voted for the president. But among those who saw the national economy as unchanged or improved, Bush received a respectable 45 percent of the vote. Clearly, citizens evaluated the candidates on the basis of their self-interest. But for more informed citizens, it was, to use de Tocqueville's phrase, self-interest *properly understood.*

Table 6.4 Percent Voting for Bush, by Personal Financial Problems and Perceptions of the National Economy, 1992 Presidential Election

	Knowledge level: bottom half		Knowledge level: top half	
	National economy is		National economy is	
Personal finances	better or same	worse	better or same	worse
< 4 troubles	55%	29%	67%	35%
4 or more troubles	19%	21%	45%	14%

Source: 1992 National Election Study.

The Situational Impact of Knowledge: A Case Study of the Abortion Issue

Our analysis of NES data shows the electoral importance of issues for knowledgeable citizens when opinions are summarized into foreign and domestic indexes. Our assumption, supported indirectly by controlling for the impact of general political interest and cognitive ability, is that *specific* information relevant to the issues at hand drives a good deal of this relation. We tested this assumption more directly with data from a 1989 Virginia survey.

Abortion is a useful topic for examining the role of information in issue voting. Few issues have commanded as much attention or generated as much controversy. The two major parties in the United States have taken nearly opposite positions on the issue over the past several presidential elections. The abortion issue has also figured prominently in several subnational races (Cook, Jelen, and Wilcox, 1994), perhaps most notably the 1989 gubernatorial election in Virginia. The Democratic candidate, Lieutenant Governor L. Douglas Wilder, campaigned on a platform promising that no restrictions would be placed on abortion in Virginia. His opponent, former state Attorney General Marshall Coleman, favored major restrictions. Wilder won the election by fewer than 7,000 votes, becoming the nation's first elected black governor.

Interest in the abortion issue in Virginia was not confined to activists: most voters said they were concerned about it. Fifty-nine percent of registered voters surveyed near the time of the election said the issue was "very important" to them (and another 23 percent said it was "somewhat important").[63] But despite considerable attention to the campaign in general and the abortion issue in particular, fewer than four in ten (36 percent) of the respondents were aware of both candidates' stands on abortion (another 22 percent were aware of only one candidate's stand). Knowledge, or lack thereof, was critical to the ability of citizens to connect their attitudes with their vote. Even among those who said the abortion issue was very important to them, knowing their personal opinion about abortion was nearly useless in predicting their vote if they did not know where the candidates stood: the correlation between the vote and a four-point abortion-opinion scale for these individuals was a meager .05. In contrast, for those who felt the abortion issue was very important *and* who knew both candidates' positions, the correlation was a striking .74. In this group, 87 percent of those who opposed any new restrictions on abortion said they would vote for Wilder. Of those who favored major restrictions, only 6 percent would vote for him.[64]

Research by Alan Abramowitz provides corroborating evidence at the national level. Although there was relatively little discussion of abortion in the 1992 presidential election, survey evidence suggests that abortion was a critical issue for many voters. Among the one-fourth of the electorate (excluding Perot voters) who were aware of the candidates' relative positions on abortion and who evidenced concern about abortion by mentioning it at least once in the open-ended questions about the parties and candidates, abortion outweighed all other issues—including economic concerns—in its impact on the vote (Abramowitz, 1995: 183–84). The situational value of knowledge is clear. In both the state and national contexts, specific knowledge of candidate positions (coupled with concern about the issue) makes issue voting possible.

The Collective Consequences of Political Ignorance: Evidence from the 1988 Presidential Election

A critical consequence of a lack of information is the potential for citizens to misperceive what the government does or does not do. In many ways, the 1988 election was a referendum on the Reagan administration, without the confounding effects of Reagan's personal charisma. An interesting set of questions on the 1988 National Election Study regarding Reagan administration policies allows a glimpse of policy misperceptions and their consequences. Respondents were asked what the federal government had done during the past eight years. The survey questions did not refer to particular pieces of legislation or executive acts, but rather to the nature of government efforts in four important policy areas: federal spending on assistance to the poor, federal spending on public schools, government spending on defense, and federal efforts to improve and protect the environment. For each, the alternative responses were that government efforts or spending "increased," "stayed about the same," and "decreased" (respondents could also say they had not followed the issue). Respondents were then asked what they thought the government should have done. The combination of the questions makes it possible to sort respondents according to their perceptions of the government's actions and whether they approved or disapproved. For example, on the question of government efforts to clean and protect the environment, one group is composed of those who said the government had decreased its efforts in this area and who also disapproved of this action. For each of the categories on the four issues we computed the percentage of voters who cast their votes for George Bush (table 6.5).

Table 6.5 The Link between Perceptions and Vote

Perception of National Government Action and Respondent's Opinion about the Perceived Action	Environmental Protection		Defense Spending		Spending on the Poor		Spending on Public Schools	
	Voted for Bush (%)	All Voters (%)	Voted for Bush (%)	All Voters (%)	Voted for Bush (%)	All Voters (%)	Voted for Bush (%)	All Voters (%)
Haven't paid attention	51	20	56	10	59	19	57	23
Increased and I approve	75	24	74	43	65	19	66	21
Decreased and I disapprove	27	23	40	2	23	25	31	24
Stayed the same, but should have increased	53	21	50	2	35	16	43	19
Stayed the same, and I approve	64	7	68	4	83	9	72	6
Decreased and I approve	67	2	56	1	79	5	71	3

Table 6.5 The Link between Perceptions and Vote (*continued*)

Perception of National Government Action and Respondent's Opinion about the Perceived Action	Environmental Protection		Defense Spending		Spending on the Poor		Spending on Public Schools	
	Voted for Bush (%)	All Voters (%)	Voted for Bush (%)	All Voters (%)	Voted for Bush (%)	All Voters (%)	Voted for Bush (%)	All Voters (%)
Increased and I disapprove	47	2	25	37	81	5	78	4
Stayed the same, should have decreased	—	0	67	1	73	2	50	0.4
N		971		955		928		937

Source: 1988 National Election Study.

There is a strong relation between disapproving of Reagan's policies and voting against George Bush. However, the instrumental rationality of this vote is sharply curtailed by misperception of what actually occurred during the Reagan-Bush years. Eighty percent of voters correctly perceived that defense spending increased during the Reagan years. But only a quarter to a third of voters knew that federal efforts on behalf of the environment, the poor, and the schools declined during this period.[65] Indeed, of the 60 to 68 percent of voters who believed that federal aid in these three domestic policy areas should have increased, substantially less than half knew that it had not. Perhaps most strikingly, a sizable minority of the voting public (from one-fifth to one-fourth) thought the federal government had increased spending on the environment, the poor, and schools and said they approved of that action. In each case, a large majority of these citizens voted for Bush—in essence to continue policies that were the opposite of what they wanted. Even among respondents whose personal situations would lead to the expectation of a Democratic vote—those with incomes below $20,000 and those who were worse off financially than one year before—about one-fifth fell into the misperceiving group, and majorities (56–60 percent) voted for Bush. Inattention was also consequential. A group comparable in size to the misperceivers said they had not paid much attention to these issues. For the items on spending for defense, the poor, and the public schools, majorities of these inattentive individuals reported voting for Bush.

In this chapter we have documented a range of sizable differences in the political opinions and behaviors of well and poorly informed citizens. These differences are manifested in several important ways. Much of the public lacks adequate information about basic democratic norms and may, as a consequence, be less committed to those norms. Poorly informed citizens hold fewer, less stable, and less consistent opinions. They are more susceptible to political propaganda and less receptive to relevant new information. They are less likely to connect objective group conditions to their policy views or to connect their policy views to evaluations of public officials and political parties in instrumentally rational ways. Poorly informed citizens are less likely to participate, and when they do participate, they are less likely to tie their actions effectively to the issue stands and political orientations they profess to hold. Because so many of these differences bear on the issue of political power, a key implication of these findings is that the maldistribution of political knowledge has consequences: it threatens the basic democratic principle of political equality among citizens.

Although these findings would be troubling under any circumstances, they are especially so because political knowledge is not randomly distributed in the population. The very groups who are disadvantaged economically and socially are also less politically informed and, thus, disadvantaged in the struggle over the political allocation of scarce goods, services, and values. The net result is a less effective translation of their collective interests into public opinion and political behavior. Whether examining such attitudes as party identification, such opinions as the approval ratings of the president, or such behaviors as vote choice, the more informed one is, the more likely one is to send clear, policy-oriented messages to political elites (Althaus, 1994). To the extent that political elites respond to such signals—a central tenet of any theory of representative democracy—informed citizens are likely to have their concerns taken more seriously.

Despite the real challenge presented by these findings, there is good news as well. The benefits of political knowledge are not out of the reach of ordinary Americans. As Philip Converse has observed, a major argument against radical notions of the social contract and consent of the governed in the late eighteenth century was that "the common 'citizen' simply lacked the information necessary for any sensible contribution to debates over the grand policies of state," and that even if provided with adequate information, most citizens would be unable to make wise or efficient use of it (1990: 369). The evidence presented in this chapter indicates that such pessimism is not warranted. Although it is demonstrably true that many citizens are innocent of any but the most trivial political cognitions, many others—perhaps a large minority—appear knowledgeable enough to shoulder the responsibilities of republican government quite well.

Taken together, our findings constitute powerful evidence that a rational, informed public, acting in ways consistent with classical norms of citizenship, is not an unrealistic ideal for America. Consider the best-informed quartile of citizens from the surveys we examined. This group is certainly not superhuman—they are, for the most part, simply people who have been afforded the social and economic benefits promised by the American dream. Yet they were highly likely to express a considered, genuine opinion on most issues—as demonstrated, for example, by the fact that a majority of them provided the same response when asked the questions months later, and by the fact that their opinions on related questions of the appropriate scope of government activities in the domestic sphere were highly interrelated, just as is the case among political elites. This group was also highly likely to vote (80 percent did so in 1988). The vast majority of voters in this group chose a presidential candidate whose views were consistent with theirs on a range of issues. By almost any standard of democratic behavior, these are desirable characteristics and would, taken together, satisfy quite rigorous standards for a rational public. That they are exhibited by a sizable minority of the public—citizens who also hold jobs, raise children, and pursue other interests in life—suggests that substantial improvement in the quality of our democracy is surely attainable without extraordinary or unrealistic changes in the citizens or the system.[66]

The implications of our findings for improving civic literacy depend in large part on the extent to which good citizenship is a result of knowledge rather than other civic characteristics. Our belief that knowledge is the critical factor is based on two considerations. First, in all of the analyses, plausible alternative explanations were tested statistically, usually in head-to-head contests with knowledge. In all instances knowledge emerged as the principal factor accounting for the behavior. We do not claim that simply by "injecting" adequate political information into less informed citizens, they would promptly manifest the qualities of citizenship that are related to political knowledge. Yet the interconnectedness of political interest and motivation, knowledge, and participation strongly suggest that a boost in any of these elements would lead to gains in the others.

Second and more important, for all of the phenomena we examined, a strong theoretical case exists that knowledge promotes or facilitates the behavior in question. Tolerance is logically higher among citizens who are aware of constitutional provisions for civil liberties. Attitudes about issues are doubtless more stable and better connected to values and interests among citizens who know a lot about the issues. Instrumentally rational voting behavior must be more common among citizens who know how candidates stand on the issues that matter to them. And perceptions of one's interests, and how the political world affects them, must be clearer for citizens whose views are not, as Robert Lane put it, morselized or personalized (1962).

The behavior and capabilities of the public are important not only for their role in empowering (or enfeebling) individual citizens. They also set the context for the behavior of public officials and other political actors. Numerous observers have remarked on the deplorable state of contemporary public discourse over issues and the trivial and misleading style of election campaigns. These problems could be mitigated by broader and deeper public comprehension of politics. The irony is that such improvement on the public's part probably cannot occur without substantial change in the behavior of political elites. As long as the latter have incentives to polarize the public with false choices (Dionne, 1991), or to shroud themselves in ambiguity that leads ill-informed voters to view them simply as moderates (Alvarez and Franklin, 1994), it will be difficult for the public to learn what they need to learn. The public's gullibility increases the incentives for elites to employ such tactics. The consequence of this is, as E. J. Dionne, Jr., has argued, ineffective and often paralyzed government, which leads in turn to cynical and withdrawn citizens who are even more susceptible to the techniques of modern campaigns (Dionne, 1991; Entman, 1989). There is no magic way out of this conundrum. But we hope this chapter, and indeed all of what we have attempted to demonstrate in this book, show that the goal of an informed citizenry is not utopian, and that the effort to achieve one is well worth the effort.

CHAPTER SEVEN

Informing the Public's Discretion

[These and other cases raise the question of] whether peace is best preserved by giving energy to the government, or information to the people. This last is the most certain, and the most legitimate engine of government. Educate and inform the whole mass of the people. . . . They are the only sure reliance for the preservation of our liberty. —THOMAS JEFFERSON, letter to James Madison

We have frequently printed the word Democracy. Yet I cannot too often repeat that it is a word the real gist of which still sleeps, quite unawakened, not withstanding the resonance and the many angry tempests out of which its syllables have come, from pen or tongue. It is a great word, whose history, I suppose, remains unwritten, because that history has yet to be enacted.—WALT WHITMAN, *Democratic Vistas*

The American political system is an enigma. It celebrates the individual while longing for a sense of community. It allows almost unlimited participation while doing little to facilitate it. It combines thick civic responsibilities with thin civic identities. It has emerged as the world's leading democracy, but it is designed to limit the impact of the vox populi. And, perhaps most fundamentally, it is built upon both an abiding faith in and a deep-seated suspicion of the public. In his later years, Thomas Jefferson often lamented the lack of trust most of his contemporaries had in the general public. Although he agreed that people often fell short of the civic ideal, he argued that the political system, by minimizing what was expected of citizens, guaranteed the nature of their public behavior: "We think one side of this experiment has been long enough tried, and proved not to promote the good of the many; and that the other has not been fairly and sufficiently tried" (1939: 67).

We share Jefferson's concern about the lack of trust in the people themselves, a suspicion that, in many respects, is as prevalent today as it was in the late eighteenth and early nineteenth centuries. We also share his beliefs that an informed citizenry is the only true repository of the public will; that, given the incentive, education, and opportunity, the general public is capable of exercising political power in an enlightened way; and that the context in which citizens operate—the social, political, and economic structure—is a critical factor in determining whether or not they are motivated and capable.

Ironically, the belief that most citizens simply cannot or will not acquire sufficient political knowledge drives the arguments of both the proponents and critics of contemporary democracy. It is our view, however, that attempts to salvage democratic theory and practice by downplaying the responsibilities of citizens or the importance of an informed public do an injustice to the very values they seek to defend. Regardless of what conception of democracy one holds—whether thin or thick, direct or indirect—information is necessary for citizens to function effectively. Further, the real world of American politics makes a surprisingly large number of demands on citizens. Whereas it is impossible to identify the specific pieces of information necessary for assuring good citizenship, clearly some information is important, and all other things being equal, more information is better than less information. Arguments that it is irrational for citizens to become politically informed are based on economic models of rational choice, when civic models are normatively and empirically more appropriate. And although it is certainly true that we all take advantage of heuristics that reduce the amount of information necessary for making political decisions, these shortcuts require a nontrivial amount of knowledge to be used effectively.

Principal Findings

Throughout this book we have attempted to provide empirical support for the Jeffersonian vision of the importance and possibility of an informed citizenry, while at the same time confronting those places where the American public falls short of this vision. Our analyses suggest the following.

First, it is nearly meaningless to talk about how much the "public" knows about politics. Although political knowledge levels are, in many instances, depressingly low, they are high enough among some segments of the population, and on some topics, to foster optimism about democratic possibilities. More than a small fraction of the public is reasonably well informed about politics—informed enough to meet high standards of good citizenship. Many of the basic institutions and procedures of government are known to half or more of the public, as are the relative positions of the parties on many major issues of the day. Further, knowledge levels are too high for us to accept the view, offered by some proponents of the rational choice school, that acquiring and retaining information is fundamentally irrational.[1] Indeed, given their socioeconomic and educational status, the people who are politically well informed are precisely the kind we would expect to engage in rational behavior. None of this discounts the need for increasing the level of public knowledge, nor does it ignore the fact that large numbers of American citizens are woefully underinformed and that overall levels of knowledge are modest at best. Nor is it to downplay the often dramatic disparities in knowledge found between the most and least informed citizens, disparities that rival those found in the distribution of income and wealth in the United States. Rather it demonstrates that enough citizens are able to obtain and retain information in the current political environment—an environment that is only partially supportive of this task—to believe that a more fully and equally informed public is possible.

Second, despite the numerous political, economic, and social changes that have occurred since World War II, overall political knowledge levels in the United States are about the same today as they were forty to fifty years ago. This stability presents the greatest challenge to our notion that political knowledge levels are strongly affected by structural and contextual conditions. At a minimum it underscores how difficult raising aggregate levels of knowledge may be, and it could be construed as evidence of the fundamental intransigence of political ignorance. It is important to keep in mind, however, that many of the changes of the past half century seem as likely to depress as increase citizens' civic knowledge. For example, while educational attainment levels have risen, other changes have clearly depressed levels of public interest and engagement in politics among citizens of all educational levels. Thus, the stability in political knowledge is the result of offsetting forces. Further, while long-term trends show little change in what citizens know, short-term patterns suggest that, given the right mix of ability, opportunity, and motivation, citizens are capable of significant political learning. This, coupled with our analyses in later chapters that find a strong and significant relation between socioeconomic status, the political and information environment, and political knowledge levels, strongly suggests the potential for improvement.

Third, most citizens are political generalists, meaning that those who are knowledgeable about one aspect of politics tend to be knowledgeable about others. Several exceptions to this general pattern were found, most notably that women, blacks, and partisans were relatively more informed about gender, race, and party issues, respectively, than they were about other political topics and that knowledge of local politics was somewhat distinct from knowledge of state or national government. Taken as a whole, these findings suggest that different socioeconomic groups are drawn to politics through a variety of distinct pathways, but that in the long run, differences in the ability, opportunity, and motivation to learn about *politics in general* outweigh differences in the ability, opportunity, and motivation to learn about *specific domains of politics*. At the individual level this means that someone who has the resources to learn about one aspect of politics is also likely to have the resources to learn about other aspects of politics. At the aggregate level this means that rather than a pluralist information society in which different groups and classes bring different information to the marketplace of ideas, political information of all kinds tends to be concentrated in the same hands.

A fourth conclusion follows from the third. Inequality in citizen knowledge is not simply an idiosyncratic characteristic of individuals. Groups of citizens vary in knowledge in ways that mirror their standings in the social, political, and economic world, calling into question the fundamental democratic principle of equality among citizens. In particular, women, African Americans, the poor, and the young tend to be substantially less knowledgeable about politics than are men, whites, the affluent, and older citizens. Much of the knowledge gap between these groups persists even when such relevant personal characteristics as education or occupation are taken into account, pointing to a legacy of the long-term exclusion of socioeconomically disadvantaged citizens from many aspects of the public sphere. These systematic differences in political knowledge have serious implications for the ability of some groups to perceive and act on their self-interest or their notion of the public interest. If Jefferson is right that the people themselves are the best protectors of their own interests, then many groups are hindered in this effort by their relative lack of political information.

Fifth, being politically informed is the result of many factors. As in most spheres of life, motivation is important in learning about politics. Motivation increases with age, education, social status, a sense of efficacy, and a belief that the political world is directly relevant to the individual. But motivation is only one influence. Individuals with higher levels of cognitive skill and relevant contextual knowledge will tend to learn much more about politics than will others. Cognitive skill and contextual knowledge fall under the rubric of "ability" and are strongly related to one's level of formal education. Indeed, education is the strongest single predictor of political knowledge. Yet while personal factors such as ability or motivation strongly affect knowledge levels, our analysis of the persistent gender gap in knowledge suggests that these characteristics are greatly influenced by cultural and structural factors and are not solely the result of autonomous personal choices. Moreover, a key element for political learning is the opportunity to do so, which is neither as constant nor as vast as commonly believed. Where adequate political information is available in a form easily comprehended, citizens learn more. Indeed, the relation between availability of information and citizen knowledge levels is so strong in certain situations that the nature of the information environment is the most important predictor of knowledge, surpassing education and interest. Overall, while it is true that individuals with the greatest cognitive skills are likely to learn the most about politics, the type of political information needed to function effectively as a citizen is not especially complex and is well within the reach of individuals with modest cognitive ability—given the motivation and opportunity to do so. With all due respect to Albert Einstein, politics is not harder than physics![2]

Finally and perhaps most important, informed citizens are demonstrably better citizens, as judged by the standards of democratic theory and practice underpinning the American system. They are more likely to participate in politics, more likely to have meaningful, stable attitudes on issues, better able to link their interests with their attitudes, more likely to choose candidates who are consistent with their own attitudes, and more likely to support democratic norms, such as extending basic civil liberties to members of unpopular groups. Differences between the best- and least-informed citizens on all of these dimensions are dramatic. In our analyses, the impact of political knowledge is independent of, and thus over and above, that of other such factors as interest in politics and political efficacy.[3]

What Can Be Done?

One perspective on the extent of public understanding of politics is that information is widely available, and thus it is a citizen's own fault if he or she is uninformed. Yet if an informed public is important to the workings of an effective democracy, this is as unacceptable a response as saying that doctors have ample opportunity to learn about innovations in medicine and it's their problem if they fail to do so. We all suffer from an underinformed citizenry as surely as we would if the medical profession were inadequately trained; there is a public, as well as a private, good at stake. Although increasing a sense of civic responsibility among individuals is certainly part of the solution, the multiplicity of paths to knowledge suggest that there are many other ways we can improve the political knowledge levels of the public. The interrelatedness of knowledge, interest, and engagement means that, absent strong countervailing forces, a gain in any of these elements will tend to raise the others.

News and the Information Environment

The primary source of information about much of contemporary politics is the mass media. In many respects, politically relevant information is more widely available now than at any time in history. Primarily because of the spread of cable television, most households in the United States have access to broadcast news at any hour of the day, as well as to such specialized and in-depth programming as C-SPAN. Public affairs radio in various forms—from NPR's "All Things Considered" to G. Gordon Liddy's talk show—is attracting growing audiences. And on-line information services and computer bulletin boards, accessible from home or office via personal computer and modem, provide news, reference services, and a forum for public discussion of issues to millions of users. Citizens who use these electronic networks can exchange opinions and information directly with White House staff, members of Congress, journalists, and many local governments. These services provide citizens with quick access to information ranging from schedules of local political and cultural events to the full texts of presidential statements and Supreme Court decisions. The ability to access the full text of wire service stories allows citizens literally to construct their own newspapers. Concurrent access to on-line encyclopedias and other reference material allows citizens to research topics when they are most relevant, increasing the likelihood that they will engage in such information seeking and that they will retain the information. Interactive services also allow citizens to engage in electronic conversations with people in their community, around the nation, and around the world.

Many trends that have enriched the information environment also raise concerns. Access to cable television, computer bulletin boards, and other information services can be costly and, at present at least, require users to have certain communication and technical skills that are not evenly distributed throughout the populace. This raises the specter of an accelerating knowledge gap between the haves and the have-nots (Delli Carpini and Singh, 1987). Not surprisingly, there are significant economic biases in who is and is not "wired" to the new technology. For example, among households earning over $50,000 a year, 75 percent have cable, 56 percent have a home computer, and 27 percent have a modem. Among families earning between $20,000 and $29,000, however, only 58 percent have cable, 23 percent have a computer, and 7 percent have a modem (Times Mirror Center, 1994a). More dramatically, while over one in five college graduates from households earning over $50,000 a year have and use a modem at home, a mere one in fifty noncollege graduates with family incomes less than $30,000 a year do so. There are also significant differences between men and women and between whites and blacks in both computer and modem ownership, with whites and men more likely than blacks and women to be owners. Thus, the public is dramatically divided in how the new information technology affects their lives.[4] The information explosion that created the news-oriented media also brought a new wave of entertainment media that dwarfs the increases in public affairs programming and threatens to divert citizens—especially the young—from news and other informative programming.[5]

There is also reason for concern about the content of information presented by the media. The media have long been the subject of intense criticism for various sins of omission and commission (see, for example, Postman, 1985; Entman, 1989). Typical of the many discouraging trends in recent years is the drastic decline in the length of direct quotes by candidates (from 42.3 seconds in 1968 to 9.8 seconds in 1988, according to Kiku Adatto, 1990), and the rise of tabloid news formats in local television news (Kurtz, 1993a). The tendency of many newspapers to compete with television by shifting to shorter, more entertaining, and less fact-oriented stories is also troubling.

It seems clear that to raise levels of political knowledge it is necessary both to increase accessibility to quality information sources and to improve the quality of information that is accessible. Regarding the former, the technology of fiber optics means that within the next few years any household with a telephone will also have access to a range of video- and computer-information services. But the failure of nearly four-in-ten American households to have cable television is only partly due to a lack of availability—many households cannot afford it. Cable television has become a central source of information, and with the increased use of fiber optics, is likely to become more important to the interactive exchange of information between government and its citizens. One solution to the problem of unequal access would be for the United States to adopt a policy, analogous to that in many states promoting universal telephone service, in which all households were connected to the Internet (or its successor) and to a basic cable television service that would include C-SPAN, CNN, and other public affairs–oriented programming (including local programming). The government could also subsidize the purchase of hardware and software necessary to allow all households to make use of the Internet, community bulletin boards, and other local information services.

Promoting universal access to specialized news and to computer information services is not an unreasonable long-term goal and is consistent with plans to increase the economic competitiveness of the U.S. workforce.[6] In the meantime, access to information can be improved within the current media environment. This would require news organizations to take seriously the role of informing, even educating, citizens. Information could be packaged in a way that makes it more understandable,[7] more relevant, more frequent,[8] and more interesting. Few news organizations—even the elite—make a systematic effort to determine what, if anything, citizens actually learn from the news. Absent such research, little effort is made to adopt practices that enhance learning by the audience.[9]

Journalists and editors need to take more seriously John Dewey's (1927) model of "scientific journalism" or its contemporary reincarnation in Phillip Meyer's (1991) notion of "precision journalism." Both Dewey and Meyer emphasize the importance of blending the techniques of social scientific research and quality journalism to provide the general public with valid, reliable, useful, and accessible information about the social and political world.[10] As part of this, journalists and editors could combine their interest in holding the reader's attention with a concern about informing him or her about the relevant facts.

Currently much of what the press focuses on and how it presents information is determined not by a judgment of what citizens need to know, but rather by institutional needs, bureaucratic routines, and other forces (Epstein, 1973; Gans, 1979; Sigal, 1973). Furthermore, reporters and editors do not always have accurate images of their audiences and so cannot fully anticipate their needs and interests (Gans, 1979: 236–41). Efforts to take account of citizen needs have been made by some news organizations (see, for example, Teixeira, 1992) but more could be done (Graber, 1994). One simple—and potentially popular—approach would be to offer readers and viewers a formal opportunity to influence the news agenda. Except in the case of tips about crimes, pothole alerts, and the like, input by readers does not appear to affect what is covered—at the least, such influence is rarely acknowledged by editors and thus little reinforcement is provided. Citizens should be encouraged to write with questions about the activities of government, business, interest groups, and other potentially powerful institutions, and editors should print these queries and assign reporters to obtain answers to some of them.[11] In addition to providing important feedback for editors and reporters and suggesting possible story topics, such a system might give readers a sense of empowerment and a feeling of investment in what journalists do, leading to greater engagement in politics (Kurtz, 1993a).

Perhaps more important than encouraging citizen participation in journalism is promoting direct involvement in politics by providing audiences with the information they need to take action. Neuman, Just, and

Crigler's study found that part of citizen apathy about the topics covered in the news "results from a profound sense of powerlessness. . . . Our subjects reacted with special enthusiasm to information about how to take control of public issues" (1992: 111). James Lemert calls this "mobilizing information," which he defines as "information that helps people act on attitudes they already have" (1981: 118). Mobilizing information is abundant in advertising (phone numbers, addresses, prices) but largely absent from the news, especially stories about policy conflicts. Although Lemert's research has found that journalists often omit mobilizing information for fear of appearing partisan, providing such information would be consistent with the broader journalistic norm of empowering the citizenry. If political knowledge and participation are closely linked in a spiraling process, any increase in participation spurred by mobilizing information should lead to increases in knowledge. At a minimum, the local print and electronic media could be much more effective at reporting on the voting behavior and other activities of public officials.[12]

Promising efforts on the part of the media to provide mobilizing information are exemplified by the work of a daily newspaper in Columbus, Georgia (Rosen, 1991; 1992). Faced with dwindling circulation and producing a news product that was viewed by citizens, editors, and public officials alike as increasingly irrelevant, editors of the Columbus *Ledger-Enquirer,* a Knight-Ridder affiliate, coordinated a series of stories on local economic development with a concurrent series of public meetings—organized by the newspaper—between local citizens and public officials. The result was increased newspaper circulation, a more informed and engaged citizenry, and tangible movement on a number of local policy issues. Similar experiments have been tried in other communities around the country.[13]

A different kind of collaboration between journalism and the public is the *Utne Reader's* "Neighborhood Salon Association" (NSA). Salons, which date back to seventeenth-century France (and have relatives in the eighteenth- and nineteenth-century English coffeehouses), are regular gatherings of a small number of people who come together to talk about social and political issues of the day (Sandra, 1993).[14] Some salons involve structured discussion on topics about which participants have completed common readings, while others allow the topic of the day to emerge from less formal conversations. The NSA now boasts over three hundred registered salons in North America. Other media organizations have also begun to organize salons, roundtables, and discussion groups.[15]

Perhaps the most difficult issue the media face is providing relevant information while also holding the reader's or viewer's attention. One consequence of the television networks' growing concern with profitability in the face of a declining share of the audience is the near total demise of the news documentary and the concurrent rise of the docudrama. This trend is problematic. Documentaries provide a unique opportunity to address important social and political issues in depth and in a way less fettered by the restrictions of objective reporting. Although more documentaries and other forms of educational public affairs broadcasting are needed, docudramas—properly used—can be an effective tool in educating citizens about public affairs. Docudramas can contain as much factual information about events as traditional news broadcasts and also attract much larger audiences (Delli Carpini and Williams, 1994). Because the journalistic norms governing docudramas are unclear, however, news divisions need to play a more active role in their production and oversight and in assuring the development of rules of accuracy and fairness similar to those applied to documentaries.[16]

The range of media and the variety of uses we suggest may seem a bit far-fetched to some readers, yet all these things are already being tried to some degree. As the 1992 presidential campaign dramatized, the lines between entertainment and public affairs broadcasting, between journalist and host, between traditional and interactive media, and between mass and interpersonal communications are rapidly blurring. The central role played by television and radio talk shows; the direct exchanges between candidates and citizens, such as those in the second presidential debate; the controversies generated by rappers Ice-T and Sister Souljah and by the television character Murphy Brown; the emergence of MTV news as a central power broker in the battle for the youth vote; the use of computer and satellite technology both within campaigns and as a way of reaching the public; the use of 800 and 900 telephone numbers for fund raising and information sharing; Ross Perot's half-hour "infomercials"; the increasing role of the traditional press as fact-checker—these demonstrate the rapid pace at which the information environment is shifting. What we are suggesting is simply that a more conscious and coordinated effort be made to use the changing media environment and evolving media policy to educate citizens.

Education

Reflecting the view of many theorists and practitioners, Amy Gutmann has written that "political education—the cultivation of the virtues, knowledge, and skills necessary for political participation—has moral primacy over other purposes of public education in a democratic society" (1987: 287). Two central findings of our research are that formal education is a key determinant of how knowledgeable citizens are about politics and that citizens who are knowledgeable about politics are the most likely to acquire new information. Nonetheless, how well the schools are succeeding at political education is a matter of debate—a debate that we believe should be intensified. Although the available evidence indicates that schooling promotes the acquisition of political knowledge, several steps could increase the role played by the schools in democratic education.

Higher education clearly promotes political engagement and learning about politics. The fact that English and biology majors are as politically knowledgeable, on average, as social science majors and that citizens with college experience are far more knowledgeable and politically active than those without it suggests that a broad liberal education yields significant dividends in preparing students for a life of citizenship. Thus an effort should be made to ensure that higher education is available to everyone.

Unfortunately, the political climate for higher education is changing. Public institutions throughout the United States have experienced substantial reductions in state funding and have been forced to raise tuition. Many private schools are experiencing fiscal problems, with the result that costs are escalating rapidly. These trends have had the effect of pricing education out of the reach of some students while causing many others to spend more time earning money, thus diverting much of their attention and energy away from their classes. As financial barriers to college remain high or become higher, substantial differences between advantaged and disadvantaged citizens and groups in access to political knowledge (and the means for efficiently acquiring it over a lifetime) will remain. Greater government support for students could be the most significant single step toward greater civic literacy—and civic equality.

As political science instructors, we of course think that all students should take one or more courses in government and politics during their years in college and hope that such courses teach—in addition to the substance of politics—such skills of citizenship as critical thinking, how to read the newspaper and watch the news effectively, and how to gather information about elected officials and substantive issues. But college courses can do more—they can initiate the student to a life of political engagement through internships and service programs. The Civic Education and Community Service Program now underway at Rutgers University in New Jersey (Barber, 1992; Barber and Battistoni, 1993) combines structured community service with required readings and writing assignments on topics related to citizenship and its obligations. According to its directors, the primary justification for the program is pedagogical, not philanthropic (Barber and Battistoni, 1993: 236). Its courses are credit-bearing and range well beyond the political science department.

Whereas colleges have the advantage of dealing with students who are relatively self-motivated and who, as eighteen-year-olds, have been granted the full privileges and responsibilities of citizenship, primary and secondary schools have the advantage of reaching almost all members of a particular age cohort and of reaching them relatively early in their intellectual and civic development. Of course, reformers hoping the schools will do more to promote civic literacy will have to stand in a long line to make their case; nearly everyone wants the schools to do more than they are doing now. Nonetheless, in prioritizing the goals of education (especially public education) a strong case can be made for the importance of creating effective citizens. At a minimum, civics education could be given a more central and regular place on the curricula of both grade schools and high schools.[17] Civics should be taught in a realistic manner, introducing students to the conflictual, often unsettling nature of politics. This would not be an easy change for many teachers. Perhaps even more than with sex education, teachers are uncomfortable dealing with political controversies in the classroom. Yet the disjuncture between the overwhelmingly positive view of government provided by primary school socialization and the reality of clashing interests that the young adult sees when viewing the real world of politics is apt to result in cynicism and withdrawal. Students need an introduction that is realistic without being alienating, encouraging without being propagandizing, and that promotes participation as well as simply learning. High school programs combining civic education and community activism, similar to the Rutgers community service program, are undergoing successful tests in many locations around the country (Jordan, 1992b; Sullivan, 1992).

Finally, civic education need not and should not end when formal schooling does. One of the great failures of the American political system is the almost complete absence of public forums and public spaces for the continuing civic education of citizens. Grade schools, high schools, and colleges could serve much more effectively both as resources for this continuing education and as the public sphere in which political discourse occurs. Schools could play a role in establishing information hot lines and electronic community bulletin boards, such as the Cleveland "Free Net" supported by Case Western Reserve University. It is imperative that citizens learn the basic skills necessary to access (and add to) the growing body of information available through electronic data bases and bulletin boards (Jordan, 1992a). Teaching computer literacy with a special emphasis on its relevance to civic engagement should be a high priority beginning in primary school and continuing through adult education.[18]

Politics

Much of the responsibility for informing the public and stimulating citizens to become more engaged in the process of self-governance rests with political candidates, public officials, the parties, and public interest groups. As Benjamin Page has noted, there is persuasive evidence that many of the perceived failings of citizens, such as a lack of awareness of candidate positions, "result at least in part from the behavior of candidates . . . from the sorts of candidates cast up by the electoral system, and the incentives with which those candidates find themselves" (1978: 187). Can the candidates' incentives—which now influence them to be ambiguous—be changed? Page suggests persuading voters "to put an increased value on candor and specificity, even when it disagrees with their policy views" (191). The media would have to cooperate in any shift in criteria for evaluation. Although journalists frequently bemoan the lack of specificity by candidates, television news in particular appears unwilling to provide candidates an adequate forum for detailed policy proposals (witness the ten-second average for sound bites). Moreover, specificity by candidates makes them vulnerable to attacks by individuals and groups likely to be adversely affected by the proposed policies—a phenomenon journalists encourage because conflict is a comfortable theme for them (Entman, 1989: 128). Improvements in the quantity and quality of information provided during campaigns could be enhanced by a number of proposals currently under consideration, for example, campaign finance reform that would promote greater equality in the resources available to candidates or regulations that would increase the media's responsibility for providing candidates with more equitable and frequent opportunities to address the public. Such reforms are relevant to the issue of what citizens know because the evidence strongly suggests that voters have a greater opportunity to learn when opposing candidates are able to mount relatively equal campaigns (Clarke and Evans, 1983: 51–72; 86–100; Zaller, 1995).

Another of Page's suggestions would require candidates to submit to direct questioning about their policy proposals (191). Perhaps the most common format for such questioning is the debate. The three presidential debates of 1992 were exceedingly popular, and the national television audiences increased over the series. The "People's Debate," which involved a live audience asking questions of the candidates, had a substantial impact on public opinion and political knowledge in a random sample of undecided voters we recruited to watch it. Although many pundits derided the debate as a softball affair, our panelists praised the format, and the audience was larger than that of the first debate (Delli Carpini, Keeter, and Webb, 1993).

The debate format has great potential to focus public attention on politics in ways other means of disseminating information do not. The gladiatorial element of debates, along with public interest in the personalities of leaders, is a strong attraction even to relatively disengaged citizens. Debates between candidates should be encouraged, but the potential utility of the debate as a tool for stimulating public engagement in politics extends beyond elections. An American version of the question-and-answer period for British prime ministers could be enormously engaging and potentially enlightening political theater. The 1993 debate between Vice President Albert Gore and citizen-politician Ross Perot attracted a large audience (despite the fact that it was not available to most over-the-air broadcast outlets) and arguably affected the level of public engagement on the North American Free Trade Agreement (NAFTA). Such debates between elected officials and citizens should be encouraged and expected. Given the public's evident fascination with law and the legal process, as demonstrated in the popularity of real and fictional courtroom dramas and novels, the Supreme Court would seem to have great potential to stimulate public interest. Lifting the traditional veil over the Supreme Court would enable the public to learn more about the judicial branch and the democratic process. The simplest and most effective way to accomplish this—without interfering with the Court's settled procedures and customs—would be to televise oral arguments and the reading of decisions. As the enthusiastic reception accorded Peter Irons's and Stephanie Guitton's 1993 compilation of Supreme Court tapes of oral arguments attests, the Supreme Court is often fine theater. Objections to broader dissemination of these aspects of the Court's operations have less legitimacy than did those surrounding the decision to televise the House and Senate. Supreme Court justices have tenure for life and thus have little incentive to grandstand or otherwise alter their normal practices and behavior.

A poorly used but potentially educational tool is the Congressional franking privilege and other governmental mailings. During nonelection years members of Congress send out more than 500 million pieces of mail to their constituents, and during election years the total is over 750 million. Such mailings, along with the mailings of other elected officials and government agencies, could serve as a valuable source of information and as a forum for the exchange of information and ideas. (Members of the

House and Senate receive more than 100 million mailings from their constituents each year, and the replies they send are often remarkably informative.) Of course name recognition and credit claiming—not the general education of the American public—is the principal purpose of most member-initiated mailings. But more specific regulations regarding the use and content of these mailings, if not a greater sense of civic responsibility on the part of government officials, could improve their educational value.[19] Shifting at least some of the budget for constituency mailings to the General Accounting Office or the Congressional Research Service might prove a more effective way to assure that such mailings are informative.[20]

As de Tocqueville observed, "better use has been made of association and this powerful instrument of action has been applied to more varied aims in America than anywhere else in the world (1969: 189). His admiration for the role of voluntary associations in America was based on their special character: "There has been no sacrifice of will or of reason, but rather will and reason are applied to bring success to a common enterprise." He contrasts this to associations in Europe, where "the main aim of these associations being to act and not to talk, to fight and not to convince, there is naturally nothing civilian about their organization. . . . Members of these associations . . . have made a complete sacrifice of their judgement and free will" (195).

Unfortunately, intermediary organizations, such as political parties and public interest groups, have lost much of the deliberative, participatory character de Tocqueville found so critical and have more in common with his portrayal of nineteenth-century European associations than their American progenitors. Nonetheless, such organizations remain essential components of democracy in America and provide fertile ground for improving the information environment—and thus the political knowledge—of citizens. Evidence for this is found in our research, which suggests that partisans are more likely to learn facts with a partisan hue and that contact by the parties modestly increases a citizen's level of general political knowledge. But parties and interest groups seldom take their educational function as seriously as their mobilizing one.[21] By making a more conscious effort to educate citizens (both during elections and throughout the governing cycle), such organizations could play a central role in raising aggregate levels of knowledge.

The political parties are of special significance in this regard because they are among the few overtly political organizations that reach out (with modest effectiveness) to socially and economically disadvantaged groups (Verba and Nie, 1972: 209–28). Thus, they are in a unique position to aid those who are the most likely to be uninformed. Unlike most interest groups and political associations, the parties address a broad range of issues that force citizens to consider their views on particular issues in the context of a broader agenda. Information from even two parties with moderately distinct stands would help assure some degree of balance to the information environment. Reforms intended to strengthen political parties and improve their ability to educate citizens (for example, those that encourage contributions to political parties as opposed to individual candidates or that allow parties to use "soft money" as a way of increasing voter interest, registration, and turnout), if properly designed and implemented, could be effective at increasing levels of political knowledge.

Other political organizations could serve a similar educational function, augmenting their often emotional appeals with the presentation of relevant facts and the encouragement of public debate. This role is very much within the tradition of voluntary associations in America. The League of Women Voters has long seen its primary function as providing political information to citizens. Similarly, the Center for National Independence in Politics/Project Vote Smart publishes a *Voter's Self-Defense Manual* that provides citizens with nonpartisan, practical information of relevance to national elections; and a biannual publication (*U.S. Government: Owner's Manual*) designed to present citizens with more basic information about the institutions, processes, people, and issues of national government. Most innovative, they provide a twenty-four-hour 800 number citizens can call for information about candidates, officeholders, political issues, and so forth. More partisan groups have also begun to educate citizens regarding their stands on particular issues like gun control and health care.[22]

Several other proposals for improving the quality—if not the quantity—of citizen participation in government have been made in recent years. Among the more radical is the *minipopulous* proposed by Robert Dahl (1989) and the *deliberative opinion poll* proposed by James Fishkin (1991). Although neither of these would lead directly to increases in knowledge by most citizens (unless instituted on a very wide scale), they might do so indirectly by stimulating interest in politics and providing a greater sense of efficacy to the public. Dahl's notion of the minipopulous calls for the selection of one thousand citizens at random, who would communicate electronically with each other and deliberate on an important national issue for an extended period of time (for example, a year), at the end of which they would announce their decisions. One version of Fishkin's deliberative opinion poll would assemble two large, randomly selected groups of citizens (one for each party) for several days before the start of the presidential nominating season. The groups would study and discuss issues and interact with candidates. At the end, the citizens would express preferences among the candidates, which would be reflected in the selection of convention delegates. The goal of both the minipopulous and the deliberative opinion poll is to reconcile the oft-competing democratic values of equality and deliberation. By using randomly selected groups of citizens who are compensated for their time, equality is promoted. And by providing information and opportunities for the orderly development of informed preferences, these proposals allow for much greater deliberation than exists in typical opinion polls or elections.

Although neither the minipopulous nor the deliberative opinion poll has been attempted in the United States, more modest variations on the theme are appearing.[23] Perhaps the most noteworthy of these is the *citizen jury,* typically a small panel of randomly selected citizens who assemble to consider issues or to question candidates (Fishkin, 1991: 96–97). During the 1992 U.S. Senate campaign in Pennsylvania, citizen juries questioned Senator Arlen Specter and his Democratic challenger, Lynn Yeakel. Their favorable judgment on Specter was thought to have provided him with an important advantage in his close victory. Other citizen juries were convened shortly after President Bill Clinton took office and wrestled with ways to reduce the federal budget deficit (Claiborne, 1993).

Nearly all of these suggestions are applicable to state and local politics, where the closer connection between government, community, and the individual increases the likelihood that citizens will see the relevance of political information and be able to turn information into action. And given both the sizable correlation between knowledge of local politics and knowledge of state and national politics, and the unavoidable link between local, state, and national issues in our "marble cake" model of federalism (Grodzins, 1990), citizens who become engaged (and informed) at the local level are more likely to become engaged and informed at the other levels. Local politics may be the door through which citizens of all economic and social backgrounds are brought into the political arena more generally.

The Citizen

Throughout this book we have attempted to defend—some might say apologize for—the individual citizen. Our central thesis is that the pathways to political knowledge, and thus the likelihood that a particular individual or group is informed, are determined as much by systemic as individual forces. Were political ignorance and knowledge randomly distributed among the various demographic and economic groups in society, this argument would be difficult to defend. But the close connection between socioeconomic resources and political knowledge provide powerful evidence that access to the latter is heavily dependent on prior access to the former.

Of course, our evidence demonstrates that individual motivation and attitudes play an important role in political learning. But individual motivation has systemic roots as well. Political interest, feelings of personal efficacy, or a sense of civic duty, all emerge out of real-world experiences that vary dramatically by social and economic class. Indeed, even the rational ignorance argument is more applicable to economically and socially disadvantaged citizens because it is more true that their participation is unlikely to be effective. In the end, most citizens who are given the best of what this society offers in terms of the ability and opportunity to learn about politics demonstrate reasonably extensive knowledge of it. It is citizens who have been afforded these resources but who continue to remain ignorant of politics for whom the issue of personal responsibility is most applicable.

Nonetheless, along with many democratic theorists, we believe that citizenship is—to borrow an infamous phrase from the 1992 presidential campaign—"not just another lifestyle choice."[24] In profound ways, citizenship as a role is different from other roles. The role of the citizen in a democracy is not simply a right but a responsibility. We have evidence that many people see it that way—half of those who claim to keep up with politics on a regular basis say they do it because it's their duty, not because they like it. These individuals are only slightly less knowledgeable than those who say they genuinely enjoy politics, and they are significantly more informed than those who neither enjoy politics nor feel a duty to follow it.

Of course, a free society carries with it the right to shun politics (as articulated by the character of Rabbit in John Updike's novel *Rabbit Redux*), and we are wary of efforts to compel political engagement through such methods as mandatory voting. Nevertheless, the withdrawal of some citizens from the political process entails hidden costs for other citizens, if not for themselves. A principal cost of disengagement for the polity is the difficulty, or impossibility, for the disengaged to develop a sophisticated and broad sense of the public, as opposed to purely private, interest (Popkin and Dimock, 1995). Evidence in support of this view was offered in chapter 6, where we saw that uninformed citizens were much more likely to vote solely on the basis of how their financial situation had changed in the past year and were much less likely to be tolerant of groups whose views differed from theirs. More generally, disengagement from politics denies to individuals a critical forge for intellectual and moral development (Barker, 1970; Barber, 1992).

Ironically, political science and other academic disciplines also share responsibility for the lowered expectations we have of citizens. In response to the disappointing findings of early survey research about citizen competence, many scholars and theorists strove for a more realistic democratic theory that brought normative expectations into line with empirical realities. This democratic revisionism, disseminated to leaders and taught to a generation of students, undoubtedly affected the views of many regarding the capabilities of citizens. Furthermore, it induced rational leaders to try to structure institutions to function better without the involvement of the public or, less nobly, to take advantage of the public. The normative implications of the revisionist view have met with resistance since its birth, and in recent years the empirical basis of it has been challenged by works with titles such as *The Reasoning Voter* (Popkin, 1991) and *The Rational Public* (Page and Shapiro, 1992). We hope that our study contributes to this challenge as well.

In the end, however, there remain things that all of us can do as individuals to increase our own, and thus the general citizenry's, knowledge of politics. Among the most obvious is to increase one's exposure to political information. At the simplest level this would mean spending a little more time reading the newspaper, watching the evening news, or reading a weekly news magazine. Beyond this, it would entail a more active search for information, such as using reference material (for example, an almanac) to research something read or heard on the news. Indeed, if every household had a handful of basic reference books sitting atop the television, and if family members got in the habit of using them with any regularity, levels of political knowledge would assuredly increase in the United States.

Sharing political information through conversations with family members, friends, and coworkers would also likely increase political knowledge. For those things about which one is ignorant, ask questions. For those about which one is knowledgeable, share the wealth (according to Ralph Waldo Emerson, "The intelligent have a right over the ignorant; namely the right of instructing them" [1908: 196]). And for those issues about which no one in a group is informed, make it a point to follow up and find out.[25] In short, we are suggesting that as a society we need to thicken our civic identities, raising our self-image as citizen to the status of worker, parent, mother, athlete, friend, lover, and so on.

Finally, we would urge citizens to become involved with and connected to their communities by joining their fellow citizens in secondary associations—clubs, groups, or organizations formed around mutual interests or concerns. As noted above, memberships in such groups was a strong predictor of political knowledge. Civic sociability may, as Robert Putnam's research in Italy discovered, be a key determinant of the quality and responsiveness of government (1993).

Lifting the Bottom

One of the central—and most disturbing—findings of our research is the sizable gaps in knowledge found between socioeconomically disadvantaged groups and their more advantaged counterparts. These originate both from inequities in the structural resources that aid political learning and from the legacy of a system (and a political philosophy) originally designed to limit the public role of women, blacks, the poor, and, to a lesser degree, the young. These gaps in knowledge have tangible consequences for individuals and groups who are less informed.

The relatively low level of knowledge found among these groups offers a unique opportunity for increasing the aggregate level of political knowledge in the United States. It also raises the danger of increasing the divide between the information rich and the information poor. On the one hand, because these citizens are the most uninformed, efforts aimed at improving their ability, motivation, and opportunity to learn about politics are likely to produce the greatest gains. This seems especially true given that many members of these groups have already experienced significant improvement in the political, economic, and social circumstances correlated with political knowledge (for example, education, occupational status, and political participation). On the other hand, since knowledge begets knowledge, many of our suggestions for improving the information environment could easily benefit those who are already well informed to a greater degree than those who are not.

In the long run, and despite the apparent intransigence of aggregate levels of political knowledge over the past half century, continued gains in education, occupational status, and income will assuredly help to narrow these gaps.[26] In the shorter run, suggestions similar to those we have made in this chapter could also make a difference. This puts an added burden on the schools, the media, public officials, political parties, and public interest groups to aim their greatest efforts for improving levels of civic knowledge at the least-informed portion of the citizenry. This burden (and this opportunity) is especially great for those who claim to represent or speak for women, blacks, the young, and the economically disadvantaged:

inner city schools; black and women's colleges; black and women's studies departments; city newspapers; publications and electronic media that target black, female, or young audiences; and candidates, public officials, parties, interest groups, and government agencies that represent these groups and their interests.[27] Although efforts to promote political learning among these groups are of obvious import to members of these groups themselves, in the end, a broadly and equitably informed citizenry is beneficial to the entire polity. Achieving this goal should be a central item on national educational, media, and political agendas.

It would be a mistake to see these recommendations and the concerns that motivate them as wishful thinking. Information is already the most important asset of postindustrial democracies, and the information environment is changing at a breathtaking pace. It is no longer a question of whether or not change occurs, but to what ends change is put and who benefits from it. The information superhighway provides a telling and ironic metaphor for the future of mass communications. Speeding down a superhighway conjures images of adventure, connection with others, freedom. But these images are for those who are on the highway. There is another image that this metaphor evokes. Interstates passing through urban areas are often built through the poorest neighborhoods and seldom provide entrance ramps at these locations. For people in these neighborhoods, the highway represents a disruption, a further example of a public world that affects one's daily life but to which one has no easy access. As we continue to construct the information superhighway we should keep this alternative image in mind and be sure that entrance ramps, vehicles, and road maps are accessible to citizens of all walks of life.

Is an Informed Public Possible?

As we discuss the means by which the U.S. public could approach the democratic ideal of a competent citizenry, one must wonder whether this goal, perhaps attainable in the early days of the republic, is still feasible given the complexity of society and its dependence on technology. Earlier in this century, skepticism on this point suffused the writings of Walter Lippmann; in the years since, technical experts have become more autonomous and seemingly indispensable. Sociologist Robert Bellah and his colleagues write that the "exploitative" path chosen for the development of the American political economy "led to the development of large economic and governmental structures that grew 'over the heads' of the citizens and beyond their control, making a mockery of the most fundamental principle of Lockean political philosophy: government by consent of the governed. When this was followed not only by plundering the natural resources of the North American continent but by the development of an imperial military state, operating with the secrecy and arbitrary domination that empires always employ, the eighteenth-century notion of a republican polity, answerable to its citizens in the full light of day, was hardly recognizable" (Bellah et al., 1991: 266). Far from rendering public opinion irrelevant, we believe that modern (even postmodern) society and the moral choices it presents—from genetic engineering to nuclear power—make it imperative that government reflect the judgment of an informed citizenry. Informed choices do not require citizens to become experts, but they do require an understanding of the terms of the debate, a goal that does not appear unreachable (Graham, 1988: 327; Kuklinski, Metlay, and Kay, 1982). And many of those who acknowledge that citizens often lack the information necessary to engage meaningfully in public discourse about the issues of the day also contend that this ignorance results from identifiable (and remediable) failures in the way the media and public officials present information, biases in the type of information they present, and the lack of public forums for citizens to exchange ideas and information (Rosen, 1988).

Ultimately, political knowledge is a key resource in the battle between the present and the future. Economist Lester Thurow has said, with perhaps only a little hyperbole, that "the function of government is to represent the interests of the future to the present." And yet for citizens to act as agents for the future, they must fight the imperatives of the present, which are well organized and politically powerful. Indeed, the dilemma is that this battle is also fought *within* each citizen. The incentives to lead privatized and atomized lives are forceful, causing many well-intentioned citizens to retreat into the havens of their families. But as Bellah and his colleagues point out, "We cannot be the kind of caring people whom our children need us to be and ignore the world they will have to live in" (1991: 276). Not knowing what particular fortune—good or bad—will befall oneself and one's progeny, it is manifestly rational for a guarantor of the future to be concerned with the public interest, as opposed to a narrowly private one. Developing a sense of the public interest requires a level of cognitive engagement with the political world that is both broader and deeper than that found today. More than most challenges facing citizens, gauging the impact of today's political choices on the future and influencing those choices—whether the topic is the national debt, global warming, or the health care system—requires political knowledge. As Bellah and his colleagues put it, "Democracy means paying attention" (254).

In a world where reason prevails, information is power. Those with more information, *ceteris paribus,* will be more powerful. But it is our great fortune that information is unlike other sources of power in two important respects. First, there is no finite quantity of it, such that its acquisition by one citizen means that others necessarily do without. And second, although information assuredly helps one to pursue private interests, greater knowledge is also apt to promote a fuller appreciation of the community and interdependence of all people, of the consequences of one's private actions, and of the means for reconciling one's private interest with the public interest. In the struggle between liberty and authority, skepticism about democracy may sometimes be justified. But it is through greater knowledge for all citizens that the safest resolution of this struggle will be found.

APPENDIX ONE

Overview of Data Sources

We relied on three main sources of data for this research: the National Election Studies conducted by the University of Michigan, a data base of survey questions covering the period from the 1940s to the 1990s developed and maintained by the Roper Center for Public Opinion Research, and a number of studies we designed and conducted between 1989 and 1992. Among these studies were two national surveys (a mail survey of political scientists and the 1989 Survey of Political Knowledge conducted by telephone with 610 randomly selected adults), eight statewide Virginia telephone surveys, three telephone surveys of residents in the Richmond, Virginia, area, four focus groups, and a panel study of individuals recruited to watch the second presidential debate of 1992 (the "People's Debate"). All these studies were conducted by the Survey Research Laboratory (SRL) at Virginia Commonwealth University. The telephone surveys employed computer-assisted telephone interviewing (using a system developed by the Computer Assisted Survey Methods [CSM] program at the University of California at Berkeley), and most used commercial random samples prepared by Survey Sampling, Incorporated of Fairfield, Connecticut.[1] Interviewing for all except two of the surveys was conducted by the regular paid interviewing staff of the SRL.[2] Council of American Survey Research Organizations (CASRO) response rates for the state and local surveys varied from 55 to 72 percent. Table A1.1 is a description of the fifteen studies.

Table A1.1 Description of Data Surveys

Dates	Population and Survey Method	Sample Size	Content
Jan.-Mar. 1989	Members of the American Political Science Association (mail)	111	Opinions regarding what the public should know about politics

Table A1.1 Description of Data Surveys (*continued*)

Dates	Population and Survey Method	Sample Size	Content
Mar.-May 1989	Adult residents of the U.S. (telephone)	610	Knowledge of institutions and processes, issues, political leaders, history
Sept.-Oct. 1989	Adult residents of Virginia (telephone)	468 likely voters	Knowledge of gubernatorial candidates' position on abortion
Oct.-Nov. 1989	Adult residents of Virginia (telephone)	801 likely voters	Knowledge of gubernatorial candidates' position on abortion
Jan.-Feb. 1990	Adult residents of Virginia (telephone)	805	Knowledge of state elected officials, national institutions and processes, state issues
July-Sept. 1990	Adult residents of Virginia (telephone)	885	Knowledge of state elected officials, national institutions and processes, state issues
Oct. 1990	Adult residents of Richmond, Va. (telephone)	409	Knowledge of local political issues, elected officials, government processes
Dec. 1990-Jan. 1991	Adult residents of Virginia (telephone)	814	Knowledge and attitudes about the Persian Gulf crisis
Mar.-Apr. 1991	Adult residents of Chesterfield County, Va. (telephone)	329	Knowledge of local issues, party control of county board, superintendent of schools, U.S. representative, national institutions and processes
Apr.-May 1991	Adult residents of Chesterfield County, Va. (in person)	21	Four focus group sessions with subjects recruited from the Chesterfield County telephone survey respondent pool
July-Aug. 1991	Adult residents of Virginia (telephone)	804	Knowledge about *Rust v. Sullivan,* Clarence Thomas, public schools, Sandra Day O'Connor, Bill of Rights, presidential veto, term of office for senators
Oct. 1991	Adult residents of Richmond, Va. (telephone)	804	Knowledge of local elected officials, local issues, national institutions and processes
Nov.-Dec. 1991	Adult residents of Virginia (telephone)	800	Knowledge of national politics; distractions while attending to the news media
Sept. 1992	Adult residents of Virginia (telephone)	666 likely voters	Knowledge of issue positions of Clinton, Bush, and Perot; knowledge of national politics
Oct.-Dec. 1992	Adult residents of Richmond, Va. metro area (telephone and in person)	104 likely voters	Panel recruited by random telephone survey to watch the second presidential debate on Oct. 15; 99 interviewed by telephone during Nov. and Dec.

The 1989 Survey of Political Knowledge

Respondents within households were selected randomly by the computer-assisted telephone interviewing (CATI) software following a household enumeration. Interviews averaged twenty-three minutes in length. The sample was weighted on gender, race, and education according to 1986 population estimates of the U.S. Census Bureau. The CASRO response rate, which is adjusted for "no answer" and "busy" outcomes, was 36 percent. Despite the low response rate, the sample appears valid on a number of criteria. Compared with the samples for recent National Election Studies and General Social Surveys, the sample was nearly identical in the distribution of partisanship and very similar in most reported levels of political activity, including turning out to vote, reading a daily newspaper, watching network television news, and discussing politics with family and friends. Knowledge questions available for comparison with the 1991 NES and 1987 General Social Survey also indicate no serious bias. For a further discussion of this survey, see Delli Carpini and Keeter, 1991.

The Focus Group Study

To examine how individuals use factual knowledge about politics in conversation, we conducted an exploratory study consisting of four focus groups with individuals who had responded to one of our local telephone surveys. The telephone survey included eight factual questions, four on national politics and four on local politics. These items were used for selecting focus group participants. We contacted 134 of the survey respondents who met our screening criteria, invited them to come to the university for a small group discussion, and offered them a twenty dollar honorarium. There was a strong positive correlation between knowledge level and willingness to participate in the groups.

Three of the focus groups were relatively homogeneous with respect to level of knowledge (high, medium, and low), and the fourth was mixed. Each group met for about two hours. The groups were moderated by one of the authors, who asked the participants general questions designed to stimulate political discussion about national, state, and local issues. If the issues did not come up spontaneously, they asked specifically about the participants' views of the Persian Gulf war (recently concluded), the savings and loan scandal, the state's budget problems, and the issue of development in the county where the participants lived. The sessions were taped and transcribed and later coded to permit an analysis of the use of factual information by each participant.

APPENDIX TWO

The Conceptualization and Measurement of Political Knowledge

Political knowledge as used in this book is a simple concept. We define it as the range of factual information about politics stored in long-term memory. It is our view that factual political knowledge is the most important component of a broader notion of political sophistication. But exactly *what* factual knowledge—out of all that could be known about politics—is important? This question speaks to the *content validity* of a knowledge measure and is fundamental to much of the analysis we present in this book. Because we rely on data from many sources in exploring various aspects of political knowledge, it is essential that the validity of these different measures be established. The fundamental issue in content validity is "the extent to which a set of items taps the content of some domain of interest" (Zeller and Carmines 1980: 78). We attempt to specify the domain of interest in chapter 2 where we discuss the basic categories of what citizens should know: fundamental facts about the rules of the game, the substance of politics, and people and parties that are central to the conduct of politics. To identify specific survey items tapping knowledge in this domain, we turned to a variety of sources. We drew on our own experience as teachers of political science courses. We examined a diverse collection of materials ranging from high school texts to works by democratic theorists and others who wrote on citizenship and civic education. And we reviewed several decades of public opinion surveys. We also employed expert judgment via a mail survey of a random sample of 111 U.S. political scientists. These educators were asked for their views on both the general topics and specific facts that a citizen should know. In the various citizen surveys we conducted, we used many of the items endorsed or suggested by the sample of political scientists.

A key issue in designing knowledge tests or in using knowledge questions found on surveys is whether for most purposes political knowledge is a unidimensional or a multidimensional phenomenon. To the extent that people tend to specialize—that is, they are well informed about some aspects of politics but not about others—then an appropriate measure of political knowledge must reflect the various domains in which citizens specialize, or separate measures must be created. In contrast, if people are generalists, a single common scale may suffice for valid measurement. Furthermore, if certain kinds of facts are reliably known by individuals at certain levels of knowledge and not by those below that level, political knowledge levels can be gauged with relatively few questions—an important practical advantage given the reluctance of survey researchers to test their respondents.

Our examination of the structure of political knowledge indicates that citizens tend to be generalists, at least for the type of knowledge we think is important for exercising basic rights of citizenship in a republican polity. The practical consequence of this is that many different kinds of knowledge measures, regardless of their particular content (e.g., whether dealing with current issues, public officials, or rules of the game) may provide a valid measure of political knowledge. This is not to say that any old knowledge question will do; far from it (Delli Carpini and Keeter, 1993). But it does mean that such data collections as the National Election Studies may contain the ingredients of a valid knowledge scale—even if the components were not initially intended to measure knowledge—provided that the validity of individual items can be established through traditional means.[1]

Another issue in developing measures of political knowledge is more technical and pragmatic. How does one best test for knowledge in the typical research setting—the sample survey? A significant concern is the assumption that survey respondents don't like to be tested (and shown to be ignorant). Researchers are ordinarily reluctant to risk damaging the rapport they develop with their subjects. This is a principal reason why relatively little knowledge testing has been done on surveys of political attitudes and behavior.[2] Beyond this sticky problem is the more general question of how to construct reliable measures. Fortunately, there is a vast literature on the development and application of achievement tests to gauge factual knowledge in a particular domain. This body of research is highly applicable to the measurement of political knowledge, and so we drew on it and devoted substantial attention to the development of appropriate measures.

In conducting our surveys, we found that the fears of knowledge testing's damage to rapport are exaggerated. Although some respondents complained during our knowledge quizzes, many of the complaints were about their own ignorance. We saw no evidence that their level of cooperation was diminished by the experience. Furthermore, because of the general nature of political knowledge, knowledge levels of citizens can be reliably assessed with relatively few questions, thus minimizing the negative reactions to the testing. And finally, the evidence indicates that political knowledge is a highly stable construct amenable to highly reliable measurement. Even with the guessing that invariably accompanies factual questions, the reliability of many knowledge measures for the same respondents surveyed at two different times equaled or exceeded that of any political attitude, including party identification.

The Performance of Specific Knowledge Items

Most tests of ability are composed of several—sometimes a great many—individual items. These may be thought of as sampled from the large domain of items related to the trait under study. This sampling process is not random since the population of items cannot be specified. And clearly some items are better than others. Under the assumptions of *classical test theory* (also called *true score theory*), an observed score on a test (X) is equal to the true score (T) plus measurement error (e). All things being equal, a better measure is one with less measurement error. A measure with a relatively high proportion of true variance to observed variance (which includes error variance) is said to be a more reliable measure (Zeller and Carmines, 1980: 13).

Perhaps the most common and useful method for evaluating individual items is the *item-total correlation* (the item's correlation with the total test score).[3] If the items in the test can be assumed to measure the trait under study (and only that trait), then the relative item-total correlations reflect how much measurement error is present in each item. The most reliable overall set of items (shorter than the original test) will be those with the highest item-total correlations.[4]

Another method of evaluating items is *stepwise multiple regression*, in which the total test score is regressed on the component items. The first item selected will be the one with the highest item-total correlation, but subsequent items chosen will not necessarily be those with the highest zero-order correlations. In essence, the procedure seeks out those items that best resolve the remaining variance. In so doing, inherent multidimensionality in the set of items is at least partially accounted for. Items highly correlated with those already in the model will usually not be chosen because they provide little additional predictive value. This method is completely atheoretical, however, and should be used with caution (see Lewis-Beck, 1978: esp. 218–24). It is also characterized by diminishing returns following the selection of about one-fifth to one-fourth of the items. Discrimination among the remaining items is poor.

Another common criterion of evaluation is *item difficulty,* which is usually defined as the proportion correct for the item (the *p* value). A test composed of items with a *p* value of .5 will have a larger variance than if those of greater or lesser difficulty are included. This may be an attractive quality for some testing purposes, especially those where discrimination among subjects in the middle range of ability is desired. But better discrimination among subjects across a range of ability levels is achieved by using items of varying levels of difficulty. No standard for choosing items based on difficulty exists, and some specialists argue that item difficulty should not be a consideration, except insofar as extreme *p* values (like .1 or .9) should be avoided (Nunnally, 1978: 270–74).

Item-total correlation and item difficulty are the two most common statistics used in item analysis, and both are closely related to classical test theory. An alternative model finding increasing acceptance in the construction and analysis of ability tests is *item response theory* (IRT), which is based upon the broader notion of *latent trait theory.*[5] Item response theory holds that a subject's test performance can be explained by his or her level of an hypothesized latent trait or ability and that the probability of correctly answering a given test item can be expressed as a monotonically increasing function called an *item characteristic curve* (ICC). If appropriate assumptions are met, techniques utilizing item response theory can yield estimates of both the discriminating power and the difficulty of a test item—independent of the particular sample on which they are tested.[6] Conversely, using a test composed of items for which the discrimination and difficulty parameters have been established, the latent ability of the examinees can be estimated—again, regardless of the average level of ability of the sample being tested. The quality of *sample invariance* is one of the most appealing aspects of IRT and has led to its use in a wide variety of applied settings.[7]

The item characteristic curve simply plots the probability of a correct response to a given item as an increasing function of the latent ability of the test-taker. In item response theory, the shape of this function is typically hypothesized to be that of the normal ogive or the logistic curve. Three hypothetical ICCs are shown in figure A2.1. Ability is on the x-axis, and the probability of a correct response is on the y-axis. The curve on the left is typical of a relatively easy item that appears to discriminate rather well (the steepness of the curve indicates the extent to which the probability of a correct response increases rapidly relative to changes in ability). The middle curve is a more difficult item but with poorer discrimination. Increases in ability do not bring very dramatic increases in the probability of a correct answer. The curve on the right would have the same discriminating power as the one on the left, but its discrimination occurs at a higher level of ability.

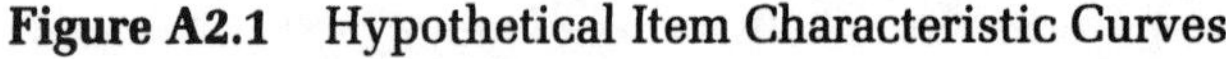

Figure A2.1 Hypothetical Item Characteristic Curves

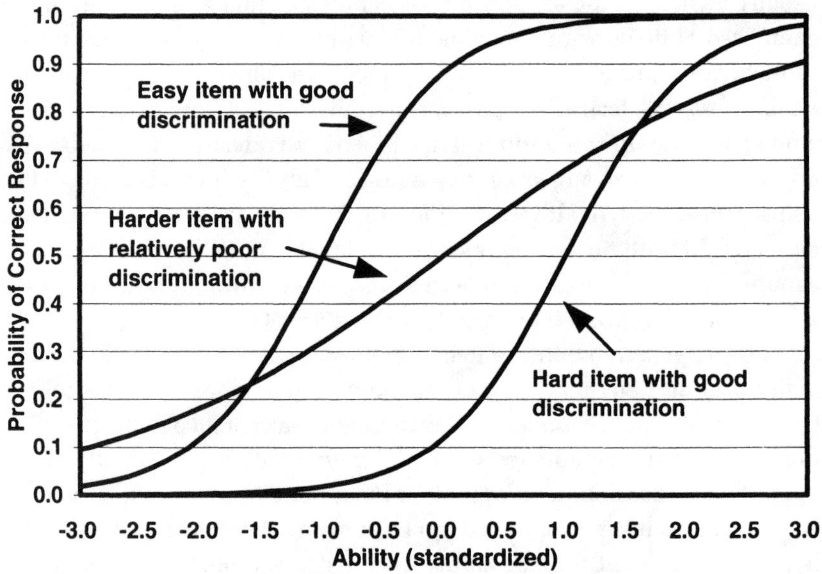

Item characteristic curves can be created by simply plotting the mean *p* value for all subjects at each of several levels of the total test score. But this method at best permits only a visual comparison of the steepness of the curves as a way of estimating the discrimination parameters. By using logistic regression to regress a dichotomous test item on the standardized total test score (adjusted by removing the item being tested), estimates of both the discrimination and difficulty parameters can be obtained.[8] The discrimination parameter, which is the coefficient from the logistic regression analysis, is proportional to the slope of the ICC at the point where the predicted *p* value is .5 (the x-axis value where this occurs is the difficulty parameter for the item). A larger coefficient implies a steeper slope, and thus greater discrimination. This statistic is analogous to the item-total correlation in that it reflects (comparatively) the presence of greater or lesser amounts of measurement error. Reliability decreases when there is a large range of ability over which we are unable to predict accurately whether a correct response will be given. The discrimination parameter and the item-total correlation tend to be correlated with one another, but not perfectly so. For many of the items described below, the discrimination parameters for the very easy and very hard ones were quite high.[9]

Five statistics for thirty-nine items from the 1989 Survey of Political Knowledge are presented in table A2.1.[10] The table is sorted by the item-total correlation. Even with a variety of statistical aids (and, to some extent, *because* of the variety), the selection of specific items remains fairly subjective, guided by the goals of the research and influenced by factors not easily quantified. For example, the desire to maintain respondent morale in the interview may necessitate the inclusion of easier items than the item analysis would dictate.

Table A2.1. Item Performance Statistics for Questions from the 1989 Survey of Political Knowledge

	Proportion Correct (p value)	Discrimination Parameter (logistic regression coefficient)	Difficulty Parameter (logistic regression intercept)	Corrected Item-Total Correlation	Step on Which the Item Entered a Multiple Regression (r^2 after inclusion)
Arms control knowledge	.47	1.44	–0.17	.54	1 (.34)
Knows Bill of Rights	.46	1.42	–0.27	.53	2 (.52)
U.S. supported Contras	.66	1.48	0.95	.53	4 (.72)
Judicial review	.66	1.36	0.88	.51	
Veto override %	.34	1.42	–0.92	.51	8 (.84)
Appoint judges	.58	1.27	0.41	.50	
Party control of House	.68	1.35	1.04	.50	
Name vice president	.74	1.45	1.46	.49	
Party control of Senate	.55	1.15	0.26	.47	7 (.82)
FDR party ID	.63	1.17	0.67	.47	3 (.64)
Truman party ID	.58	1.13	0.42	.46	
Government budget deficit	.78	1.40	1.73	.46	
Name U.S. Senators	.25	1.39	–1.52	.45	5 (.76)
U.S. has trade deficit	.82	1.48	2.08	.45	6 (.79)
What is "recession"	.57	1.04	0.35	.44	9 (.86)
New Deal knowledge	.15	1.81	–2.61	.43	
Describe Superfund	.12	2.17	–3.28	.43	
Percent unemployed	.24	1.27	–1.54	.42	
Nixon party ID	.78	1.20	1.60	.42	
Fifth Amendment	.50	0.92	0.02	.40	
Communist run for president	.50	0.85	–0.01	.38	10 (.88)
Women's suffrage	.90	1.57	2.99	.37	
Name governor	.73	0.92	1.19	.36	
Name U.S. representative	.29	0.89	–1.06	.35	
First Amendment	.35	0.82	–0.73	.35	
Effect of high tariff on U.S. trade	.52	0.76	0.08	.34	
Pledge of allegiance	.75	0.88	1.31	.34	
Rehnquist ideology	.30	0.82	–0.96	.33	
Who declares war	.34	0.73	–0.74	.31	
Education spending	.24	0.79	–1.29	.30	
Can your state prohibit abortion	.72	0.70	1.07	.29	
Date of New Deal	.12	1.08	–2.39	.29	

Table A2.1. Item Performance Statistics for Questions from the 1989 Survey of Political Knowledge (*continued*)

	Proportion Correct (p value)	Discrimination Parameter (logistic regression coefficient)	Difficulty Parameter (logistic regression intercept)	Corrected Item-Total Correlation	Step on Which the Item Entered a Multiple Regression (r^2 after inclusion)
% black	.12	0.99	−2.28	.28	
% poor	.18	0.81	−1.68	.28	
Size of U.S. budget	.49	0.57	−0.07	.27	
U.S. supported whom in El Salvador	.43	0.49	−0.30	.23	
Length of presidential term	.96	1.19	3.66	.21	
Date of women's suffrage	.10	0.78	−2.49	.20	
Defense spending	.28	0.41	−0.97	.18	
Mean for all items	.48	1.11	−0.08	.39	
Mean for top 20 items	.53	1.37	0.08	.47	

$N = 610$

Our item analysis had several goals: to determine if certain topics could be measured more effectively than others; to evaluate the performance of different question formats; to identify good questions to use (and bad questions to avoid) on subsequent surveys; and, if possible, to select items to use in a short scale for measuring political knowledge. The data in table A2.1 support the following generalizations. First, no particular topic area appeared easier or harder to measure than the others. The top ten items (in terms of item-total correlations) included four civics items, four party and people items, and two issues. Second, there was no penalty in using a particular question format. Open- and closed-ended formats were represented among the best and worst performers. For example, one open-ended item (knowledge about arms control) was at the top in item-total correlation and very high on the discrimination parameter, but another with nearly the same p value (knowledge of the effect of high tariffs on U.S. trade) performed quite poorly. Similarly, closed-ended items with as few as two fixed alternatives, despite their susceptibility to guessing, did as well as open-ended questions. It all depends on the item.

As for specific items, some questions with good face validity were mediocre performers: naming one's governor or U.S. Representative, stating one provision of the First or Fifth Amendments, and knowing which side the U.S. government supported in El Salvador were below average on all performance measures. As a general rule, items requiring respondents to state a number or a percentage did poorly, although the unemployment rate was an exception to this.

Finally, the item analysis indicated that a short scale covering a modest range of topics can constitute a reliable measure of general political knowledge. For example, according to the multiple regression analysis, five items explained over three-quarters of the variance in the full thirty-nine-variable measure, and ten variables accounted for nearly 90 percent of the variance.

Items on the National Election Study Surveys

The most common source of data for analysts of public opinion and voting behavior is the series of national surveys conducted in election years as part of the National Election Studies at the University of Michigan. Direct measures of political knowledge on the NES surveys are not common, especially before 1988. Nevertheless, valid knowledge scales can be constructed from most NES surveys (see Zaller, 1992: 337–44, for suggested scales).

The ability to construct valid and reliable knowledge scales on the NES surveys depends in part on the unidimensional nature of political knowledge. The item analysis of our 1989 survey, however, indicates that some knowledge measures are better than others (and that face validity is not a reliable guide). Thus we conducted an item analysis of a variety of NES questions that can be used as knowledge measures.

We used the 1990–91 NES pilot study for this analysis, owing to the unusually wide range of knowledge variables it contained.[11] To facilitate an evaluation of a broader measure of knowledge, the NES board placed six civics knowledge items on the 1991 survey, including the four best civics items from our 1989 survey. A twenty-item criterion knowledge index for the item analysis was constructed by combining the civics items with a number of measures from the 1990 survey. This index scaled well (alpha = .87) and had good correlations with several criterion variables. The knowledge variables are described in table A2.2, and the performance data for the component items are presented in table A2.3.

Table A2.2. Description of Items in the 1990–91 NES Surveys

Variable	Variable # (NES)	% Correct	% Incorrect or Incomplete	% Don't Know
People				
Quayle	v395	84	1	14
Gorbachev	v398	71	14	15
Thatcher	v399	53	29	18
Name one candidate (and his/her party) for U.S. House	v111	23	11	66
Mandela	v400	17	51	32
Foley	v401	12	10	78
Rehnquist	v397	5	19	76
Mitchell	v396	3	12	85
Party				
Relative ideological location of the two parties	v413; v414	57	25	18
Party with most seats in the House	v402	55	16	29
Relative location of parties on defense spending	v443; v444	52	23	25
Party with most seats in the Senate	v403	47	17	36
Relative location of parties on federal spending	v456; v457	45	26	29
Relative location of parties on aid to blacks	v449; v450	42	30	28
Civics				
Times a president can be elected	v2852	73	16	11
Whose responsibility is judicial review	v2849	68	23	9
Whose responsibility is it to nominate federal judges	v2850	51	32	17
What are the first ten amendments called	v2848	43	6	50
What majority is needed to override a presidential veto	v2851	37	17	46
How long is a senator's term	v2853	25	49	26

N = 449

Table A2.3. Item Performance Statistics for Questions from the 1990–91 NES Surveys

	Proportion Correct (*p* value)	Discriminating Power (logistic regression coefficient)	Difficulty (logistic regression intercept)	Corrected Item-Total Correlation	Step on Which the Item Entered a Multiple Regression (r^2 after inclusion)
House party	.55	1.79	.35	.60	1 (.43)
Veto override %	.37	1.67	–.81	.58	3 (.72)
Senate party	.47	1.42	–.18	.54	
Ideological party	.57	1.48	.43	.54	2 (.61)
Defense party	.52	1.43	.14	.53	

Table A2.3. Item Performance Statistics for Questions from the 1990–91 NES Surveys (*continued*)

	Proportion Correct (*p* value)	Discriminating Power (logistic regression coefficient)	Difficulty (logistic regression intercept)	Corrected Item-Total Correlation	Step on Which the Item Entered a Multiple Regression (r^2 after inclusion)
Judicial review	.68	1.64	1.18	.52	5 (.82)
Nominate judges	.51	1.36	.08	.52	
Mandela	.17	2.16	–2.70	.52	10 (.93)
Thatcher	.53	1.29	.16	.51	4 (.78)
Gorbachev	.71	1.72	1.43	.51	8 (.90)
Spend party	.45	1.30	–.28	.51	
Black party	.42	1.26	–.42	.49	6 (.85)
Bill of Rights	.43	1.24	–.35	.49	
Quayle	.84	2.52	3.20	.48	
Senator's term[a]	.25	1.32	–1.50	.45	7 (.88)
Name one House candidate[a]	.23	1.15	–1.54	.40	9 (.91)
Foley	.12	1.76	–2.98	.40	
Rehnquist	.05	2.59	–5.14	.33	
Times a president can be elected[a]	.73	.71	1.08	.29	
Mitchell	.03	2.95	–6.43	.28	
Mean for all items	.43	1.64	–.71	.47	

N = 449
[a] Dropped in subsequent analyses.

Most of the questions did well in the item analysis; fifteen of the twenty had corrected item-total correlations of .45 or higher. Three of the remaining five were difficult identification items whose correlations were low because of their extreme *p* values; these had high values on the discrimination parameter.[12]

The four civics items from our national survey performed about as well on the NES survey as they had in the 1989 survey, but the other two civics items (length of a senator's term and number of times a person can be elected president) did less well and were dropped in subsequent analyses. Most of the knowledge items traditionally found on the NES surveys also performed very well. The best question in terms of item-total correlation was "House party" (.60); its very high discrimination parameter (1.79) was especially noteworthy for an item susceptible to guessing. The "Senate party" item was good but did not discriminate as well as the House item (a pattern also seen in the 1989 survey).[13] The party placement questions were generally strong performers, too. The best in terms of both item-total correlation and discrimination was the ideology scale, followed closely by defense spending.

The other item in the index that is commonly found on the NES surveys is naming a House candidate. It was a fairly weak performer, with an item-total correlation of .40 and a discrimination parameter of 1.15. This is not surprising, given the considerable variation in the prominence of House races across the nation, an external factor that undoubtedly introduces its own variance into the measure. We dropped this item in subsequent analyses.

We tested a few additional items commonly found on the NES surveys, although for various reasons we did not include them in the index. In his analyses of presidential elections using NES data, Kessel (1988) measured knowledge with a simple index of the total number of likes and dislikes about the parties and presidential candidates. Although this measure rewards the garrulous and penalizes the laconic (and thus also measures a trait other than political knowledge), our analysis suggests that it is nevertheless a valid measure of knowledge—the item-total correlation was .57. This measure is found on NES surveys dating back to 1952, and its value in analyses over time is considerable. A potential limitation, as with several other NES items adapted to the measurement of information, is that the likes-dislikes items are commonly used as dependent variables in substantive analyses; one would not want to use such items on both sides of the equation.

A Recommended Five-Item Knowledge Index

Our analysis above suggests that researchers using NES data can adequately measure the general concept of political knowledge with available items. Those collecting their own data, however, may have a need for a dependable knowledge index that is more parsimonious than the large set of NES items just discussed. An important application of item analysis techniques is the derivation of short scales that provide reliable and valid measurement with relatively few individual items.

Using the data in table A2.3, we derived a five-item index from the 1990 and 1991 NES questions. The items, and the rationale for their inclusion, are:

Party control of the House. A good performer in our 1989 survey, and picked first by the stepwise regression in the 1990–91 data, this item has good discriminating power as measured by the logistic regression (fifth overall). It has strong face validity.

Veto override percent. Picked third by the regression, this is the most difficult of the recommended items. Its discriminating power is good, and it was strong in the 1989 survey.

Party ideological location. Picked second by the regression, this item had the highest discriminating power of the four party placement questions. As another key concept at the heart of contemporary U.S. politics, it has strong face validity.

Judicial review. A relatively easy civics item (68 percent correct), this question had good discriminating power. It was selected fifth by the regression analysis. The veto item taps familiarity with both Congress and the presidency, and this item ensures that the judiciary is represented.

Identifying the vice president. This item had high discriminating power according to the logistic regression and was also a strong variable in our 1989 national survey. It is the easiest of the NES items tested, serving to distinguish those who are completely disconnected from politics. And this is one "people" variable that may remain relatively consistent in its contribution to the scale over time. Despite Dan Quayle's high profile, the percentage of the public able to name him in the 1989 survey or to identify his position in the 1990 NES survey was comparable to that for other vice presidents: Alben Barkley in 1952, Richard Nixon in 1953, Walter Mondale in 1978, and Albert Gore in 1994.

This five-item index scaled well (alpha = .71). Three of the items provide comparability with NES data, and one of the two civics items (judicial review) was added to the 1992 NES general election survey and may be used regularly on future studies.[14] In tests of construct validity, this index was a strong performer in comparison with longer indexes.

Question Wording for a Recommended Five-Item Knowledge Index

For researchers interested in including a measure of political knowledge on their own survey, we recommend the following introduction and question wording: "Last, here are a few questions about the government in Washington. Many people don't know the answers to these questions, so if there are some you don't know just tell me and we'll go on."

1. "Do you happen to know what job or political office is now held by [insert current vice president]?" (Original wording in NES: Now we have a set of questions concerning various public figures. We want to see how much information about them gets out to the public from television, newspapers, and the like. The first name is Dan Quayle: what job or political office does he now hold?)
2. Whose responsibility is it to determine if a law is constitutional or not . . . is it the president, the Congress, or the Supreme Court?
3. How much of a majority is required for the U.S. Senate and House to override a presidential veto?
4. Do you happen to know which party had the most members in the House of Representatives in Washington before the election this/last month?
5. Would you say that one of the parties is more conservative than the other at the national level? Which party is more conservative? (In the item analysis, the party ideology item is constructed from the respondent's placement of the parties on an ideology scale. An item based on the direct question of which party is more conservative, however, works as well and is much easier to administer.)

APPENDIX THREE

Knowledge over Time

Table A3.1 Over-Time Knowledge of Institutions and Processes

Question Wording	T1	T2
For how many years is a president of the United States elected—that is, how many years are there in one term of office?	93% (1952)	95% (1989)
Will you tell me what the term *veto* means to you? For example, what does it mean when the president vetoes a bill sent him by Congress?	80% (1947)	89% (1989)
Will you tell me what the initials FBI stand for?	78% (1949)	78% (1965)
Do you happen to know how many times an individual can be elected president?	73% (1972)	73% (1991)
If the president vetoes a bill, can Congress override his veto?	70% (1947)	83% (1989)
Which of the following best describes a political party platform?	71% (1952)	61% (1987)
Just in your own words, will you tell me what a monopoly is?	69% (1949)	64% (1950)
Will you tell me what your understanding is of the term *wiretapping*?	67% (1949)	67% (1950)
Will you tell me what the United Nations Organization is?	64% (1950)	66% (1951)
What percentage vote of Congress is needed to override a veto by the president—a bare majority, two-thirds, three-fourths, or 90%?	63% (1975)	63% (1985)
Do you think the U.S. dollar's decreasing value abroad makes things made in foreign countries and imported into the United States cost more here, or cost less here, or don't you think it has any effect?	62% (1978)	52% (1986)
True or false: A district attorney's job is to defend an accused criminal who cannot afford a lawyer.	61% (1977)	47% (1983)
Do you happen to know in what country the headquarters and general assembly of the United Nations are located?	58% (1985)	49% (1989)
1989: Whose responsibility is it to appoint judges to the federal courts? 1991: Whose responsibility is it to nominate judges to the federal courts?	58% (1989)	51% (1991)
True or false: In a criminal trial, it is up to the person who is accused of the crime to prove his innocence.	56% (1977)	46% (1983)

Table A3.1 Over-Time Knowledge of Institutions and Processes (*continued*)

Question Wording	T1	T2
When you hear that we have a foreign trade deficit, which of these things does it mean to you?	54% (1977)	63% (1985)
1947: When you read about a business recession, what does that mean to you? 1989: When you read about an economic recession, what does that mean to you?	52% (1947)	57% (1989)
1959: Do you see any connection between an unbalanced budget and the prices of the things you buy? 1960: Do you see any connection between an unbalanced budget and the value of the dollar?	52% (1959)	44% (1960)
1985: Here is a list of three statements. Would you please read down that list and tell me which statement comes closest to your understanding of the definition of the federal deficit? 1987: As you may know, there are many different complicated terms used in news stories to describe the economy and the stock market. Many people understand these terms but many people do not. I'm going to mention some terms which are sometimes used in news stories about the economy and the stock market. After each, I would like you to tell me briefly what each means to you or if, perhaps, you are not familiar with it. . . . What is the federal budget deficit, or don't you know enough about it to say?	54% (1985)	52% (1987)
From what you've heard, what kind of effect to you think a high American tax on foreign goods would have on our trade?	51% (1949)	52% (1989)
Do you happen to know what a tariff is? What is it?	51% (1946)	46% (1947)
1957: Please tell me in your own words how you would describe someone who is a liberal in politics. 1960: Do you happen to know what is meant when someone is called a liberal in politics? What?	46% (1957)	47% (1960)
1985: I am going to read you a list of individuals, groups, and terms. Please try to identify each. . . . the Dow Jones index. 1987: As you may know, there are many different complicated terms used in news stories to describe the economy and the stock market. Many people understand these terms but many people do not. I'm going to mention some terms which are sometimes used in news stories about the economy and the stock market. After each, I would like you to tell me briefly what each means to you or if, perhaps, you are not familiar with it. . . . Would you tell me what the Dow Jones industrial average is, or don't you know enough about it to say?	43% (1984)	34% (1987)
1943: Will you tell me what the term *farm subsidy* means to you? 1953: Just in your own words, would you tell what is meant by the term *farm price supports.*	42% (1943)	54% (1953)
When you hear or read anything about the Fifth Amendment, what does it mean to you?	42% (1957)	57% (1989)
There has been some talk lately about the welfare state. What does the expression *welfare state* mean or refer to, as you understand it?	36% (1949)	36% (1950)
1951: Will you tell me what the North Atlantic Treaty Organization is? 1985: I am going to read you a list of individuals, groups, and terms. Please try to identify each. . . . NATO.	35% (1951)	36% (1985)

Table A3.1 Over-Time Knowledge of Institutions and Processes (*continued*)

Question Wording	T1	T2
1977: Can you name any of the agencies or institutions that are part of the United Nations? 1985: Can you name any of the agencies that are part of the United Nations?	32% (1977)	19% (1985)
How long is the term of office for a United States senator?	30% (1972)	25% (1991)
And do you think the U.S. dollar's decreasing value abroad makes things made in the United States and sold abroad cost more here, or cost less here, or don't you think it has any effect?	30% (1978)	33% (1986)
Everywhere we go people seem to have different ideas about what reciprocal trade agreements mean. Would you mind telling me just what reciprocal trade agreements mean to you?	30% (1945)	29% (1950)
What do you know about the Bill of Rights? Do you know anything it says?	23% (1943)	21% (1945)
Would you tell me what is meant by the fallout of an H-bomb?	17% (1957)	57% (1961)
Do you think the U.S. dollar's decreasing value abroad makes things made and sold in the United States cost more here, or cost less here, or don't you think it has any effect?	15% (1978)	18% (1986)
True or false: Every decision made by a state court can be reviewed and reversed by the U.S. Supreme Court.	12% (1977)	11% (1983)
Out of every 100 people who are employed, how many would you say work for some parts of government—city, state, or federal, and either the government itself or some government unit like police, post office, or army?	10% (1976)	10% (1979)

Question Wording	T1	T2	T3
1977: Here is a list of statements about the courts. Please tell me whether you think each statement is correct or incorrect. . . . Everyone accused of a serious crime has the right to be represented in court by a lawyer. 1983: True or false: Everyone accused of a serious crime has the right to be represented in court by a lawyer. 1989: If someone is accused of a very serious crime but they can't afford a lawyer, does the Constitution require the government to provide them with a lawyer?	93% (1977)	97% (1983)	90% (1989)
1951: What would you say is the main purpose of the United Nations Organization? 1976: Just as you understand it, what is the purpose of the United Nations? 1988: What is the general purpose of the United Nations?	80% (1951)	82% (1976)	83% (1988)
1986: The Constitution of the United States is continually reinterpreted to accommodate social change, among other reasons. Who is the final authority on the interpretation of the Constitution? 1989; 1991: Whose responsibility is it to determine if a law is constitutional or not?	59% (1986)	66% (1989)	68% (1991)
Will you tell me what the term *cold war* means?	54% (1948)	58% (1950)	55% (1951)

Table A3.1 Over-Time Knowledge of Institutions and Processes (*continued*)

Question Wording	T1	T2	T3
1947: If anything should happen to President Truman, do you know who would become president? 1985: If something happens to the president of the United States, the vice president is next in line to take his place. Who is third in line—the chief justice of the Supreme Court, or the secretary of state, or the Speaker of the House of Representatives?	46% (1947)	22% (1947)	47% (1985)
1954: When someone is referred to as a conservative, what does this mean to you? What kinds of things and ideas is he likely to stand for? 1957: Please tell me in your own words how you would describe someone who is a conservative in politics. 1960: Do you happen to know what is meant when someone is called a conservative in politics? What?	46% (1954)	46% (1957)	48% (1960)
Do you happen to know what is meant by the term *balancing the federal budget*?	45% (1959)	47% (1960)	44% (1962)
How much of a majority is required for the Senate and House to override a presidential veto?	44% (1947)	35% (1989)	37% (1991)
What are the first ten amendments to the Constitution called?	33% (1954)	46% (1989)	43% (1991)

Question Wording	T1	T2	T3	T4
1945: How many senators are there in Washington from your state? 1951: How many U.S. senators are there from each state? 1954; 1978: How many U.S. senators are there from your state?	55% (1945)	60% (1951)	49% (1954)	52% (1978)
Can you tell me what the term *filibuster* in Congress means to you?	48% (1947)	54% (1949)	54% (1950)	53% (1963)
When banks speak of the prime rate, what do they mean—the highest interest rate at which they lend money, or the rate at which they lend money to the greatest number of their customers, or the lowest rate at which they lend money?	23% (1975)	16% (1979)	15% (1981)	26% (1985)

Question Wording	T1	T2	T3	T4	T5
1973; 1974a; 1974c; 1974d: There has recently been talk of impeachment of the president (Nixon), and people seem to have different understandings of what impeachment means. Some say that if a president is impeached it means he is thrown out of office. Others say if a president is impeached it only means that he is put on trial by Congress for the charges brought against him to determine whether or not he is guilty. What do you think impeachment means—that a president is thrown out of office, or that he is put on trial by Congress?					

Table A3.1 Over-Time Knowledge of Institutions and Processes (*continued*)

Question Wording	T1	T2	T3	T4	T5
1974b: There's a great deal of confusion about what impeachment means. When you personally think of impeachment, do you think mostly of the president being forced to leave office, or do you think mostly of the president being tried by the Senate—or aren't you quite sure what impeachment means?	52% (11/73)	57% (2/74)	51% (3/74)	61% (4/74)	66% (5/74)

Question Wording	T1	T2	T3	T4	T5	T6	T7	T8
Will you tell me what is meant by the electoral college?	34% (1950)	35% (1951)	36% (1954)	33% (1954)	38% (1955)	31% (1960)	20% (1960)	40% (1961)

Table A3.2 Over-Time Knowledge of Public Figures and Political Parties

Question Wording	T1	T2
1971: I'm going to read off the names of some people whom you may know, some of whom you may not. Can you tell me who the following men are or what they do. . . . Hubert Humphrey? 1975: Please look at this card and tell me whether each of the people I mention is a writer, someone in sports, a politician, or an entertainer. Very few people would know all of the names, so if you don't know someone, just say so. . . . Hubert Humphrey.	91% (1975)	87% (1971)
1947: Will you please look over this list of names and tell me which of these people you have heard of? Will you tell me who each one is or what he does. . . . Robert Taft. 1952: Here is a list of people in the news. Will you tell me who each one is or what he does. . . . Robert Taft.	82% (1947)	74% (1952)
1944: Can you tell me who Henry Wallace is or what he does? 1947: Will you please look over this list of names and tell me which of these people you have heard of? Will you tell me who each one is or what he does. . . . Henry Wallace.	79% (1944)	75% (1947)
Here's a sort of quiz, such as you might participate in on a radio or television show. I'll read you the names of some people who have been in the news lately. Please tell me who these people are, what it is they do. . . . Joe McCarthy.	70% (1954)	77% (1954)
1944: Can you tell me who Harry Truman is or what he does? 1947: Will you please look over this list of names and tell me which of these people you have heard of? Will you tell me who each one is or what he does. . . . Harry Truman.	68% (1944)	98% (1947)
1953: Which (of President Eisenhower's) appointments can you recall?—Secretary of defense. 1977: How many members of Jimmy Carter's cabinet can you name?—Secretary of defense.	68% (1953)	2% (1977)
Here is a list of people in the news. Will you tell me who each one is—or what he does. . . . Estes Kefauver.	67% (1952)	83% (1956)
Can you tell me who the following men are or what they do? . . . Charles de Gaulle.	64% (1962)	73% (1964)

Table A3.2 Over-Time Knowledge of Public Figures and Political Parties (*continued*)

Question Wording	T1	T2
1953: Which (of President Eisenhower's) appointments can you recall?—Secretary of state. 1977: How many members of Jimmy Carter's cabinet can you name?—Secretary of state.	59% (1953)	12% (1977)
1957: Will you tell me who each of these men is—that is, what he does? . . . Orval Faubus. 1958: Can you tell me who Orval Faubus is?	57% (1957)	67% (1958)
1990a: Do you happen to know who Nelson Mandela is? (If "yes," ask: Who is he?) 1990b: Do you happen to know what job or political office Nelson Mandela holds now?	56% (1990)	17% (1990)
1947: Will you please look over this list of names and tell me which of these people you have heard of? Will you tell me who each one is or what he does. . . . Harold Stassen. 1952: Here is a list of people in the news. Will you tell me who each one is or what he does. . . . Harold Stassen.	50% (1947)	46% (1952)
Do you know how old Ronald Reagan is? (Ask: Would you say he's in his early sixties or late sixties?)	47% (1980)	45% (1980)
1983: Please tell me whether the following are in Congress, are a judge, or are in the cabinet. . . . Warren E. Burger. 1984: Now, I'd like to ask you about a number of people, some of whom are better known than others. Using this card, would you tell me to your knowledge who these people are? . . . Warren Burger.	41% (1983)	51% (1984)
1971a: I'm going to read off the names of some people whom you may know, some of whom you may not. Can you tell me who the following men are or what they do? . . . . Ralph Nader 1971b: Can you tell me who Ralph Nader is or what he does?	40% (1971)	43% (1971)
1950: Here are some organizations that are usually referred to by their initials. Can you tell me what each one stands for? . . . GOP 1952: Will you tell me what the initials GOP stand for?	36% (1950)	47% (1952)
Here is a list of people in the news. Will you tell me who each one is or what he does? . . . Adlai Stevenson.	34% (1952)	88% (1956)
1953: Which (of President Eisenhower's) appointments can you recall?—Secretary of labor. 1977: How many members of Jimmy Carter's cabinet can you name?—Secretary of labor.	32% (1953)	1% (1977)
1979: Do you happen to know the name of the local superintendent of schools? (If "yes," ask: What is the name of the local superintendent of schools?) 1987: What is the name of the head of the local school system?	32% (1979)	32% (1987)
Now, I'd like to ask you about a number of people, some of whom are better known than others. Using this card, would you tell me to your knowledge who these people are? . . . Lee Iacocca.	31% (1980)	61% (1984)
Here is a list of people in the news. Will you tell me who each one is or what he does? . . . Averell Harriman.	25% (1952)	55% (1956)
1970: The next question is like a quiz show on television. Do you happen to know the name of . . . the U.S. attorney general? 1989: Do you happen to know the name of the person that Bush selected to be his attorney general?	24% (1970)	3% (1989)

Table A3.2 Over-Time Knowledge of Public Figures and Political Parties (*continued*)

Question Wording	T1	T2
1985: Who is the most important leader in the Soviet Union today? 1986: Do you happen to know the name of the leader of the Soviet Union?	24% (1985)	45% (1986)
1970: The next question is like a quiz show on television. Do you happen to know the name of . . . the chief justice of the Supreme Court? 1989: Please tell me, if you know, who is the chief justice of the United States Supreme Court?	22% (1970)	9% (1989)
1953: Which (of President Eisenhower's) appointments can you recall?—Secretary of agriculture. 1977: How many members of Jimmy Carter's cabinet can you name?—Secretary of agriculture.	15% (1953)	2% (1977)
Now I'd like to ask you about a number of people, some of whom are better known than others. Using this card, would you tell me to your knowledge who these people are? . . . James Schlesinger. (*Note*: First percent given is knowing he is in cabinet; second is for at least knowing he is government official.)	15% 45% (1975)	20% 52% (1978)
Now I'd like to ask you about a number of people, some of whom are better known than others. Using this card, would you tell me to your knowledge who these people are? . . . Robert MacNeil.	15% (1978)	16% (1980)
1989: Do you happen to know who Thomas Foley is? (If "yes," ask: Who is he?) 1990: Do you happen to know what job or political office Tom Foley holds now?	14% (1989)	12% (1990)
1953: Which (of President Eisenhower's) appointments can you recall?—Attorney general. 1977: How many members of Jimmy Carter's cabinet can you name?—Attorney general.	11% (1953)	14% (1977)
1989: (Asked of respondents who said they know who Marion Barry is.) Who is Marion Barry? 1990: Do you happen to know who Marion Barry is? (If "yes," ask: Who is he?)	7% (1989)	40% (1990)
1953: Which (of President Eisenhower's) appointments can you recall?—Secretary of the treasury. 1977: How many members of Jimmy Carter's cabinet can you name?—Secretary of the treasury.	5% (1953)	3% (1977)
1953: Which (of President Eisenhower's) appointments can you recall?—Secretary of the interior. 1977: How many members of Jimmy Carter's cabinet can you name?—Secretary of the interior.	3% (1953)	1% (1977)
I'd like to ask you about a number of people, some of whom are better known than others. Using this card, would you tell me to your knowledge who these people are? . . . Thomas A. Murphy.	3% (1975)	4% (1978)
1953: Which (of President Eisenhower's) appointments can you recall?—Secretary of commerce. 1977: How many members of Jimmy Carter's cabinet can you name?—Secretary of commerce.	2% (1953)	3% (1977)
Now I'd like to ask you about a number of people, some of whom are better known than others. Using this card, would you tell me to your knowledge who these people are? . . . John DeButts.	1% (1975)	3% (1978)

Table A3.2 Over-Time Knowledge of Public Figures and Political Parties (*continued*)

Question Wording	T1	T2	T3
1970: The next question is like a quiz show on television. Do you happen to know the name of . . . the governor of this state? 1987: We would want to know how well known the different governmental leaders are around here. Could you tell me the name of the governor of this state? 1989: Can you tell me the name of the current governor of your state?	86% (1970)	79% (1987)	73% (1989)
1953: Will you tell me who Richard Nixon is? 1963: Can you tell me who the following persons are or what they do? . . . Richard Nixon. 1985: I am going to read a list of individuals, groups and terms. Please try to identify each . . . Richard Nixon.	79% (1953)	84% (1963)	84% (1985)
Can you tell me who the following men are or what they do? . . . Nelson Rockefeller.	78% (1963)	84% (1963)	84% (1967)
1952; 1989: Will you tell me who the vice president of the United States is? 1978: Who is the vice president of the United States?	69% (1952)	79% (1978)	74% (1989)
1947: Will you please look over this list of names and tell me which of these people you have heard of? Will you tell me who each one is or what he does? . . . Earl Warren. 1952: Here is a list of people in the news. Will you tell me who each one is or what he does? . . . Earl Warren. 1964: Can you tell me who the following people are? . . . Earl Warren.	41% (1947)	65% (1952)	62% (1964)
1950: Here are some organizations which are usually referred to by their initials. Can you tell me what each one stands for? . . . NAM 1975, 1985: The initials NAM stand for a certain organization. Do you think the NAM is a political organization, a labor organization, a business organization, or a farm organization.	17% (1950)	22% (1975)	15% (1985)
1990a; 1991: Can you name any of the five U.S. senators who are being investigated in the savings and loan scandal, the so-called Keating Five? 1990b: Can you name any of the five U.S. senators who are being investigated in the savings and loan situation for receiving over $600,000 in campaign funds from a S&L bank executive? The five senators are sometimes called the "Keating Five."	14% (1990)	17% (1990)	27% (1991)
I'd like to ask you about a number of people, some of whom are better known than others. Using this card, would you tell me to your knowledge who these people are? . . . Kurt Waldheim	13% (1975)	14% (1978)	39% (1980)
I am going to read you the names of some people. Will you please tell me who each is—that is, what they do? . . . Elmo Roper.	6% (1955)	4% (1956)	6% (1960)
1985; 1988: Do you know the name of the prime minister of Japan? 1986: Thinking of countries around the world, can you tell me the name of . . . the prime minister of Japan?	4% (1985)	19% (1986)	1% (1988)
I am going to read you the names of some people. Will you please tell me who each is—that is, what they do? . . . Samuel Lubell.	1% (1956)	2% (1960)	1% (1964)

Table A3.2 Over-Time Knowledge of Public Figures and Political Parties (*continued*)

Question Wording	T1	T2	T3	T4
Do you happen to know the religious preference of the following men? . . . John Kennedy.	48% (1959)	46% (1959)	69% (1960)	84% (1960)
Do you happen to know the religious preference of the following men? . . . Richard Nixon.	36% (1959)	39% (1959)	59% (1960)	56% (1960)

Question Wording	T1	T2	T3	T4	T5
1945; 1954; 1957: Do you happen to know the names of the two senators from this state? 1985: Can you tell me the names of the two U.S. Senators from (name state)? 1989: Do you happen to know the names of the two U.S. Senators from your state? (Note: First percentage = name at least one senator; second = name both.)	57% 35% (1945)	31% (1954)	44% 22% (1957)	62% 35% (1985)	55% 25% (1989)
With what country do you associate General Franco?	53% (1948)	58% (1949)	56% (1949)	56% (1950)	57% (1953)
1949: Do you happen to know who is secretary of state in the government at Washington (that is, the member of President Truman's cabinet who is in charge of our relations with other countries)? 1958: Can you recall offhand the name of the U.S. secretary of state? 1970: The next question is like a quiz show on television. Do you happen to know the name of . . . the U.S. secretary of state? 1978: Who is the current United States secretary of state? 1985: Do you know the name of the United States secretary of state?	36% (1949)	57% (1958)	18% (1970)	34% (1978)	25% (1985)

Question Wording	1948	1952	1960	1964	1968	1976	1980	1988
1948: Will you tell me the names of the presidential and vice presidential candidates for the Republican party? 1952: Can you recall, offhand, the name of the Republican candidate for vice president? 1960: Can you recall the name of the (1960) vice presidential candidate nominated by . . . the Republicans? 1964; 1968: Can you recall the name of the man who was nominated as the vice presidential candidate on the (1964) Republican ticket? 1976: Do you happen to know the names of the two men running for vice president (in 1976)? Who are they?								

Table A3.2 Over-Time Knowledge of Public Figures and Political Parties (*continued*)

Question Wording	1948	1952	1960	1964	1968	1976	1980	1988
1980: Do you happen to know who is the (1980) Republican vice presidential running mate with Ronald Reagan? (If respondent answered "yes" but did not mention running mate's name, ask: Who is it? 1988: Do you happen to know who Vice President George Bush has chosen to be his vice presidential running mate on the (1988) Republican presidential ticket?	58%	45%	60%	62%	62%	72%	84%	64%
Same as above, but for Democrats.	49%	32%	69%	80%	55%	66%		

Question Wording	1960	1964	1968	1972	1976	1980	1984	1988	1992
Would you say that one of the parties is more conservative than the other at the national level? (if "yes": Which party is more conservative.) (If "no": Do you think that people generally consider the Democrats or the Republicans more conservative, or wouldn't you want to guess about that.)	61%	58%	62%	57%	53%	41%[a]	53%	57%	58%
Do you happen to know which party had the most members in the House of Representatives in Washington before the elections (this/last) month? Which one.	64%	62%	68%	64%	60%	71%	55%	59%	60%
Do you happen to know which party had the most members in the Senate in Washington before the elections (this/last) month? Which one.							30%	54%	52%

Question Wording	1958	1964	1966	1968	1970	1972	1974
(Nonincumbents)							
Do you happen to remember the names of the candidates for Congress—that is, for the House of Representatives—who ran in this district this November?	28%	32%	23%	34%	16%	19%	16%

Table A3.2 Over-Time Knowledge of Public Figures and Political Parties (*continued*)

Question Wording	1942	1947	1957	1958	1964	1965	1966	1966	1968
(Incumbents/ Representatives) In election years: Do you happen to remember the names of the candidates for Congress—that is, for the House of Representatives-who ran in this district this November? In nonelection years: Can you remember offhand the name of the person who represents your district in the House of Representatives—that is, your congressman (or congresswoman)?	50%	42%	35%	44%	52%	43%	46%	40%	50%

Continued	1970	1970	1972	1974	1977	1978	1978	1987	1989	1989
	53%	35%	36%	34%	30%	32%	35%	38%	28%	29%

[a] The question directly asking which party is more conservative was not asked in 1980. Instead we used two questions asking respondents to rank the two parties on a liberal-conservative scale and used the relative placement of the parties to determine if a respondent correctly ranked the Republican party as the more conservative. Although this percentage seems unusually low, for the three following election years in which both forms of the question were asked, the percentage ranking the Republican party more conservative using the relative ranking scale was within one to three percentage points of the percentage doing so using the more direct question.

Table A3.3 Over-Time Knowledge of Foreign Affairs

Question Wording	T1	T2
1948: Which of the countries on the card would you say are communist? . . . Russia. 1985: As you know, different types of governments are found in various countries. I want you to check off the answer which comes closest to describing your own impression of the kind of government in each of several countries. Look at the top of each column for the description of each type of government. Then place an *X* in the box that best describes each country. In a democratic, civilian authoritarian, military authoritarian, mixed military-civilian authoritarian, communist . . . USSR (Russia).	78% (1948)	87% (1985)
1988: Please tell me for each of the following countries if you think the country sells more to the United States than it buys, or buys more than it sells. . . . South Korea.		

Table A3.3 Over-Time Knowledge of Foreign Affairs (*continued*)

Question Wording	T1	T2
1989: When the United States sells more goods to other countries than it buys from them, it has a trade surplus. When the United States buys more goods from other countries than it sells to them, it has a trade deficit. For the following countries, tell me if you think the United States has a trade surplus or a trade deficit? . . . South Korea.	67% (1988)	53% (1989)
1978: As you probably know, for many years two rival governments have called themselves Korea: on one hand, the Democratic People's Republic of Korea (or North Korea) is the northern part of the Korean peninsula and, on the other, the Republic of Korea (or South Korea) in the south. Do you happen to know if North Korea does or does not have a communist government? 1985: As you know, different types of governments are found in various countries. I want you to check off the answer that comes closest to describing your own impression of the kind of government in each of several countries. Look at the top of each column for the description of each type of government. Then place an *X* in the box that best describes each country. . . . North Korea.	66% (1978)	60% (1985)
As far as you know, is Russia now able to make the atomic bomb, or not?	63% (1948)	65% (1949)
From what you know about the situation, which side is the United States backing—the government of El Salvador or those who are opposed to the government?	62% (1981)	46% (1983)
1982: Do you think that . . . free elections . . . exist in Japan, or not? 1986: Please tell me whether you think the following information about Japan is true or not. . . . It has a democratic election system.	57% (1982)	48% (1986)
As far as you know, is the United States trying to get other countries to agree to the international control of atomic energy or not?	54% (1947)	56% (1947)
1978: As you probably know, for many years two rival governments have called themselves Korea: on one hand, the Democratic People's Republic of Korea (or North Korea) in the northern part of the Korean peninsula and, on the other, the Republic of Korea (or South Korea) in the south. Does South Korea have a communist government or not? 1985: As you know, different types of governments are found in various countries. I want you to check off the answer which comes closest to describing your own impression of the kind of government in each of several countries. Look at the top of each column for the description of each type of government. Than place an *X* in the box which best describes each country. . . . South Korea.	52% (1978)	57% (1985)
1948: Here is a list of different countries. Which of those would you say are democracies, which are not democracies, and which aren't you sure about? . . . Mexico. 1988: Here are five countries and I'd like you to tell me if each of these countries has a pro-Soviet, communist government, a democratic government, or neither one. If you are not sure, just tell me. . . . Mexico.	50% (1948)	48% (1988)
Do you happen to know whether or not black South Africans have the right to vote?	48% (1985)	51% (1985)
1984: Do you happen to know which side the United States is backing in the Central American country of El Salvador: the government or the rebels trying to overthrow the government?		

Table A3.3 Over-Time Knowledge of Foreign Affairs (*continued*)

Question Wording	T1	T2
1989: And what about El Salvador. . . . Does the U.S. support the government of El Salvador or the rebels there?	45% (1984)	43% (1989)
1977: As you probably know, for many years two rival government have called themselves China: on the one hand, the People's Republic or mainland China on the continent of Asia and, on the other hand, the Republic of China on the island of Taiwan (or Formosa, as it is sometimes called). Do you happen to know, does the Republic of China or Taiwan have a communist government or not? 1985: As you know, different types of governments are found in various countries. I want you to check off the answer that comes closest to describing your own impression of the kind of government in each of several countries. Look at the top of each column for the description of each type of government. Then place an *X* in the box that best describes each country. . . . Taiwan.	44% (1977)	50% (1985)
1985a: As you know, different types of governments are found in various countries. I want you to check off the answer that comes closest to describing your own impression of the kind of government in each of several countries. Look at the top of each column for the description of each type of government. Then place an X in the box that best describes each country. . . . Japan. 1985b: What kind of government does Japan have? Is it a democratic government, a military government, a communist government, or a monarchy where the emperor makes all the important decisions?	35% (1985)	35% (1985)
About what proportion of its oil would you say the United States imports from other countries? Would you say two-thirds or more, about half, about one-third, or less than one-third?	33% (1984)	49% (1990)
Does Nicaragua have a communist government, or a right-wing dictatorship, or does it have some other kind of government?	32% (1986)	42% (1986)
Just your best guess. . . . How many U.S. soldiers do you think we now have in Vietnam?	25% (1965)	29% (1967)
How many U.S. soldiers do you think have been killed so far in the Vietnam war?	17% (1965)	6% (1967)
I'd like to ask you whether several countries are members of NATO (North Atlantic Treaty Organization) or not. How about Russia—is it a member?	15% (1964)	21% (1989)
To the best of your knowledge, how much do the biggest U.S. aircraft carriers and supertankers now use the Panama Canal—a great deal, quite a lot, not very much, or not at all?	15% (1977)	17% (1978)
Here is a list of some different companies. All of them have operations here in the United States. But, would you go down that list and for each one would you tell me whether, to your knowledge, the main headquarters is located here in the United States or located in a foreign country? . . . Toyota.	91% (1978)	91% (1986)
. . . Volkswagen	87% (1978)	85% (1986)
. . . Exxon	78% (1978)	76% (1986)
. . . Sony	77% (1978)	79% (1986)
. . . Nestles	76% (1978)	77% (1986)
. . . Lever Brothers	65% (1978)	60% (1986)

Table A3.3 Over-Time Knowledge of Foreign Affairs (*continued*)

Question Wording	T1	T2
. . . Panasonic	54% (1978)	51% (1986)
. . . Shell Oil	17% (1978)	19% (1986)
Now, here is a list of some different kinds of materials and products. Would you go down that list, and for each one tell me whether you think we have adequate supplies of it in this country for our needs, or need to import some from other countries, or need to import most or all of it to meet our needs? . . . Wheat.	92% (1975)	95% (1977)
. . . Meat	90% (1975)	93% (1977)
. . . Cotton	87% (1975)	89% (1977)
. . . Oil	54% (1975)	49% (1977)
. . . Coffee	53% (1975)	59% (1977)
. . . Tea	45% (1975)	47% (1977)
. . . Rice	42% (1975)	38% (1977)
. . . Wool	19% (1975)	20% (1977)
. . . Leather	19% (1975)	20% (1977)
. . . Iron and steel	18% (1975)	18% (1977)
. . . Textiles	16% (1975)	18% (1977)
. . . Tin	9% (1975)	10% (1977)

Question Wording	T1	T2	T3
I'd like to ask you whether several countries are members of NATO (North Atlantic Treaty Organization) or not. First, is the U.S. a member?	61% (1964)	59% (1988)	60% (1989)
1981; 1983: One of these two nations, the United States or the Soviet Union, is a member of what is known as the NATO (North Atlantic Treaty Organization) alliance. Do you happen to know which country that is, or are you not sure? 1986: Do you happen to recall whether the U.S. or the USSR (Soviet Union/Russia) is in NATO—that is, the North Atlantic Treaty Organization?	47% (1981)	43% (1983)	56% (1986)
As far as you know, will the United States have the right to defend the Panama Canal against third-nation attacks after Panama takes full control?	43% (1978)	44% (1978)	54% (1978)
Using the card, at the present time, how much of the oil used in the United States would you say we have to import from other countries? (Five choices.)	29% (1977)	30% (1978)	27% (1981)

Table A3.3 Over-Time Knowledge of Foreign Affairs (*continued*)

Question Wording	T1	T2	T3
As far as you know, in what year is the Panama Canal to be turned over completely to the Republic of Panama, by terms of the treaties?	27% (1977)	21% (1978)	31% (1978)
Which side does the U.S. government support in Nicaragua—the current government, or the people fighting against the government, or haven't you been following this closely enough to say?	26% (1985)	38% (1986)	58% (1986)
1979a; 1979b: Can you tell me which countries are involved in the SALT (Strategic Arms Limitation Talks/Treaty) negotiations—the negotiations for a treaty that would limit strategic military weapons? 1986: Do you recall which two nations took part in the SALT (Strategic Arms Limitation) talks, now known as the START talks?	23% (1979)	30% (1979)	47% (1986)
1989: If you had to guess, who would you say is the U.S.'s biggest trading partner? 1990: Please tell me which of these countries is the largest trading partner of the United States. 1991: Can you tell me what country is America's largest trading partner, that is, with what country the United States conducts the greatest amount of foreign trade?	12% (1989)	20% (1990)	8% (1991)

Question Wording	T1	T2	T3	T4
1949: Which would you say is larger—the amount of goods we send to other countries or the amount of goods we get from other countries? 1977; 1985: When it comes to exporting U.S. goods to other countries and importing goods from other countries, is it your impression that at the present time we export more goods than we import, or import more than we export, or that imports and exports are about equally balanced? 1989: And in the past few years have people in the U.S. bought more foreign goods than we've sold to people overseas, or have we sold more to them than we have bought, or has it pretty much balanced out?	73% (1949)	53% (1977)	75% (1985)	83% (1989)
Do you think the United States has to import oil to meet our needs, or do we produce as much oil as we need?	48% (1977)	51% (1979)	63% (1980)	50% (1991)
1985: As far as you know, is the U.S. backing the Sandinista government in Nicaragua, or are we backing the rebel forces—the so-called Contras—trying to overthrow the Sandinista government? 1988: Over the past several years, has the Reagan administration favored sending military aid to (rotate:) the Sandinistas, the Contras, or neither one? 1986; 1989: Do you happen to recall whether the Reagan administration is backing the Sandinistas or the Contras in Nicaragua?	38% (1985)	52% (1986)	69% (1988)	66% (1989)
What percentage of our oil do you think we now import? (Don't read answers.)	15% (1977)	12% (1978)	6% (1990)	5% (1991)

Table A3.3 Over-Time Knowledge of Foreign Affairs (*continued*)

Question Wording	T1	T2	T3	T4	T5
1945: As far as you know, has the United States already agreed to join a world organization, or hasn't this been decided yet? 1946a: Here is a list of international organizations. Would you mind telling me which of them you have heard of? (For each one marked "heard," ask: Do you happen to know whether or not the United States is a member of the . . . United Nations Organization?) 1946b: As far as you know, is or is not our country a member of the United Nations organization—sometimes called the UNO? 1976: Do you happen to know whether this nation is a member or is not a member of the United Nations? 1985: Is the United States a member of the United Nations?	40% (1945)	75% (1946)	84% (1946)	85% (1976)	96% (1985)
1978: Is it your impression that the United States now sells more goods to Japan than it buys, does the United States buy more goods from Japan than it sells, or are sales between the United States and Japan about equal? 1985; 1986: Who sells more products to the other country? Does Japan sell more products to the United States, or does the United States sell more products to Japan? 1988: Please tell me for each of the following countries if you think the country sells more to the United States than it buys, or buys more than it sells. . . . Japan. 1989: When the United States sells more goods to other countries than it buys from them, it has a trade surplus. When the United States buys more goods from other countries than it sells to them, it has a trade deficit. For the following countries, tell me if you think the United States has a trade surplus or a trade deficit? . . . Japan.	70% (1978)	87% (1985)	85% (1986)	88% (1988)	83% (1989)

Question Wording	8/83	5/84	3/85	6/85	3/86	3/86	4/87	6/87	8/87	1/88
Do you happen to know which side the U.S. is backing in Nicaragua, the rebels or the government?	29%	33%	37%	46%	50%	59%	45%	52%	54%	55%

Table A3.4 Over-Time Knowledge of Domestic Affairs

Question Wording	T1	T2
1974: Which of the benefits listed on this card are you fairly sure there are under Social Security? . . . Disability benefits. 1981: Which of these programs are included in the Social Security system? . . . Disability insurance.	67% (1974)	54% (1981)
The federal government publishes unemployment figures for different racial groups. As far as you know, is the rate of unemployment among blacks lower, about the same, or higher than the rate for whites? (If higher: Is it slightly higher or more than twice as high?)	50% 31% (1977)	59% 28% (1980)
In any given year, the government both takes in Social Security money from those who are working and pays out money to those receiving Social Security benefits. Which of the statements on this card comes closest to expressing the way you think these funds are handled by the government? (Three options.)	38% (1975)	43% (1984)
1979: I am going to read you some statements about the Social Security program. For each one, I would like you to tell me whether it is true or false. If you are not sure, just say so. . . . All federal employees pay into the Social Security system. 1981: As far as you know, do all workers who work for pay outside their own homes make payments into the Social Security system?	37% (1979)	31% (1981)
1977: Do you happen to know what the minimum wage per hour allowed by law now is? 1987: From what you understand, what is the federal minimum wage today?	36% (1977)	43% (1987)
1979: From what you've heard or read, do you think a nuclear power plant accident could cause an atomic explosion with a mushroom-shaped cloud like the one at Hiroshima? 1980: Do you think that it is possible for a nuclear power plant to explode and cause a mushroom-shaped cloud like the one at Hiroshima, or don't you think that is possible?	33% (1979)	31% (1980)
1980: Do you know what the rate of inflation is now—that is, the rate at which prices are going up? 1985: What do you think is the current rate of inflation—that is, by what percent have prices increased this year over last?	31% (1980)	42% (1985)
In terms of what it will buy, about how many cents would you say the dollar is worth today compared with 1939? With 1946?	29% (1951)	23% (1957)
1944: We now have around 56 million people employed in this country, not counting those in the armed forces. Which of these figures do you think comes closest to the number of people in the United States now belonging to the national labor unions? 1984: About what percentage of Americans today belong to a union?	23% (1944)	18% (1984)
1950: And just your best guess again—about how much would you say the total public debt now is of the U.S. government? 1951: Roughly how much would you guess our national debt is today?	20% (1950)	14% (1951)
1989: What is your best guess as to what percentage of the U.S. population is black? 1990: What percent of the U.S. population today would you say is black?	13% (1989)	17% (1990)
1944: Just as a rough guess, what percent profit would you say the average manufacturer makes in peacetime? 1969: Just as a rough guess, what percent profit on each dollar of sales do you think the average manufacturer makes, after taxes?	10% (1945)	9% (1969)

Table A3.4 Over-Time Knowledge of Domestic Affairs (*continued*)

Question Wording	T1	T2
Businesses in this country aim to make a profit, of course. What profit do you think business as a whole makes as a percentage of sales—less than 10%, 10% to 20%, 20% to 30%, or over 30%?	10% (1975)	10% (1985)
1984: What percent of the national budget do you think the United States spent in 1983 on social programs, including Social Security? 1989: And how many cents of your federal tax dollar are spent on Social Security and Medicare?	8% (1984)	5% (1989)
To your knowledge, what percentage of the nation's electric power is currently supplied by nuclear power plants?	5% (1979)	6% (1986)

Question Wording	T1	T2	T3
1978; 1981: As far as you know, do the Social Security taxes people pay get set aside in a fund for their own retirement, or are they used to pay for Social Security benefits that people are collecting today? 1979: I am going to read you some statements about the Social Security program. For each one, I would like you to tell me whether it is true or false. If you are not sure, just say so. . . . The Social Security tax money collected from an individual is set aside specifically for his or her retirement benefits.	78% (1978)	62% (1979)	75% (1981)
1974: Which of the benefits listed on this card are you fairly sure there are under Social Security? . . . Survivor benefits. 1979: I am going to read you some statements about the Social Security program. For each one, I would like you to tell me whether it is true or false. If you are not sure, just say so. . . . Social Security pays benefits to the families of workers who die.	74% (1974)	87% (1979)	63% (1981)
1984: Do you happen to know, is the deficit larger or smaller now than it was five years ago? 1985: Is the federal budget deficit larger or smaller than it was when President Reagan first took office? 1987: Compared to five years ago, has the federal budget deficit increased, decreased, or stayed about the same?	62% (1984)	83% (1985)	74% (1987)
1975; 1984: At the present time, do you think the government is taking in more Social Security money than it is paying out, or paying out more than it is taking in, or that Social Security payments and receipts are about in balance? 1989: To the best of your knowledge, is the amount of money collected from payroll taxes for Social Security greater than the amount the government pays out to people receiving Social Security, or is the amount collected less than the amount paid out, or is the amount collected about equal to the amount paid out?	34% (1975)	46% (1984)	45% (1989)
Have you heard or read anything about the Herbert Hoover Commission reports? If "yes": What is your understanding, in general, of the purpose of the Hoover Commission?)	28% (1949)	31% (1950)	24% (1951)
1980: Can you tell me what percentage of the workforce in this country is currently unemployed, that is, the percentage of people out of work? 1985: What do you think is the current national unemployment rate? 1989: And what percentage of the U.S. population is currently unemployed, according to the government?	26% (1980)	42% (1985)	27% (1989)

Table A3.4 Over-Time Knowledge of Domestic Affairs (*continued*)

Question Wording	T1	T2	T3
1969; 1976: Do you happen to recall about how much of every dollar is now spent for military and defense purposes? 1989: And about how many cents of your federal tax dollar are going to the Defense Department these days?	4% (1969)	7% (1976)	8% (1989)

Question Wording	T1	T2	T3	T4
1962: Have you heard or read about the Medicare plan proposed by the Kennedy administration? (If "yes," ask: Do you happen to know how the Medicare plan would be paid for?) 1974; 1981: Which of the benefits listed on this card are you fairly sure there are under Social Security? . . . Medicare. 1979: I am going to read you some statements about the Social Security program. For each one, I would like you to tell me whether it is true or false. If you are not sure, just say so. . . . Social Security taxes pay for hospital care benefits (Medicare) for the elderly.	41% (1962)	75% (1974)	69% (1979)	54% (1981)

Question Wording	1976	1977	1982	1983	1984	1989	1989
1976; 1977: Do you happen to know if the federal budget is balanced—that is, does the federal government take in as much as it spends? 1982; 1983: Do you happen to know whether the government is or is not operating at a loss? 1984; 1989a: Do you happen to know, is the federal government spending more money than it is taking in this year, or is it spending less money than it is taking in? 1989b: In the past few years, has the U.S. government taken in more money in taxes than it has spent, has it spent more than it has taken in, or has it pretty much balanced the money it taxes and spends?	72%	67%	63%	70%	77%	81%	80%

Table A3.5 Over-Time Knowledge of Geography

Question Wording	T1	T2
Will you please tell me the number on this map which locates each of the following states? . . . California?	82% (1948)	89% (1988)
. . . Texas	82% (1948)	91% (1988)
. . . Pennsylvania	59% (1948)	62% (1988)
. . . New York	58% (1948)	55% (1988)

Table A3.5 Over-Time Knowledge of Geography

Question Wording	T1	T2
. . . Illinois	50% (1948)	52% (1988)
. . . Ohio	46% (1948)	50% (1988)
. . . Michigan	45% (1948)	48% (1988)
. . . New Jersey	45% (1948)	42% (1988)
. . . Massachusetts	43% (1948)	39% (1988)
. . . Missouri	43% (1948)	45% (1988)
Will you please tell me the number on this map that locates each of the following countries? . . . Brazil	60% (1947)	61% (1988)
. . . Argentina	49% (1947)	47% (1988)
. . . Chile	44% (1947)	45% (1988)
. . . Holland	38% (1947)	30% (1988)
. . . Greece	33% (1947)	34% (1988)
. . . Czechoslovakia	25% (1947)	19% (1988)
. . . Peru	21% (1947)	23% (1988)
. . . Hungary	18% (1947)	14% (1988)
. . . Bolivia	17% (1947)	17% (1988)
. . . Paraguay	16% (1947)	13% (1988)
. . . Ecuador	16% (1947)	13% (1988)
. . . Colombia	16% (1947)	19% (1988)

Question Wording	T1	T2	T3
Will you please tell me the number on this map that locates each of the following countries. . . . England.	72% (1947)	65% (1955)	57% (1988)
. . . Italy	72% (1947)	74% (1955)	74% (1988)
. . . France	65% (1947)	63% (1955)	54% (1988)
. . . Spain	53% (1947)	57% (1955)	50% (1988)
. . . Poland	41% (1947)	32% (1955)	28% (1988)

Table A3.5 Over-Time Knowledge of Geography (*continued*)

Question Wording	T1	T2	T3
. . . Yugoslavia	22% (1947)	16% (1955)	14% (1988)
. . . Rumania	17% (1947)	11% (1955)	11% (1988)
. . . Bulgaria	13% (1947)	10% (1955)	12% (1988)

Question Wording	T1	T2
1978: Which one of these statements about Japan is correct? . . . Japan is a nation of islands. 1982: As far as you know, is Japan part of the Asian continent or a separate island country?	66% (1978)	57% (1982)

Question Wording	1951	1952	1958	1965
1951; 1952; 1965: Just your best guess—what is the population of communist China? 1958: Incidentally, could you tell me what the population of communist China is?	12%	14%	10%	11%

Table A3.6 Over-Time Knowledge of History

Question Wording	T1	T2	T3
Now, here are some questions that may be used in a quiz program. Some of them are easy, but most of them are hard. I think you'll find them all interesting. Who was . . . Columbus?	90% (1955)	92% (1975)	
. . . Napoléon Bonaparte	67% (1955)	58% (1975)	
. . . Aristotle	34% (1955)	44% (1975)	
. . . Karl Marx	33% (1955)	41% (1975)	
. . . Sigmund Freud	22% (1955)	47% (1975)	
1975: Can you tell me what important events occurred in the following years? . . . 1776. 1989: We're interested in knowing how familiar Americans are with the history of their country. . . . What happened on July 4, 1776?	73% (1975)	88% (1989)	
1985: Which side did the United States support in the war—North Vietnam or South Vietnam? 1990: In the Vietnam war, was the United States fighting on the side of the North Vietnamese or the South Vietnamese?	63% (1985)	67% (1990)	
1985: In World War II, did the Soviet Union and the United States fight on the same side or on opposite sides? 1986: To the best of your knowledge, during World War II, was the Soviet Union an ally of the United States or not?	56% (1985)	67% (1986)	

Table A3.6 Over-Time Knowledge of History (*continued*)

Question Wording	T1	T2	T3
1982a; 1982b: On another matter, can you tell me which two nations, aside from the United States, were involved in the Camp David peace talks? 1983: Can you tell me which two countries, aside from the United States, were involved in the Camp David peace talks when Jimmy Carter was president?	45% (1982)	36% (1982)	38% (1983)

APPENDIX FOUR

Details of the Structural Analysis Used in Chapter 4

The principal method used in determining the dimensionality of knowledge in various surveys was confirmatory factor analysis with LISREL. We chose confirmatory rather than exploratory factor analysis because, for each of the data sets examined, we had specific expectations concerning the structure of knowledge. Exploratory factor analysis simplifies the relation among variables without regard to the substantive meaning of the resulting factors. Consequently, the results of exploratory factor analysis can often be difficult to interpret. Confirmatory factor analysis, because it allows the researcher to set certain interrelations at zero, often produces more easily interpretable results if the hypothesized relations are theoretically well conceived.

The adequacy of a LISREL model is judged on the basis of several measures of statistical fit. Perhaps the most important is the ratio between the chi-square and the degrees of freedom. The smaller the chi-square–degrees of freedom ratio the better, with ratios of less than five to one considered evidence of an acceptable model for large sample (Wheaton et al., 1977; Sullivan, 1981; Hayduk, 1987). The adjusted goodness of fit index, or AGFI, is another measure of the hypothesized model's fit with the data and ranges from zero to one with higher scores indicating a better fit. The coefficient of determination (CD) serves as a measure of overall model reliability. The epistemic correlations are analogous to factor loadings and when squared indicate the percent of each item's variance that is shared with the other variables in the factor. They thus serve as conservative indicators of an item's reliability. The fit of a model is typically assessed not only by the absolute level of these different measures, but also relative to the fit of other models (Wheaton, 1988).

The key indicator of dimensionality in the model is the interfactor correlation. Normally, interfactor loadings of greater than .9 are considered evidence of insignificant differences across factors, although Hayduk (1987) argues that such decisions should be made on a case-by-case basis and should be informed by theoretical expectations.

The number of variables that can be used in a LISREL analysis is limited by the available sample size. In our analyses of the 1989 Survey of Political Knowledge, the sample size of 610 limited us to no more than eighteen variables. Consequently, in our analysis of the subdomains of knowledge (e.g., rules of the game), we identified the most reliable items (as indicated by the epistemic correlations) and used these in subsequent tests of dimensionality across domains (table A4.1).[1] A similar approach was taken with the 1985 and 1991 NES pilot surveys.

Given that the knowledge items are almost exclusively dichotomous, we opted for using a weighted least squares estimation procedure of a correlation matrix of tetrachoric correlations (see Joreskog and Sorbom, 1988). All analyses were replicated using both covariance and Pearson correlation matrices, however, and these produced results similar to, if less strong than, those reported here.

Table A4.1 LISREL Analyses of Eighteen "Best" Items

	Model A4.1a	Model A4.1b			Model A4.1c				
Contras	.68	.71			.71				
Arms treaty	.65	.68			.68				
Trade deficit	.62	.65			.65				
Budget deficit	.67	.69			.69				
Superfund	.76	.79			.79				
New Deal	.72	.75			.74				
Bill of Rights	.67		.69			.70			
Fifth Amendment	.68		.70			.72			
Judicial review	.67		.69			.71			
Veto	.54		.56			.57			
Abortion	.38		.39				.48		
Suffrage	.55		.56				.68		
House party	.67			.72				.77	
Truman party	.72			.77				.82	
FDR party	.76			.81				.86	
Senators	.62			.67					.69
Vice president	.68			.73					.75
U.S. representative	.52			.56					.57
	CD = .93	CD = .98			CD = .98				
	chi-sq./df = 288/135 = 2.1	chi-sq./df = 223/132 = 1.7			chi-sq./df = 185/125 = 1.5				
	AGFI = .97	AGFI = .98			AGFI = .98				

Table A4.1 LISREL Analyses of Eighteen "Best" Items (*continued*)

Interfactor Correlations

	1	2	3
1	1.00		
2	.97	1.00	
3	.80	.83	1.00

	1	2	3	4	5
1	1.00				
2	.94	1.00			
3	.89	.70	1.00		
4	.72	.75	.52	1.00	
5	.83	.83	.77	.80	1.00

Source: 1989 Survey of Political Knowledge.

Table A4.2 Description of Independent Variables

Variable Name	Variable Description	Range
Motivational variables		
Discussion of politics	How often do you discuss politics with your family or friends	1–5
Attention to politics	Follow what's going on in government and public affairs	1–4
Internal efficacy	People like me have a say in government Public officials care People like me should stay informed Government and politics not too complicated	0–4 (higher is more efficacious)
Political trust	Trust government to do what is right (1 = trust "most" or "some of the time")	0–1
Party strength	True independent to strong partisan	1–4
Behavioral variables		
Television news	Days watched television last week times level of attention to news about politics and government	0–21
Newspapers	Days of reading newspaper last week times level of attention to news about politics and government	0–21
Newsmagazines	Respondent volunteers that he or she reads newsmagazines	0–1
Radio	Respondent volunteers that he or she listens to news about politics and government on the radio	0–1
Educational variables		
Schooling	No high school; no high school diploma; high school graduate; some college; college degree; graduate school	1–6
Civics	Did you study civics in high school (0 = no, 1 = as part of other courses, 2 = separate course)	0–2
Demographic variables		
Age	Actual age	18–86
Income	<$10,000; $10,000–19,999; $20,000–34,999; $35,000–49,999; $50,000+	1–5
Gender	Male (0); Female (1)	0–1
Race	White/Asian (0); black/Hispanic (1)	0–1
Region (South)	Nonsouth (0); South (1)	0–1

Source: 1989 Survey of Political Knowledge.

Table A4.3 LISREL Analyses of Virginia Data

	Model A4.3a	Model A4.3b		Model A4.3c		
Attorney general	.84	.86		.91		
Senators	.74	.76		.81		
Lieutenant Governor	.71	.72		.76		
State senate in session	.63	.65		.69		
Governor	.57	.58		.63		
U.S. representative	.49	.51		.53		
Pension issue	.42	.43		.46		
Party: House of Delegates	.78	.81			.85	
Party: State Senate	.72	.74			.79	
Party: U.S. Senate	.80		.84		.86	
Party: U.S. House	.82		.87		.89	
Truman's party	.58		.60		.63	
Pledge	.28		.30			.35
Bill of Rights	.59		.62			.72
Contras	.57		.61			.70
Trade deficit	.59		.62			.71
	CD = .94 chi-sq./df = 545/104 = 5.2 AGFI = .96	CD = .98 chi-sq./df = 482/103 = 4.7 AGFI = .96		CD = .99 chi-sq./df = 182/101 = 1.8 AGFI = .99		

Interfactor Correlations

	Model A4.3b			Model A4.3c		
		1	2		1	2	3
	1	1.00		1	1.00		
	2	.85	1.00	2	.66	1.00	
				3	.74	.66	1.00

Source: 1990 statewide Virginia survey.

Table A4.4 LISREL Analyses of Richmond Data

	Model A4.4a	Model A4.4b	
City council action	.64	.71	
How mayor is elected	.67	.74	
How city council is elected	.77	.88	
Richmond city manager	.59	.66	
Superintendent of schools	.28	.34	
Party: House	.84		.88
Boris Yeltsin	.77		.81
Judicial review	.72		.77
Veto %	.73		.77
	CD = .91 chi-sq./df = 165/27 = 6.1 AGFI = .96	CD = .98 chi-sq./df = 53/26 = 2.0 AGFI = .99	

Interfactor Correlations

	1	2
1	1.00	
2	.69	1.00

Source: 1991 Richmond city survey.

APPENDIX FIVE

Methodology of the Analysis of Information's Impact on Opinion in Chapter 6

Political knowledge can influence both the *variability* and the *central tendency* of opinions. As Bartels (1994) notes, it is unrealistic to expect that information would have the same effect on all citizens, given the variability in their circumstances and interests. We argue that political knowledge matters in part by helping individuals to identify their political interests and connect those interests to an appropriate opinion. To the extent that this is true, it may be possible to observe differences in opinion between better- and lesser-informed individuals whose personal characteristics are similar.

Since there are insufficient cases in a typical survey to permit a fine-grained comparison of better- and lesser-informed citizens with similar social and demographic characteristics, we attempted to simulate the comparison through a multivariate regression analysis that would allow us to estimate how knowledge affected opinions both directly and through its role in strengthening or weakening the impact of social characteristics. Using the 1992 National Election Study, we developed indexes of citizen opinion in five issue areas and used these as dependent variables in a regression analysis. The independent variables in each analysis were similar and included our standard political knowledge index, a large set of demographic variables, and interactions between knowledge and each demographic variable. The demographic variables included the following: age; education; family income; race (black or nonblack); sex; presence of children in the home; marital status (married versus not married); home ownership; homemaker status; retirement status; employment in a clerical position; employment in a professional position; union membership in household; residence in an urban area; residence in the eastern United States; residence in the southern United States; residence in the western United States; Protestant religious affiliation; Catholic religious affiliation; Jewish religious affiliation.

The domestic issues index was a factor score scale of support for or opposition to government spending and action on seven domestic issues. Variables included government services and spending (v3701), health insurance (v3716), government guarantee of a job and good standard of living (v3718), government spending on food stamps (v3725), assisting the unemployed (v3816), assisting blacks (v3729), and public schools (v3818). Higher values of the scale mean less support for these government activities. Alpha for the items comprising the scale was .65. The adjusted r^2 of the regression predicting attitudes with personal characteristics and knowledge was .27.

Four abortion items were combined using factor analysis to form the abortion opinion scale. The variables were: supporting restrictions on abortion (v3732); opposing public funding of abortions for poor women (v3737); supporting a law requiring women to inform their husbands before obtaining an abortion (v3739); and supporting a law requiring parental consent for a minor's abortion (v3735). Alpha for the items comprising the scale was .65. The adjusted r^2 of the regression was .20.

Four questions relating to government efforts to assist blacks were factor analyzed to create a racial attitudes scale. The items were: government aid to blacks (v3724); spending on programs that assist blacks (v3729); civil rights people pushing too slow or too fast (v5929); and government should help blacks get fair treatment in jobs (v5938). Alpha for these items was .62. The adjusted r^2 of the regression was .23.

The homosexual rights measure was a factor score scale of responses to three questions dealing with support for or opposition to homosexuals in the military (v5926), prohibition of job discrimination against homosexuals (v5924), and adoption rights for homosexual couples (v5928). Alpha for the items comprising the scale was .70. The adjusted r^2 for the regression was .23.

The social issues scale used in the generational analysis included three scales, two of which were described above (abortion and gay rights) and a third dealing with the role of women in society, constructed using v3801, v6006, v6008, and v6011). Alpha for these items was .65. The adjusted r^2 of the regression was .22.

For each analysis, a multiple regression was used to estimate the coefficients for political knowledge, the demographics, and the interactions. To simulate the effect of greater and lesser degrees of political knowledge on the direction of opinions, data for each individual in the survey were used to impute two hypothetical opinion positions: an uninformed opinion and a fully informed opinion. The actual scores on each variable for an individual were inserted into the equation with the political knowledge variable set at zero (the lowest possible score) for one analysis and 28 (the highest possible score) for the other. Simply put, the goal of this was to answer the question of "Given how various personal characteristics influence opinions, what opinion would this person have if he or she had scored zero (or 28) on political knowledge?" After this imputation process was done for all respondents in the survey, the sample was divided according to the groups of interest in each analysis (e.g., blacks and non-blacks in the analysis of racial attitudes, three different age groups in the generational analysis, and so on), and the imputed opinions were aggregated (as means). These imputed group means, for uninformed and fully informed individuals, were then plotted to create the graphs shown in chapter 6.

Since each scale was based on factor scores, the original metric of the scale entailed a mean of zero and a standard deviation of one. This metric provides a basis for evaluating the size of the changes in opinion associated with increases in political knowledge. For example, for people who do not believe that the Bible is the word of God, the difference between the imputed mean attitude on gay rights for the fully informed mean versus the uninformed is .83, or over three-fourths of one standard deviation. Standard errors for the imputed means ranged from .01 to .04, with most falling between .01 and .02. Thus all of the shifts in opinion reported in this analysis would be statistically significant by conventional t-tests. It should be noted, however, that the imputation process takes us a considerable distance away from the actual data and that no known sampling distribution exists for these hypothetical variables.

Notes

PREFACE

1. The analysis of advertising and media coverage described here was reported by Jamieson (1994).

2. Habermas's definition of the "ideal speech situation" is controversial and in its pure form is undoubtedly utopian (see, e.g., Rorty, 1987a; 1987b). Our point is simply that the closer one comes to approximating the conditions of equal information and power in political discourse, the more democratic the process and the outcome.

INTRODUCTION. POLITICAL KNOWLEDGE, POLITICAL POWER, AND THE DEMOCRATIC CITIZEN

1. Of course there are limits to this analogy: knowledge is not as effectively finite, tradeable, and spendable as money, for example. Nor is this to suggest that money itself is not an important political currency in its own right.

2. Lance Bennett calls the tendency to treat the attributes of citizens as purely psychological—and thus to reify the status quo—the "state of consciousness fallacy." He contrasts this to a "situational perspective" in which public opinion emerges from the interaction of individual, systemic, and situational factors (1980: 94–131). Our approach to the acquisition of political knowledge builds on Bennett's general theory of public opinion.

3. Our distinction between information provided at a particular moment and the stored information individuals bring to that moment is similar to Downs's (1957) distinction between "information" and "contextual knowledge." Of course even contextual knowledge is ultimately dependent on the range and quality of information provided by the larger environment. In addition, all information is filtered through individual and group belief systems—or schema—and so is subject to interpretation or bias. Nonetheless, information stored in long-term memory is more likely to be drawn from a variety of sources and collected over a longer period of time, and thus it is less likely to be charged with the specific systemic biases and limitations associated with that provided at the time a particular issue is under discussion. As such it allows citizens to make more independent, reasoned decisions.

4. On this issue, see the exchange between Estlund, Waldron, and Grofman and Feld (1989).

CHAPTER 1. FROM DEMOCRATIC THEORY TO DEMOCRATIC PRACTICE

1. Macpherson overstates his case regarding Aristotle. Aristotle does criticize pure democracy, which he defines as rule by the poor. He also doubts the ability of the poor (along with women and certain working classes) to deliberate wisely or to act on behalf of the public good. Nonetheless, his writings form the basis for much of the modern notion of middle-class, representative democracy.

2. Of course the debate over the strengths and weaknesses of democratic governance extend beyond issues of the civic competence of citizens. For a full discussion of these issues, see Dahl (1989).

3. Significantly, Aristotle (1946) suggests that the larger the middle class, the larger the pool of citizens who will be able to both deliberate and rule (181–86).

4. Technically, citizens do not voluntarily "enter into" the social contract because in most cases the contract is implicit, and citizens are usually born into a system that already exists. More accurate, perhaps, is to speak of citizens' decisions to "not resist" the rules presented to them.

5. But Rousseau hesitates to call his system a democracy because his citizens do not actually execute the laws.

6. For this reason, Rousseau argues that all citizens should own some property, but that there be a limit on the amount of property one can own. This situation of relative economic equality helps assure political equality because "no citizen shall be rich enough to buy another and none so poor to be forced to sell himself" (1762: 96).

7. It has also been adapted to advanced socialist systems. See, e.g., the work of G. D. H. Cole, 1919; 1920.

8. Like Rousseau, however, Mill argued that the extremes of wealth found in mid-nineteenth-century England worked against the possibility of laborers and the poor achieving their full potential. As he saw it, the system allocated the fruits of labor "almost in an inverse ratio to labour—the largest portions to those who never worked at all, the next largest to those whose work is almost nominal, and so in a descending scale" (1871: v. 3, 207).

9. In addition, the early development of the U.S. system affected, and in turn was affected by, the theories of Bentham and both Mills.

10. In some ways the American variant of republicanism is more reminiscent—and perhaps consciously so—of the Roman than the Greek republic (see, e.g., Mullett, 1939–40; Wood, 1969). Although the differences between Greek and Roman republics are significant, they are not central to our purposes, which are to highlight their notions of civic virtue and natural hierarchy and to show how these notions are integrated into the U.S. system.

11. The inconsistency of the sentiment expressed in this quote from Adams as compared to that expressed in the quote from him used earlier in this chapter reflects the extent to which the founders' were torn regarding the civic potential of the general public.

12. As one recent textbook on curriculum development asserts: "A . . . tenet of democracy is the right of all citizens to be informed, that is, to have knowledge. Participation in a democracy is meaningless unless citizens have full access to information. . . . Therefore, the education of the masses is a central concern of a democracy" (Engle and Ochoa, 1988: 10).

13. It also suggests that even when information is processed on-line, political sophisticates do not discard it but store some of it for later use; they are also most efficient at retrieving it when it is needed.

14. Although it is true, for example, that the most informed citizens, regardless of their underlying political values, were the most supportive of the war in Vietnam during the early 1960s when information was tightly controlled and very one-sided, it is also true that more informed citizens who held dovish attitudes were generally the first and strongest opponents of the war once a greater range of information became available (Zaller, 1992: chap. 9).

15. It is in the normative assumptions about what is and is not open to negotiation that the central differences between the civic knowledge and heuristic schools are found. Downs is clearly troubled by the ineffectiveness and inequity found in contemporary democracies. He argues, however, that this situation is "rooted in the very nature of society" (236). Furthermore, efforts by government to coerce citizens to become more informed, while collectively beneficial, are unacceptable because there "is no reliable, objective, inexpensive way to measure how well-informed a man is," there is "no agreed-upon rule for deciding how much information of what kinds each citizen should have," and "the loss of freedom involved in forcing people to acquire information would probably far outweigh the benefits to be gained from a better-informed electorate" (247). Such contemporary studies as those done by Sniderman et al. and by Popkin are more upbeat in their assessment that ordinary people can make reasonably good judgments despite their "modest level of political information" and their "similarly modest abilities to process it" (Sniderman et al., 1991: 1). Implicit in these arguments, however, is the same underlying belief that because of a lack of interest, ability, or opportunity, this muddling through is the most we can hope for from ordinary citizens.

16. Indeed, the consequences of different heuristics for the quality of decision making is the focus of much of the work by Sniderman and his colleagues.

17. Of course, statistically three points can be arrayed in a multidimensional space. The point, however, is that in a choice between two options, the voter's decision is ultimately based on his or her relative distance from the parties and candidates, and this distance can be measured on a single dimension.

18. As the work of Fiorina (1981) and others shows, voters do make retrospective decisions about parties and officeholders. Indeed, these evaluations affect the subsequent party identification of voters. Our point here is not that most voters behave in the simple-minded way we describe, but rather to explore if such a mode of decision making would eliminate the need for more specific information.

19. This is an intriguing idea, however, that ought not to be dismissed out of hand. Consider, for example, James Fishkin's (1991) arguments in favor of deliberative opinion polls and citizen juries (both of which are based on the random selection of citizens for the purpose of legislating) and Ernest Callenbach's and Michael Phillips's (1985) argument in favor of a randomly selected national citizen legislature.

20. The story, which is probably apocryphal, has been retold in several fashions. This version is found in Stephen Hawking's *A Brief History of Time* (1988).

CHAPTER 2. WHAT AMERICANS KNOW ABOUT POLITICS

1. One reason for this dearth of studies is the tendency to ask very few factual questions in most surveys. This tendency was first noted by Hazel Gaudet Erskine in 1963a (133) and has been reiterated time and again (Converse, 1975: 101;

Neuman, 1986: 9; Luskin, 1987: 882; Smith, 1989: 160). For a review of factual questions asked before 1964, see Erskine, 1962, 1963a, 1963b, and 1963c.

2. Additional evidence on behalf of the importance of such information is provided by citizens. Those who are well informed about issues, parties, and leaders are also well informed about the rules of the game. This suggests that the most engaged citizens apparently think such information is important and useful.

3. For most of these items, determining the correct answer was fairly straightforward if occasionally time-consuming. When more than one answer could reasonably be considered correct, we were generous in our scoring.

4. Many survey respondents would express exasperation when they could not recall a fact they felt they knew; often they would remember the answer after the interview had proceeded and would ask the interviewer to go back. We attempted to accommodate these requests, but we have no doubt that this type of test-taking anxiety caused some respondents to miss items that, for all practical purposes, they actually knew. In surveys with a relatively large number of knowledge questions, this problem may be less serious. For example, 94 percent of the respondents for our national Survey of Political Knowledge said the questions constituted a fair test of what they knew about politics.

5. Still, it should be noted that the over-time reliability of factual knowledge questions (measure through test-retest procedures) exceeds that of most other phenomena measured in attitude surveys, including party identification.

6. For purposes of counting, each part of a multipart survey item is treated as a separate question. For example, a survey item asking respondents to identify ten people from a list of names would count as ten separate questions. Identical questions asked at different points in time are also counted separately.

7. We have organized our review around the categories of the rules of the game, people and players, and the substance of politics. The conceptual and empirical distinctions among these categories, however, are not always clear-cut. We use them as organizing principles rather than as definitive and mutually exclusive categories.

8. The following discussion of the patterns of public knowledge is based on a reading of the full set of items, as is the analysis presented later in this and in subsequent chapters. But because presenting the marginal percentages for all the items would be unwieldy, we present a sampling of items, selected to reflect the substantive pattern of knowledge found more generally in the larger data set.

9. The exceptions to this were the more visible runs for the presidency of George Wallace in the late 1960s and early 1970s, John Anderson in 1980, and Ross Perot in 1992—all of whom achieved much higher levels of recognition.

10. We included questions here if they addressed issues of domestic public policy issues or if they involved information relevant to making a public (as opposed to a purely private) choice. Although some deal with public health, we did not include most items about AIDS, cancer prevention, or cholesterol and heart problems.

11. The percent correct for questions requiring that respondents give a number or percentage (for example, regarding the minimum wage or the unemployment rate) is obviously dependent on question format (for example, open-ended versus multiple choice) and coding (for example, the range deemed close enough to be coded "correct"). We shall address these issues more directly later. In this overview, correct is used more loosely to mean within the context of question wording and based on the decision rules implemented by the original researchers or, when possible, by us.

12. The specific questions asked varied from nation to nation, making comparisons of specific scores somewhat problematic. Nonetheless, the general point—that Americans are less informed about their national legislature than are citizens of Canada or Great Britain—is compelling.

13. The survey included a mix of items measuring knowledge of the institutions and processes of government, political leaders, political parties, and substantive issues. The items also varied by degree of difficulty and question format. The percentage correctly answering the questions ranged from a low of 2 percent able to identify three Fifth Amendment rights to a high of 96 percent able to name the length of a presidential term. The mean percentage correct across all items was 48, and the median was 49.

14. We found a similar percentage of uninformed responses in the larger set of marginals we collected from other surveys, but we could not determine whether respondents were encouraged or discouraged from guessing. In our survey we discouraged guessing by prefacing the factual questions with the statement, "Most people will not know the answers to many of these—if you don't know, don't worry about it, just tell me and we'll move on to the next one."

15. Correct is defined here as between 10 and 15 percent.

16. These figures are based on only the items for which we could disaggregate wrong answers or for which the total percent misinformed was less than 10 percent.

17. This percentage was nearly identical to that found for the larger set of marginal items for which we could disentangle incorrect answers.

18. The average percent giving an explicitly wrong answer (as opposed to admitting they don't know) was 9 percent for the open-ended questions, compared to 20 percent for the multiple choice and either/or formats. Interestingly, the questions asking for percentages (for example, the percentage without health insurance) had the highest percent of respondents who gave wrong answers. We suspect this is because the boundaries set by percentages (0 to 100) made guessing more enticing, but the wide range possible made guessing correct unlikely.

19. An experiment we conducted with part of the 1989 sample indicated that over 15 percent of respondents did not understand the concept of percentage. Such respondents would no doubt have difficulty with questions referring to percentages or requiring them as responses, even if they had relevant knowledge of the part-whole relations implied in the questions.

20. Consistent with our notion of lagged attention, although a majority of citizens mistakenly thought that the Republicans had taken control of the House of Representatives in the 1980 elections, by 1984 a majority knew that the Democrats still controlled the House.

21. Indeed, voter turnout in most of Western Europe is higher than in the United States, but many other forms of participation are more common in the United States (Dalton, 1988).

22. Data from the 1992 NES survey.

CHAPTER 3. STABILITY AND CHANGE IN POLITICAL KNOWLEDGE

1. Of course, few if any of these abilities are sine qua non for learning—being blind or deaf is not an insurmountable impediment, for example. Further, the importance of any particular attribute or skill likely varies depending on the subject matter being learned.

2. A possible exception to this is the argument that industrial pollutants like

lead and mercury have in fact lessened the cognitive abilities of at least a segment of the population, and one might argue that this could result in lower aggregate levels of intelligence.

3. See also Meyrowitz (1985), Illich and Sanders (1989), and Mander (1978).

4. In a 1990 address to the German Informatics Society, provocatively entitled "Informing Ourselves to Death," Postman argues that the explosion of information provided by new electronic technology actually works against citizens' ability to inform themselves about social and political matters of import by inundating them with essentially irrelevant information.

5. As a concession to the relatively few items repeated over time, we do not limit our analysis to items asked by the same survey organization. As a result, some variation may reflect the sampling and surveying techniques used by different organizations. Because our basic conclusion is that little change occurred, such house differences are unlikely to be of major significance to our analysis.

6. For example, if a question is asked at time 1 (T1) and time 2 (T2), it provides a single observation—the change that occurred between those two points in time. However, if it is asked a third time (T3), then there are three comparisons: T1–T2, T1–T3, and T2–T3.

7. Surveys conducted in the same calendar year are treated as having occurred one year apart. We experimented with various ways of coding these relatively few surveys and found it had little impact on the substantive conclusions.

8. We use inferential statistics on the assumption that our collection of questions represents a sample of all possible facts about politics. We recognize that this sample is not, strictly speaking, random. Nevertheless, measures of statistical significance provide a gauge of how confident we can be in our conclusions.

9. An indication that our simple analysis is inadequately modeling all the sources of stability and change is provided by the constant term (a significant 5.0) that would cancel out most of the losses produced by the length of time variable.

10. In this model, the constant term is reduced to an insignificant 1.7.

11. This argument should not be taken too far, since we have no way of knowing if the issues are really new, nor do all the five-year intervals consist of change over the first five years of any set of variables. Nonetheless, given that most polls are conducted when an issue emerges as important, that 70 percent of the survey items we use were repeated only once, and that the T1 for more than 80 percent of our 749 observations was the first time the survey item was asked, this interpretation seems reasonable.

12. A third type of knowledge (*taught* knowledge about civics, geography, and history) and an additional time period, the 1940s through the 1950s, are not included so as to keep the model identified. The impact of these variables is captured in the constant term. We tested other models that included these variables and eliminated others, but they resulted in poorer statistical fits with the data and produced insignificant coefficients for these excluded variables.

13. This pattern holds for knowledge of both domestic and foreign politics when entered as separate variables in the equation, although the effect appears stronger for the latter type of knowledge.

14. Rogers did serve as legal counsel to a Senate committee and was a member of the U.S. delegation to the United Nations in the 1960s, but neither was a visible position.

15. The statement, which was made in response to a question regarding whether he felt he could, as secretary of defense, make a decision that might

adversely affect General Motors, was intended to show that he could. It is often quoted in reverse, thus suggesting that Wilson was putting General Motors in the driver's seat, so to speak.

16. Although he had served as secretary of the Air Force under President Johnson, for the nine years before his nomination he had been president of the California Institute of Technology.

17. Although not among the regression analysis's outliers, the other cases of lagged attention discussed in chapter 2 provide additional examples of the degree of public surveillance and the pace of public learning (e.g., the case of John L. Lewis and Philip Murray). Similarly, in late January and early February of 1949, only 36 percent of those asked could name the newly appointed secretary of state, Dean Acheson. Another 24 percent were aware that a change had been made, but they could not name the new secretary. In 1986, while 43 percent of the public knew that William Rehnquist was the Chief Justice of the Supreme Court, an additional 29 percent named Warren Burger, who had only recently stepped down from that position. And the 1990 NES survey captured the steady, if partial, diffusion of information regarding Margaret Thatcher's resignation as prime minister.

18. We were unable to uncover a plausible, substantive explanation for why the percentage correctly answering that survivor's benefits are part of the Social Security program dropped 24 percent between 1979 and 1981.

19. The revelations regarding Waldheim's wartime association with the Nazis occurred after he had left the United Nations and so do not explain this jump in recognition.

20. Although not as dramatic an increase as others, knowledge of the technical definition of impeachment rose from 52 percent in early November 1973, when the House Judiciary Committee first took up the issue of President Nixon's impeachment, to 66 percent in May 1974, two months before the Judiciary Committee voted for impeachment.

CHAPTER 4. WHO'S INFORMED?

1. The methodology of the focus groups is described in Appendix 1.

2. The reliability and validity of knowledge measures depend on many other factors in addition to the range of topics covered by the questions. For further discussion of the methodological issues in measuring political knowledge see Delli Carpini and Keeter (1993) and Appendix 2.

3. The notion of information specialists is the logical extension of the more general theory of pluralism (Truman, 1951; Dahl, 1961) and has been developed in the work of Iyengar (1990). For a review and critique of this view, see Neuman, 1986: 30–39.

4. This would be true even if citizens tended to be specialists because there could be variation in knowledge among citizens who profess an interest in particular issues or domains of politics.

5. Although we occasionally adopt Zaller's terminology of political knowledge as a trait, we see knowledge more as a resource.

6. A third possible structure is worth noting—no structure at all. According to some critics of contemporary society, America's media environment presents information in contextless disconnected fragments, which are perceived by a citizenry that has become physically and psychologically distant from many aspects of politics (see, e.g., Postman, 1985; Meyerowitz, 1985; Hanson, 1985; Bennett,

1986). This view would lead to the expectation of generally lower levels of knowledge and the lack of a systematic structure to what people know about politics. Were this true, we would expect to find few significant correlations among the specific facts people know. But even at the level of correlations between individual knowledge items, substantial structure is evident. For example, the median inter-item correlation among forty-three independent measures of factual knowledge included on the 1989 Survey of Political Knowledge, though small (.17), is both substantively and statistically significant.

7. The schema concept has found widespread use in political science during the past decade, but it has also been criticized as providing few new insights—"old wine in new bottles," according to one critic. For a lively exchange on this issue, see the symposium in the *American Political Science Review*: an attack by Kuklinski, Luskin, and Bolland, and replies by Lodge and McGraw, Conover and Feldman, and Miller (all 1991).

8. At the individual level, well-organized but idiosyncratic schemata, as well as strong relations among schemata, could exist. Idiosyncratic belief systems have received serious treatment from a number of political scientists (see, e.g., Lane, 1962; Dawson, 1979; Hochschild, 1981). But unless an adequate number of individuals displayed the same pattern, this structure of political knowledge would not be evident in the types of statistical procedures used in this chapter (see Brown and Taylor, 1973).

9. Our sample size of 610 limited the LISREL analysis to eighteen variables and prevented us from including all of our items in a single model. We were forced to use a two-step process. We first used LISREL to examine the interrelations among items within the three domains of knowledge discussed above. Knowledge about the substance of politics (i.e., issues) provides the strongest theoretical expectations for multidimensionality because it seems most likely to be driven by motivations that would vary among different types of citizens. Despite the plausibility of this argument, this type of political knowledge is well summarized by a unidimensional model. Distinguishing knowledge of domestic politics from knowledge of foreign affairs produced almost no improvement in the fit of the model, and the extremely high correlation between the two factors (.96) further discounts the utility of this distinction. With two exceptions, analyses of rules of the game and people and players showed that subdividing the data into theoretically plausible models with additional factors failed to improve (and in most cases were worse than) the models presented in the text. The two exceptions were that gender-related rights (e.g., knowledge that women were not always allowed to vote) showed some distinctiveness from knowledge of other rules, and partisan knowledge (e.g., knowing which party controlled the House) showed some distinctiveness from knowledge of public figures. Although in both cases the improvement in the models was small, where appropriate we drew on this distinction in subsequent analysis. We then chose six items from each of the three domains (taking into account the possible subdomains of gender and partisanship). These items were selected based on the size of their epistemic correlations, which, when squared, indicate item reliability (Joreskog and Sorbom, 1988).

10. Normally, interfactor loadings of greater than .9 are considered evidence of insignificant differences across factors, although Hayduk (1987) argues that such decisions should be made on a case-by-case basis and should be informed by theoretical expectations.

11. The people-and-parties scale is a combination of the items included in

the public-leaders scale with those items from the party-knowledge scale that include references to individual public figures (for example, identifying the party affiliation of Richard Nixon).

12. There is an ongoing debate in the literature on the use of standardized betas and r^2 statistics in regression analyses (King, 1986, 1991; Luskin, 1991; Bennett and Bennett, 1991). For most of the comparisons across scales, we refer to the betas; however, both *b*s and betas are reported in table 4.1.

13. Curiously, however, newspaper reading was not significantly associated with knowledge of substantive issues.

14. The relation between age and political knowledge is further clarified by more detailed analysis. Age is significantly associated with knowledge of political processes (beta = .14), but not with knowledge of political rights, a finding consistent with a shifting emphasis in what aspects of the rules of the game are emphasized in the schools (Janowitz, 1983). And, consistent with our argument that associations with demographic variables reflect differences in interest not captured by our broad measures of motivation, age is positively associated with knowledge of domestic affairs (.13), but not with knowledge of foreign affairs. Finally, age is strongly associated with knowledge of twentieth-century political history (.46). This finding is hardly surprising, given that for older citizens, such information is often learned not only through schools, but also as part of their longer surveillance of politics.

15. Given that a LISREL analysis with only 345 cases (the size of the pilot sample) should not exceed thirteen variables, we first ran separate analyses for each of the three issue areas. For both racial information and foreign affairs, a unidimensional model proved the best summary of the data, producing coefficients of determination (CDs) of .89 and .91, respectively, chi-square ratios of 1.2 in both cases, and adjusted goodness of fit indexes (AGFIs) of .99 and .98. In addition, epistemic correlations for these two domains ranged from .53 to .86 and averaged .75 for racial issues and .63 for foreign affairs. Knowledge of economic issues produced a satisfactory one-dimensional model (CD = .86; chi-square ratio = 3.6; and AGFI = .95). But a two-dimensional model distinguishing national political economy (inflation rate, unemployment rate, growth in the national deficit, and identification of Paul Volcker) from Wall Street politics (defining the Dow Jones index and characterizing the partisan leanings of stockbrokers and corporate executives) did somewhat better (CD = .96; chi-square ratio = 1.3; AGFI = .98). In addition, the average epistemic correlation increases from .67 to .74, and the interfactor correlation is .64. We then chose the four best indicators of each of these three issue areas (the same four economic items had the highest reliabilities regardless of which of the models was used). These twelve items were used in a LISREL analysis.

16. Betas for race on the foreign affairs and general knowledge scales were both .09, with the former significant at the .06 level and the latter at .05. The beta for economic knowledge was .16 ($p < .001$). The beta for race-specific knowledge, though not significant, was negative (–.05), indicating greater knowledge among blacks. These findings paralleled those reported by both Iyengar (1986) and Zaller (1986) in their analyses of these data.

17. This is not, of course, to suggest that pluralism need be rejected as the way organized interests do or should vie for influence in the political arena. Consistent with many critiques of this model of democracy, however, it does suggest that certain segments of the population lack the resources (in this case, the resource of political knowledge) to effectively organize their interests.

18. Actual scores ranged from 3 to 43. Because of the number of questions

asked, the top and bottom tenths of the scale are each actually 11.5 percent of the scale, and the remaining eight tenths are each 9.6 percent of the scale.

19. The one exception was race, where the knowledge gap was less dramatic than in the 1989 survey (approximately three-quarters of blacks scored below the median for whites). We attribute the smaller knowledge gap to the predominance of party-oriented questions in the 1988 survey.

20. Although likes and dislikes are not direct measures of knowledge, research by Kessel (1988) and Delli Carpini and Keeter (1993) demonstrates that they function well as surrogate measures. For a further discussion, see Appendix 2.

21. The analysis of the structure of knowledge earlier in this chapter suggested that partisan knowledge was more sensitive to age differences than such other domains as knowledge of institutions and processes. Thus, the patterns reported above are probably more applicable to certain kinds of knowledge than to others.

22. The additional eight questions were: knowing the first ten amendments to the Constitution are called the Bill of Rights; naming a right mentioned in the Fifth Amendment; saying what a presidential veto is; knowing which party controls the House; knowing the length of a president's term; naming both U.S. senators; naming one's U.S. representative; and naming the vice president.

23. The five questions were: knowing the length of a president's term; naming one's U.S. representative; naming the vice president; knowing which party controlled the House of Representatives; and knowing which party controlled the Senate. These five were also used in the age comparisons discussed in the next paragraph. We were not able to make comparisons based on income with the Gallup data.

24. The exception was the gender-issues scale in the 1989 Survey of Political Knowledge.

CHAPTER 5. EXPLAINING POLITICAL KNOWLEDGE

1. Learning about politics is a dynamic process. An ideal approach to explaining political knowledge would entail following samples of individuals over a long period and observing what and how they learned about politics. In practice, this approach has unavoidable limitations. The best example of such a study is the Jennings-Niemi panel study of adolescents and their parents, which began in 1965 (Jennings and Niemi, 1974; 1981). This project has yielded many important insights about the development of political attitudes and orientations. Yet significant differences in political knowledge levels were already apparent among the adolescent sample when it was first interviewed, and they have persisted over time. In addition, the scope of knowledge questions used in the study was necessarily narrow, and most of the college-bound students could correctly answer five or six of the six items before they entered college.

2. This focus on individual-level variables may underestimate the importance of factors not easily captured in surveys of individual citizens—in particular, variations in the information and political environments. We shall address this later in the chapter.

3. We used the 1988 and 1992 National Election Studies, along with the 1989 Survey of Political Knowledge, for the statistical analyses. Most—though not all—of the relevant variables were measured in each of the surveys. For the sake of economy, we do not always report the findings from all three sets of analyses, but where differences were found, we address them in the text.

4. Our model implies that causation runs only one way—an assumption we know to be false but make for convenience in estimating the parameters. A model that fully captured the interactive and reciprocal nature of the relations would be extremely complex. Nonrecursive methods (i.e., those that allow factors to affect each other simultaneously) are more satisfying theoretically but require unrealistic assumptions in order to identify the model (Smith, 1989: 191–96). We choose instead, as Smith did, to use a simple recursive model. We recognize that some bias in our results is inevitable as a consequence of this decision. An alternative approach using a nonrecursive model is employed by Luskin (1990).

One concession to the fact that causation runs in both directions is that we omit participation variables (e.g., voting) from our model, believing them to be more dependent upon knowledge than vice versa. See Bennett (1994) for a somewhat similar approach.

5. The composite variables are used to simplify the presentation, but they are defensible as measures of broader concepts using multiple indicators. Indeed, the behavioral composite was created using factor scores from a principal components factor analysis of the indicators. This factor analysis suggested that the indicators were highly enough intercorrelated to justify treating the cluster as a single variable.

6. Of course, it is hard to see how gender could directly affect knowledge. It should be possible to identify the mechanism by which this relation operates, but as the discussion below indicates, this search is complicated.

7. We tested a large array of other theoretically relevant variables in these models. These other variables did not achieve statistical significance or contribute to the overall explained variance of the model and thus were not included in the version presented here.

8. The fact that much of the statistical relation between race and knowledge can be explained by controlling for income and other intervening variables does not diminish the political significance of the fact that blacks as a group know less than nonblacks.

9. Although the motivation to attend to the media belongs under the rubric of "interest and engagement," the consequences of actual use of media depend not only on the individual but on what information is available and how it is presented.

Krassa (1990) offers another intriguing finding that bears on motivation. Using NES data combined with county-level voting results, he found that citizens who live in a setting where most other residents have political attitudes unlike theirs are apt to be more knowledgeable than those who live in politically homogeneous environments. Although Krassa is unable to pinpoint the mechanism by which this occurs, political minorities evidently make a greater effort to obtain political information than they would if they lived in a more hospitable setting.

10. Those who said they enjoyed politics were more knowledgeable (mean knowledge score = 3.47, compared with 3.18 for those who considered following politics an obligation), but the difference was not statistically significant.

The tendency for some survey respondents to overreport their interest in politics contributes to uncertainty about the relation between knowledge, interest, and engagement. This phenomenon is well documented in the chronic overreporting of voter turnout, wherein approximately 10–15 percent of respondents claim to have voted when they have not. How this response error affects the correlation between knowledge and engagement is unclear. Although it is plausible that the unknowledgeable will exaggerate their level of interest and engagement, the data on voting indicate that the truth may be more complicated. With voting, better-informed individuals are a little more likely than others to say they voted when they did not. Such behavior is likely to strengthen inappropriately the correlations between measures of engagement and levels of knowledge.

11. In contrast, enthusiasm about the candidates did not directly influence learning, although it did affect involvement in the campaign.

12. Both reported television viewing and newspaper use, however, were insignificant predictors of knowledge in our 1989 Survey of Political Knowledge, once other factors (including other forms of media use) were controlled for.

13. One possible explanation is that survey measures of attention to the news media fail to capture variation in the extent of true cognitive engagement with the media. On one of our state surveys, we asked respondents what else—if anything—they usually did while watching television news or reading the newspaper. Many respondents said they were regularly distracted by cooking, eating, cleaning, or child care. For a discussion of these data, see Kennamer, 1992.

14. The relative weakness of most survey measures of media use is undoubtedly partially responsible for these low correlations. On this topic see Zaller, 1995.

15. The recall assessed by Price and Zaller is somewhat different from the type of political knowledge our surveys measure. Yet one might reasonably conclude that recall of news stories is a precursor to the embedding of factual information about the issue in long-term memory.

16. Luskin found that variations in attention to the media may be inconsequential in comparison with variations in cognitive skill and political interest. He suggests that skilled and interested citizens can learn much from even a brief exposure to the news, whereas less skilled and interested citizens can spend a great deal of time with the media and learn very little (1990). We tested a variety of interaction terms (e.g., media use with education) but were unable to confirm his findings.

17. These were the twenty-five most reliable and valid questions, based on an item analysis. See Appendix 2 for details about the item analysis.

18. That is, the partial correlation between knowledge and education, controlling for age, is even higher than the zero-order correlation.

19. Although it is true that earlier research by Jennings, Langton, and Niemi concluded that civics instruction did not boost knowledge levels of white students, they found evidence of a measurable effect on black students (1974: 194–96).

20. Recent research in Sweden and Great Britain points to the potential for civics education to matter. Denver and Hands (1990) found that courses in politics had substantial positive effects on the political knowledge levels of secondary school pupils in English schools. And scholars studying a panel of Swedish adolescents concluded that the social studies curriculum does have an impact on political knowledge among adolescents (Westholm, Lindquist, and Niemi, 1990: 199). Their large study was especially valuable in that it permitted the disentangling of selection effects from the direct effects of schooling. Students high in prior civics knowledge were much more likely than others to choose a course of study that included a large social studies component. The authors noted, however, that students exposed to social studies instruction learned a great deal from it and that the impact was actually greater on those who started out knowing less. They conclude that the potential equalizing effects of a high school social studies curriculum are substantial (200–201).

As discussed in chapter 3, there is a marked degree of pessimism about and dissatisfaction with the performance of the schools in several germane areas, including the teaching of history and politically relevant knowledge (Ravitch and Finn, 1987; Hirsch, 1988). The Ravitch and Finn data have been challenged by one critic who questioned their relevance for a comparison of the schools' performance today with those of the past. In fact, where comparisons with older tests are possible, it appears that "students of the 1980s are not demonstrably different from their parents' or grandparents' generation in terms of their knowledge of American history" (Whittington, 1991: 776).

21. On the importance of shared contextual, factual knowledge of this nature, see Hirsch (1988).

22. Gould also provides an enlightening presentation of the history of hereditarian arguments and their political consequences. See his book *The Mismeasure of Man* (1981).

23. As evidence of the validity of the NES intelligence measure, Luskin notes that in other surveys, interviewer ratings of intelligence were correlated with vocabulary tests of cognitive ability (themselves an imperfect measure of intelligence), and that the NES intelligence measure is correlated with education at about the same level as education is correlated in other studies with more direct measures of intelligence (Luskin, 1990: 341–42, 347–50).

24. It is also possible that differences in the ratings of men and women result from more deep-seated stereotypes, although we have no evidence to support this contention.

25. They employed two standardized tests from the Educational Testing Service's Factor Referenced Cognitive Inventory: the Advanced Vocabulary Test, part 1, and the Inference Test, part I (Neuman, Just, and Crigler, 1992: 137–38).

26. See Finkel, Guterbock, and Borg (1991) for an example of this technique.

27. One could argue that in the past a meritocratic selection process for college was impeded by the significant financial obstacles facing talented students of modest financial means. Dull but affluent students were much more likely to find their way into college. Now both the bright and the dull have greater opportunities to attend. This may mean that the selectivity of higher education in the past—with respect to individuals of high ability—was actually not as great as generally assumed; regardless, it is certainly no more selective today.

28. The schools may bear some responsibility in this trend. Morris Janowitz argues that the schools have been doing a poorer job of instilling a sense of civic duty in students since 1945 (1983).

29. Depending on the type of political knowledge, the relation between age and knowledge is slightly curvilinear. But statistical corrections for this phenomenon, such as those suggested by Bennett (1990) using polynomial terms, do not improve the overall performance of models that include age. In the interest of simplicity we use age in years as reported by the respondents.

30. The betas for the 1989 data are nearly identical: –.17 for structural variables and +.18 for the behavioral variables.

31. The net effect of age on knowledge shown in table 5.1 is, in fact, a slight underestimate of its total effect. If the statistical analysis functions properly, the regression coefficient for age should reflect age's influence, controlling for all other variables. The suppressor effects of education are removed, but so, too, are the indirect but positive effects of age on knowledge. Age boosts interest in politics, which, as we have seen, boosts knowledge. In figure 5.1, age has a negative effect on the structural variables (chiefly education) but a positive effect on the attitudinal ones (although the path is smaller than .10 and is not shown in the figure).

Adding the direct and indirect paths from age to knowledge yields a total effect slightly larger than the net effect.

32. We suspect that the difference between the findings across the two surveys results from the wider range of factual items included in the 1989 survey, from the large number of partisan-oriented items found in the 1988 survey, and from having fewer measures of structural circumstances in the 1989 survey.

33. See Sapiro, 1983; Jennings and Niemi, 1981.

34. Jennings (1993) found a similar effect of children on the mother's knowledge, but unlike our results his analysis showed that fathers were affected as well.

35. Truly capturing structural and situational differences through surveys is obviously a difficult task. For example, women and men—even those in similar structural situations—often do different things with their time, and much of the difference results from the sexual division of labor. Our 1991 Virginia survey on reading and viewing habits found that a similar proportion of women and men reported engaging in other activities while watching television news or reading the newspaper. *What* they were doing was highly gender specific, however: 32 percent of women were cooking, cleaning, or caring for children while watching television news, compared with only 12 percent of men (who were more likely to be eating or reading). Such differences presumably have consequences for the comparative level of political engagement of women and men.

36. Doris Graber observed substantial gender differences in her subjects' reported childhood socialization to politics, with men able to recall far more specific politically relevant incidents than were women (Graber, 1988, 134; for a related argument and evidence see Rapoport, 1982; 1985; also see Jennings and Niemi, 1981; Orum et al., 1974).

The legacy is not simply a matter of women's socialization, of course. Ample evidence exists that women continue to confront resistance from men when they take part in politics (e.g., Schumaker and Burns, 1988). Such experiences also have socializing effects by lowering one's sense of efficacy.

37. We found similar patterns in other questions about abortion that were not directly tied to electoral politics in the 1989 Survey of Political Knowledge and in statewide Virginia surveys.

38. The most extensive of our local surveys was conducted in 1991 with 804 residents of the city of Richmond. This survey had eight knowledge items, four on national and four on local politics. The local items included explaining how the city council and the mayor are selected and naming the city manager and the superintendent of schools. Another Richmond city survey conducted in 1990 also included the item on how the mayor is selected, asked who was the incumbent, and asked about exposure to news of a dispute over the placement of a monument to civil rights leaders. A survey of suburban Chesterfield County (in the Richmond metropolitan area) had four national knowledge items and four local items. The local items were naming the local U.S. representative and county school superintendent, stating whether the county imposes an environmental impact fee on developers, and stating which party had a majority on the county Board of Supervisors. In addition to these local surveys, the 1987 General Social Survey conducted by the National Opinion Research Center at the University of Chicago asked respondents to name the head of their local school system, their U.S. representative, and their governor.

39. Some of this variation is captured by personal characteristics such as employment or income, but changes in the political Zeitgeist over time—the

occurrence of such events as the Watergate affair or a particularly important election—cannot be.

40. While affording the opportunity for us to conduct the "natural experiment" described below, the relative lack of coverage of state politics is a significant shortcoming in terms of the opportunity of the American public to learn about this important arena of politics. State government has been called the "hidden layer of government, the stepchild of American politics and the soft underbelly of journalism" (Wolfson, 1985: 137). By any textbook definition of newsworthiness, state government ought to be very newsworthy. Compared with the federal government, state governments have grown more dramatically in the past thirty years and have become responsible for a vast range of activities with palpable consequences for citizens.

41. The content analysis covered four five-day periods during 1990: two periods selected at random during the 1990 General Assembly session (January 21–25, February 7–11), one selected at random in May (May 13–17), and another selected at random in July (July 9–13, before the summer survey). We coded every appearance of a news story, photograph, editorial, opinion essay, or letter to the editor that dealt with any aspect of state government and politics. For each item we coded the date, placement, and major topics covered. See Delli Carpini, Keeter, and Kennamer (1994) for details.

Although we did not analyze the content of television news, structural differences between the Richmond and Washington markets make clear that Virginia state news will receive far greater attention in the Richmond market than in northern Virginia.

42. We also conducted the analyses without controlling for national political knowledge. The results are very similar to those reported below, and the substantive conclusions we draw would be unchanged.

43. In each analysis, the independent variables included the respondent's tenure in Virginia since age eighteen (coded 1 = 0–5 years, 2 = 6–10 years, 3 = more than 10 years), educational level (coded 1 = no high school diploma, 2 = high school diploma, 3 = some college, 4 = college grad, 5 = post-graduate), knowledge of national politics (a six-item additive index in the winter survey coded 0–6, and a three-item index in the summer survey coded 0–3), reported attention to politics (a standard item coded 1 = pays attention hardly ever, 2 = only now and then, 3 = sometimes, 4 = most of the time), gender, and family income. Region of residence was coded as separate dummy variables for Richmond and northern Virginia, with the rest of the state as the baseline. Full results from the logistic regression models are not shown in order to conserve space.

For purposes of estimating a probability, the typical Virginia resident was defined as a female with some college experience who has been a Virginia resident at least ten years, follows politics some of the time, has a family income between $35,000 and $50,000, and scored 3 on our national knowledge scale in the winter survey. The death penalty item was taken from a different survey; variables in the model were identical with the exception of the national knowledge index, which included only two items.

44. It is possible, of course, that many residents of northern Virginia have little or no identification with the state, regarding themselves as residents of the Washington area. Such a phenomenon, if widespread, could be a consequence of the low level of media attention to state political news. We question the assumption that residents of northern Virginia would be measurably less interested in state

politics than any other in-migrant who shares a similar length of residence. Indeed, there is reason to believe just the opposite: because many people move to the Washington area to work in government and related industries, it is reasonable to assume that the receptivity of northern Virginia residents to political information of any type is greater than average for the state.

A similar concern might be raised for residents of the Richmond area: perhaps they are more knowledgeable about state politics because of their direct connection with state government. But state government in Richmond is a relatively small part of the local economy of the Richmond metropolitan area. State employees in the area constitute approximately 39,000 out of a total employment of 455,000 (about 9 percent—compared with a statewide average of 4.3 percent—although the number of households affected would be higher). Furthermore, most state employees are in distinctly nonpolitical jobs that are unrelated to policy making.

45. Undoubtedly the impact of contact would be greater for knowledge about specific facts that are directly relevant to the elections in which the contact occurred.

46. Blacks, however, report being contacted to register at a slightly greater rate than nonblacks, and they are only slightly less likely to be contacted in an attempt to influence their vote.

47. For example, the headline of a newspaper opinion column discussing one of our surveys read "People Will Learn about Politics Only If They Care" (Gottleib, 1989: 10).

48. Much interesting work on the influence of political context has been done. For an overview, see Huckfeldt and Sprague, 1993.

49. Many would argue that recognizing the name of the chief justice is a highly obscure piece of trivia. We would agree that knowing this is less important than knowing the ideological direction of recent Court appointments or trends in the Court's recent decisions in key areas of the law. But name recognition is a likely indicator of more substantive knowledge. Further, the public fascination with the people who occupy important political positions would suggest that lack of knowledge about the chief justice is not a result of its perceived irrelevance but the lack of easy availability of such information in an appropriate context.

CHAPTER 6. THE CONSEQUENCES OF POLITICAL KNOWLEDGE AND IGNORANCE

1. There is little evidence regarding the consequences of intolerant attitudes. The expression of intolerant opinions in a survey does not prove that citizens with such attitudes would, in fact, behave intolerantly. There is ample evidence, however, that people do sometimes act in an intolerant fashion; consider the nation's experiences during the 1950s, the periodic confrontations between blacks and Hasidic Jews in New York City, the battle over fishing rights between Vietnamese immigrants and white residents in several Texas coastal communities, the success of anti-gay referenda in states like Colorado, and, most recently, the efforts by some residents of a rural Mississippi community to block a lesbian couple from establishing a women's retreat on their property.

2. Our choice of measures reflects concerns raised by Sullivan and his colleagues (1982). As they demonstrated, studies of tolerance that compare the findings of the 1950s with those of recent years are potentially flawed because feelings about the particular groups referred to in the 1950s surveys—in particular, communists—have moderated, leading to a possibly erroneous conclusion that toler-

ance has increased. Accordingly, a more valid measure of tolerance would ask citizens about their willingness to extend civil liberties to groups they disliked, without assuming what those groups were. Using this content controlled measure, Sullivan and his colleagues demonstrated that the apparent increases in the public's tolerance since the 1950s may have been illusory.

To ease the administration of the survey, which was conducted by telephone, we did not present respondents with an extensive list of groups from which to choose (as Sullivan et al. had done). The effect of this modification is apt to be relatively minor. The goal of the method is to ensure that the respondent is reacting to a truly disliked group. In the 1978 National Opinion Research Center study, 61 percent of respondents chose one of the three groups we listed. It is reasonable to assume, based on the other groups chosen (e.g., Symbionese Liberation Army, Black Panthers, pro-abortionists, etc.) that most respondents in our survey actually disliked at least one of the groups we offered, even if their least-liked group was not among the trio.

3. They were also asked the public school question about one of the groups they did not choose. Response options for these items included "strongly agree," "agree," "disagree," and "strongly disagree."

4. These results are similar to those from the 1978 National Opinion Research Center study.

5. We recognize that a simple index such as this one provides only a rough measure of the concept of tolerance. We are certainly not justified in labeling respondents as "intolerant" based, for example, on their response that they are unwilling to let a member of the Ku Klux Klan teach in the public schools. An extensive discussion of issues in the measurement of political tolerance can be found in Sniderman, Brody, and Tetlock (1991: chap. 7).

6. Other influences include such personality characteristics as dogmatism and self-esteem (Sullivan, Piereson, and Marcus, 1982; McClosky and Brill, 1983), religiosity (McClosky and Brill, 1983), political involvement (Stouffer, 1955), and the perceived threat of target groups (Sullivan, Piereson, and Marcus, 1982).

7. The questions included knowledge of Chief Justice Rehnquist's ideology, the name of the first ten amendments, whether a communist can run for president, who appoints Supreme Court justices, and what branch of government has the power to declare laws unconstitutional. These items had the strongest loadings on the first rotated factor of a principal components factor analysis of ten variables related to civil liberties. We are not arguing that knowledge of these specific facts increases political tolerance; rather, the scale serves as an indicator of a broader understanding of civil rights and liberties and of the institutions designed to protect and adjudicate them.

8. Engagement was a two-item index (following and discussing politics); ideology was a two-item index, including self-placement on the liberal-conservative scale and support for or opposition to a larger national government.

9. This is based on the validated vote from the 1988 NES survey.

10. Neuman's analysis is based on a broader concept—sophistication—which includes knowledge as one of its components. He notes, however, that of the three component parts of sophistication, knowledge's relation with turnout is the strongest.

11. This was determined through a logistic regression analysis. The strong connection between knowledge and caring about the election, however, can be seen in the simple bivariate relation. Ninety percent of the best-informed quartile of respondents said they cared a great deal about the election, compared with only 53 percent of the least-informed quartile.

It is certainly plausible that concern about the outcome of the election could lead a voter to gather information about the candidates, and if so, the causal direction of the relation between concern and knowledge would be reversed. For the logistic regression analysis described here, however, we used a measure of political knowledge that included no variables directly relevant to the 1992 election. Thus it is highly unlikely that this knowledge was acquired as a result of the voter's concern about the outcome of the election.

12. We conducted this analysis with both the 1988 National Election Study and our 1989 Survey of Political Knowledge. In the NES study we employed the validated vote variable; in the 1989 study reported vote was used. Not all of the independent variables were available in the 1989 Survey of Political Knowledge, but the models were made as similar as possible.

See Wolfinger and Rosenstone, *Who Votes?* (1980) for a discussion of the determinants of voter turnout.

13. The overall model is a reasonably good one, with a pseudo-r^2 of 40 percent and acceptable goodness-of-fit statistics. The model correctly predicts 75 percent of the cases, compared with a baseline of 58 percent. (The *baseline* is the percentage of responses in the modal category. It is the level of accuracy one would achieve simply by predicting the mode, in the absence of any other information. The performance of logistic regression models is often judged by how much they improve predictions over the baseline.)

14. Although it is important to demonstrate that knowledge has identifiable, independent effects on participation, there remains something artificial in the use of traditional statistical techniques that control for confounding variables. We use such controls in this and subsequent analyses, but these tests should be viewed as conservative estimates of the full impact of political knowledge.

15. Although the terms *attitude* and *opinion* tend to be used interchangeably in the public opinion literature, we will try to maintain a distinction in our discussion. But as Price (1992, 46–49) notes in his review, most scholars (including L. L. Thurstone, who is credited with first making the distinction) have had difficulty remaining consistent in their usage of the terms.

16. Zaller has described "considerations" as "any reason that might induce an individual to decide a political issue one way or the other" (Zaller, 1992: 40). These are analogous in many respects to "beliefs" as defined earlier.

17. Neuman (1986: 57–61) argues that the relation between knowledge and opinionation is of little significance, given the paltry amount of variability in opinion holding found in the typical survey. He writes: "80 percent of the people will voice an opinion 80 percent of the time." As a practical matter, we agree with Neuman. But we think the variability that is observed—however small—is an indicator of the citizens' underlying propensity to develop meaningful attitudes and not simply a direct manifestation of that propensity. Accordingly, the finding that knowledge is its strongest correlate is important. Some of the opinions expressed in surveys are "considered opinions," while others are "doorstep opinions" that might not be offered if the dynamics and perceived expectations of the survey process were different. Declining to offer opinions on one or more items may be a marker for a more significant absence of considered opinions. The greater reluctance of the well informed to offer opinions on obscure or nonexistent issues, however, also suggests that the degree of opinionation they exhibit in surveys is a more valid indicator of their true level than is the case for the less informed.

18. Our measure was an index of nine items chosen to maximize the variability of the index.

19. As one might expect, the pattern is even stronger when domain-specific knowledge is considered. For example, Faulkenberry and Mason (1978) found that substantive knowledge about wind power was the most potent predictor of opinionation about the use of wind power for the generation of electricity.

20. There is nothing wrong with changing one's mind, of course. But the pattern of response instability found in many panel surveys does not appear to be a result of genuine attitude change.

21. The 1984 NES conducted preelection and postelection surveys of the same individuals, with most pairs of interviews separated by one to three months. The 1991 pilot study involved interviews during the summer of 1991 with respondents from the 1990 postelection survey; the 1992 survey also reinterviewed some of the 1990 respondents. Except for the 1990–92 panel, most of these pairs of interviews were conducted within six to nine months of each other.

22. These categories are the two polar directions—i.e., codes 1, 2, 3 and 5, 6, 7—and the middle position.

23. Of course, the consequences of having an unstable opinion or having no opinion are quite similar.

24. Our results are consistent with those of Zaller, who performed a similar analysis with the 1974–76 waves of the NES major panel study in the 1970s (1990; also see Zaller, 1986, for his work with the 1984–85 NES pilot study). He concluded that "information is approximately 3.6 times more important than its nearest competitor" (Zaller, 1990: 135).

The loss of respondents from one wave of a panel study to the next may also weaken the apparent relation between knowledge and attitude stability. Attrition is greater among less interested and less knowledgeable respondents. For example, 19 percent of respondents in the initial interview of the 1984 NES survey who were rated below average on information were not reinterviewed, compared with only 8 percent among those rated above average. If the dropouts are also less likely to manifest stable attitudes than those who remain in the sample, the resulting analysis may understate the extent of variability in attitude stability and, hence, the potential strength of the correlation with political knowledge. See Rapoport (1979) and Schuman and Presser (1981: 337–40) for further discussion of this issue. Brehm's (1993) treatment of nonresponse in surveys is also highly relevant to this issue.

25. Such political observers as Thomas Byrne Edsall and Mary D. Edsall have argued that race has been the preeminent political issue in the United States during the past thirty years, underlying and suffusing many other issues (1991; for a dissenting view, see Hagen, 1993).

According to Sniderman and his colleagues (1991: chaps. 4 and 5), attitudes toward blacks constitute an important heuristic for some whites in generating their political views toward government policies. Since we might expect attitudes about blacks to be highly stable, political attitudes derived from them should be relatively more stable than other attitudes—exactly the pattern seen here.

26. This conclusion is based on logistic regression analyses of the three items in the 1984 NES survey (the dependent variable was 1 = stable, 0 = not stable). We also used ordinary least squares regression on an additive index of stability combining the three items. In all analyses, the knowledge variable dwarfed the other predictor variables.

27. One reason our results differ from Neuman's (1986: 61–64) is that our underlying spatial model is different from his. We assume that such survey questions as the seven-point issue scales are tapping respondents' preferences regarding the *direction* in which policy should go, rather than a preferred policy *position* along a hypothetical continuum. Rabinowitz and MacDonald (1989) have demonstrated that a *directional model* is much more consistent with respondent voting behavior than the more traditional *positional model*. Using the positional model, Neuman considered an opinion as unstable if it varied by more than one scale point across waves. Our standard considers an opinion as unstable if the direction changes, for example, if a respondent moves from the favorable side of the scale to the unfavorable side (or to neutral).

28. Zaller's research also demonstrates the importance of the information environment to democratic discourse. Absent a range of elite opinions regarding an emerging issue, politically knowledgeable citizens, because they are most likely to be exposed to media messages, can be—at least temporarily—more susceptible to manipulation than less informed, interested citizens. Under these conditions Edelman's argument regarding the value of political indifference is most compelling (see chap. 1).

29. Over the years, a great deal of scholarly attention has been paid to the question of attitude consistency or constraint. See, e.g, Luttbeg, 1968; Nie, Verba, and Petrocik, 1979; Judd and Milburn, 1980; Converse, 1980; Hurwitz and Peffley, 1985; Bardes and Oldendick, 1990.

30. Of course there are important exceptions, and it depends on how general one wishes to make the argument. As Sniderman and his colleagues argue, "political awareness and sophistication . . . favor constraint selectively." Better-informed citizens may bring a wider range of considerations (or values) to bear on a given issue and thus find themselves cross-pressured; assuming that the considerations do not all point to the same outcome, the decision is likely to be inconsistent with some underlying value or predisposition (Sniderman, Brody, and Tetlock, 1991, 5–6).

31. Converse's original article on belief systems (1964) demonstrated large differences in consistency, but his comparison was between mass and elite samples, not better- and lesser-informed citizens among the general public. Neuman's analysis of five NES surveys and the 1948 Elmira data found average correlations between opinion items that were not much higher for the most sophisticated than for the least-sophisticated thirds of the samples (1986: 64–67). Nie, Verba, and Petrocik found differences in constraint between the politically interested and the uninterested, but the size of the differences varied considerably across elections (1979: 154). Zaller's analysis of the 1985 NES pilot study (and the 1984 study linked to it) found reasonably large—though not dramatic—differences in consistency between the best- and least-informed respondents (1986: 10–11). McClosky and Zaller report substantially higher levels of consistency in attitudes toward capitalism among the most sophisticated citizens compared with the least sophisticated (1984: 250–51).

32. Stimson's first factor explained 39 percent of the common variance. His test was a fairly difficult one because he included social and international issues along with economic ones. It is thus quite interesting that a single dimension did so well in capturing the variability among the high-knowledge group.

33. We also conducted an analysis with these eight variables plus four that dealt with foreign and military policy. We observed the same general pattern of increasing simplicity with higher knowledge, except that two factors were ex-

tracted for the top knowledge quartile (five factors were extracted for the bottom quartile, four for the second quartile, and three for the third). After the solution was rotated, the two factors in the top quartile were clearly interpretable as foreign and domestic issues. Before rotation, however, the foreign items loaded reasonably well on the first principal component, constituting the second, sixth, ninth, and eleventh ranking items in terms of their correlation with the first factor.

We also conducted the analysis with education held constant. Although the sample size limits the precision of this analysis, the results showed the same pattern of increasingly simplicity in the structure of knowledge as information levels rose.

34. For a description of the specific items used in these analyses and details of the scale construction, see Appendix 5.

35. See Bartels (1994) for a similar analysis of voting behavior. Our list of demographic and personal variables is quite similar to his.

36. Because the estimates are derived from a linear model, it is necessary to compute only the endpoints; all intermediate points will fall on a straight line connecting the two endpoints. An examination of the residuals suggests that the simplifying assumption of linearity is generally supported by the actual relations.

37. The financial problems index included the following: put off buying things that were needed; put off needed medical or dental treatment; had to borrow to make ends meet; dip into savings to make ends meet; in order to make ends meet, respondent looked for a job, second job, or worked more hours at present job; unable to save money this year; fallen behind in rent or mortgage payments; any family member received food stamps; any family member received Medicaid; any family member received unemployment compensation; any family member received Aid to Families with Dependent Children (AFDC). One point was added to the index for each type of problem reported. Neither of the standard measures of class—family income or self-identification—adequately gauges the concept we are interested in.

38. We use the term *fully informed* to mean scoring 100 percent on the twenty-eight-point scale of political knowledge. This, of course, is not meant to imply that such citizens are fully informed in any absolute sense.

39. The point of this analysis is to demonstrate that a more informed citizenry can have collective opinions that differ systematically from those of the citizenry as currently constituted. For a variety of reasons, the statistical significance of this and other shifts we report is not easily interpreted. In all our examples, the shifts in opinion would be statistically significant by conventional t-tests, but the use of such tests is somewhat problematic. For a discussion of this issue, see Appendix 5.

40. More controversially, these differences have also been attributed to socialization and even biological differences between men and women that lead the latter to be more nurturing in their approach to domestic social issues (see Tolleson Rinehart, 1992: 1–17).

41. The debate over whether such programs create a dependency on welfare complicates this issue, although this belief is often based on more deep-seated attitudes regarding racial differences.

42. Tellingly, and further evidence that political knowledge can promote a broader notion of self-interest, among whites, experience with financial problems promotes greater support for assistance to blacks.

43. Of course we recognize that the Bible is not the basis of religious beliefs for citizens outside the Judeo-Christian tradition.

44. This promotion of greater tolerance for homosexuals and greater willingness to grant civil rights to them is similar to the one demonstrated earlier in this chapter on the issue of political tolerance.

45. We call this *instrumental rationality,* in that it is not dependent on the specific ends involved but merely refers to the ability to connect self-professed ends to appropriate means.

46. These graphs plot the estimated mean party identification based on regression analyses in which party identification was regressed on a set of independent variables that included the political knowledge scale, the domestic issue index, controls for a wide range of demographic variables, and interaction terms for political knowledge and the demographic variables. Adjusted r^2 for the regression was .32.

We recognize that party identification depends on many factors other than opinions on domestic issues. Nevertheless, the current partisan alignment in the United States continues to be based on domestic, scope-of-government issues of the sort tapped by the domestic-issue index. To the extent that partisanship can serve as an effective heuristic for the expression of group-related interests, we would argue that, in general, self-identified Democrats and Republicans ought to differ on these issues in predictable ways. Perhaps the best evidence for the reasonableness of this assumption is how strong, in fact, is the relation between these issues and party identification among the most knowledgeable quartile.

47. Presidential approval was regressed on knowledge, demographic variables, domestic issue opinions, and interaction terms for knowledge and the other predictors. Coefficients from this model were then used to estimate presidential approval for individuals in different knowledge groups across a range of domestic opinions. Adjusted r^2 for the regression was .22.

48. The importance of information in voting extends beyond general elections. For example, in primary elections, partisanship is not available as a guide. In addition to concerns with issues, voters may also consider a candidate's viability in the general election. For a discussion of how knowledge affects the judgments of presidential primary voters, see Brady and Ansolabehere (1989).

Information should also help participation beyond voting and outside the electoral arena. Because of the lack of data for examining other forms of political participation, however, our focus in this section will be on voting, the most prevalent mode of political participation for U.S. citizens. Even when data are available, the way knowledge strengthens the linkage between attitudes and the direction of other forms of participation is difficult to demonstrate, in part because citizens who make use of other modes of participation tend to be relatively high and somewhat homogeneous in political knowledge. Still, the connection with voting is visible, however faintly, with data on campaign contributions in the 1988 NES.

49. In spite of the enormous attention paid to voting behavior, relatively little research has focused on how citizens differ from each other in the process of making up their minds in elections. In the past, most models of voter behavior implicitly assumed that everyone decided how to vote in the same fashion, using more or less the same considerations. Students of voting behavior are increasingly concluding that these procrustean voting models are misleading and that realistic theories of voting must allow for the possibility that citizens differ in the criteria they employ in voting (Stimson, 1975; Knight, 1985; Rivers, 1988; Moon, 1990; Sniderman, Brody, and Tetlock, 1991).

Recent studies have demonstrated that political knowledge is a key variable in distinguishing how voters decide. For example, David Moon's analysis of the 1976 presidential election (1990) found low-information voters to be more heavily influenced by their party affiliations and by candidate personal characteristics, whereas those with an average level of information relied more heavily on perceptions of how the candidates would affect different groups in the society—heuristics that our earlier analysis of second-order opinions suggests are least valuable for the very citizens who are most dependent on them. The best-informed voters appeared to use a very wide range of information including the issue stances of the candidates. Sniderman and his colleagues, examining the same data with a different model, reached a similar conclusion about the greater role of policy considerations among better-educated voters (Sniderman, Brody, and Tetlock, 1991: 170–73). They also concluded that national economic conditions had a direct impact on the vote of the less educated, whereas the effect for the high-information voters was indirect. In effect, less educated voters looked at the economy, decided whether they liked it, and used that judgment in making a vote choice. Better-educated voters used the economy as one among many criteria for rating the incumbent party's performance, which then directly affected the vote.

Similarly, Thomas R. Palfrey's and Keith T. Poole's (1987) analysis of the 1980 election found that an issue-based model produced much more accurate forecasts of the vote among the better informed than among the less informed, suggesting that issues were a more important criterion for the knowledgeable voter. And Neuman's examination of election data from 1948 to 1980 found, for each election, that correlations between issue-distance measures and the vote increased as political sophistication increased (1986: 110; see also Erikson, Luttbeg, and Tedin, 1991: 246–49). We draw on all these studies to fashion a straightforward test of how knowledge affects voting.

50. Although there are many different conceptions of issue voting in the scholarly literature, all have in common the notion that issue voting requires citizens to choose candidates primarily on the basis of issues, rather than on candidate personal qualities, general dissatisfaction with the status quo, or idiosyncratic factors. An incomplete but representative sampling of major issue-voting studies would include the following: Nie, Verba, and Petrocik, 1979; Page and Brody, 1972; Repass, 1971; Kessel, 1988; Pomper, 1975; Rabinowitz and MacDonald, 1989; Asher, 1992.

51. In addition, although we agree that presidential character, experience, and other personal qualities are important and legitimately can affect the vote of a conscientious citizen, these are certainly criteria where the quality of judgments can benefit from greater information just as much as issue voting can. The best guide to a candidate's character may be his or her past actions rather than, for example, his or her television persona (Keeter, 1987). The facts about a candidate's past constitute political information of the same type and available through much the same channels as information about issue stances.

52. Of course, this assumes that the Democratic candidate behaves like a Democrat. But the ability of less knowledgeable citizens to rely on the heuristic of party is heavily dependent on the behavior of knowledgeable voters. Given that primaries dominate the party nomination process, the key mechanism for ensuring the fidelity of candidates to their party's philosophy is the behavior of knowledgeable partisan voters who are able and willing to reject candidates who don't behave like a Democrat (or a Republican, as the case may be).

53. This simplification is subject to many criticisms, of course. Some issues

are easier than others; that is, some pertain more to policy outcomes than policy instruments, hindering the determination of what is a rational vote (Fiorina, 1981: 144; Carmines and Stimson, 1980). In addition, issues can work at cross purposes with each other (especially when comparing social issues with those arrayed along the traditional New Deal cleavage). As noted in the previous section, however, the pattern of interrelationships among issues for the most knowledgeable voters was simpler than for less knowledgeable ones.

54. For all years, the dependent variable was coded as follows: 0 = Democratic candidate, 1 = Republican candidate. The attitude indexes were constructed as follows:

Domestic attitudes: An additive index of support for government spending and action on domestic issues. In all three years, variables were the same as those described earlier in the analysis of knowledge's impact on opinions.

Foreign attitudes: An additive index of attitudes on foreign policy issues. In 1984 and 1988, variables included defense spending and cooperation with the Soviet Union. In 1984 another defense spending variable was added. In 1988, the index also included support for the Strategic Defense Initiative and aid to the Contras. In 1992, the index included defense spending, importance of military strength, and opinion about the Persian Gulf war. Higher numbers mean more conservative views.

Ideology: In all three years, a seven-point self-identified ideology scale from extremely liberal to extremely conservative. Respondents who had "not thought much" about this were assigned a code of 4 (moderate).

This analysis is based on a directional spatial model rather than a positional model (Rabinowitz and MacDonald, 1989; MacDonald, Listhaug, and Rabinowitz, 1991). The indexes reflect the cumulative direction and intensity of opinions. Unlike the Rabinowitz-MacDonald analysis, our measure does not explicitly include terms for candidate positions, but these positions are implicitly accounted for in that the candidates were assumed to take opposite (and directionally consistent) positions on all of the issues included in the indexes.

55. We omit party identification for two reasons. First, we are interested in assessing the consistency of one's vote with one's opinions on issues. Although partisanship is one means this consistency is promoted, its presence is irrelevant to whether, in fact, such a correspondence exists. Second, the inclusion of partisanship would obscure the apparent importance of issues because of the consistency between party identification and opinions. See Page (1978: 103) for an elaboration of this argument.

Knowledge promotes a closer connection between party identification and a citizen's political attitudes in much the same manner as it strengthens the linkage between attitudes and the vote. Thus, even the effective functioning of such common heuristics as partisanship depends on the availability of sufficient information.

56. The interaction variables were (1) knowledge index multiplied by the domestic policy index, (2) knowledge index multiplied by the foreign policy index, and (3) knowledge index multiplied by the ideology scale.

57. The knowledge measure used here was our summary index, composed of many factual questions. An index composed only of electorally relevant items—questions regarding the placement of parties and candidates on issue and ideological scales—performed as well or better than the larger, more general measure.

The 1992 analysis shown here excludes Perot voters, but the same pattern is evident when Perot's vote is included.

58. Another measure of effectiveness is the percentage of votes we can correctly forecast knowing the issue positions of the voters. In the lowest knowledge group, the model correctly predicted 65, 68, and 68 percent in 1984, 1988, 1992, respectively, compared with baselines of 52, 54, and 63 percent—sufficient improvement over guessing the modal category to indicate that at least some low-knowledge voters are able to connect their opinions with their vote. As we would expect, however, the predictive accuracy of the model increases with the knowledge level of the sample: the percentage correctly predicted for the second quartile was 76, 73, and 77; for the third quartile it was 81, 82, and 88; and among the high-knowledge group, 91, 91, and 88 percent of the votes were accurately predicted by the model.

59. The scales were standardized to have a mean of zero and a standard deviation of one. This allows us to compare the relative impact of each on the vote.

60. Part of the effect of knowledge may be attributed to the fact that better-informed voters have more intense opinions on issues (i.e., the variance of their opinions is greater), which means that correlations with other variables, such as the vote, can be higher (see Palfrey and Poole, 1987). This phenomenon is exacerbated by the fact that citizens expressing no opinion on issues that made up the scales had to be assigned to centrist categories to keep the sample size from shrinking. This, however, is not simply a methodological issue: the absence of an opinion on an issue, or the presence of a weak predisposition, by definition can make it difficult to vote on the basis of issues. Political information is necessary to develop opinions that reflect one's interests. Or, put in practical terms, if we excluded everyone with weak, missing, or centrist views on issues we would be eliminating a large portion of the poorly informed voters. A variety of tests using alternative treatments for centrist voters or those with no opinion did not change the fundamental conclusion that knowledge promotes the linkage of attitudes with votes.

We tried two ways to gauge the effects of imputing centrist views to those expressing no opinion: one was to exclude individuals with no opinion and then estimate the model. A second involved estimating the model using an averaged index of attitudes—taking the mean issue position across all issues for which an opinion was offered—rather than an additive one. This did not let centrists off the hook, but it also did not deflate the variance of the overall scale for some types of voters by assigning them a centrist position when they expressed no opinion. Neither variation on our original method changed the results: the explanatory power of the model remained quite high, and all the interactions between attitudes and knowledge were statistically significant.

61. In general, sociotropic voting appears to be more common than egocentric voting, although the distinction masks some of the ways personal circumstances may influence views of the national economy. The relative power of the two explanations also varies as a function of the trajectory of the economy at a given election and where citizens place responsibility for their economic condition (Brody and Sniderman, 1977; Weatherford, 1986).

62. As Kinder and Herzog (1993) have pointed out, judgments about the success of government in such areas as managing the economy are "among the most arbitrary of political constructions" (368). Although elements of judgments about the state of the economy certainly constitute political knowledge as we have defined it (e.g., whether the unemployment rate is higher or lower compared with a year ago), summary judgments about the role of government are apt to be freighted with many considerations beyond the strictly factual. In this regard, Edelman (1988) and Iyengar (1991) provide useful analyses and caveats.

63. The survey was conducted by telephone between October 23 and November 6, 1989, with a sample of 803 registered voters.

64. A statewide survey we conducted earlier in the campaign produced results nearly identical to this one.

65. The "correct" answers to the defense spending and environmental protection items are unambiguous. The other two items are somewhat problematic, in that some types of federal spending on the poor and the public schools declined in absolute terms, other types increased in dollars but declined relative to inflation, and still others increased in real terms. Nonetheless, the consensus among political practitioners and scholars is that overall federal support in both areas declined during the 1980s. Even if those who said spending on the poor and schools stayed about the same during the Reagan years are included among knowledgeable citizens, only about a third of voters would have been counted as correctly informed.

66. It is also noteworthy that these relations are clearly evident in the data, in spite of the ubiquitous presence of measurement error that tends to weaken the appearance of consistent or rational behavior on the part of respondents.

CHAPTER 7. INFORMING THE PUBLIC'S DISCRETION

1. Morris Fiorina (1990) offers a thoughtful essay on the dilemma this poses to the rational choice school.

2. Of course Einstein was not talking about the cognitive ability needed to process information regarding politics versus information regarding physics but meant, instead, that solving the world's political problems was a more difficult task than solving the riddles of the physical world. We make no claims that all political problems can be solved if people simply know enough, as most of politics is inherently contestable. Our point is simply that mastering the facts about politics structures political discourse in ways that increase the likelihood of decisions that are equitable and that approximate the public will. To the extent that this is true, the ability to master facts of the sort examined in this book is well within the reach of the vast majority of American adults if given the opportunity.

3. Indeed, because political knowledge is likely to increase one's sense of efficacy or interest in politics, our analyses likely underestimate its full impact on citizenship. Further, we suspect—but lack the data to demonstrate—that the benefits of being informed go well beyond the kinds of civic attitudes and actions specifically tested in our empirical research.

4. Evidence suggests that there are also regional and local disparities in access to the information superhighway. For example, a March 13, 1994, *New York Times* article reported that while half the population of Palo Alto, California, has home computers, modems, and access to the Internet, significantly less than 10 percent of Chicago residents can make this claim.

5. Whereas newspaper readership has been declining in all age cohorts, the fall off in readership among the young is particularly alarming (Times Mirror Center, 1990).

6. For example, such a program has been initiated in Paris, France, where the government has attempted to provide every household with a personal computer linked via modems to databases that provide various forms of political information. This network has also been used to conduct citywide discussions about local and national political issues and to hold citywide referenda on some of these

issues. The current, early proposals of the Clinton-Gore administration regarding the creation of the information superhighway also include plans for assuring that all citizens have access to the network via personal computers.

7. Much of the style of journalism works against the comprehension of news stories. For instance, recent research indicates that the inverted pyramid format probably hinders comprehension of the news, especially for readers with modest cognitive skills (Neuman, Just, and Crigler, 1992). The inverted pyramid style is a convention employed primarily for the convenience of editors and could certainly be changed.

8. To be more informative, journalists may need to make greater use of repetition, a well-understood aid to learning (Graber, 1988: 259). Repetition of stories is thought to violate journalistic canons, but this rule is applied selectively at best.

9. The absence of serious efforts to determine how well citizens learn from the news is ironic in that most reporters and editors would, no doubt, agree that the principal function of a free press is to provide information about the workings of the government so that citizens can exercise their discretion wisely. Research aimed at answering the question of what citizens learn and how standard journalistic practices promote or discourage learning would be, in the long run, of both civic and commercial value to the news industry. An educated public is more likely to seek out news, thus enlarging the audience and potential subscription and advertising revenues.

10. For a fuller discussion of Dewey's notion of scientific journalism, see Carey, 1988; 1989.

11. Of course, editors would retain their autonomy, and many queries would not be pursued if judged to be too idiosyncratic, repetitive of recent stories, or simply uninteresting. The publication of queries, even if unanswered, would be important because some of these might generate further reader (or official) response, suggesting greater interest in the topic than editors first judged.

12. For example, borrowing a technique used to update sports scores or present-breaking news, local stations could scroll the telephone numbers of relevant members of Congress and senators across the bottom of the television screen while airing stories about particular pieces of legislation, and they could scroll the votes of local representatives during reports on the final passage or defeat of pieces of legislation (similarly, newspapers could include a sidebar with this information).

13. Jay Rosen, a journalist and media scholar at New York University who has studied and written about the Columbus, Georgia (and other), experiments has received several grants to train interested journalists and editors in the techniques of integrating journalism and civic organizing. Related work is being done by Mercedes Lynn de Uriarte of the School of Communications at the University of Texas, who works with local reporters and editors in an effort to help newspapers rethink the concept of newsworthiness in a way that is meaningful to the diverse ethnic communities that increasingly make up the potential readership of many local newspapers.

14. Salons in the United States date from the turn of the century. A notable salon was organized by Mabel Dodge with the help of Lincoln Steffens and Hutchins Hapgood.

15. For example, in fall 1992 the Minneapolis/St. Paul *Star Tribune* in conjunction with a local civic group began organizing a series of neighborhood roundtables across the state. Each month the paper selected a different topic for discussion (past topics have included health care, racism, the economy, welfare

reform, and crime), "told its readers where to obtain low-cost study materials, framed the issue from several perspectives, and reported on the resulting conversations in a monthly series called 'Minnesota's Talking'" (Wigley, 1993: 53). Public radio stations in Minnesota, Wisconsin, and Seattle have organized similar forums.

16. More generally, television programmers could consider adding politically relevant entertainment programming to their schedules during such major political events as the national party conventions, presidential debates, or the state of the union address. This could include political movies, performances by political comedians or satirists, local public forums, and the like. This approach remains true to the notion of autonomy and diversity in broadcasting and at the same time draws attention to the political world at times when this is especially appropriate.

Children's programming could also be recruited to educate the public. One of the authors teaches a course on the American Congress, and unfailingly every year several students will describe (correctly) how a bill becomes a law by reciting the "School House Rock" jingle, broadcast during the 1980s on Saturday morning television: "I'm just a bill on Capitol Hill. . . ."

17. The state of Maryland, for example, requires all high school students to pass a competency test in citizenship skills before graduation. This test has motivated schools to bolster their civics curriculum, with apparent success (Marcus, 1992).

18. President Clinton's advocacy for lifelong learning focuses largely on making America more economically productive, but it could easily be expanded to include a concern for making America civically productive as well (*Chronicle of Higher Education,* 1994: A22).

19. Of course, government mailings always raise the specter of propaganda, but here again we would argue that an emphasis on facts would provide less opportunity for such manipulation (and greater ability to dispute controversial mailings) than the current system.

20. Similar arguments could be made for other branches and levels of government, as well as for the political parties. One practical example of the use of the mails for public education was the Surgeon General's 1988 brochure on AIDS, which was mailed to every U.S. household. Similar mailings could be considered for major policy issues (for example, health care reform) and for broader issues of politics and governance (for example, a mailing on how a bill becomes a law, complete with the phone numbers and mailing addresses of local representatives, or a discussion of the budget process, including pie charts on where the current fiscal year's revenues come from and how they are being spent).

21. Although, ironically, our research suggests that by informing citizens, parties would be more likely to mobilize them, and to do so in ways that would more firmly tie their behavior to the policies and platforms of the parties and other organizations.

22. For example, in 1994 several groups used paid political advertisements to argue for or against the Clinton health care proposal. While much of this debate was emotional or misleading, several ads based their arguments on relevant and accurate factual information. Many also offered additional information through 800 numbers.

23. Deliberative polls have been experimented with in Great Britain (Fishkin, 1994), and as of this writing one is planned for the U.S. in January 1996.

24. Of course, politics is, and perhaps long has been, an enjoyable spectator sport for many. Apart from whatever participation they engage in or tangible benefits they receive (or think they receive) from the political system, some people find politics interesting and fun in the same way others enjoy sports or soap operas.

Many people are political junkies, a category of citizen that has probably increased since the advent of CNN and C-SPAN.

25. To those who suggest that there is no time for this kind of civic engagement, we point out that people currently spend more time in front of the television than in any other leisure activity except sleeping.

26. There is, of course, no guarantee that socioeconomic gains will continue unabated. Indeed, for blacks, the poor, and, to a lesser extent, women, the last fifteen years have brought mixed success at best, and in many cases, real declines in income, education, occupational status, and political power (Delli Carpini, 1994; Phillips, 1990).

27. Such efforts are not utopian. Although flawed in many ways, MTV's coverage of the 1992 presidential campaign and its "Rock the Vote" campaign no doubt brought some young Americans into the political sphere. Similarly, many women's magazines that have traditionally focused on cultural issues (for example, *Vogue*) have increased their coverage of political and politically relevant issues. And black- and Hispanic-oriented electronic networks (the Black Entertainment Network, the National Black Network, Sheridan, and Caballero) provide alternative public affairs programming of special relevance to people of color.

APPENDIX 1. OVERVIEW OF DATA SOURCES

1. The most common sample employed was the "Super B," which is list-assisted in the selection of working blocks but which randomly alters the last two digits to achieve a quasi-random digit dial result. The October 1990 Richmond survey utilized a listed sample (from the telephone directory) with the last two digits randomly altered. The October 1991 Richmond survey and the survey used to recruit panelists for the presidential debate study used listed samples prepared by Survey Sampling, Incorporated.

2. Interviewing for the October 1990 Richmond survey and the September 1992 statewide survey was conducted by students in upper-level undergraduate research methods and public opinion courses, under the supervision of the SRL's regular telephone facility staff.

APPENDIX 2. THE CONCEPTUALIZATION AND MEASUREMENT OF POLITICAL KNOWLEDGE

1. We offer three important caveats here. First, there *is* a discernible multidimensional structure in the sets of national knowledge questions we examined. This structure is not pronounced but it is evident, and we conclude that the best measure of knowledge will include items that capture a variety of subdimensions. Second, detailed knowledge of a particular issue area is undoubtedly more consequential for attitudes and behaviors in that domain than is general political knowledge. We do not want to deny the importance of specialization for some purposes. Third, the unidimensional structure characterizes national political knowledge but does not fully encompass local knowledge (knowledge of state politics appears more akin to national than local politics).

2. As a consequence, many researchers have simply used surrogates, such as educational achievement or reported media use. These surrogates are exceedingly weak as measures of the underlying concept.

3. The item-total correlations are "corrected" by removing the item from the total score before computing the correlation.

4. Items with highly skewed distributions (i.e., very difficult or very easy items) will have attenuated correlations with the total test score as a result of how the product-moment correlation coefficient is calculated (Nunnally, 1978: 140–46). Choosing items solely on item-total correlation would lead to the omission of very hard and very easy items, even though they might be highly content-valid and reliable.

5. The literature on item response theory is considerable. For useful overviews see Hambleton, Swaminathan, and Rogers, 1991; Hambleton and Swaminathan, 1985; Thorndike, 1982; Allen and Yen, 1979; Lord, 1980. Latent trait theory is described by Lazarsfeld and Henry, 1968.

6. Two critical assumptions are (1) unidimensionality of the trait being measured and (2) local independence of the test items (the assumption that for any pair of items on a test, only a test-taker's ability affects the likelihood of correctly answering each of them—in the language of causal analysis, that no spurious influences will affect the correlation between the items).

7. Sample invariance means that an item's performance parameters will hold regardless of the sample to which it is administered (unlike the *p* value and item-total correlations, which would vary according to the mean and variance of the sample's ability level). The sample invariant quality of IRT measures has led to their application in discovering biased items in standardized tests.

8. The use of IRT to estimate item and ability parameters requires specialized computer software (e.g., LOGIST or BILOG), which at present is not included in the basic version of statistical packages commonly used by social scientists (e.g., SPSSX, SAS, BMDP). Approximations of the parameters for the item characteristic curve, however, can be obtained with the logistic regression module found in most statistical packages.

9. The difficulty parameter is related to the *p* value in nearly linear fashion (except at the extremes) and so for our limited purposes does not provide any additional information beyond that of the conventional item analysis statistics. But when IRT is used with specialized software to estimate ability levels of subjects, the difficulty parameter is a critical variable (see, e.g., Hambleton and Swaminathan, 1985).

10. In item analysis it is important that the criterion scale be a reasonable measure of the underlying construct. Unusually poor items may contaminate or weaken the item analysis. An initial examination of item-total correlations led us to reject three of the original forty-two items: right to counsel (-.01), abortion rights before *Roe v. Wade* (.07), and the percentage of the federal budget spent on Social Security (.10).

11. The pilot study was conducted by telephone during summer 1991. The civics items were administered to one of three randomly divided subsamples of the original 1990 NES sample. The *N* of cases was 449.

12. Politician-feeling thermometer items that included a response of "doesn't recognize" were also tested; their performance was adequate. They would be acceptable components of a knowledge scale if direct identification measures were not available.

13. It should be noted, though, that these items get some of their strength from each other because they are so highly intercorrelated.

14. An additional civics item—appointing judges—was also included on the 1992 NES survey.

APPENDIX 4. DETAILS OF THE STRUCTURAL ANALYSIS USED IN CHAPTER 4

1. We also used composite variables, combining two or more indicators into one, as an alternative way of achieving the eighteen-variable limit. The results were nearly identical to those reported in table A4.1.

Bibliography

Abramowitz, Alan. 1995. "It's Abortion, Stupid: Policy Voting in the 1992 Presidential Election." *Journal of Politics* 57:176–86.

Abramson, Jeffrey B., F. Christopher Arterton, and Gary R. Orren. 1988. *The Electronic Commonwealth: The Impact of New Media Technologies on Democratic Politics*. New York: Basic Books.

Abramson, Paul R. 1983. *Political Attitudes in America: Formation and Change*. San Francisco: W. H. Freeman.

Achen, Christopher H. 1975. "Mass Political Attitudes and the Survey Response." *American Political Science Review* 69:1218–23.

Adams, Henry. 1920. *The Degradation of the Democratic Dogma*. New York: Macmillan.

Adams, John. [1776] 1954. "Thoughts on Government." In *The Political Writings of John Adams*. New York: Liberal Arts Press.

———. [1788] 1971. "A Defence of the Constitutions of Government of the United States of America," vol. 3. In *The Works of John Adams* vol. 6. New York: AMS Press.

Adatto, Kiku. 1990. "The Incredible Shrinking Sound Bite." *The New Republic*, 28 May, 20–23.

Allen, Mary J., and Wendy M. Yen. 1979. *Introduction to Measurement Theory*. Monterey, Calif.: Brooks/Cole.

Almond, Gabriel. 1950. *The American People and Foreign Policy*. New York: Harcourt, Brace.

Almond, Gabriel, and Sidney Verba. 1963. *The Civic Culture*. Boston: Little, Brown.

Althaus, Scott L. 1994. "The Conservative Nature of Public Opinion." Paper presented at the annual meeting of the American Association for Public Opinion Research, Danvers, Mass., May 12–15.

———. 1995. "Can Collective Opinion Redeem an Ill-Informed Public?" Paper presented at the annual meeting of the American Association for Public Opinion Research, Fort Lauderdale, Fla., May 18–21.

Alvarez, R. Michael, and Charles H. Franklin. 1994. "Uncertainty and Political Perceptions." *Journal of Politics* 56:671–88.

Andersen, Kristi. 1979. *The Creation of a Democratic Majority, 1929–1936*. Chicago: University of Chicago Press.

Aristotle. 1946. *The Politics of Aristotle*. Trans. Ernest Barker. Oxford: Oxford University Press.

———. 1985. *The Nicomachean Ethics.* Trans. Terence Irwin. Indianapolis: Hackett.

Ashcraft, Richard. 1987. *Locke's Two Treatises of Government.* London: Allen and Unwin.

Asher, Herbert B. 1992. *Presidential Elections and American Politics: Voters, Candidates, and Campaigns since 1952.* Pacific Grove, Calif.: Brooks/Cole.

Bagdikian, Ben H. 1992. *The Media Monopoly.* Boston: Beacon Press.

Baker, John R., Linda L. Bennett, Stephen E. Bennett, and Richard S. Flickinger. 1994. "Looking at Legislatures: Citizens' Knowledge and Perceptions of Legislatures in Canada, Great Britain, and the United States." Paper presented at the 16th Congress of the International Political Science Association, Berlin, August 21–25.

Barber, Benjamin. 1984. *Strong Democracy.* Berkeley: University of California Press.

———. 1992. *An Aristocracy of Everyone: The Politics of Education and the Future of America.* New York: Ballantine.

———. 1993. "Reductionist Political Science and Democracy." In *Reconsidering the Democratic Public,* ed. George E. Marcus and Russell L. Hanson. University Park: Pennsylvania State University Press.

Barber, Benjamin, and Richard Battistoni. 1993. "A Season of Learning: Introducing Service Learning into the Liberal Arts Curriculum." *PS: Political Science and Politics* 26 (June): 235–40, 262.

Barber, James David. 1973. *Citizen Politics.* 2d ed. Chicago: Markham Publishing.

Bardes, Barbara A., and Robert W. Oldendick. 1990. "Public Opinion and Foreign Policy: A Field in Search of Theory." In *Research in Micropolitics,* vol. 3, ed. Samuel Long. Greenwich, Conn.: JAI Press.

Barker, Ernest. 1970. "Democracy as Activity." In *Frontiers of Democratic Theory,* ed. Henry S. Kariel. New York: Random House.

Bartels, Larry M. 1990. "Public Opinion and Political Interests." Paper delivered at the annual meeting of the Midwest Political Science Association, Chicago, April 5–7.

———. 1994. "Uninformed Votes: Information Effects in Presidential Elections." Unpub. paper, Princeton University.

Beck, Paul Allen. 1974. "A Socialization Theory of Partisan Realignment." In *The Politics of Future Citizens,* ed. Richard G. Niemi. San Francisco: Jossey-Bass.

Bell, Daniel. 1973. *The Coming of Post-Industrial Society.* New York: Basic Books.

Bellah, Robert, Richard Madsen, William M. Sullivan, Ann Swidler, and Steven M. Tipton. 1985. *Habits of the Heart.* New York: Harper and Row.

———. 1991. *The Good Society.* New York: Vintage.

Bennett, W. Lance. 1980. *Public Opinion in American Politics,* ed. Samuel L. Long. New York: Harcourt Brace Jovanovich.

Bennett, Linda L. M., and Stephen Earl Bennett. 1989. "Enduring Gender Differences in Political Interest: The Impact of Socialization and Political Dispositions." *American Politics Quarterly* 17:105–22.

———. 1991. "Out of Sight, Out of Mind: Americans' Knowledge of Party Control of the House of Representatives, 1960–1984." Unpub. paper, University of Cincinnati.

Bennett, Stephen Earl. 1986. *Apathy in America*. Dobbs Ferry, N.Y.: Transnational Publishers.

———. 1988. "Know-Nothings Revisited: The Meaning of Political Ignorance Today." *Social Science Quarterly* 69:476–90.

———. 1989. "Trends in Americans' Political Information, 1967–1987." *American Politics Quarterly* 17:422–35.

———. 1990. "The Dimensions of Americans' Political Information." Paper presented at the annual meeting of the American Political Science Association, San Francisco, August 29-September 2.

———. 1994. "The Persian Gulf War's Impact on Americans' Political Information." *Political Behavior* 16:179–201.

Bentham, Jeremy. [1830] 1962. *The Works of Jeremy Bentham*, ed. John Bowring. New York: Russell and Russell.

Berelson, Bernard. 1952. "Democratic Theory and Public Opinion." *Public Opinion Quarterly* 16 (fall): 313–30.

Berelson, Bernard R., Paul F. Lazarsfeld, and William N. McPhee. 1954. *Voting: A Study of Opinion Formation in a Presidential Campaign*. Chicago: University of Chicago Press.

Bishop, George F., Robert W. Oldendick, Alfred J. Tuchfarber, and Stephen Earl Bennett. 1980. "Pseudo-Opinions on Public Affairs." *Public Opinion Quarterly* 44:198–209.

Bishop, George F., Alfred J. Tuchfarber, and Robert W. Oldendick. 1986. "Opinions on Fictitious Issues: The Pressure to Answer Survey Questions." *Public Opinion Quarterly* 50:240–50.

Bloom, Allan David. 1987. *The Closing of the American Mind: How Higher Education Has Failed Democracy and Impoverished the Souls of Today's Students*. New York: Simon and Schuster.

Blumberg, Paul. 1990. "The Politics of Ignorance." Unpub. paper, Queens College.

Bobo, Lawrence, and Frederick C. Licari. 1989. "Education and Political Tolerance: Testing the Effects of Cognitive Sophistication and Target Group Affect." *Public Opinion Quarterly* 53 (fall): 285–308.

Bogart, Leo. 1989. *Press and Public*. Hillsdale, N.J.: Lawrence Erlbaum.

Bowles, Samuel, and Herbert Gintis. 1976. *Schooling in Capitalist America: Educational Reform and the Contradictions of Economic Life*. New York: Basic Books.

Boyte, Harry C. 1980. *The Backyard Revolution: Understanding the New Citizens' Movement*. Philadelphia: Temple University Press.

———. 1984. *Community Is Possible*. New York: Harper and Row.

Brady, Henry E. 1987. "Knowledge, Strategy, and Momentum in Presidential Primaries." Unpub. paper.

Brady, Henry E., and Stephen Ansolabehere. 1989. "The Nature of Utility Functions in Mass Publics." *American Political Science Review* 83 (March): 143–63.

Brehm, John. 1993. *The Phantom Respondents: Opinion Surveys and Political Representation.* Ann Arbor: University of Michigan Press.

Brigham, John. 1990. "Bad Attitudes: The Consequences of Survey Research for Constitutional Practice." *Review of Politics* 52:582–602.

Brody, Richard A., and Paul M. Sniderman. 1977. "From Life Space to Polling Place: The Relevance of Personal Concerns for Voting Behavior." *British Journal of Political Science* 7:337–60.

Brooks, Phill, and Bob M. Gassaway. 1985. "Improving News Coverage." *State Legislatures,* March, 29–31.

Brown, Steven R., and Richard W. Taylor. 1973. "Frames of Reference and the Observation of Behavior." *Social Science Quarterly* 54:29–40.

Burdick, Eugene. 1959. "Political Theory and Voting Studies." In *American Voting Behavior,* ed. Eugene Burdick and Arthur J. Brodbeck. New York: Free Press.

Burnham, Walter Dean. 1970. *Critical Elections and the Mainsprings of American Politics.* New York: Norton.

———. 1978. "American Politics in the 1970s: Beyond Party?" In *Parties and Elections in an Anti-Party Age,* ed. Jeff Fishel. Bloomington: Indiana University Press.

———. 1982. *The Current Crisis in American Politics.* New York: Oxford University Press.

Callenbach, Ernest, and Michael Phillips. 1985. *A Citizen Legislature.* Berkeley, Calif.: Banyan Tree Books.

Campbell, Angus, Philip E. Converse, Warren E. Miller, and Donald E. Stokes. 1960. *The American Voter.* New York: John Wiley.

Campbell, James E. 1992. "Forecasting the Presidential Vote in the States." *American Journal of Political Science* 36:386–407.

Carey, James. 1988. *Communication as Culture: Essays on Media and Society.* London: Unwin Hyman.

———. 1989. "Commentary: Communication and the Progressives." *Critical Studies and Mass Communication* 6:264–82.

Carmines, Edward G., and James A. Stimson. 1980. "The Two Faces of Issue Voting." *American Political Science Review* 74:78–91.

———. 1989. *Issue Evolution: Race and the Transformation of American Politics.* Princeton: Princeton University Press.

Center for the American Woman and Politics. 1991. *The Impact of Women in Public Office: An Overview.* New Brunswick, N.J.: Eagleton Institute of Politics, Rutgers, The State University of New Jersey.

Chaffee, Steven H., and Donna G. Wilson. 1977. "Media Rich, Media Poor: Two Studies of Diversity in Agenda Holding." *Journalism Quarterly* 54:466–76.

Chronicle of Higher Education. 1994. March 2.

Claiborne, William. 1993. "'Citizen Jury' Demand Strong Action on Budget." *Washington Post.*

Clarke, Peter, and Susan H. Evans. 1983. *Covering Campaigns: Journalism in Congressional Elections.* Stanford: Stanford University Press.

Clarke, Peter, and Eric Fredin. 1978. "Newspapers, Television, and Political Reasoning." *Public Opinion Quarterly* 42:143–60.

Cole, G. D. H. 1919. *Labor in the Commonwealth.* London: Headley Brothers.

———. 1920. *Social Theory*. London: Methuen.

Connolly, William E. 1972. "On 'Interests' in Politics." *Politics and Society* 2:459–77.

———. 1983. *The Terms of Political Discourse*. 2d ed. Princeton: Princeton University Press.

Conover, Pamela Johnston, and Stanley Feldman. 1984. "Group Identification, Values, and the Nature of Political Beliefs." *American Politics Quarterly* 12:151–75.

———. 1991. "Where Is the Schema? Critiques." *American Political Science Review* 85:1364–69.

Conover, Pamela Johnston, Ivor Crewe, and Donald D. Searing. 1991. "The Nature of Citizenship in the United States and Great Britain: Empirical Comments on Theoretical Themes." *Journal of Politics* 53:800–832.

Converse, Philip E. 1962. "Information Flow and the Stability of Partisan Attitudes." *Public Opinion Quarterly* 26:578–99.

———. 1964. "The Nature of Belief Systems in Mass Publics." In *Ideology and Discontent*, ed. David E. Apter. New York: Free Press.

———. 1970. "Attitudes and Non-Attitudes: Continuation of a Dialogue." In *The Quantitative Analysis of Social Problems*, ed. Edward R. Tufte. Reading, Mass.: Addison-Wesley.

———. 1975. "Public Opinion and Voting Behavior." In *Handbook of Political Science*, ed. Fred I. Greenstein and Nelson W. Polsby. Reading, Mass.: Addison-Wesley.

———. 1976. *The Dynamics of Party Support*. Beverly Hills: Sage.

———. 1980. "Comment: Rejoinder to Judd and Milburn." *American Sociological Review* 45:644–46.

———. 1990. "Popular Representation and the Distribution of Information." In *Information and Democratic Processes*, ed. John A. Ferejohn and James H. Kuklinski. Urbana: University of Illinois Press.

Converse, Philip E., and Gregory B. Markus. 1979. "*Plus ça Change* . . .: The New CPS Election Study Panel." *American Political Science Review* 73:32–49.

Cook, Elizabeth A., Ted G. Jelen, and Clyde Wilcox. 1994. "Issue Voting in Gubernatorial Elections: Abortion and Post-*Webster* Politics." *Journal of Politics* 56:187–99.

Coupland, Douglas. 1991. *Generation X: Tales for an Accelerated Culture*. New York: St. Martin's.

Cronbach, Lee J. 1984. *Essentials of Psychological Testing*. 4th ed. New York: Harper and Row.

Cronin, Thomas E. 1989. *Direct Democracy: The Politics of Initiative, Referendum, and Recall*. Cambridge: Harvard University Press.

Dahl, Robert A. 1956. *A Preface to Democratic Theory*. Chicago: University of Chicago Press.

———. 1961. *Who Governs? Democracy and Power in an American City*. New Haven: Yale University Press.

———. 1989. *Democracy and Its Critics*. New Haven: Yale University Press.

Dalton, Russell J. 1988. *Citizen Politics in Western Democracies*. Chatham, N.J.: Chatham House Publishers.

Darcy, R., Susan Welch, and Janet Clark. 1987. *Women, Elections, and Representation.* New York: Longman.

Dawson, Paul A. 1979. "The Formation and Structure of Political Belief Systems." *Political Behavior* 1:99–122.

de Tocqueville, Alexis. [1850] 1969 . *Democracy in America.* Garden City, N.Y.: Doubleday.

Delli Carpini, Michael X. 1994. "The Making of a Consensual Majority: Political Discourse and Electoral Politics in the 1980s." In *An American Half Century: Postwar Culture and Politics in the USA,* ed. Michael Klein. London: Pluto Press.

———. 1989. "Age and History: Generational and Sociopolitical Change." In *Political Learning in Adulthood: A Sourcebook of Theory and Research,* ed. Roberta S. Sigel. Chicago: University of Chicago Press.

———. 1986. *Stability and Change in American Politics: The Coming of Age of the Generation of the 1960s.* New York: New York University Press.

Delli Carpini, Michael X., and Ester Fuchs. 1993. "The Year of the Woman: Candidates, Voters, and the 1992 Elections." *Political Science Quarterly* 108:29–36.

Delli Carpini, Michael X., and Scott Keeter. 1991. "Stability and Change in the U.S. Public's Knowledge of Politics." *Public Opinion Quarterly* 55:583–612.

———. 1993. "Measuring Political Knowledge: Putting First Things First." *American Journal of Political Science* 37:1179–1206.

Delli Carpini, Michael X., and Indu Singh. 1987. "Political Development and the New Information Technology." In *Dynamics of Information Management,* ed. Indu Singh. Norwood, N.J.: Ablex.

Delli Carpini, Michael X., and Bruce Williams. 1994. "'Fictional' and 'Non-Fictional' Television Celebrates Earth Day: Or, Political Is Comedy Plus Pretense." *Cultural Studies* 8:74–98.

Delli Carpini, Michael X., Scott Keeter, and J. David Kennamer. 1994. "Effects of the News Media Environment on Citizen Knowledge of State Politics and Government." *Journalism Quarterly* 71:443–56.

Delli Carpini, Michael X., Scott Keeter, and Sharon Webb. 1993. "Effects of 'The People's Presidential Debate' on Undecided Voters in the Richmond Area." Paper presented at the annual meeting of the American Association for Public Opinion Research, St. Charles, Ill., May 20–23.

Denver, David, and Gordon Hands. 1990. "Does Studying Politics Make a Difference? The Political Knowledge, Attitudes, and Perceptions of School Students." *British Journal of Political Science* 20:263–79.

Dewey, John. [1916] 1966. *Democracy and Education.* New York: Free Press.

———. [1927] 1954. *The Public and Its Problems.* Athens, Ohio: Swallow Press.

———. [1900] 1956. *The School and Society.* Chicago: University of Chicago Press.

Dimock, Michael A., and Samuel L. Popkin. 1995 "Who Knows: Political Knowledge in Comparative Perspective." Paper presented at the annual meeting of the Midwest Political Science Association, Chicago, April 6–8.

Dionne, E. J., Jr. 1991. *Why Americans Hate Politics.* New York: Simon and Schuster.

Downs, Anthony. 1957. *An Economic Theory of Democracy.* New York: Harper and Row.

Drew, Dan, and David Weaver. 1991. "Voter Learning in the 1988 Presidential Election: Did the Debates and the Media Matter?". *Journalism Quarterly* 68:27–37.

Dye, Thomas R., and L. Harmon Zeigler. 1990. *The Irony of Democracy: An Uncommon Introduction to American Politics.* 8th ed. Pacific Grove, Calif.: Brooks/Cole.

Easton, David. 1965. *A Systems Analysis of Political Life.* New York: John Wiley.

Easton, David, and Robert D. Hess. 1962. "The Child's Political World." *Midwest Journal of Political Science* 6:229–46.

Edelman, Murray. 1988. *Constructing the Political Spectacle.* Chicago: University of Chicago Press.

Edsall, Thomas Byrne. 1984. *The New Politics of Inequality.* New York: Norton.

Edsall, Thomas Byrne, and Mary D. Edsall. 1991. *Chain Reaction: The Impact of Race, Rights, and Taxes on American Politics.* New York: Norton.

Elshtain, Jean Bethke. 1981. *Public Man, Private Woman.* Princeton: Princeton University Press.

Emerson, Ralph Waldo. [1850] 1908. *English Traits, Representative Men, and Other Essays of Ralph Waldo Emerson.* New York: E. P. Dutton.

Engle, Shirley H., and Anna Ochoa. 1988. *Education for Democratic Citizenship: Decision Making in the Social Studies.* New York: Teacher's College of Columbia University.

Entman, Robert. 1989. *Democracy without Citizens: Media and the Decay of American Politics.* New York: Oxford University Press.

Epstein, Edward Jay. 1973. *News from Nowhere.* New York: Vintage.

Erikson, Robert S. 1979. "The SRC Panel Data and Mass Political Attitudes." *British Journal of Political Science* 9:89–114.

Erikson, Robert S., and Kathleen Knight. 1993. "Ideological Sophistication and the Stability of Ideological and Partisan Sentiment." Paper presented at the annual meeting of the American Political Science Association, Washington, D.C., September 2–5.

Erikson, Robert S., Norman R. Luttbeg, and Kent L. Tedin. 1991. *American Public Opinion.* 4th ed. New York: Macmillan.

Erskine, Hazel Gaudet. 1962. "The Polls: The Informed Public." *Public Opinion Quarterly* 26:669–77.

———. 1963a. "The Polls: Textbook Knowledge." *Public Opinion Quarterly* 27:133–41.

———. 1963b. "The Polls: Exposure to Domestic Information." *Public Opinion Quarterly* 27:491–500.

———. 1963c. "The Polls: Exposure to International Information." *Public Opinion Quarterly* 27:658–62.

Estlund, David, Jeremy Waldron, Bernard Grofman, and Scott Feld. 1989. "Democratic Theory and the Public Interest: Condorcet and Rousseau Revisited." *American Political Science Review* 83:1317–40.

Fair, Ray. 1988. "The Effect of Economic Events on Votes for President: 1984 Update." *Political Behavior* 10:168–79.

Faulkenberry, G. David, and Robert Mason. 1978. "Characteristics of Non-opinion and No Opinion Response Groups." *Public Opinion Quarterly* 42:533–43.

Feldman, Stanley. 1989. "Measuring Issue Preferences: The Problem of Response Instability." *Political Analysis* 1:25–60.

Ferejohn, John A. 1990. "Information and the Electoral Process." In *Information and Democratic Processes,* ed. John A. Ferejohn and James H. Kuklinski. Urbana: University of Illinois Press.

Finkel, Steven E., Thomas M. Guterbock, and Marian J. Borg. 1991. "Race-of-Interviewer Effects in a Preelection Poll: Virginia 1989." *Public Opinion Quarterly* 55:313–30.

Fiorina, Morris P. 1981. *Retrospective Voting in American National Elections.* New Haven: Yale University Press.

———. 1990. "Information and Rationality in Elections." In *Information and Democratic Processes,* ed. John A. Ferejohn and James H. Kuklinski. Urbana: University of Illinois Press.

Fishkin, James S. 1991. *Democracy and Deliberation: New Directions for Democratic Reform.* New Haven: Yale University Press.

———. 1994. "Britain Experiments with the Deliberative Poll." *The Public Perspective* 5 (July/August): 27–29.

Fiske, Susan T., and Shelley E. Taylor. 1984. *Social Cognition.* New York: Random House.

Flanigan, William H., and Nancy H. Zingale. 1987. *Political Behavior of the American Electorate.* 6th ed. Boston: Allyn and Bacon.

Gamson, William. 1992. *Talking Politics.* New York: Cambridge University Press.

Gans, Herbert. 1979. *Deciding What's News.* New York: Vintage.

Gibson, James L. 1992. "The Political Consequences of Intolerance: Cultural Conformity and Political Freedom." *American Political Science Review* 86:338–56.

Gilligan, Carol. 1982. *In a Different Voice: Psychological Theory and Women's Development.* Cambridge: Harvard University Press.

Gilmour, Richard, and Richard Lamb. 1975. *Political Alienation in Contemporary America.* New York: St. Martin's.

Ginsberg, Benjamin. 1982. *The Consequences of Consent.* Reading, Mass.: Addison-Wesley.

Ginsberg, Benjamin, and Martin Shefter. 1990. *Politics by Other Means.* New York: Basic Books.

Glenn, Norval. 1972. "The Distribution of Political Knowledge in the United States." In *Political Attitudes and Public Opinion,* ed. Dan Nimmo and Charles Bonjean. New York: McKay.

Gormley, William T., Jr. 1978. "Television Coverage of State Government." *Public Opinion Quarterly* 42:354–59.

Gottlieb, Martin. 1989. "People Will Learn about Politics Only If They Care." *The Stars and Stripes,* 10 June, 10.

Gould, Stephen Jay. 1981. *The Mismeasure of Man.* New York: Norton.

Graber, Doris A. 1988. *Processing the News.* 2d ed. New York: Longman.

———. 1994. "Why Voters Fail Information Tests: Can the Hurdles Be Overcome?" *Political Communication* 11:331–46.

Graham, Thomas W. 1988. "The Pattern and Importance of Public Knowledge in the Nuclear Age." *Journal of Conflict Resolution* 32:319–34.

Greenberg, Edward S., and Benjamin I. Page. 1993. *The Struggle for Democracy.* New York: Harper Collins.

Greenstein, Fred I. 1965. *Children and Politics.* New Haven: Yale University Press.

Grodzins, Morton. 1990. "The Federal System." In *American Government: Readings and Cases,* ed. Peter Woll. New York: Harper Collins.

Gutmann, Amy. 1987. *Democratic Education.* Princeton: Princeton University Press.

Habermas, Jürgen. 1984. *A Theory of Communicative Action,* trans. Thomas McCarthy. Boston: Beacon Press.

Hagen, Michael G. 1993. "The Salience of Racial Issues." Occasional Paper 93–11, Center for American Political Studies, Harvard University.

Hambleton, Ronald K., and Hariharan Swaminathan. 1985. *Item Response Theory: Principles and Applications.* Boston: Kluwer-Nijhoff Publishing.

Hambleton, Ronald K., H. Swaminathan, and H. Jane Rogers. 1991. *Fundamentals of Item Response Theory.* Newbury Park, Calif.: Sage.

Hamill, Ruth, and Milton Lodge. 1986. "Cognitive Consequences of Political Sophistication." In *Political Cognition,* ed. Richard R. Lau and David O. Sears. Hillsdale, N.J.: Lawrence Erlbaum.

Hamill, Ruth, Milton Lodge, and Frederick Blake. 1985. "The Breadth, Depth, and Utility of Class, Partisan, and Ideological Schemata." *American Journal of Political Science* 29:850–70.

Hamilton, Alexander, James Madison, and John Jay. [1787–88] 1961. *Federalist Papers.* Garden City, N.Y.: Anchor Books.

Hanson, Russell. 1985. *The Democratic Imagination.* Princeton: Princeton University Press.

Hart, James D. 1950. *The Popular Book.* New York: Oxford University Press.

Hastie, Reid. 1986. "A Primer of Information-Processing Theory for the Political Scientist." In *Political Cognition,* ed. Richard R. Lau and David O. Sears. Hillsdale, N.J.: Lawrence Erlbaum.

Hawking, Stephen. 1988. *A Brief History of Time.* New York: Bantam.

Hayduk, Leslie A. 1987. *Structural Equation Modeling with LISREL.* Baltimore: Johns Hopkins University Press.

Hirsch, Fred. 1976. *The Limits to Social Growth.* Cambridge: Harvard University Press.

Hirsch, E. D., Jr. 1988. *Cultural Literacy: What Every American Needs to Know.* Boston: Houghton Mifflin.

Hirschman, Albert O. 1982. *Shifting Involvements.* Princeton: Princeton University Press.

Hochschild, Jennifer L. 1981. *What's Fair? American Beliefs about Distributive Justice.* Cambridge: Harvard University Press.

Hollander, Richard S. 1985. *Video Democracy: The Vote-from-Home Revolution.* Mt. Airy, Md.: Lomond Publications.

Holsworth, Robert D. 1980. *Public Interest Liberalism and the Crisis of Affluence: Reflections on Nader, Environmentalism, and the Politics of a Sustainable Society.* Boston: G. K. Hall.

Huckfeldt, Robert, and John Sprague. 1993. "Citizens, Contexts, and Politics." In *Political Science: The State of the Discipline II,* ed. Ada W. Finifter. Washington, D.C.: American Political Science Association.

Hurwitz, Jon , and Mark A. Peffley. 1985. "A Hierarchical Model of Attitude Constraint." *American Journal of Political Science* 29:871–90.

Hyman, Herbert H., and Paul B. Sheatsley. 1947. "Some Reasons Why Information Campaigns Fail." *Public Opinion Quarterly* 11:412–23.

Hyman, Herbert H., Charles R. Wright, and John Shelton Reed. 1975. *The Enduring Effects of Education.* Chicago: University of Chicago Press.

Illich, Ivan, and Barry Sanders. 1989. *ABC: The Alphabetization of the Popular Mind.* New York: Vintage.

Inglehart, Ronald. 1977. *The Silent Revolution: Changing Values and Political Styles among Western Publics.* Princeton: Princeton University Press.

Irons, Peter H., and Stephanie Guitton. 1993. *May It Please the Court.* New York: New Press.

Iyengar, Shanto. 1986. "Whither Political Information." Report to the Board of Overseers and Pilot Study Committee, National Election Studies.

———. 1990. "Shortcuts to Political Knowledge: The Role of Selective Attention and Accessibility." In *Information and Democratic Processes,* ed. John A. Ferejohn and James H. Kuklinski. Chicago: University of Illinois Press.

———. 1991. *Is Anyone Responsible? How Television News Frames Political Issues.* Chicago: University of Chicago Press.

Jackson, John E. 1979. "Statistical Estimation of Possible Response Bias in Close-Ended Issue Questions." *Political Methodology* 6:393–424.

Jamieson, Kathleen Hall. 1994. "Political Ads, the Press, and Lessons in Psychology." *Chronicle of Higher Education,* September 28, A56.

Janowitz, Morris. 1983. *The Reconstruction of Patriotism.* Chicago: University of Chicago Press.

Jefferson, Thomas. [1804] 1939. Letter to Abigail Adams in *Democracy,* ed. Saul Kussiel Padover. New York: Appleton-Century.

———. 1944. *The Life and Selected Writings of Thomas Jefferson,* ed. Adrienne Koch and William Peden. New York: Modern Library.

Jennings, M. Kent. 1993. "Political Knowledge over Time and across Generations." Paper presented at the annual meeting of the American Political Science Association, Washington, D.C., September 2–5.

Jennings, M. Kent, and Richard G. Niemi. 1974. *The Political Character of Adolescence.* Princeton: Princeton University Press.

———. 1981. *Generations and Politics: A Panel Study of Young Adults and Their Parents.* Princeton: Princeton University Press.

Jennings, M. Kent, and Harmon Ziegler. 1970. "The Salience of American State Politics." *American Political Science Review* 64:523–35.

Jennings, M. Kent, Kenneth P. Langton, and Richard G. Niemi. 1974. "Effects of the High School Civics Curriculum." In *The Political Character of Adolescence,* ed. M. Kent Jennings and Richard G. Niemi. Princeton: Princeton University Press.

Jhally, Sut, Justin Lewis, and Michael Morgan. 1991. *The Gulf War: A Study of the Media, Public Opinion, and Public Knowledge.* Amherst: Center for the Study of Communication, University of Massachusetts.

Jordan, Mary. 1992a. "More Adults Are Hooking Up to Higher Education." *Washington Post,* August 14.

———. 1992b. "Nader, Educators Rewrite the Civics Textbook to Cultivate Student Activism." *Washington Post,* December 2.

Joreskog, Karl G., and Dag Sorbom. 1988. LISREL 7: A Guide to the Program and Applications. Chicago: SPSS Inc.

Judd, Charles M., and James W. Downing. 1990. "Political Expertise and the Development of Attitude Consistency." *Social Cognition* 8:104–25.

Judd, Charles M., and Michael A. Milburn. 1980. "The Structure of Attitude Systems in the General Public: Comparisons of a Structural Equation Model." *American Sociological Review* 45:627–43.

Junn, Jane. 1991. "Participation and Political Knowledge." In *Political Participation and American Democracy,* ed. William Crotty. New York: Greenwood Press.

Kahneman, Daniel, and Amos Tversky. 1972. "Subjective Probability: A Judgment of Representativeness." *Cognitive Psychology* 3:430–54.

———. 1973. "On the Psychology of Prediction." *Psychological Review* 80: 237–251.

Keeter, Scott. 1987. "The Illusion of Intimacy: Television and the Role of Candidate Personal Qualities in Voter Choice." *Public Opinion Quarterly* 51: 344–358.

Keeter, Scott, and Harry Wilson. 1986. "Natural Treatment and Control Settings for Research on the Effects of Television." *Communication Research* 13: 37–53.

Keeter, Scott, and Cliff Zukin. 1983. *Uninformed Choice: The Failure of the New Presidential Nominating System.* New York: Praeger.

Kennamer, J. David. 1992. "Active Audience or Busy Audience? Attention Operationalized as Lack of Distractions." Paper presented to the annual meeting of the Midwest Association for Public Opinion Research, Chicago, November 19–20.

Kernell, Samuel. 1986. *Going Public: New Strategies of Presidential Leadership.* Washington, D.C.: CQ Press.

Kessel, John H. 1988. *Presidential Campaign Politics: Coalition Strategies and Citizen Response.* 3d ed. Chicago: Dorsey Press.

Key, Jr., V. O. 1966. *The Responsible Electorate: Rationality in Presidential Voting 1936-1960.* New York: Vintage.

Kiewiet, D. Roderick. 1983. *Macroeconomics and Micropolitics: The Electoral Effects of Economic Issues.* Chicago: University of Chicago Press.

Kinder, Donald R., and Don Herzog. 1993. "Democratic Discussion" In *Reconsidering the Democratic Public,* ed. George E. Marcus and Russell L. Hanson. University Park: Penn State University Press.

Kinder, Donald R., and Lynn M. Sanders. 1990. "Mimicking Political Debate with Survey Questions: The Case of White Opinion on Affirmative Action for Blacks." *Social Cognition* 8:73–103.

Kinder, Donald R., Gordon S. Adams, and Paul W. Gronke. 1989. "Economics and Politics in the 1984 American Presidential Election." *American Journal of Political Science* 33:491–515.

King, Gary. 1986. "How Not to Lie with Statistics: Avoiding Common Mistakes in Quantitative Political Science." *American Journal of Political Science* 30:666–87.

———. 1991. "Truth Is Stranger than Prediction, More Questionable than Causal Inference." *American Journal of Political Science* 35:1047–53.

Klein, Ethel. 1984. *Gender Politics: From Consciousness to Mass Politics.* Cambridge: Harvard University Press.

Knight, Kathleen. 1985. "Ideology in the 1980 Election: Ideological Sophistication Does Matter." *Journal of Politics* 47:828–53.

Kozol, Jonathan. 1991. *Savage Inequalities: Children in America's Schools.* New York: Crown Publishers.

Krassa, Michael A. 1990. "Political Information, Social Environments, and Deviants." *Political Behavior* 12:315–30.

Kriesberg, Martin. 1949. "Dark Areas of Ignorance." In *Public Opinion and Foreign Policy,* ed. Lester Markel. New York: Harper.

Krosnick, Jon A., and Donald R. Kinder. 1990. "Altering the Foundations of Support for the President through Priming." *American Political Science Review* 84:497–512.

Krosnick, Jon A., and Michael A. Milburn. 1990. "Psychological Determinants of Political Opinionation." *Social Cognition* 8:49–72.

Kuklinski, James H., Daniel S. Metlay, and W. D. Kay. 1982. "Citizen Knowledge and Choices on the Complex Issue of Nuclear Energy." *American Journal of Political Science* 26:615–42.

Kuklinski, James H., Robert C. Luskin, and John Bolland. 1991. "Where Is the Schema? Going Beyond the "S" Word in Political Psychology." *American Political Science Review* 85:1341–56.

Kurtz, Howard. 1993a. "Click! On-Line Newspaper Is a Mixed Read." *Washington Post,* October 23.

———. 1993b. "Tabloid Sensationalism Is Thriving on TV News." *Washington Post,* 4 July.

Lambert, Ronald D., James E. Curtis, Barry J. Kay, and Steven D. Brown. 1988. "The Social Sources of Political Knowledge." *Canadian Journal of Political Science* 21:359–74.

Lane, Robert E. 1962. *Political Ideology.* New York: Free Press.

Lanoue, David J. 1992. "One That Made a Difference: Cognitive Consistency, Political Knowledge, and the 1980 Presidential Debate." *Public Opinion Quarterly* 56:168–84.

Lasch, Christopher. 1979. *The Culture of Narcissism: American Life in an Age of Diminishing Expectations.* New York: Warner Books.

Lasswell, Harold D. 1958. *Politics: Who Gets What, When, How.* Cleveland: World Publishing Company.

Lau, Richard R., and David O. Sears. 1986. "Social Cognition and Political Cognition: The Past, the Present, and the Future." In *Political Cognition,* ed. Richard R. Lau and David O. Sears. Hillsdale, N.J.: Lawrence Erlbaum.

Lazarsfeld, Paul F., and Neil W. Henry. 1968. *Latent Structure Analysis.* Boston: Houghton Mifflin.

Lazarsfeld, Paul F., Bernard Berelson, and Hazel Gaudet. 1944. *The People's Choice: How the Voter Makes Up His Mind in a Presidential Campaign.* New York: Columbia University Press.

Leighley, Jan E. 1991. "Participation as a Stimulus of Political Conceptualization." *Journal of Politics* 53:198–211.

Lemert, James B. 1981. *Does Mass Communication Change Public Opinion after All?* Chicago: Nelson-Hall.

———. 1992. "Effective Public Opinion." In *Public Opinion, the Press, and Public Policy,* ed. J. David Kennamer. Westport, Conn.: Praeger.

Lever, Janet. 1976. "Sex Differences in the Games Children Play." *Social Problems* 23:478–87.

———. 1978. "Sex Differences in the Complexity of Children's Play and Games." *American Sociological Review* 43:471–83.

Lewis-Beck, Michael S. 1978. "Stepwise Regression: A Caution." *Political Methodology* 5:213–40.

Lewis-Beck, Michael S., and Tom W. Rice. 1992. *Forecasting Elections.* Washington, D.C.: CQ Press.

Lewis, Justin, and Michael Morgan. 1992. *Images/Issues/Impact/: The Media and Campaign '92.* Amherst: Center for the Study of Communication, University of Massachusetts.

Lippmann, Walter. 1922. *Public Opinion.* New York: Free Press.

———. 1925. *The Phantom Public.* New York: Harcourt, Brace.

———. 1955. *Essays in the Public Philosophy.* Boston: Little, Brown.

Lodge, Milton, and Ruth Hamill. 1986. "A Partisan Schema for Political Information Processing." *American Political Science Review* 80:505–19.

Lodge, Milton, and Kathleen M. McGraw. 1991. "Where is the Schema? Critiques." *American Political Science Review* 85:1357–64.

Lodge, Milton, Kathleen M. McGraw, and Patrick Stroh. 1989. "An Impression-Driven Model of Candidate Evaluation." *American Political Science Review* 83:399–419.

Lord, Frederick M. 1980. *Applications of Item Response Theory to Practical Testing Problems.* Hillsdale, N.J.: Lawrence Erlbaum.

Loverich, Nicholas P., John C. Pierce, Tsurutani Taketsugu, and Abe Takematsu. 1986. "Gender Differences in Policy-Relevant Knowledge Holding: A Cross National Analysis of Environmental Information in the United States and Japan." In *Women and Politics: Activism, Attitudes, and Office Holding,* ed. Gwen Moore and Glenna Spitze. Greenwich, Conn.: JAI Press.

Luskin, Robert C. 1987. "Measuring Political Sophistication." *American Journal of Political Science* 31:856–99.

———. 1990. "Explaining Political Sophistication." *Political Behavior* 12:331–61.

———. 1991. "Abusus Non Tollit Usum: Standardized Coefficients, Correlations, and r^2s." *American Journal of Political Science* 35:1032–46.

Luttbeg, Norman R. 1968. "The Structure of Beliefs among Leaders and the Public." *Public Opinion Quarterly* 32:398–409.

MacDonald, Stuart Elaine, Ola Listhaug, and George Rabinowitz. 1991. "Issues and Party Support in Multiparty Systems." *American Political Science Review* 85:1107–31.

Macpherson, C. B. 1977. *The Life and Times of Liberal Democracy.* New York: Oxford University Press.

Madison, James. [1832] 1865. *Letters and Other Writings of James Madison,* vol. 3. Philadelphia: Lippincott.

Mander, Jerry. 1978. *Four Arguments for the Elimination of Television*. New York: Morrow.

Mann, Horace. [1848] 1957. "Twelfth Annual Report to the Massachusetts Board of Education." In *The Republic and the School: Horace Mann on the Education of Free Men*. New York: Teacher's College of Columbia University.

Mansbridge, Jane J. 1983. *Beyond Adversary Democracy*. Chicago: University of Chicago Press.

Marcus, Erin. 1992. "Montgomery 10th-Graders Pass Test at Record Rate." *Washington Post*, May 12.

Marcus, George E., and Michael B. MacKuen. 1993. "Anxiety, Enthusiasm, and the Vote: The Emotional Underpinnings of Learning and Involvement during Presidential Election Campaigns." *American Political Science Review* 87:672–85.

McClosky, Herbert, and Alida Brill. 1983. *Dimensions of Tolerance: What Americans Believe about Civil Liberties*. New York: Russell Sage Foundation.

McClosky, Herbert, and John Zaller. 1984. *The American Ethos: Public Attitudes Towards Capitalism and Democracy*. Cambridge: Harvard University Press.

McGraw, Kathleen, Milton Lodge, and Patrick Stroh. 1990. "Processes of Candidate Evaluation: On-line or Memory Based?". Paper presented to the Political Psychology Group of Columbia University and SUNY-Stony Brook.

Merelman, Richard M. 1980. "Democratic Politics and the Culture of American Education." *American Political Science Review* 74:319–37.

Merriam, Charles E. 1931. *The Making of Citizens: A Comparative Study of Methods of Civic Training*. Chicago: University of Chicago Press.

Meyer, Philip. 1991. *The New Precision Journalism*. Bloomington: Indiana University Press.

Meyrowitz, Joshua. 1985. *No Sense of Place*. New York: Oxford University Press.

Milbrath, Lester W., and M. L. Goel. 1977. *Political Participation*. 2d ed. Chicago: Rand McNally.

Mill, James. [1825] 1937. *An Essay on Government*, ed. E. Barker. Cambridge: Cambridge University Press.

Mill, John Stuart. [1861] 1910. *Representative Government*. London: Everyman.

———. [1835] 1963. "De Tocqueville on Democracy in America." In *Essays on Politics and Culture*, ed. G. Himmelfarb. Garden City, N.Y.: Doubleday.

———. [1871] 1965. "Principles of Political Economy." In *Collected Works*, ed. J. M. Robson. Toronto: University of Toronto Press.

———. [1859] 1975. *On Liberty*. New York: Norton.

Miller, Arthur H. 1991. "Where Is the Schema? Critiques." *American Political Science Review* 85:1369–76.

Miller, Arthur, Edie N. Goldenberg, and Lutz Erbring. 1979. "Type-Set Politics: Impacts of Newspapers on Public Confidence." *American Political Science Review* 73:67–84.

Miller, Jon D. 1983. *The American People and Science Policy*. New York: Pergamon Press.

Miller, Jon D., Robert W. Suchner, and Alan M. Voelker. 1980. *Citizenship in an Age of Science: Changing Attitudes among Young Adults.* New York: Pergamon Press.

Miller, Nicholas R. 1986. "Information, Electorates, and Democracy: Some Extensions and Interpretations of the Condorcet Jury Theorem." In *Information Pooling and Group Decision Making: Proceedings of the Second University of California, Irvine, Conference on Political Economy,* ed. Bernard Grofman and Guillermo Owen. Greenwich, Conn.: JAI Press.

Miller, Warren E., and the National Election Studies. 1992. *American National Election Study, 1992: Pre- and Post-Election Survey.* Conducted by the Center for Political Studies of the Institute for Social Research, The University of Michigan. Ann Arbor: Inter-University Consortium for Political and Social Research.

———. 1988. *American National Election Study, 1988: Pre- and Post-Election Survey.* Conducted by the Center for Political Studies of the Institute for Social Research, The University of Michigan. Ann Arbor: Inter-University Consortium for Political and Social Research.

"Mississippi Town Roiled by Lesbians' Plan for Women's Camp." 1994. *New York Times,* January 9.

Mondak, Jeffrey. 1994. "Cognitive Heuristics, Heuristic Processing, and Efficiency in Political Decision Making." In *New Directions in Political Psychology,* ed. Michael X. Delli Carpini, Leonie Huddy, and Robert Y. Shapiro. Greenwich, Conn.: JAI Press.

Moon, David. 1990. "What You Use Depends on What You Have: Information Effects on the Determinants of Electoral Choice." *American Politics Quarterly* 18:3–24.

Morone, James. 1990. *The Democratic Wish: Popular Participation and the Limits of American Government.* New York: Basic Books.

Mueller, John. 1992. "Democracy and Ralph's Pretty Good Grocery: Elections, Equality, and the Minimal Human Being." *American Journal of Political Science* 36:983–1003.

Mullett, Charles F. 1939–40. "Classical Influences on the American Revolution." *Classical Journal* 35.

Nadeau, Richard, and Richard G. Niemi. 1992. "Gaining Knowledge about the Sources of Political Knowledge: A Multivariate Perspective." Unpublished paper, University of Rochester.

National Task Force on Citizenship Education. 1977. *Education for Responsible Citizenship.* New York: McGraw-Hill.

Neuman, W. Russell. 1981. "Differentiation and Integration: Two Dimensions of Political Thinking." *American Journal of Sociology* 86:1236–68.

———. 1986. *The Paradox of Mass Politics: Knowledge and Opinion in the American Electorate.* Cambridge: Harvard University Press.

Neuman, W. Russell, Marion R. Just, and Ann N. Crigler. 1992. *Common Knowledge: News and the Construction of Political Meaning.* Chicago: University of Chicago Press.

Neustadt, Richard. 1976. *Presidential Power.* New York: John Wiley.

Nie, Norman H., Sidney Verba, and John R. Petrocik. 1979. *The Changing American Voter.* Cambridge: Harvard University Press.

Niemi, Richard G., and Jane Junn. 1993. "Civics Courses and the Political Knowledge of High School Seniors." Paper presented at the annual meeting of the American Political Science Association, Washington, D.C., September 2–5.

Nunn, Clyde Z., Harry J. Crockett, and J. Allen Williams. 1978. *Tolerance for Nonconformity.* San Francisco: Jossey-Bass.

Nunnally, Jum C. 1978. *Psychometric Theory.* 2d ed. New York: McGraw-Hill.

Orum, Anthony M., Roberta S. Cohen, Sherri Grasmuck, and Amy W. Orum. 1974. "Sex, Socialization and Politics." *American Sociological Review* 39:197–209.

Owen, Diana, and Marianne Stewart. 1987. "Explaining Political Knowledge: Problems of Conceptualization and Measurement." Paper presented at the annual meeting of the Southern Political Science Association, Charlotte, N.C.

Oxford English Dictionary (compact edition). 1971. . Oxford: Clarendon Press.

Page, Benjamin I. 1978. *Choices and Echoes in Presidential Elections: Rational Man and Electoral Democracy.* Chicago: University of Chicago Press.

Page, Benjamin I., and Richard A. Brody. 1972. "Policy Voting and the Electoral Process: The Vietnam War Issue." *American Political Science Review* 66:979–95.

Page, Benjamin I., and Robert Y. Shapiro. 1992. *The Rational Public.* Chicago: University of Chicago Press.

Palfrey, Thomas R., and Keith T. Poole. 1987. "The Relationship between Information, Ideology, and Voting Behavior." *American Journal of Political Science* 31:511–29.

Pateman, Carole. 1970. *Participation and Democratic Theory.* Cambridge: Cambridge University Press.

Patterson, Thomas E. 1993. *Out of Order.* New York: Alfred A. Knopf.

Phillips, Kevin P. 1990. *The Politics of Rich and Poor: Wealth and the American Electorate in the Reagan Aftermath.* New York: Random House.

Piazza, Thomas. 1980. "The Analysis of Attitude Items." *American Journal of Sociology* 86:584–603.

Pomper, Gerald. 1975. *Voter's Choice: Varieties of American Electoral Behavior.* New York: Dodd, Mead.

Popkin, Samuel L. 1991. *The Reasoning Voter: Communication and Persuasion in Presidential Campaigns.* Chicago: University of Chicago Press.

Popkin, Samuel L., and Michael A. Dimock. 1995. "Cognitive Engagement and Citizen World Views." Paper presented at the Conference on Citizen Competence and the Design of Democratic Institutions, Washington, D.C., February 10–11.

Postman, Neil. 1979. *Teaching as a Conserving Activity.* New York: Delacorte Press.

———. 1985. *Amusing Ourselves to Death.* New York: Viking.

Price, Vincent. 1992. *Public Opinion.* Newbury Park, Calif.: Sage.

Price, Vincent, and John Zaller. 1993. "Who Gets the News? Alternative Measures of News Reception and Their Implications for Research." *Public Opinion Quarterly* 57:133–64.

Prothro, James W., and Charles W. Grigg. 1960. "Fundamental Principles of Democracy: Bases of Agreement and Disagreement." *Journal of Politics* 22:276–94.

Putnam, Robert. 1993. *Making Democracy Work: Civic Traditions in Modern Italy.* Princeton: Princeton University Press.

Rabinowitz, George, and Stuart Elaine MacDonald. 1989. "A Directional Theory of Issue Voting." *American Political Science Review* 83:93–121.

Rahn, Wendy M. 1989. "The Role of Partisan Stereotypes in Information Processing about Political Candidates." Paper presented at the annual meeting of the American Political Science Association, Atlanta.

Rapoport, Ronald B. 1979. "What They Don't Know Can Hurt You." *American Journal of Political Science* 23:805–15.

———. 1981. "The Sex Gap in Political Persuading: Where the "Structuring Principle" Works." *American Journal of Political Science* 25:32–48.

———. 1982. "Sex Differences in Attitude Expression: A Generational Explanation." *Public Opinion Quarterly* 46:86–96.

———. 1985. "Like Mother, Like Daughter: Intergenerational Transmission of DK Response Rates." *Public Opinion Quarterly* 49:198–208.

Ravitch, Diane. 1983. *The Troubled Crusade.* New York: Basic Books.

Ravitch, Diane, and Chester Finn. 1987. *What Do Our 17-Year-Olds Know?* New York: Harper and Row.

RePass, David E. 1971. "Issue Salience and Party Choice." *American Political Science Review* 65:389–400.

Rivers, Douglas. 1988. "Heterogeneity in Models of Electoral Choice." *American Journal of Political Science* 32:737–57.

Robinson, Michael J. 1976. "Public Affairs Television and the Growth of Political Malaise." *American Political Science Review* 70:409–42.

Robinson, John P., and Mark R. Levy. 1986. *The Main Source: Learning from Television News.* Beverly Hills: Sage.

Rokeach, Milton. 1968. "The Nature of Attitudes." In *International Encyclopedia of the Social Sciences,* vol. 1, ed. David L. Sills. New York: Macmillan.

———. 1973. *The Nature of Human Values.* New York: Free Press.

Rorty, Richard. 1987a. "Posties." *London Review of Books,* September, 11–12.

———. 1987b. "Thugs and Theorists: A Reply to Bernstein." *Political Theory* 15:564–80.

Rosen, Jay. 1988. "Democracy Overwhelmed: Press and Public in the Nuclear Age." Occasional Paper #4. New York: Center for War, Peace, and the News Media, New York University.

———. 1991. "Journalism as Political Action: The Case of the *Columbus (Ga.) Ledger Enquirer.*" Unpublished Paper, New York University.

———. 1992. "Forming and Informing the Public." *Kettering Review* (winter): 60–70.

Rosen, Jay, and Paul Taylor. 1992. *The New News v. the Old News: Press and Politics in the 1990s.* New York: Twentieth Century Fund Press.

Rosenstone, Steven J. 1983. *Forecasting Presidential Elections.* New Haven: Yale University Press.

Rosenstone, Steven J., and John Mark Hansen. 1993. *Mobilization, Participation, and Democracy in America.* New York: Macmillan.

Rousseau, Jean-Jacques. [1762] 1968. *The Social Contract.* Harmondsworth, Eng. Penguin.

Sandra, Jaida n'ha. 1993. "How to Start a Salon (Or Jump Start One)." *Utne Reader* 58 (July/August): 53–55.

Sapiro, Virginia. 1983. *The Political Integration of Women.* Urbana: University of Illinois Press.

Schattschneider, E. E. 1942. *Party Government.* New York: Farrar and Rinehart.

———. 1960. *The Semisovereign People: A Realist's View of Democracy in America.* New York: Holt.

Schumaker, Paul, and Nancy Elizabeth Burns. 1988. "Gender Cleavages and the Resolution of Local Policy Issues." *American Journal of Political Science* 32:1070–95.

Schuman, Howard, and Stanley Presser. 1981. *Questions and Answers in Attitude Surveys: Experiments on Question Form, Wording, and Content.* New York: Academic Press.

Schumpeter, Joseph A. 1942. *Capitalism, Socialism, and Democracy.* New York: Harper and Row.

Shapiro, Robert Y., and Harpreet Mahajan. 1986. "Gender Differences in Policy Preferences: A Summary of Trends from the 1960s to the 1980s." *Public Opinion Quarterly* 50:42–61.

Sigal, Leon V. 1973. *Reporters and Officials.* Lexington, Mass.: D. C. Heath.

Smith, Eric R. A. N. 1989. *The Unchanging American Voter.* Berkeley: University of California Press.

Sniderman, Paul M., and Thomas Piazza. 1993. *The Scar of Race.* Cambridge: Harvard University Press.

Sniderman, Paul M., Richard A. Brody, and Philip E. Tetlock. 1991. *Reasoning and Choice: Explorations in Political Psychology.* New York: Cambridge University Press.

Sorauf, Frank, and Paul Allen Beck. 1987. *Party Politics in America.* 6th ed. Glenview, Ill.: Scott, Foresman.

Stimson, James A. 1975. "Belief Systems: Constraint, Complexity and the 1972 Election." *American Journal of Political Science* 19:393–417.

Stokes, Donald. 1967. "Parties and the Nationalization of Electoral Forces." In *The American Party Systems: Stages of Political Development,* ed. W. N. Chambers and W. D. Burnham. New York: Oxford University Press.

Stouffer, Samuel. 1955. *Communism, Conformity, and Civil Liberties.* New York: Doubleday.

Sullivan, Christopher. 1992. "Charlotte Schools Registering Their Seniors to Vote." *Raleigh [N.C.] News and Observer,* June 14.

Sullivan, John L., George E. Marcus, Stanley Feldman, and James E. Piereson. 1981. "The Sources of Political Tolerance." *American Political Science Review* 75:92–106.

Sullivan, John L., James Piereson, and George E. Marcus. 1982. *Political Tolerance and American Democracy.* Chicago: University of Chicago Press.

Tan, Alexis S. 1980. "Mass Media Use, Issue Knowledge, and Political Involvement." *Public Opinion Quarterly* 44:241–48.

Tannen, Deborah. 1990. *You Just Don't Understand: Women and Men in Conversation.* New York: Ballantine Books.

Teixeira, Ruy A. 1992. *The Disappearing American Voter.* Washington: Brookings Institution.

Thorndike, Robert L. 1982. *Applied Psychometrics.* Boston: Houghton Mifflin.

Tichenor, P. J., G. A. Donahue, and C. N. Olien. 1970. "Mass Media Flow and Differential Growth in Knowledge." *Public Opinion Quarterly* 34:159–70.

Times Mirror Center for the People and the Press. 1990. "The Age of Indifference." Survey report. Washington, D.C.

———. 1994a. "Technology in the American Household: The Role of Technology in American Life." Survey report. Washington, D.C., May.

———. 1994b. "Mixed Message about Press Freedom on Both Sides of Atlantic." Survey report. Washington, D.C., March 16.

Tolleson Rinehart, Sue. 1992. *Gender Consciousness and Politics.* New York: Routledge.

Toffler, Alvin. 1980. *The Third Wave.* New York: Morrow.

Truman, David. 1951. *The Governmental Process.* New York: Alfred A. Knopf.

Tufte, Edward R. 1978. *Political Control of the Economy.* Princeton: Princeton University Press.

Tully, James. 1979. *A Discourse on Property: John Locke and His Adversaries.* Cambridge: Cambridge University Press.

Tussman, Joseph. [1922] 1970. "The Citizen as Public Agent." In *Frontiers of Democratic Theory,* ed. Henry S. Kariel. New York: Random House.

Verba, Sidney. 1990. "Women in American Politics." In *Women, Politics, and Change,* ed. Louise A. Tilly and Patricia Gurin. New York: Russell Sage Foundation.

Verba, Sidney, and Norman H. Nie. 1972. *Participation in America.* New York: Harper.

Weatherford, M. Stephen. 1986. "Economic Determinants of Voting." In *Research in Micropolitics,* vol. 1, ed. Samuel Long. Greenwich, Conn.: JAI Press.

Weaver, Paul H. 1975. "Newspaper News and Television News." In *Television as a Social Force,* ed. Douglas Cater and Richard Adler. New York: Praeger.

Weisberg, Herbert F. 1987. "The Demographics of a New Voting Gap: Marital Differences in American Voting." *Public Opinion Quarterly* 51:335–43.

Welch, Susan, and John Hibbing. 1992. "Financial Conditions, Gender, and Voting in American National Elections." *Journal of Politics* 54:197–213.

Westholm, Anders, Arne Lindquist, and Richard G. Niemi. 1990. "Education and the Making of the Informed Citizen: Political Literacy and the Outside World." In *Political Socialization, Citizenship Education, and Democracy,* ed. Orit Ichilov. New York: Teachers College Press.

Wheaton, Blair. 1988. "Assessment of Fit in Overidentified Models with Latent Variables." In *Common Problems/Proper Solutions,* ed. J. Scott Long. Newbury Park, Calif.: Sage.

Wheaton, Blair, Bengt Muthen, Duane F. Alwin, and Gene F. Summers. 1977. "Assessing Reliability and Validity in Panel Models." In *Sociological Methodology,* ed. David R. Heise. San Francisco: Jossey-Bass.

Whitney, D. Charles, and Ellen Wartella. 1988. "The Public as Dummies." *Knowledge: Creation, Diffusion, Utilization* 10:99–110.

Whittington, Dale. 1991. "What Have 17-Year-Olds Known in the Past?". *American Educational Research Journal* 28:759–80.

Wigley, Griff. 1993. "Salon Update." *Utne Reader* 58 (July/August): 53–54.
Wolfinger, Raymond E., and Steven J. Rosenstone. 1980. *Who Votes?* New Haven: Yale University Press.
Wolfson, Lewis. 1985. *The Untapped Power of the Press.* New York: Praeger.
Wood, George. 1982. "Beyond Radical Educational Cynicism." *Educational Theory* 32 (spring): 55–71.
Wood, Gordon. 1969. *The Creation of the American Republic, 1776–1787.* New York: Norton.
———. 1980. "Democracy and the Constitution." In *How Democratic Is the Constitution?* ed. Robert A. Goldwin and William A. Schambra. Washington, D.C.: American Enterprise Institute.
———. 1992. *The Radicalism of the American Revolution.* New York: Alfred A. Knopf.
Woolf, Virginia. 1938. *Three Guineas.* New York: Harcourt, Brace.
Zaller, John. 1986. "Analysis of Information Items in the 1985 NES Pilot Study." Report to the Board of Overseers for the National Election Studies.
———. 1990. "Political Awareness, Elite Opinion Leadership, and the Mass Survey Response." *Social Cognition* 8:125–53.
———. 1991. "Information, Values, and Opinion." *American Political Science Review* 85 (4): 1215–37.
———. 1992. *The Nature and Origins of Mass Opinion.* New York: Cambridge University Press.
———. 1995. "The Myth of Massive Media Effects Revived: Empirical Suport for a Discredited Idea." In *Political Persuasion and Attitude Change,* ed. Diana Mutz, Paul M. Sniderman, and Richard A. Brody. Ann Arbor: University of Michigan Press.
Zaller, John, and Stanley Feldman. 1992. "A Simple Theory of the Survey Response: Answering Questions versus Revealing Preferences." *American Journal of Political Science* 36:579–616.
Zeller, Richard A., and Edward G. Carmines. 1980. *Measurement in the Social Sciences: The Link between Theory and Data.* New York: Cambridge University Press.
Zukin, Cliff, and Robin Snyder. 1984. "Passive Learning: When the Media Environment Is the Message." *Public Opinion Quarterly* 48:629–38.

Index

Ability: civic, x, 2, 3, 7–8, 19, 25, 26, 27, 29, 30–31, 32–33, 33–35, 36, 41, 106–10, 179, 190, 216–17, 339n; cognitive, 2, 7–8, 10, 140, 179, 186, 257–58, 271–72; and education, 190, 193–99
Abramowitz, Alan, 262
Abramson, Jeffrey, 112, 115
Achen, Christopher, 232
Adams, Gordon, 259
Adams, Henry, 39, 107
Adams, John, 35, 37, 338n
Adatto, Kiko, 274
Adversarial democracy, 15, 155
African-Americans. *See* Race
Age: and differences in opinions, 240, 245–247; and knowledge of politics, 18, 146, 149, 150, 156, 157–63, 170–71, 172, 173–74, 176–77, 179, 180–81, 182–84, 188, 191–92, 199–203, 205, 206, 345n, 349n
Allen, Mary, 366n
Almond, Gabriel, 90, 139
Althaus, Scott, 265
Alvarez, Michael, 266
Andersen, Kristi, 54
Ansolabehere, Stephen, 358n
Anxiety, and political knowledge, 185
Aristotle, 2, 22, 26–28, 32, 34, 35, 38, 43, 338n
Arterton, Christopher, 112
Ashcraft, Richard, 29, 40
Asher, Herbert, 359n
Athens, 2, 25, 34
Attentive publics, 3, 23
Attitudes, 219; defined, 228–30; instrumentally rational, 251–254, 358n; and issue consistent voting, 254–58; and opinions, 228, 230–31; responsiveness of, 234–35; stability of, 231–34; structure of, 235–38. *See also* Opinions

Bacon, Sir Francis, 1
Bagdikian, Ben, 113
Baker, John, 90
Barber, Benjamin, xii, 39, 49, 112, 278–79, 286
Barber, James David, 63, 65
Bardes, Barbara, 356n
Barker, Ernest, 286
Barry, W. T., 22
Bartels, Larry, 238, 334, 357n
Battistoni, Richard, 278–79
Beck, Paul, 54
Behavioral sources of political knowledge, 180–81, 184–87, 188, 200, 201, 203, 204–205. *See also* Civic duty; efficacy; interest; mass media; trust
Beliefs, 228–29
Bell, Daniel, 114
Bellah, Robert, 40, 288–89
Bellamy, Edward, 105
Bennett, Lance, 337n
Bennett, Linda, 206, 345n
Bennett, Stephen, 42, 116, 139, 140, 175, 179, 184, 206, 343n, 345n, 347n, 349n
Bentham, Jeremy, 30–31, 34, 38, 338n
Berelson, Bernard, 2, 22, 42, 46, 54, 64
Bishop, George, 229, 231

Blacks. *See* Race
Blake, Frederick, 140
Bloom, Allan, 17, 62, 105, 108, 109
Blumberg, Paul, 23
Bobo, Lawrence, 221
Bogart, Leo, 113
Bolland, John, 344n
Borg, Marian, 349n
Bowles, Samuel, 109–10
Boyte, Harry, 147
Brady, Henry, 56, 358n
Brehm, John, 66, 355n
Brigham, John, 99
Brill, Alida, 220, 221, 353n
Brody, Richard, 3, 51–52, 232, 353n, 356n, 358n, 359n, 361n
Brooks, Phill, 211
Brown, Steven, 344n
Burdick, Eugene, 49
Burnham, Walter Dean, 54, 114, 215
Burns, Nancy, 350n

Callenbach, Ernest, 339n
Campbell, Angus, 41
Campbell, James, 259
Capitalism, 28, 30
Carey, James, 363n
Carmines, Edward, 141, 248, 294, 296, 360n
Center for the Study of Communication, 63, 99–100
Chaffee, Steven, 210
Children, impact of having on political knowledge, 148, 150, 183, 204–05
Citizen juries, 284, 339n
Citizenship: and collective rationality, 23, 43–44, 46, 60; constructionist approach to, 13–14; in early America, 35–39; elite theories of, 36, 42–43, 46–48, 60, 61, 172–74; in Greek city states, 25–27, 34, 338n; and impression driven decisionmaking, 45–46, 339n; improving, 20–21; and informed indifference, 48–49; and liberalism, 4, 28–29, 34, 36, 37; limits on, 13, 16, 25–26, 27, 30–31, 32–33; and low-information decisionmaking, 3, 23, 44–45, 46, 51–55, 60, 61, 63, 339n; in participatory democracies, 31–33, 34–35, 37; in protectionist democracies, 29–31, 34; requirements for, x–xii, 1–3, 5–7, 8, 10–11, 13, 18, 19, 22–23, 24–25, 33, 40, 41, 49–51, 59–61, 63–65, 218; responsiblities of, 3, 4, 8, 14–17, 24–25, 33, 39–40, 41, 49–51, 55–59, 59–61, 63, 284–87; in Roman republic, 27–28, 338n; thick, 5, 40, 55, 268, 269; thin, 4, 39–40, 55, 268, 269; in a two-party system, 53–55. *See also* Democracy, knowledge, political
Civic duty, and knowledge of politics, 49, 180, 182–85
Civic virtue, 8, 24, 28, 34, 35, 37, 38, 42, 105, 338n
Claiborne, William, 284
Clark, Janet, 148, 206
Clarke, Peter, 210, 280
Classical test theory, 296
Class. *See* Income; occupation
Clymer, Adam, x
Cole, G.D., 338n
Collective rationality (aggregate opinion, collective judgements, collective opinion, collective wisdom), 2, 3, 23, 26–27, 36, 43–44
Colonies, American, 37–38
Common good. *See* Public good
Communal democracy, 4, 24, 38, 39, 218
Competent democrat, requisites and responsibilities, 55–59
Competent voter, requisites and responsibilities, 49–55
Connolly, William, xi, xii, 5–6, 238, 239
Conover, Pamela, 39, 40, 140, 344n
Construct validity, 141–42; 143–46; 148–50
Constructionism, 13–14, 69
Content valisity, 294
Converse, Philip, 3, 22, 41, 42, 54, 115, 137, 230, 231–32, 235–36, 265, 339n, 356n
Cook, Elizabeth, 262
Coupland, Douglas, 105
Crewe, Ivor, 39, 40
Crigler, Ann, 13–14, 69, 186, 195–96, 276, 349n, 363n
Crockett, Harry, 221
Cronin, Thomas 57

Dahl, Robert, 8, 24, 25, 238, 283–284, 338n, 343n
Dalton, Russell, 341n
Darcy, R., 148, 207
Data sources, 66–67, 291–93
Dawson, Paul, 228, 344n
Debates, presidential, 280–81

Deliberative opinion polls, 283–84, 339n
Delli Carpini, Michael, 114, 200, 245, 273, 277, 281, 295, 343n, 346n, 351n, 365n
Democratic values (norms), and political knowledge, 5, 220–24
Democratic dread and yearning, 2
Democracy (democratic theory), 10, 14, 15, 16, 18, 20, 24, 33–35, 41, 45, 47, 52, 53, 54, 61, 177, 268–69; communal, 4, 24, 38, 39, 218; direct 2, 4, 25, 32, 59; elite, 2, 23, 36, 42–44, 46, 61, 172–74; in Greek city states, 24, 25–28, 34; and health care reform debate, ix–x; hybrid, 35–40; and an informed citizenry, xi–xii, 1–7, 22–22–23, 288–290; liberal, 4, 23, 24, 28–29, 34, 35, 36, 37, 38, 40, 44, 46, 49, 55; limited, xii, 2, 16, 24, 36, 42–43; managerial, 152, 154; mass-based, 2; paradox of, 16–17, 22–23, 49, 60; participatory, 31–33, 34, 37–38, 55, 59; pragmatic, 152–53, 154; protectionist, xii, 24, 29–31, 44, 49, 55, 56; skepticism of, 2, 13, 14, 16, 22–23, 24, 26, 33, 35, 36, 37, 42; stratified, 3–4, 9, 40; strong, xii, 26, 152–153, 154. *See also* Citizenship
Denver, David, 348n
Dewey, John, xi, 39, 48, 106, 107, 108–09, 178, 194, 275, 363n
Dimock, Michael, 89, 251, 285
Dionne, E.J., 266
Direct democracy, 2, 4, 25, 32, 59
Distributive justice, 27–28
Dodge, Mabel, 363n
Donahue, G.A., 175
Downing, James, 235
Downs, Anthony, 51–53, 54, 337n, 339n
Doyle, Sir Arthur Conan, 135
Drew, Dan, 185
Dye, Thomas, 42

Easton, David, 12, 54
Economic voting, 259–61
Edelman, Murray, 47–48, 361n
Edsall, Mary, 247, 248, 355n
Edsall, Thomas Byrne, 215, 247, 248, 355n
Education, civic xi, 25, 31, 32–33, 39, 106–07, 107–09, 279–80, 338n
Education, civics, 144–45, 183, 190–191, 278–279, 348n
Education, formal: and ability, 106–10, 179; effects of over time, 196–99; and improving levels of knowledge, 277–80; and intelligence, 193–96; and knowledge of national politics, 19, 143, 144, 179, 180, 182–84, 188–193; and knowledge of state and local politics, 149–50, and motivation, 114–115, 179, 190; and opportunity, 110–11, 179, 190; and race, 180, 203; and tolerance, 221–22
Efficacy, political: and knowledge of politics, 6, 144, 180, 182–84
Einstein, Albert, 7, 272, 362n
Elections. *See* Participation, voting
Electronic media: attention to and knowledge of politics, 182. *See also* Television, radio
Elites. *See* Citizenship, elite theories of; democracy, elite
Elshtain, Jean Bethke, 148
Emerson, Ralph Waldo, 286
Engle, Shirley, 107, 338n
Entman, Robert, 23, 57, 274, 280
Enlightened self-interest (enlightened preferences). *See* opinions, and enlightened self-interest
Enlightenment, the, xi, 105
Epstein, Edward Jay, 275
Erbring, Lutz, 115
Erikson, Robert, 116, 232, 359n
Erskine, Hazel Gaudet, 339–40n
Essentially contestable concepts, xii, 5, 239
Estlund, David, 338n
Evans, Susan, 210, 280

Fair, Ray, 259
Faulkenberry, David, 355n
Feld, Scott, 338n
Feldman, Stanley, 140, 229, 232, 344n
Ferejohn, John, 62
Figures: Attitude crystallization by knowledge, 233; Changes in political knowledge levels, 117; Distributions of average change in knowledge, 119; Distribution of knowledge by demographic groups, 161; Hypothetical item characteristic curve, 298; Impact of domestic opinion on party identification by knowledge level, 253; Impact of domestic opinion on presidential approval by knowledge level, 254; Impact of knowledge on opinion by age, 247; Impact of knowledge on opinion

Figures: (*continued*)
by faith in bible, 251; Impact of knowledge on opinion by gender, 245, 246; Impact of knowledge on opinion by respondents' financial condition, 243; Impact of knowledge on opinion by race, 249; Issue consistent voting by knowledge levels, 256, 257, 258; Knowledge in comparative perspective, 92; Knowledge of federal spending, 97; Political participation by political knowledge, 225; Relative knowledge across selected groups, 162; Simplified path model of sources of political knowledge, 181; Tolerance by knowledge, 222; Trends in knowledge by age, 1170–71; Trends in knowledge by gender, 164–165; Trends in knowledge by income, 168–69; Trends in knowledge by race, 166–67
Finkel, Steven, 349n
Fiorina, Morris, 339n, 360n, 362n
Finn, Chester, 62, 349n
Fishkin, James, 224, 283–84, 339n, 364n
Fiske, Susan, 140
Flanigan, William, 116
Focus groups, 135–36, 293
Framers, 35–39
Franklin, Charles, 266
Fredin, Eric, 210
Friday, Joe, 62

Gallup surveys, 163, 196, 198, 202, 346n
Gamson, William, 47
Gans, Herbert, 275
Gassaway, Bob, 211
Gaudet, Hazel, 54,
Gender: and citizenship, 13, 25, 27, 30, 33, 36, 156, 203; differences in opinions, 240, 244–45, 246; and knowledge of national politics, 18, 19, 143, 144, 145–46, 151, 156–61, 162, 163–65, 172, 173–74, 175–77, 179, 180–81, 182–84, 187, 195, 197– 98, 199, 203–07, 216; and knowledge of state and local politics, 148–50, 207–09; socialization, 204, 205–07, 350n
General Social Survey (GSS), 186, 207, 208
Generalists, 18, 50–51, 55, 136–42, 174, 177, 270–71, 295
Generations and knowledge: *See* Age
Gibson, James, 220
Gilligan, Carol, 206
Gilmour, Richard, 115, 116
Ginsberg, Benjamin, 58
Gintis, Herbert, 109–10
Goel, M.L., 147
Goldenberg, Edie, 115
Gormley, William, 211
Gottleib, Martin, 352n
Gould, Stephen Jay, 194, 349n
Guessing (on surveys), 65–66, 95, 341n
Guitton, Stephanie, 281
Guterbock, Thomas, 349n
Graber, Doris, 12, 175, 187, 275, 350n, 363n
Graham, Thomas, 289
Greek city states, 24–28, 34, 338n
Greenberg, Edward, 35
Greenstein, Fred, 54
Grigg, Charles, 220
Grodzins, Morton, 284
Grofman, Bernard, 337n
Gronke, Paul, 259
Group differences: in knowledge, 156–61, 162, 199–09; in knowledge over time, 161, 163–72; in opinions, 239–51; ways of decreasing, 287–88. *See also* Age, gender, income, race, religion
Guttman, Amy, 277–78

Habermas, Jurgen, xi–xii, 6, 15, 48, 337n
Hagan, Michael, 355n
Hambleton, Ronald, 366n
Hamill, Ruth, 140, 175
Hamilton, Alexander, 36–37, 238
Hands, Gordon, 348n
Hansen, John Mark, 199, 209, 213–14
Hanson, Russell, 4, 114, 343n
Hapgood, Hutchins, 363n
Hawking, Stephen, 339n
Hayduk, Leslie, 329, 344n
Health care reform: importance of political knowledge to debate, x; role of media ix–x
Henry, Neil, 366n
Herzog, Don, 361n
Hess, Robert, 54
Heuristics. *See* Low-information decisionmaking
Hibbing, John, 259
Hirsch, E. D., 62, 108, 109, 349n
Hirsch, Fred, 155
Hirschman, Albert, 115, 121

Hochschild, Jennifer, 344n
Hollander, Richard, 112
Holsworth, Robert, 29, 40,
Huckfeldt, Robert, 352n
Hurwitz, John, 356n
Hybrid democracy, 35–40
Hyman, Herbert, 7, 193, 198

Ideal speech situations, xii, 337n
Ideology, and issue-consistent voting, 255–58
Ignorance, political, xii, 8, 14, 22, 34, 40, 47–48, 62–63, 93–95, 177; and contested truths, 95–96; and close calls, 96, 97; and lagged attention, 96, 97, 341n, 343n; and manipulation, 99–101; and projection, 98–99; and voting, 263–264. *See Also* Knowledge, political
Illich, Ivan, 342n
Impression-driven decisionmaking (on-line decisionmaking), 45–46, 339n
Income (economic class): and access to information, 273–274; and knowledge of national politics, 18, 144, 156- 63, 168–69, 173–74, 176–77, 180, 182–84, 199–200, 213–16; and knowledge of state and local politics, 149–50; and the 1988 vote, 264
Information, political, 10–11, 12. *See also* information environment; knowledge, political
Information costs, 50–55
Information environment, ix–x, 8, 19, 46, 61, 104, 122–23, 176–77; 209–213, 271, 337n, 339n, 342n, 356n; changes in, 112–14; improving, 273–77; and knowledge of state politics, 211–13
Information short cuts. *See* Low-information decisionmaking
Information superhighway (new technology), 273–75, 277, 362n
Informed indifference, 48–49
Inglehart, Ronald, 17, 105, 107
Institutions and processes (rules of the game), knowledge of, 1, 14, 63–64, 65, 67, 68–69, 69–73, 294, 340n
Intelligence, 193–196, 349n. *See also* ability, cognitive
Interest, political, 10, 19, 175–76, 347n; and knowledge of national politics, 144, 180, 182–85, 187, 214; and knowledge of state and local politics, 149, 150
Interests: individual (self), ix, 5, 6, 19, 28–29, 31, 33, 43, 49, 52, 60, 155, 219, 260–61; group, 5, 6, 9, 15, 43, 155, 239–51. *See also* opinions, and enlightened self-interest; public good
Inverted pyramid (in newspaper writing), 186, 363n
Irons, Peter, 281
Issue publics, 139. *See also* Attentive publics
Issues, political, knowledge of, 1, 14, 64–65, 67, 68–69, 79–86, 294, 340n
Item characteristic curve, 297, 298
Item response theory, 297
Iyengar, Shanto, 139, 343n, 345n, 361n

Jackson, John, 232
Jamieson, Kathleen Hall, 337n
Janowitz, Morris, 108, 109, 115, 191, 345n, 349n
Jay, John, 36–37, 238
Jefferson, Thomas, 1, 37, 112, 268, 269
Jelen, Ted, 262
Jennings, M. Kent, 54, 194, 346n, 348n, 350n
Jhally, Sut, 99
Jordon, Mary, 279
Joreskog, Karl, 330, 344n
Judd, Charles, 232, 235, 356n
Junn, Jane, 186, 190, 206, 224
Just, Marion, 13–14, 69, 186, 195–96, 275–76, 349n, 363n

Kahneman, Daniel, 52
Kay, W.D., 289
Keeter, Scott, 210, 213, 281, 295, 343n, 346n, 351n, 359n
Kennamer, David, 348n, 351n
Kernell, Samuel, 253
Kessel, John, 304, 346n, 359n
Key, V. O., 3, 20, 44, 46
Kiewiet, Roderick, 259
Kinder, Donald, 175, 234, 259, 361n
King, Gary, 345n
Klein, Ethel, 132
Knight, Kathleen, 232, 358n
Knowledge gaps. *See* Age; group differences; gender; income; race
Knowledge, non-political, 101, 102–03, 104
Knowledge, patterns of (structure of knowledge), 18–19, 136, 138–41, 343n; of national politics, 142–47, 344n, 345n; of state and local politics, 147–50

Knowledge, political: aggregate levels of, 3, 17, 41–42, 68–69, 101–02, 269; and attitudes, 227–38; changing levels of, 7, 17–18, 116–33, 161–72, 270, 307–28; and cognitive ability, 8, 106–110, 179; collective, 15–16, 219; and collective rationality, 23, 26–27, 43–44, in comparative perspective, 89–91; components of, 63–65; consequences of, 1, 5–7, 19–20, 264–67, 272, chapter 6 (passim); constructionist approach, 13–14; correlates of, 179, 180, 182–84; defined, 10–12; and democratic norms, 1, 220–24; depth of, 91–93; the distribution of, 1, 3, 8, 18–19, 137, 151–54; of domestic politics, 68–69, 79–82, 103; of economics, 1, 71–72, 73; as facilitator of other civic requisites, 1, 6–7; of foreign affairs, 68–69, 82–86; of geography and history, 67, 86–89; group differences in, 154–61, 271; and group interests, 1, 5, 6, 15, 155, 239–51; and healthcare reform debate, x; and impression-driven decisionmaking, 45–46; and individual motivation, 8, 19, 114–16, 179, 184–87, 190, 339n; and the information environment, ix–x, 8, 46–49, 209–13, 339n; and information generalists, 12, 18, 50–51, 55, 136–42, 174, 177, 270–71; and information short-cuts, 3, 44–45, 51–53, 53–55; and information specialists, 3, 12, 18, 50, 136–42, 270–71; measurement of, 15–16, 136–37, 174–75, 294–306; and opportunity, 8, 19, 21, 104, 110–14, 179, 190; and participation levels, 186–87, 219, 224–28; of political institutions and processes (rules of the game), 1, 14, 62–64, 65, 57, 68–69, 69–73; of political issues (substance of politics), 1, 14, 64–65, 67, 68–69, 79–86; of political leaders (people and parties), 1, 14, 65, 67, 68–69, 73–79; as a political resource, xi, 1, 5, 8, 59, 101, 137–138, 337n; and the public good (public interest), 1, 5, 6, 9, 12, 15, 16, 17, 20, 25, 26, 155; recommended 5-item measure, 304–06; relation to political power, 1, 3–4, 9; relation to socioeconomic power, 1, 3–4, 8, 9, 16–17, 17–18, 19–20, 22, 29, 30, 32, 34, 138, 155, 177, 213–16, 287–88; relative, 14–15, 219; and self-interest, 1, 5–6, 19, 155; situational, 14, 219, 223–24, 261–62; sources of, 7, 19–21, 271–72; structure of, 329–33; and tolerance, 219, 220–23; as a trait, 7, 138. *See also* citizenship; democracy; ignorance, political; knowledge, patterns of; knowledge, stability and change in

Knowledge, structure of. *See* knowledge, patterns of

Kozol, Jonathan, 203

Krassa, Michael, 347n

Krosnick, Jon, 175, 231

Kuklinski, James, 289, 344n

Kurtz, Howard, 274, 275

Lamb, Richard, 115, 116

Lambert, Ronald, 179

Lane, Robert, 266, 344n

Langton, P., 348n

Lanoue, David, 234

Lasch, Christopher, 47

Lasswell, Harold, 155

Latent trait theory, 297

Lau, Richard, 140

Lazarsfeld, Paul, 22, 54, 366n

Leaders, political (people and parties): knowledge of, 1, 14, 65, 67, 68–69, 73–79, 294, 340n

Learning, political, 175–77, 178–79, 204, 346n; sources of (simplified model), 180–81

Leighley, Jan, 187, 224

Lemert, James, 58, 225, 276

Lever, Janet, 206

Levy, Mark, 185

Lewis, Justin, 99

Lewis-Beck, Michael, 259, 296

Liberalism (liberal democracy), 4, 23, 24, 28–29, 34, 35, 36, 37, 38, 40, 44, 46, 49, 55

Licari, Frederick, 221

Liddy, G. Gordon, 273

Life cycle and knowledge. *See* Age

Limited democracy, xii, 2, 16, 24, 36, 42–43

Lindquist, Arne, 348n

Lippmann, Walter, 5, 219, 238

Listhaug, Ola, 360n

LISREL, 141, 142–43, 146, 147–48, 329–33, 344n, 345n

Local politics, 38, 59, 284; knowledge of, 147–150, 207–09

Locke, John, 28–30, 31, 32, 35, 288
Lodge, Milton, 45, 140, 175, 344n
Long-term memory, 10–11, 45, 337n, 348n
Lord, Frederick, 366n
Low-information decisionmaking, (heuristics, information short-cuts), 3, 23, 44–45, 46, 51–55, 60, 61, 63, 339n
Luskin, Robert, 7, 111, 179, 184, 193–94, 195, 204, 340n, 344n, 345n, 347n, 348n, 349n
Luttbeg, Norman, 116, 356n, 359n

MacDonald, Stuart Elaine, 356n, 359n, 360n
MacKuen, Michael, 185
Macpherson, C.B., 22, 28, 218, 223, 337n
Madison, John, 22, 36–37, 57, 110, 238, 268
Mahajan, Harpreet, 244
Managerial democracy, 152, 154
Mander, Gerry, 342n
Manipulation of public opinion, 46–48, 99–101, 234–35
Mann, Horace, 106, 107
Mansbridge, Jane, 15, 155, 238
Marital status: and knowledge of politics, 149; and opinions, 244, 245
Marcus, Erin, 364n
Marcus, George, 185, 220, 353n
Markus, Gregory, 54
Mason, David, 355n
Mass media 143; and coverage of state politics, 211–13, 351n; and health care reform debate, ix–x; and improving levels of knowledge, 273–77, 363n-364n; and motivation, 115; and opportunity, 112–14; use of and knowledge of national politics, 144–45, 149, 161, 175–77, 180, 182–87; use of (and knowledge of local politics), 149. *See also* Information environment, newsmagazines, newspapers, television, radio
McClosky, Herbert, 220, 221, 353n, 356n
McGraw, Kathleen, 45, 344n
McPhee, William, 22, 54
Merriam, Charles, 39, 105
Metlay, Daniel, 289
Meyer, Phillip, 275
Meyrowitz, Joshua, 342n, 343n
Milbrath, Lester, 147
Milburn, Michael, 231, 232, 356n
Mill, James, 30, 31, 34, 38, 338n
Mill, John Stuart, xi, 5, 32–33, 34, 38, 44, 48, 58, 178, 338n
Miller, Arthur, 115, 344n
Miller, Jon, 3, 139
Miller, Nicholas, 44
Miller, Warren, 67
Minipopulous, 283
Misinformation, 17
Mobilizing information, 225, 276
Mondak, Jeffrey, 52
Montesquieu, Charles, 35
Moon, David, 358n, 359n
Morgan, Michael, 99
Morone, James, 2, 4, 37–38
Motivation, and knowledge of politics, 3, 8, 19, 114–16, 179, 184–87, 190, 216–17, 271, 272
Mueller, John, 2
Mullet, Charles, 339n

Nadeau, Richard, 184
National Election Studies (NES), 66, 67, 96, 98, 139, 140, 146, 147, 151, 156, 157, 160, 161, 172, 180, 184, 186, 188, 190, 195, 199, 200, 202, 207, 210, 214, 215, 224, 226, 227, 230, 231, 232, 236, 237, 239, 242, 255, 263, 301–04; 341n, 346n, 349n, 354n, 355n, 356n, 358n, 366n
National geographic survey, 91
National Opinion Research Center (NORC), 208
Neighborhood Salon Association, 276, 363n
Neuman, Russell, 2, 7, 10, 13–14, 42, 63–64, 69, 101, 116, 139, 153, 179, 186, 187, 195–96, 224, 275–76, 340n, 343n, 349n, 353n, 354n, 356n, 359n, 363n
Neustadt, Richard, 253
News. *See* Information environment, mass media, newsmagazines, newspapers, television, radio
Newsmagazines, attention to (and impact on knowledge), 183, 184, 186. *See also* Electronic media, mass media, newspapers
Newspapers (print media): attention to (and impact on knowledge), 182–83, 184, 185–86; and healthcare reform debate, ix–x; role in improving knowledge levels, 276. *See also* Newsmagazines

Nie, Norman, 54, 107, 111, 147, 282, 356n, 359n
Niemi, Richard, 54, 184, 190, 194, 206, 346n, 348n, 350n
Nonresponse (on surveys), 66
Nunn, Clyde, 221
Nunnally, Jum, 297, 366n

Occupation (politically impinged): and knowledge of national politics, 19, 180–81, 182–84, 188, 201, 204; and motivation, 115; and opportunity, 111–12
Ochoa, Anna, 107, 338n
Oldendick, Robert, 231, 356n
Olien, C. N., 175
On-line model. *See* Impression-driven decisionmaking
Opinionation (opinion holding), 6, 230–31, 354n
Opinions, 5, 219, 227, 228; and age- based interests, 245–47; and attitude stability, 231–34; and economic interests, 242–43; and enlightened self-interest (preferences), 3, 5–7, 15, 19, 53, 219, 238–54, 334–36; and gender-based interests, 244–45, 246; and race-based interests, 247–48; and religious interests, 248–50; and responsiveness of attitudes, 234; and structure of attitudes, 235–38. *See also* Attitudes, opinionation
Opportunity: changes in, 34, 110–14; and political knowledge, 3, 8, 19, 21, 104, 179, 190, 216–17, 271–72
Orren, Gary, 112
Orum, Anthony, 350n
Orwell, George, 177
Owen, Diana, 139

Page, Benjamin, 3, 23, 35, 43–44, 46, 280, 286, 359n, 360n
Palfrey, Thomas, 359n, 361n
Paradox of democracy, 16–17, 22–23, 49, 60
Parties, political, 31, 42; and the information environment, 131–33, 213–16, 282–83; knowledge about, 76–77, 103–04; and low-information decisionmaking, 53–55. *See also* leaders, political
Participation, political, 56–59, 186–87, 218, 219, 224–28. *See also* voting
Participatory democracy, 31–33, 34–35, 37–38, 55, 59
Partisanship (party identification): instrumentally rational, 251–53, 358n; and knowledge of national politics, 140, 143, 145, 146, 172–73, 175, 176, 182–83, 201; and knowledge of state and local politics, 148–49, 150–51; as an information shortcut, 54–55, 56, 339n
Pateman, Carol, 9, 28, 218, 227
Patterson, Thomas, 115
Peffley, Mark, 356n
People and parties. *See* Leaders, political
Pericles, 2
Petrocik, John, 54, 107, 356n, 359n
Phillip, Michael, 339n
Phillips, Kevin, 365n
Piazza, Thomas, 141, 248
Piereson, James, 220, 353n
Plato, 22, 26, 28, 32, 34, 35
Pluralist model, 137, 177, 343n, 345n
Pomper, Gerald, 359n
Pope, Alexander, 218
Political environment, and knowledge, 121–22, 123–33, 213–16, 217
Political learning. *See* Learning, political
Politics: adversarial, 155; defined, 12; and improving levels of knowledge, 280–84, 364n-365n; unitary (consensual), 155
Political parties. *See* Parties, political
Political sophistication, 7, 10, 44, 294, 353n
Polity, 27
Poole, Keith, 359n, 360n
Popkin, Samuel, 3, 44, 46, 89, 108, 115, 251, 285, 286, 339n
Postman, Neil, 39, 108, 109, 112, 113, 274, 342n, 343n
Power, political: and political knowledge: 1, 3–4, 9, 20, 177, 268, 290
Pragmatic democracy, 152–53, 154
Precision journalism, 275
Presidential approval, and political knowledge, 251–54
Presser, Howard, 229, 231, 355n
Price, Vincent, 175, 185, 193, 348n, 354n
Print media. *See* Mass media, newsmagazines, newspapers
Private sphere, 28, 29, 35, 39, 207
Protectionist democracy, xii, 24, 29– 31, 34, 44, 49, 55, 56

Prothro, James, 220
Public good (common good, public interest, collective good), xi, 1, 4, 5, 6, 9, 12, 15, 16, 17, 20, 24, 25, 26, 27, 28, 29, 30, 34, 36, 37, 38, 43, 52, 58, 60, 155, 227, 338n
Public opinion. *See* Attitudes; opinions
Public sphere, xi, 4, 25, 28–29, 31, 32, 34, 37, 40, 59
Putnam, Robert, 59, 287

Rabinowitz, George, 356n, 359n, 360n
Race: and citizenship, 13, 36, 156, 209; and difference in opinions, 240, 247–48, 249; and knowledge of national politics, 18, 19, 144, 145, 146, 147, 156–63, 166–67, 172, 173–174, 175, 176–77, 180–81, 182–84, 187, 199, 203, 204, 346n, 347n; and knowledge of state and local politics, 148–49, 150–51, 187, 216, 347n
Radio: use of and knowledge of politics, 183, 184. *See also* electronic media, mass media
Rahn, Wendy, 140, 175
Rapoport, Ronald, 350n, 355n
Rational opinion (rational behavior), xii, 16, 19, 49–50, 269; instrumentally, 251–64
Ravitch, Diane, 62, 109, 349n
Reed, John Shelton, 193, 198
Region, and knowledge of national politics, 145, 180–83, 205
Relativism, 47–48
Relativity of knowledge, 14–15, 219
Religion, and opinions about gay rights, 240, 248–49
RePass, David, 359n
Representation (representatives), 4, 23, 30, 32, 34, 35, 37, 38, 39–40, 43–44, 51, 57, 338n
Republicanism (classical), 7, 24, 27, 28, 36–37, 38, 42, 55, 105, 106, 265, 338n
Rivers, Douglas, 358n
Robinson, Michael, 115
Robinson, John, 185
Rokeach, Milton, 228
Rogers, H. Jane, 366n
Roman republic, 27–28, 338n
Roper Center, 66–67, 68, 95, 202
Rorty, Richard, 337n
Rosen, Jay, 276, 289, 363n
Rosenstone, Steven, 199, 209, 213–14, 259, 354n
Rousseau, Jean Jacques, xi, 31–32, 34, 38, 39, 40, 48, 58, 108–09, 114, 155, 218, 338n
Rules of the game. *See* Institutions and processes
Russell, Bertrand, 61

Sanders, Barry, 342n
Sanders, Lynn, 234
Sandra, Jaida, 276
Sapiro, Virginia, 350n
Schattschneider, E. E., 2, 13, 14, 23, 24, 31, 42, 52, 60, 177
Schema theory, 139–141, 175, 337n, 344n
Schumaker, Paul, 350n
Schuman, Howard, 229, 231, 355n
Schumpeter, Joseph, 2, 31, 36, 42, 46
Searing, Donald, 39, 40
Sears, David, 140
Self-interest. *See* Interests, self
Sex. *See* Gender
Shapiro, Robert, 3, 23, 43–44, 46, 244, 286
Sheatsley, Paul, 7,
Shefter, Martin, 58
Sigal, Leon, 275
Simon, Paul, 218
Singh, Indu, 114, 273
Skepticism of democracy, 2, 13, 14, 16, 22–23, 24, 26, 33, 35, 36, 37, 42
Smith, Eric R.A.N., 7, 116, 139, 141, 179, 194, 340n, 347n
Sniderman, Paul, 3, 51–52, 53, 232, 248, 339n, 353n, 355n, 356n, 358n, 359n, 361n
Snyder, Robin, 210
Social contract theory, 28, 30, 31, 32, 34, 338n
Socioeconomic status: and citizenship, 13, 16, 22, 25–26, 27, 28, 29, 30–31, 32–34, 36; and differences in opinion, 240; and the 1988 vote, 264; and political knowledge, 1, 3–4, 8, 9, 13, 17–18, 19–20, 138, 155, 177, 213–216, 287–288; and the public interest, 13. *See also* Age, education, gender, income, occupation, race
Sociotropic voting, 259–61
Socrates, 2, 26, 59, 218
Sorauf, Frank, 54
Sorbom, Dag, 330, 344n
Specialists, 18, 50, 136–42, 295, 343n
Spiral of knowledge (reciprocal relation

Spiral of knowledge (*continued*) between knowledge, attitudes, and behavior), 19, 186–87, 214, 220, 227, 266, 272, 283, 347n
Sprague, John, 352n
Stability and change, in knowledge: aggregate declines, 123–26; aggregate increases, 127–30; general patterns, 17–18 116–22, 307–33; by groups, 161, 163–172; of party stands, 131–33
State politics, 38, 59, 187, 147–50, 211–13, 216, 351n
Steffens, Lincoln, 363n
Stewart, Marianne, 139
Stimson, James, 131, 132, 236–37, 248, 356n, 358n, 360n
Stokes, Donald, 114
Stouffer, Samuel, 353
Stratified democracy, 3–4, 9, 40
Stroh, Patrick, 45
Strong Democracy, xii, 26, 152–53, 154
Structural sources of knowledge 180–82, 188, 199–200, 201, 203, 204–05, 207, 209. *See also* Education, income, occupation
Substance of politics. *See* Issues, political
Suchner, Robert, 3, 139
Sullivan, Christopher, 279
Sullivan, John, 220, 329, 352n, 353n
Swaminathan, Hariharan, 366n

Tables: Actual distribution of political knowledge, 153; Attitudes structure by knowledge, 237; Aggregate distribution of knowledge, 68; Changes in knowledge of party stands, 132; Changes in knowledge of presidential succession, 126; Changes in knowledge of religious affiliations of Kennedy and Nixon, 128; Changes in knowledge of U.S. membership in U.N., 129; Changes in knowledge of U.S. policy in Nicaragua, 130; Changes in knowledge of vice presidential candidates, 128; Construct validity of knowledge domains (national politics), 144–45; Construct validity of knowledge domains (national, state, and local politics), 149–50; Correlates of political knowledge, 183; Correlates of political tolerance, 222–23; Demographic makeup of most and least informed quintiles of population, 173–74; Depth of knowledge, 92–93; Description of knowledge items in 1990–91; NES, 302; Description of variables used in construct validation, 331; Effects of education over time, 197–98; Estimates of change in knowledge for three hypothetical facts, 122; Group differences in knowledge of national politics, 158–160; Hypothetical distributions of political knowledge, 152; Item performance statistics, 299–300, 302–03; Knowledge classes, 154; Knowledge in comparative perspective, 89, 90, 91; Knowledge of domestic politics, 80–81; Knowledge by education levels, 189–90; Knowledge of foreign affairs, 83–84; Knowledge of geography, 87; Knowledge of history, 87–88; Knowledge by income, 215; Knowledge of institutions and processes, 70–71; Knowledge of judicial politics by age and education, 192; Knowledge of local politics by gender, 208; Knowledge of nonpolitical facts, 102–03; Knowledge of political figures and parties, 74–75; Knowledge of state politics by region, 213; Large declines in knowledge, 125; Large increases in knowledge, 127; Levels of ignorance, 94; Link between perceptions of Reagan record and 1988 vote, 263–64; Overview of data sources, 291–92; LISREL analyses of national data, 330–31; LISREL analyses of Richmond data, 332–33; LISREL analyses of Virginia data, 332; Over-time knowledge of domestic affairs, 323–25; Over-time knowledge of foreign affairs, 317–22; Over- time knowledge of geography, 326–27; Over-time knowledge of history, 327–28; Over-time knowledge of institutions and process, 307–11; Over-time knowledge of public figures and political parties, 311–17; Partial correlations between age and knowledge, controlling for education, 201–02; Predictors of voter turnout, 226–27; regression analysis of aggregate change in knowledge, 121; Summary of interfactor correlations, 151; Summary of over-time data, 117; vote choice by economic evaluations and knowledge level, 261
Tan, Alexis, 187
Tannen, Deborah, 206

Taylor, Richard, 344n
Taylor, Shelley, 140
Tedin, Kent, 116, 359n
Teixeira, Ruy, 116, 199, 275
Television, attention to (and impact on knowledge), 183, 185–86, 348n, 350n; and health care reform debate, ix
Tetlock, Philip, 3, 51–52, 232, 353n, 356n, 358n, 359n
Thick citizenship, 5, 40, 55, 268, 269
Thin citizenship, 4, 39–40, 55, 268, 269
Thorndike, Robert, 366n
Thurstone, L. L., 354n
Thoureau, Henry David, 112
Thurow, Lester, 289
Tichenor, P. J., 175
Times Mirror Center, 89, 202, 207, 273, 362n
Tocqueville, Alexis de, 19, 38, 62, 282
Toffler, Alvin, 112
Tolerance, political, 219, 220–23, 352n
Tolleson Rinehart, Sue, 357n
Truman, David, 343n
Trust, and knowledge of national politics, 145, 180, 183
Tufte, Edward, 259
Tuchfarber, Alfred, 231
Tully, James, 29, 40
Tussman, Joseph, 20
Tversky, Amos, 52

Unitary democracy, 4, 15, 155
Updike, John 105, 285
Uriarte, Mercedes Lynn de, 363

Verba, Sidney, 54, 90, 107, 111, 147, 282, 356n, 359n
Voting: and citizenship, 4, 30–31, 32, 35–36, 37, 38, 39–40; and economic evaluations 259–61; and information short cuts, 49–53; issue consistent, 254–58; minimally competent, 49–55; and political knowledge, 225–27, 358n-359n; in a two-party system, 53– 55; and retrospective evaluation of Reagan presidency 263–264

Waldron, Jeremy, 338n
Wartella, Ellen, 62
Weatherford, M. Stephen, 361n
Weaver, David, 185
Weaver, Paul, 186
Webb, Sharon, 281
Weisberg, Herbert, 244
Welch, Susan, 148, 207, 259
Westholm, Anders, 348n
Wheaton, Blair, 329
Whitman, Walt, 268
Whitney, D. Charles, 62
Whittington, Dale, 349n
Wigley, Griff, 364n
Wilcox, Clyde, 262
Williams, Bruce, 277
Williams, J. Allen, 221
Wilson, Donna, 210
Wilson, Harry, 210, 213
Wisdom, collective. *See* Collective rationality
Wolfinger, Raymond, 354n
Wolfson, Lewis, 351n
Women. *See* Gender
Women's rights, attitudes towards and knowledge of politics, 183
Wood, George, 109
Wood, Gordon, 38, 338n
Woolf, Virginia, 48–49, 135
Wright, Charles, 193, 198

Yen, Wendy, 366n

Zaller, John, 10, 46, 138, 139, 175, 185, 193, 229, 230, 235, 280, 301, 339n, 343n, 345n, 348n, 354n, 355n, 356n
Zeigler, L. Harmon, 42
Zeller, Richard, 141, 294, 296
Zingale, Nancy, 116
Zukin Cliff, 210